Regeneration
Songs

Alberto Duman is an artist, university lecturer and independent researcher. He teaches at Middlesex University in Art and Social Practice.

Dan Hancox is a writer on music, gentrification, pop culture and politics, writing for the *Guardian, New York Times* and others. His books include *The Village Against the World* and *Inner City Pressure*.

Malcolm James is a Lecturer in Media and Cultural Studies in the School of Media, Film and Music at the University of Sussex. He is the author of *Urban Multiculture: Youth, Politics and Cultural Transformation*.

Anna Minton is a writer, journalist and Reader in Architecture at the University of East London. She has written two books, *Ground Control* and *Big Capital*, and is a regular contributor to the *Guardian*.

Regeneration Songs:

Sounds of Investment and Loss from East London

Edited by
Alberto Duman
Dan Hancox
Malcolm James
Anna Minton

Published by Repeater Books
An imprint of Watkins Media Ltd

19-21 Cecil Court
London
WC2N 4EZ
UK
www.repeaterbooks.com
A Repeater Books paperback original 2018
1

Distributed in the United States by Random House, Inc.,
New York.

Copyright © Repeater Books 2018

Cover design: Johnny Bull
Typography and typesetting: Jasper Sidock
Typefaces: Helvetica Neue | Meridien LT

ISBN: 9781912248230
Ebook ISBN: 9781912248247

Printed and bound in the United Kingdom

To the people of Newham

Table of Contents

Fig. 1: "Fiery Pool of Asphalt". Image by Alberto Duman © 2017

Introduction

Alberto Duman, Dan Hancox, Malcolm James & Anna Minton

This book sets out to explore the relationship between culture and capital in the contemporary production of urban space in London and the co-opting of culture and art, in its various manifestations, by property finance. These spatial and ideological relationships between advertising, visual culture and the ability to displace our perceptions, were captured by Walter Benjamin almost a hundred years ago when he noted: "What, in the end, makes advertisements so superior to criticism? Not what the moving red neon sign says – but the fiery pool reflecting it in the asphalt"[1].

An object of visual culture in the shape of a promotional film about East London, aimed at global investors, is at the centre of this publication. *London's Regeneration Supernova* is a marketing film made by Newham Council, in East London, together with the London Development Agency (LDA), for screening at the Shanghai World Expo in 2010. It aimed to highlight land and property market opportunities in a large area branded as the "Arc of Opportunity". This stretches from Stratford, the heart of the London 2012 Olympics, through Canning Town, Custom House and the Royal Docks, focusing particularly on the Royal Docks area, which was described in the film as "offering regeneration opportunity on a global scale". This part of London and its people–like so many other parts of towns and cities around the UK and world–was offered as a product for sale to the capital investors gathered in Shanghai.

This particular branded area was conceived as a councilled, government-supported and market-backed commodity, suspended between the material values of land and property and the immaterial values of art and culture. A key theme explored in the book is that space and place do not merely reflect economic and social relations, rather they produce social relations through the creation of the urban imaginaries and patterns for living. Idealised and abstracted versions of those imaginaries and patterns are themselves reflected in the hundreds of strategies, promotional materials and CGI representations of possible futures. These contribute to the placemaking strategies described, which rest on the economics of "extracting value" from places–increasing land and property prices, in other words. As the late geographer Doreen Massey wrote, "spatial organization is integral to the production of social relations and power relations and not merely its result".[2] Our concern then is not only for the spectacle of Newham provided to global investors, but also what it means for residents of Newham to live in such fiery imagery.

***

The idea for the book originated in 2015 when Alberto Duman and Anna Minton secured a grant for Alberto to work as artist-in-residence at the University of East London's Master of Research (MRes) Architecture Programme, subtitled "Reading the Neoliberal City", where Anna is Programme Leader. But the genesis of the project came earlier, perhaps in 2012, when Alberto was asked to programme an event about the London 2012 Olympics for *MUTE Magazine*. As part of this he started to track down the appearance and disappearance of a strange promotional movie called *London's Regeneration Supernova*.

Alberto's first request for a copy of the film, made through

Newham Council's Media Services Department, was refused, apparently because "the material contained in the movie no longer represented Newham's regeneration priorities and branding". He then made a specific Freedom of Information request to the London Borough of Newham and managed to obtain a copy. The peculiarity of this recovered evidence was that the film provided by Newham was silent. The original on-site music for the event remains unknown, but the absence of sound for such an important piece of promotional place marketing narrative, opened the conceptual space for what became the Music for Masterplanning project, funded by the Leverhulme Trust. The aim of the project was for Alberto to work with artists and musicians across the "Arc of Opportunity" area to record an album's worth of music tracks to go with the film.

The film was produced for the 2010 Shanghai Expo, which showcased the dizzying speed of global regeneration and development which was reaching a pinnacle in the host city. In such circumstances, the idea of the sheer speed of change of a Supernova was a fitting image to bring to China. The "once in a lifetime" investment pitch was a film filled with culturally laden terms such as "prosperity"', amidst references to red telephone

Fig. 2: Screenshot from the *London's Regeneration Supernova* movie, 2010.

boxes and Big Ben, which sold the Arc of Opportunity to Asian investors–who would likely never have heard of Newham–on the basis of it being three hours from Paris and six hours from New York.

For Alberto, the paper trail goes back further to 6 July 2005, when the 2012 Olympic Games were unexpectedly awarded to London, the day before terrorist bombs struck the city.

A few weeks later, he became part of a group of artists, curators and urban geographers, who got together[3] to capture

Fig. 3: The Arc of Opportunity within a map of Newham, East London.

the last of the riverine and marshland area of light industry, artist's studios, sheltered housing, allotments, and overgrown nature that was to become the Olympic Park, before it would be fenced into the "Blue Zone" and disappear, followed by many other areas of London since.

But the Arc of Opportunity as a marketing concept and urban imaginary blueprint long predates this: it first hit the public consciousness in 1999 with an architectural competition organised by the London Borough of Newham and showcased by the Architecture Foundation, "to instil some imagination" into the recently developed idea of the Arc. PRS Architects wrote, that whilst pitted "against a backdrop of intense social and economic deprivation, Newham is preparing itself for lift-off". As then chief executive Wendy Thompson, said: "The Arc of Opportunity will happen. It's just a question of when and how and what standards we set."[4]

The Arc did happen, and continues to happen, but the question behind this project is: "Who is it for?"

This book provides a series of analytic, poetic and global encounters with this open question while acknowledging that

Fig. 4: Screenshot from the London's Regeneration Supernova movie, 2010.

the landscape of East London continues to change

***

In more detail, the book is divided into six parts.

The first part, entitled Regeneration Songs, engages with some of the main themes of the book. In the opening conversation, Andrea Phillips, Anna Minton and Alberto Duman locate the book in Newham and the Arc of Opportunity at a particular moment of transition between local and global city making, and in relation to the role of culture and art in those processes. Anna Minton's "Setting the Scene" follows this by locating the Arc of Opportunity in a thirty-year history of regeneration in East London, which includes the recent story of Robin Hood Gardens – a complex of social housing and social life destroyed as part of East London's wider regeneration programme. The demolition of Robin Hood Gardens is followed by the acquisition by the Victoria and Albert Museum of one of its surviving sections. That section is subsequently displayed at the Venice Architecture Biennale before its return to the new V&A East in the Arc of Opportunity. This again questions the role of cultural and artistic institutions in urban development.

In tension with this discussion, the part that poetry and creative writing can play, beyond compliant decoration to regeneration programmes, is briefly sketched in Gillian Swan's interlude "The Uses of Poetry". Swan's brief story and images capture the delicate moment of threshold between street writing and its removal, offering a reminder that the city–like art–is also a poetic construct even when dominant accountancy procedures very quickly take back control.

The second part of the book–Memory–explores the Arc of Opportunity through the multiple layers of its complex histories, whether repeated, buried, invisible or overlaid. First, Sue Brownill explores the ways in which the redevelopment narrative for the Royal Docks, as a place of "enterprise", "vision" and "growth" has been repeated, like a needle stuck in the groove, since the 1980s. This picture of insistence and idleness is further developed in Matthew Friday's chapter, which shows how since its demise in the 1960s, the Royal Docks have been pieced together as a set of architectural objects, designed to articulate particular messages about enterprise, vision and growth for the area.

Slipping out of the groove, we find a heterogeneous borough with multiple histories. Memories of colonialism and mercantilism, global and local labour exploitation, and their crystallised evidences are teased out in Tom Cordell's chapter, where the local infrastructure and architecture and even the ferry boats of the Woolwich crossing attest to these plural pasts. As Jane Rendell also notes when writing about Stratford, the landscape is not then what it seems. In the anodyne manicure of the Queen Elizabeth Olympic Park, we find a river with no tides and a park overbuilt with skyscrapers. Its psychic life now appears as a dream-work, in all its complex layering.

The third part of the book–Sounds and Visions–focuses on the representations of the Arc of Opportunity by looking at its visual and aural cultural production. As the *London's Regeneration Supernova* movie was delivered with no sound, this book is interested in tracking down those missing sounds. Dan Hancox, Owen Hatherley and Joy White track down the various ways in which music, musicians, music production, and musical culture have played a role in the making and unmaking of this part of London, and other cities in the UK. Dan Hancox returns to the former site of Deja Vu grime pirate radio on Waterden Road. Joy White considers the cultural and economic contribution of Newham's grime scene to the city. Owen Hatherley takes the themes of this section out of London, making links to the culture industries in the north of England.

Connecting the aural to the visual, Will Jennings explores the echoes of the 2012 Olympic Games opening ceremony by linking it to the quasi-mythical spectacle of Jean Michel Jarre's 1988 *Destination Docklands*, as well as to Derek Jarman's

1987 *Last of England*. Expanding these discussions of sense and sensation, Alberto Duman addresses the atmospheric affects of the Arc of Opportunity, understood through London Borough of Newham's livery colour, magenta. The Arc of Opportunity's model of exploitative capitalism is affectively known through this magenta haze. Developing these dimensions of contemporary place-making, Michela Pace returns more concertedly to the visual dimensions of the city to explore the interfaces between Shanghai and London. Here we find a culture-specific grammar of city branding aimed at investors in different global locations. Pushing further into the global dimension of city-making, Keller Easterling discusses the promotional movie genre for free enterprise zones and places yet to exist. By observing these "World City trailers" (*London's Regeneration Supernova* is a prime example) as visual objects with specific qualities, she deconstructs the canned fantasies of place marketing.

The fourth part of the book – The Lived City – emphasises the lived dimension of the area as told through various stories and perspectives. Robert Baffour-Awuah, a member of the Greater London Authority Royal Docks place-making team, provides an insiders account of the identity and brand process for the Royal Docks. He reflexively examines what it means to try to put the Docks "on the map". That process of rapid transformation is at the heart of Theodora Bowering's chapter on discordant city temporalities and aging, as told through her meeting with Betty, an aging resident of Newham. Through this ethnographic engagement Betty describes her life at odds with the hyper-city, opening questions about the ways in which different life stages, times and speeds can, or should, co-exist in a mutual and cooperative city.

The inherent violence of the hyper-city is further developed by Malcolm James in his discussion of authoritarianism in the populist architecture of the Arc of Opportunity. This chapter is interested in the ways in which the populist institutions of the Arc of Opportunity – the museums, universities, shopping centres and green spaces – undermine social democracy as they appeal to the popular. James argues that this move is inherently authoritarian, and that authoritarianism is evidenced in forms of racialised and classed social violence, and through the aesthetic erasure of working-class and black and minority ethnic people from the history of the borough. This process of making people and histories invisible is further developed by Douglas Murphy. Murphy addresses how the Asian Business Port (ABP), currently under development in Royal Albert Dock, came into existence and gained planning permission through a disregard for due process, lack of consultation and oversight typical of Boris Johnson's style of governance, as well as the manipulative manouvering of the global investment game at local planning level.

The fifth part of the book – Fighting Back – looks at various mapping, design, narrative, and visual responses to the multiple violences of the Arc of Opportunity. Phil Cohen questions the contrarian utopias of city acceleration and slowness in favour of the Living Maps – a project to create a London-wide platform for popular and planning. Concrete Action present their ethical architectural practice, a form of anarchic municipalism focused on the material production of the city from a community-led perspective. Their unique contribution is an open source manual for "reclaiming regeneration", based on a rework of the RIBA plan of work, a tool used by architects to organise projects from concept to completion.

David Cross shifts the activism from production to narration, investigating the money trail behind the dominant narratives of the Olympic Park. Cross examines the history of the ArcelorMittal Orbit and its history of environmental and social damage in India and Bosnia. This section ends with another interlude, presented by Amina Gichinga and Rohan Ayinde of Take Back the City, a new grassroots movement run by ordinary Londoners around the issues of social and affordable housing, a real London living wage and truly affordable transport. The interlude presents part of their spoken word performances carried out on buses in and around Newham.

The sixth and final part of the book – Future Fictions – reminds us of the power of fictions and narrative in the discourse of urban spatial politics. The Arc of Opportunity is a fictional entity whose atmospheric and infrastructural drive has produced a spatial reality. The fictional narratives in this chapter expand on and contest the dominant production of the city and seek other ways for cities yet to exist.

Dean Kenning's "The Zone" is a dystopian-comical allegory of regeneration, revisited through the filter of David Harvey's Marxist theory of value, crossed over with Arkady and Boris Strugatsky's *Roadside Picnic*. Kunal Modi's "Recurrence of All Things" goes to the heart of the relationship between cities and images, focusing on the possibility of cities becoming mere images, ideograms. Ending the book, Amy Butt and David Roberts' "Narrative Arcs" takes on the Arc of Opportunity story, multiplying the narrative of arcs towards Swansea Bay and Afghanistan, Swindon and Marrakesh. Here we see the Arc of Opportunity in Newham is resized into just another narrative, one story amongst many.

The appendix contains more information about the contributors to the Music for Masterplanning compilation album. The album was the first output of the Leverhulme project - of which the book is part – and was completed in 2016 during Alberto's period as artist-in-residence at the University of East London thanks to the support, expertise and enthusiasm of Gordon Kerr's staff and students at UEL's music production studios at the Stratford Campus, part of the Faculty of Arts and Digital Industries (ADI).

The seventeen tracks included in the Music for Masterplanning compilation are all three minutes and twelve seconds long, composed from original, repurposed or re-recorded material exclusively for Music for Masterplanning and authored by a broad spectrum of musicians covering many genres, abilities and professional status. They constitute their response in musical language to the "Arc of Opportunity" initiative and what it might mean for them as Newham residents. It is in part a fictional music playlist for an imaginary town planner caught between the competing complexities of her job and in part an intractable and incoherent musical narrative of people increasingly at odds with the place narrative as depicted in the *London's Regeneration Supernova* film.

The compilation is available as a free digital stream to listen or to download from Bandcamp or from the Music for Masterplanning website. Click on the links below to access.

***

In editing the book, Anna and Alberto collaborated with Malcolm James, cultural theorist at the University of Sussex and and author of *Urban Multiculture: Youth, Politics and Cultural Transformation in a Global City*, and Dan Hancox, author of *Inner City Pressure: The Story of Grime*.[5]

Alberto Duman
Dan Hancox
Malcolm James
Anna Minton
London, 2018

http://albertoduman.wixsite.com/music-masterplanning
https://musicformasterplanning.bandcamp.com/

The Leverhulme Trust

Endnotes

1   Walter Benjamin, "One Way Street" (1928), *One Way Street and Other Writings* (Penguin, 2009)

2   Doreen Massey, *Space, Place and Gender* (Wiley, 1994), p. 4. Doreen Massey died in March 2016, as the making of Music for Masterplanning was progressing.

3   We Sell Boxes We Buy Gold was the collaboration between curators Lucia Farinati and Louise Garrett, artists Richard Crow and Alberto Duman, and urban researcher/poet Jude Rosen. The project considered the 2012 Olympic site and the Lower Lea Valley as a context for interdisciplinary research and artistic intervention. http://boxesforgold. blogspot.co.uk/

4   Nick Mathiason, "Canning Town Masterplan - North of the Dome, a new world view", *Estates Gazette*, 13th March 1999, http://www.prsarchitects.com/news/publications/ canning-town-masterplan-north-dome-new-world-view Last Accessed on 3rd March 2018.

5   Dan Hancox, *Inner City Pressure: The Story of Grime*, (Harper Collins, 2018)

London's regeneration supernova.
Where 8million people live.
27 million people visit.
Welcome.
300 languages are spoken.
Where you'll find over 250 free attractions.
Newham London.
London's moving east.
Supernova.
Where you can catch the 2012 Games in the Olympic Stadium.
Where you can fly to New York.
And get the train to Paris and beyond.
Where you can shop in Europe's largest Urban Shopping Centre
which is part of a new metropolitan centre in Stratford.
Where you are 15 min from the World's Principal Financial Centre.
Newham is at the centre of London's growth, development and
innovation for the 21st Century.
It has been prioritised for billion of pounds of investment.
Where the scale of opportunity is 1142 hectares.
That's 2x the scale of Venice.
The Royal Docks.
Where you'll find 13 miles of river and dock frontage.
Where you'll find an airport, a university and London's international
convention centre.
Historically London's gateway to the world.
Now at the heart of London's future.
Sustainability.
Where we are creating a green business, technology and learning
district.
Where you will be able to live, work and stay in a viable low-carbon
environment.
Where we are building a better future for our people.
Where the population is the youngest in London.
Creating 100.000 new jobs.
Building 35.000 new homes.
Where there is huge potential for growth and prosperity.
Thank you.
Take your place in the future of London.
Newham London.
www.newhamshanghaiexpo.com

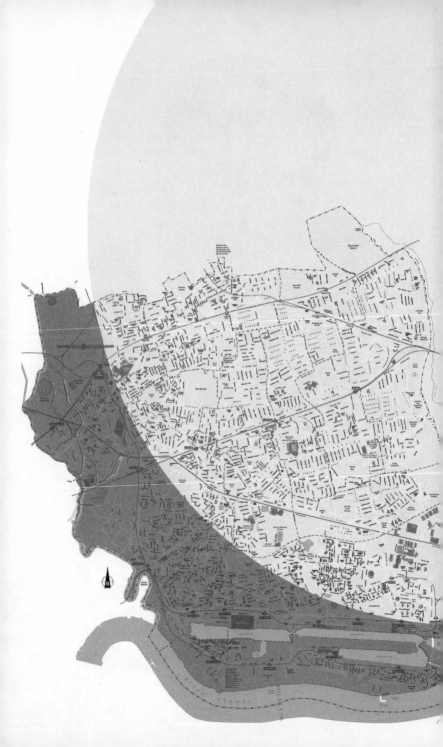

Part 1

Regeneration Songs

A Conversation

between Alberto Duman, Andrea Phillips, and Anna Minton

Andrea Phillips: My feeling is there are two elements that we could pursue in the conversation: One is a general question about rights to the city and the idea of social housing, and what policies and what ideas you think fruitful in developing a more spatially just way of organising the city based on the research that you've done. So in a way for you, Anna, it would be a bit like the next chapter of *Big Capital*. Then there's another much more specific set of questions that are around the Arc of Opportunity and the Newham projects that you're both involved in and the book focuses on. These are for me the important questions to ask: the role of the gentrifier in oppositional politics, the way in which artists contribute, or to put it another way, how can the role of "the artist" in inverted commas pursue radical agendas around housing and its lack without getting embroiled in a gentrifying process? Is there a mode through which that can happen? Because it would seem to me in the current situation it's virtually impossible, that one needs to lose one's identity as an artist in order to get involved in politics.

Alberto why don't you start by telling us where the project is at? We know from you that the *London's Regeneration Supernova* video from Newham [...] was no longer available, then through a Freedom of Information request you obtained a silent version and then your specific intervention produced the *Music for Masterplanning* album. What is happening in the area now?

Alberto Duman: It's a long and convoluted story that arises from the adoption of a New Public Management style by Newham, which aimed to transform completely the narrative of their council from being high in the deprivation index – a discredited story anyway as a description of themselves – and rewrite the way that narrative impacted on the way that their whole image is perceived. Newham really adopted this style of management as a way of narrating itself and throughout the whole period Robin Wales has been in charge, as council leader since 1995 and then Newham's first mayor from 2002 until now.

Anna Minton: Yes, Robin Wales has spanned the whole of the New Labour era and he was definitely one of the great survivors of that period very much promoting those values and that approach.[1]

AD   The story draws a huge amount of power from this kind of New Public Management and it reveals that when stories of market take-over of public assets or public administration are put forward as explanations of how we got into a neoliberal phase, it's just the opposite: the doors were held wide open by political forces and by administrative management, saying "Here we are – we are ready for business and we actually mean business". So really, whilst there is this idea of a "rape of the public services by market forces", I don't believe that for a second…

AM   I completely agree with you, the public sector is leading on it.

AP   I think you just made a big leap there with the "rape of public services by the market forces"… so let's just clarify why you both oppose that and then go back to the management aspect. So just to spell it out, what's wrong with that?

AM Well, it's essentially the public sector acting completely hand in glove with private developers and lobbyists and normally behind closed doors, working to reconfigure and reimage the city without the involvement of local communities and the democratic process. And it's presented very much today by New Labour authorities as being a case of "We don't have a choice! We're facing 40% cuts! The public sector has been decimated! If we want to do anything, if we want to build any housing and we want to create any opportunities or infrastructure in our areas we HAVE to partner with the private sector!" But actually it's not – as Alberto points out – that way round. It's the public sector who are leading on this and to a large extent that's what happened in the Docklands as well, where the public sector offered huge subsidies and tax breaks to inward investment which then piled in. So it's the same trajectory but just with a "New Labour" set of nuances compared to the Tory days of the 1980s.

AP I agree that the idea that the market has come in and decimated the public sector is completely inaccurate fiscally as well as ideologically, but what's interesting is the role of organisations like the Architecture Foundation because of course they're seen as a kind of creative political critical force that comes in and organises public thinking around the built environment. I remember a conference they organised in 2001 on the Lansbury Estate, to coincide with the fiftieth anniversary of the 1951 exhibition for which there was also an outpost in exactly the same space. It symbolised a kind of nostalgia for the Keynesian moment of the building of the welfare state, but while I was sitting

31

in that beautiful church where the conference was held I got thinking about how the Architecture Foundation epitomises a certain kind of new neoliberal force, wherein New Public Management is incorporated and quite literally taken into the body of the arts.

AM I've been thinking about the role of artists in gentrification in the last week with regard to Richard Sennett's new book which I have just reviewed (*Building and Dwelling: Ethics for the City*, Allen Lane, 2018). I think Richard Sennett has a lot of very profound things to say about the city, but at the same time he is not someone who wishes to engage with issues of race and class and structural economics. He doesn't subscribe to Henri Lefebvre's "Right to the City" approach. He's not a Marxist sociologist, he's quite the opposite. And yet what I've been wondering, as I've been thinking about his book, is if some of his ideas can be incorporated together with a more "Right to the City" approach, and how that might mean we can start to come to somewhere quite interesting with regard to the processes of gentrification and the involvement of artists in gentrification. At the moment, a lot of people take a similar view of gentrification and subscribe very much to Neil Smith's view of the rent gap, that gentrification occurs in areas where land values are low and where there is potential for those land values to increase. Artists are the shock troops of gentrification because they need cheap space in buildings, and because they are often the harbingers of fashion they act as the marketeers and propagandists of those areas – it's difficult not to subscribe to this view.

But I do think there's more to it than that – it's not just about the economic picture, it's also about the creativity of the space in terms of places of resistance that Sennett talks about in an interesting way in his latest book. There he describes his ideal place as a market on top of a car park in Delhi called Nehru Place. He describes this as a really successful part of the city probably not dissimilar to the Latin American indoor market at Ward's Corner in Tottenham that is threatened with eviction and demolition. You know the sort of space, a vibrant informal economy, street activities... now that's Richard Sennett's ideal place and part of the reason why is because it facilitates spontaneous encounters and multiple exchanges between people. But he is not interested in discussing the economics which displace that activity. What he is interested in discussing are the interactions between people which flourish in the sort of a place where you need to have your wits about you and be aware of what's going on, basically a more exciting sort of place than a Canary Wharf or a privatised space full of security guards where it's completely safe – or at least you think it is safe – but it's actually very uncreative and very boring. I'm not sure I've explained that very coherently. I've only just started thinking about it but I think if you take some of what he's saying about the importance of spaces of resistance which flourish in the informal economy and put that together with Neil Smith's rent gap ideas on gentrification, you get a more complicated picture of the role of the artist, which is not just about cheap space.

AP I think that you're absolutely right that this picture needs to be made more complex. I think that's where we need to get to. But in this and previous works of Sennett there are traces of what I might call politely a lack of racial awareness in his interest in informality. Many of my friends who are postcolonial scholars or anticolonial scholars would say actually he's excited by racial alterity and that's why he finds the market in Delhi on top of the car park which is a kind of rather bourgeois affair – in Delhi terms – exciting and interesting, but a bit like going down to Spitalfields on a Saturday or a Sunday. So I think there are some real issues with this idea of the informal sudden encounter that is dangerous because the perception of danger is potentially racially oriented.

AM   He's not offering an alternative, he just places himself as a sort of participant observer who doesn't have political opinions and says: "This is what the city created by Google (the Googleplex environment), this is what the informal economy in this particular location looks like, this is what this Columbian slum looks like, and I'm going to make some observations relating to how people communicate and how strangers interact within the space and I'm not going to link those observations to the wider socioeconomic realities", which is where I start to have difficulties... I take your point about power relations – there's another section in the book where he describes walking through Medellin in Columbia and talks about how exciting it is walking through this slum area with this eight-year-old kid who is showing him around. The point he's trying to make is about "prehension" – which is when you anticipate what might be around the corner – and he talks about how skilled this kid is at knowing exactly what's going on in his patch compared to the "stupefying smart city". I think those are really important points but at the same time you have those really problematic power relations where he's quite happy to be shown around by a kid and giving him a dollar as a thank-you... so both coexist.

AP   There's a long history within artistic work and also within architectural theory of this romanticisation of the dangerous parts of the city. You can go back to Venturi, Scott Brown's "Learning from Las Vegas", you know the "It's this exciting it's a mess" case. I'm simplifying a narrative here but the issue is the way that architectural theory—at least some of it—and sociology takes up Lefebvre is through a simplification of the narrative, to understand the production of space as being "what we do when we open a farmer's market"… and it's not! I think that's one of the problems with the way that Lefebvre has been misinterpreted. People like Neil Smith were absolutely intervening in that narrative and trying to correct it and doing it very vociferously.

Returning to the opportunity we're looking at here, the "Arc of Opportunity", let's get down to the detail of the facts here…

AD   Well the interesting thing is that the Arc of Opportunity was never really a policy, it was never really a detailed plan, it was always really just a rhetorical narrative. That's why I understood it as an atmosphere.

AM   But still I think the question is "opportunity for whom?" and this brings us back to Lefebvre. It's an opportunity alright but not for Newham's population—it's an opportunity for the people it was pitched to at the Shanghai Expo. Did it work?

AD   Considering that it's now a twenty-year-old narrative it certainly has had an effect even if only for the longevity of its persistence. So in that sense, it's been rolled out even if there was never a specificity about its plan. You cannot even call the Arc of Opportunity a "masterplan" but more a generic narrative of ambitions about how we like to see a placemaking strategy developing, really just a place-marketing narrative, so it doesn't matter how it actually works. I'm just thinking of Sue Brownill's chapter in this book. What also emerges is the extension of this kind of place-marketing strategy to the whole of the South East with the Thames Estuary Production Corridor, and of course at some point the arc overlapped with the Thames Gateway Development Corporation...

AM Can I just tell you a story about that? ...It's a funny story to do with the Thames Gateway.

AP Sure, go ahead...

AM OK, so around 2005 I was asked to do some work by CABE [the Commission for Architecture and the Built Environment], a central New Labour institution operating in the sphere that we're talking about. What they wanted to do was a piece of work that would help get the Thames Gateway off the ground. And so they asked me to write it and it was going to be a mixture of interviews with interesting people from East London who were doing interesting things and well-known artists, so I went to interview Iain Sinclair and Billy Bragg, amongst others. And I travelled throughout the area – the Medway towns, Rochester, Chatham, Canvey Island – really trying to experience the space. But there was also this set of branding workshops with Wolff Olins that we had to attend...

AD ...Who ended up doing the Olympic branding a few years later...

AM ...And this was about coming up with a branding strategy for the Thames Gateway and I just remember somebody standing up and saying: "I love my iPhone – this is the best brand I can think of, we have to think of the iPhone equivalent of the Thames Gateway", and the whole thing was beyond silly!

Anyway I wrote my piece – essentially I wasn't really allowed to write anything of interest except a travel piece so I wrote a travel piece that was quite pleasant, but there were no politics because the editors were not interested in that. And the upshot, the conclusion of the whole thing, the branding exercise and all that effort, was a report titled: "NEW THINGS HAPPEN". I mean, the cost to create this super expensive document. You know they paid me £15,000, it was a three-month project. They must have paid Wolff Olins £100K plus.

AP   Yes I would think so.

AM   Sorry, that was a tangent…

AP   No it's interesting in relation to this concept of New Public Management because this idea of pitching is one of the interesting things that happens in New Public Management – it's that local authorities had to learn to pitch and be pitched at. So that's a kind of pedagogical shift or an ideological shift if you prefer, where a transformation […] has to occur in how things are done – now people have to pitch.

I have an anecdote that I think is extremely related to this notion. When Open School East were looking for another location because their lease was coming to an end, they had a breakfast event where lots of local authorities came to pitch at them to try and get Open School East to move to their area in order to develop this process of gentrification. Barking was there and so were Newham and Margate – essentially "the poor boroughs". And they are now in Margate, so I think this concept of pitching is very important. Now we have a complete transformation within the council narrative of what you do if you're an arts officer or what you do if you are an urban-planning officer – your job is completely transformed from the job it might have been in 1980.

AD   One of the striking things about Newham's Arc of Opportunity when it comes to urban regeneration is that there is a lot of GLA-owned land within it–that's why the Arc of Opportunity could never be a specific strategy and that's why both Robin Wales and Boris Johnson went to Shanghai. Part of the difficulty is that it has a mixed ownership and governance–the Olympic Park is overseen by the London Legacy Development Corporation, which is the planning authority. Then you have the middle bit where Newham had a long-term strategy that extended from Canning Town to Custom House where the new Crossrail is coming, then there is the Royal Docks and there was another complexity there, since it's owned more by the GLA than by Newham, which is why the GLA now has an office in the Siemens Crystal to oversee the speedy placemaking of the area which has been lagging behind–[it was] one of the most intractable parts even during the days of the London Docklands Development Corporation.

AP   What you're both saying is that this shouldn't be read as lack of success on the part of the atmosphere of the Arc of Opportunity, it was actually a successful campaign.

AD   Very much so in the sense that I think it pioneered a kind of planning, a protracted way of holding a particular set of futures for a certain area in check, so that no other future can develop within that time. The Arc of Opportunity and other examples elsewhere in the world constituted this new way of narrating the future of a certain particular area from the heart of the administrative body–which amongst other things is supposed to run and deliver social care for all its citizens–and instead it constructs these narratives which are basically pitches for investments. It's a strategic and opportunistic approach to planning. And it remains the standard model for regeneration. For example, we now have a similarly long-term vague plan called the Thames Estuary Production Corridor, which is a document extending the approach of the Arc of Opportunity all the way to the coast and absorbing the Royal Docks part of it.

AM Yes, it's basically Michael Heseltine's vision from the early Eighties. I think he was the first person who came up with the idea of the East Thames Corridor, which then morphed into the Thames Gateway, and this was all laid down as part of the original Docklands Development Corporation vision, and it's still very much continuing. I mean it shows a certain lack of imagination or the persistence of an idea – thirty years later we are wedded to the same trajectory.

Some of it feels like what Docklands felt [like] in the late Eighties... empty spaces and developments that may be existing in an off-plan world but not actually in the real world. You're not sure if it's going to happen or not. It's got that sense of uncertainty and as you say too melancholy about it, slightly Derek Jarman-esque.

AP I'm interested in this atmosphere and how the atmosphere is contributed to by not only urban nostalgia – and I think you're absolutely right about that – but also a "civic" nostalgia. And here I really do think that nostalgia is very much part of kind of what I said before, as a kind of nostalgia for some [...] version of Keynesianism that never actually existed. I mean it must've existed in the NHS but I don't think it existed within the complex and antagonistic societies and communities and constituents that were living in London at the time. I'm also interested in the way that the arts have played a role in that nostalgia. I think Iain Sinclair is culpable, I think yes you're right

Jarman to a certain extent is culpable, despite the fact that I'm a huge admirer of his work.

The question of culpability is interesting, isn't it, because it's not about being culpable directly, it's an indirect culpability which is part of the problem we're trying to get to. I think it's indirect responsibility or it's retroactive agency and that's a problem for the artist who is working. A very important example is Littlewood's Fun Palace – you know, this kind of an ideological multifaceted superstructure never built that was supposed to be very much part of a kind of working relationship with an area of East London. What was very interesting was that in 2015 the Arts Council funded a huge program related to the centenary of Joan Littlewood's birth that I was repeatedly asked to be part of, as were many of my colleagues. This was Stella Duffy revisiting the Fun Palace idea, through the creation of fun palaces up and down the country but entirely denuded of their ideological imperative. And of course those that made those fun palaces weren't critical artists, but they were people that were members of local communities, so in a way the organisers ticked all the boxes in terms of, you know, gathering together on a certain day and animating the spaces and having fun. And it's very interesting how easy the Cedric Price and Joan Littlewood vision gets mobilised as – what you called – an atmospheric or an ideological perversion into New Public Management and placemaking.

AD   Of course, but remember that placemaking has entered officially the Arts Council language as one their main reasons to fund the arts. Placemaking intended really clearly as a sense of economic trigger/redevelopment trigger, leaving the principle of "arm's length" well behind.

AM   What does placemaking really mean apart from economic regeneration with decorative elements and emphasising community involvement? The kind of engaged citizen, the sort of Jane Jacobs type, but missing the overview of the social and economic forces that actually see most of the original community displaced from "the place". It's a very apolitical idea of placemaking.

AP   It's not apolitical; it's deliberately depoliticised.

AM   If we just look at placemaking in a Lefebvrian terms, a place used primarily as a product and as a space for investment, that's what contemporary placemaking is. What I wonder is what role can the artist play – any creative role – within this kind of situation? Can today, in our current climate, the artist play any useful role in this context?

AD   I think it begins with Foucault and *homo economicus*, his narrations of how neoliberal ideas in their early days really looked out for subjectivities, and where they go in order to find them. It then reconnects with Boltanski and Chiapello and the "New Spirit of Capitalism" for which the artist is being called out as directly culpable for having provided neoliberalism with the subjectivity it was looking for. At the same time I read Matteo Pasquinelli's work in a much more confident kind of way that gives me some rather convincing answers as an artist without thinking that all I'm trying to do is seek some redemption or way out from the self-flagellating option of total collusion with capital forces shaping the urban environment. I have lived in London since 1990 and have seen this process emerging in all the "hot" areas. I didn't venture into Newham in those days but it was enough to be in Dalston in the Nineties and so on. So the way I see this articulated is through these questions that I have also asked in several other situations: "What does art want from capital?" and then of course "What does capital want from art?" and why do the two have a certain trajectory that correlates at some point even if it's not causal. There's a correlation there but not necessarily causality in the way art and capital became implicated, at least from the point of view of the artist.

The animated discussions of artwashing we witness these days really come from the implications of art and capital in urban development understood as that direct causality. Of course it's also a reaction to the fact that the kind of dispersed atmospheres of placemaking are very difficult to confront directly as politics on the ground because there's no direct target in an atmosphere (unless there is a cereal café as a handy target!). Atmospheres are created by documents which are scoping studies in which the small disclaimer asterisk tells us that they are just momentary constructs, and they tell us not to believe in this narrative at the same time that is pitched and covertly operative.

AP   It tells us it's a future fantasy.

AD   But this is exactly the issue, because of this increased production of the visualisation of future fantasies – well not just because of this, but – art has changed hugely. It's not at all what it was even twenty years ago and my feeling is that it has all to do with how this proximity with capital has altered its nature in ways that the arts community still doesn't really want come to grips with. It is very reluctant to say "Look what we have become", since such view would debase some of its traditional legitimacy arguments. Only through that way of looking at what we have become can one see possible ways out of this place. I'm trying to kind of get to the end of this because it's something that pains me immensely, I suffer every time we get called "artwashers" – particularly when the accusations are right! I think it's happening because we live in these particular situations and we haven't come to grips with these changes and the way capital articulates our language on our behalf. In order to take a stance into a mode of resistance it's tempting to stay just at the ground level and meet people and let the people and the participatory environment give us potential answers. It's understandable that one could think that by doing that one hopes to divert towards the participants/the people, the agency that we find difficult to articulate otherwise in our own individual agency. On the other hand, the way in which we can also intervene is exactly in the production of these dreams, these future stories, which are exactly where capital has extracted and absorbed from the artist the vision of future previsualisation, the "oracular" at work in the speculative production of world futures. And that's where I think the main energy drive of capital is at the moment, in this "future production". It is actually in this industry of future production that artists should enter and intervene.

AM And what shape would that intervention take?

AD By entering the discursive spaces where these materials circulate unseen by the public and redeeming them from the kind of disregarded, nonconsequential marketing dross they seem to signify as opposed to art. *Music for Masterplanning* strived to enter into these discursive spaces – not necessarily at first to do with art – where these materials circulate and become operative on many different levels. We often start from the ground level to see things, but we should also go to the top level, at the level where atmospheres are generated.

43

AM Is it not also the case that there is no funding – hardly at all – for this sort of project? That comes back to the points about the institutional framework. I guess if you as an artist want to make critical work you simply have to accept that you occupy outsider status, which some people might be happy with but other people have to feed their families and, you know, keep a roof over their heads... I mean isn't it just that simple?

AD Not at all... the simple "artists must eat" response skews the debate from what artists actually do towards another conversation where it goes off the rails and loses its focus...

AP I think it's not [that simple], although the pragmatics of feeding your family and keeping a roof over your head are very important aspects of any discussion. Alberto, I think that your narrative is really interesting and hopeful although I would say that there is however within it also a fantasy, which is that capitalisation of the arts started only twenty years ago: capitalisation of the arts has always existed.

AM Couldn't it just mean "Don't take on certain jobs"... as in, "Don't work with Lendlease!" It's the same conversation for architects who are constantly saying "What do I do?" Kate Macintosh comes to mind. She was asked this question at an Architectural Workers event and she just said "Maybe think of doing something else for a while". I mean it gets to that point.

AD And I think for artists the predicament is the same.

Recorded at Showroom Gallery, 16 January 2018.

Endnotes

1   Robin Wales was deselected as Newham's Mayoral candidate in March 2018 after twenty-three years as Mayor

Setting the Scene: Thirty Years of Regeneration in East London

Anna Minton

Every year the University of East London's postgraduate Master of Research course in Architecture, subtitled "Reading the Neoliberal City", begins with a walk around the wider local area – and every year what we experience is substantially different.

From Cyprus we take the Docklands Light Railway into the heart of the original Docklands developments, to start to investigate the origins of the heavily contested story of Docklands. We walk through the private estates at South Quay and pass what feel like endless hoardings for new luxury developments which line the route to Canary Wharf, the privately owned, high-security estate which in the 1980s pioneered "regeneration" – a *tabula rasa* model of development which saw former low-value industrial land repurposed as private space for investment, which would command high property prices and rents. Passing by the barriers, bollards, and uniformed guards who police the ninety-seven-acre Canary Wharf Estate, we cross the footbridge to West

India Quay where an exhibition at the Museum of London is all that remains of the history of the old docks and the community campaign for an alternative plan. A hundred metres on, we hit a hard boundary where the estate comes to an abrupt end at Aspen Way, the dual carriageway separating Canary Wharf from Poplar on the other side.

When I first took students on this walk five years ago, the footbridge over the dual carriageway was a stark transition point between the two different worlds of the gleaming finance centre and Poplar's shabby housing estates. The skyscrapers still loom over the estates but now it's Poplar that is the contested area, with bitter battles raging over the future of Chrisp Street Market, Balfron Tower, and Robin Hood Gardens. Poplar Harca, the housing association set up by Tower Hamlets Borough Council to manage its nine thousand homes and regenerate the area, is at the centre of plans to reconfigure and reimage the area, proposing to replace the market with new shops, a cinema, and 650 mostly luxury apartments. Following a public outcry, closely linked to decisions made on nearby Balfron Tower and Robin Hood Gardens, planning permission was postponed.

Grade II-listed Balfron Tower, built by Erno Goldfinger in 1967, has been at the centre of another gentrification battle after Poplar Harca began refurbishment of the block with a view to converting all the properties into luxury apartments for private sale–despite earlier promises that the social-housing residents who wished to would be able to return. Balfron Tower is a listed building so it escapes the fate of so many other housing estates across London which now face demolition, to be replaced by developments of yet more luxury apartments with limited amounts of affordable housing. We always end our walk at neighbouring Robin Hood Gardens, just a few minutes away. While the walk changes every year, this place is now the most traumatically different; at the time of writing bulldozers are on-site and through a gouged-out section the HSBC tower block is visible, a fitting symbol of the impact of global capital on run-down housing estates ripe for development. An accompanying symbol of global property finance has been doing the rounds on social media in the shape of an advertisement for a launch event for the new Blackwall Reach development which will replace Robin Hood Gardens. Held at the Mandarin Oriental Hotel in Hong Kong in October 2017, when the bulldozers had barely got onto the site, the event boasted "East London's Best Value 2 Bedroom Apartments from £565,000".

Built by Peter and Alison Smithson in 1972, Robin Hood Gardens was, like Balfron Tower, considered by many to be a modernist masterpiece and on previous walks we have encountered visiting architects from all over the world. A campaign to gain listed status included support from preservation bodies, architectural historians, Richard Rogers, and Zaha Hadid, who said it was her favourite building in London. It failed and was followed by a second application by the Twentieth Century

Fig. 1: Robin Hood Gardens being demolished, to make way for Blackwall Reach. © Andrew Parnell 2018.

Fig. 2: Advertisement for Blackwall Reach launch event at the Mandarin Oriental Hotel, Hong Kong. Seen in Mark Baines, "Want to live in Tower Hamlets? Best you pop over to Hong Kong then", Lovewapping.org, last accessed 3 March 2018.

Society, which also failed. The addendum to this story is that the Victoria and Albert Museum recently acquired a three-storey section of the estate, including the exterior facades and the interiors of a maisonette flat. The nine-metre-high section is likely to be exhibited in the new entrance to the V&A East which will open at the Olympic Park, with the V&A arguing that the acquisition is not only about preservation, but about maintaining conversations about social housing. But critics have rounded on the museum, pointing out that the V&A – which did not back the listing campaign – should have intervened earlier when it could have wielded considerable influence on ministers. Instead the irony is that a public institution is viewed as making cultural capital from a section of an iconic building which was not deemed worth saving as housing for people to live in.

Placemaking and the "Rent Gap"

The conversion of Balfron Tower into luxury apartments and the replacement of Robin Hood Gardens by Blackwall Reach, alongside a regenerated Chrisp Street Market quite unlike the current version, are part of a "placemaking" strategy to reconfigure and reimage Poplar. Similar placemaking strategies are in play across neighbouring Newham's "Arc of Opportunity" area, at the Greenwich Peninsula, at Kings Cross, in Elephant and Castle, and throughout London and other British – and North American – cities. The strategy (in)famously popularised in Richard Florida's landmark book, *The Rise of the Creative Class*,[1] holds that knowledge workers – in design, technology, education, arts, and entertainment – are the spur for growth through innovation, and placemaking should aim to attract these types who power forward the new economy and cleave to hip locations. Creating "innovation clusters"[2] – which ideally include a university, commercial space, shops, restaurants, and perhaps an art gallery, alongside housing in the form of luxury apartments – is the model generally favoured, most often in a Canary Wharf-style privately owned, high-security environment.

Stratford Waterside in the Cultural and Educational District and HereEast in the Olympic Park are flagship examples, with global museums and cultural institutions, a tech hub, UAL's London College of Fashion, and UCL's Engineering School and Bartlett School of Architecture. At Greenwich Peninsula, the presence of the art school Ravensbourne brings activity and a "sense of place" to the area, which also boasts the O2 venue and Emirates Air Line among the attractions for those seeking to invest in the forest of luxury apartment towers going up. At Kings Cross, another art school, Central Saint Martin's, provides the cultural capital for what is billed as the largest redevelopment in northern Europe, set in a private estate of two thousand homes alongside an "innovation cluster" which includes Google's headquarters, with Facebook apparently set to follow. And in Elephant and Castle, where the Heygate Estate was demolished in the face of huge local opposition and replaced by the luxury housing complex Elephant Park, the London College of Communication has partnered with developer Delancey to redevelop the shopping centre in a scheme that uncannily mirrors what is happening in Poplar.

"Placemaking" is a vague term, which seems to have originated in the US, at the behest of the American policy makers who have been so influential in shaping UK policy towards cities. Bruce Katz–a specialist in "global urbanisation" at the American thinktank the Brookings Institution, where he founded the "Metropolitan Policy Programme" twenty years ago–has been a leading player in developing placemaking strategies, which closely cross-fertilised with New Labour during the late 1990s and 2000s, and it's a terms he favours in his book *The New Localism*.[3] For him, placemaking is a process whereby former industrial and inner-city areas are regenerated by "extracting value" through "increasing commercial yield"–which means that the potential for relatively low-priced former industrial and inner-city areas to produce far higher returns attracts developers. In turn, the tendency is for existing communities to be displaced as the cost of housing soars. *The New Localism* acknowledges that the outcome is to "typically see tenant replacement" as "yesterday's artist's lofts become tomorrow's investment banker's condos,"[4] but while housing affordability is seen as an issue it is not addressed–almost as though it were collateral damage, the price that must be paid for this model.

An alternative lens through which to look at similar processes is provided by the late geographer Neil Smith, who developed his theory of the rent gap as far back as 1979, as an economic explanation for gentrification.[5] This held that when the gap between the current "rent" or income from a property and the potential income was large enough, developers would become interested and private capital would flow in. Smith's insights provide an explanation for British urban policy in Docklands during the 1980s and beyond as incentives and tax breaks were provided to developers to invest in formerly run-down industrial areas. By the 1990s self-styled urbanists such as Bruce Katz were putting forward the value of "placemaking" as a rationale and justification for these often contested approaches. In the late 1990s and 2000s New Labour governments were also driven by the desire to "extract value" from places, which led to the scandal of "Pathfinder", the "Housing Market Renewal Programme" that aimed to increase property prices in areas of low value in Northern towns–which also tended to be well-located and therefore identified as ripe for property price increases. While areas where prices had collapsed were the initial focus of the programme, it rapidly expanded far beyond this and resulted in the demolition of tens of thousands of properties and the destruction of communities in towns across the North of England.[6]

More recently, the determined attempt by London councils to partner with developers to raze their housing estates has seen the revival of this approach, which was spearheaded by the former Labour Cabinet Minister Andrew Adonis, after former Chancellor George Osborne appointed him chair of the National

Infrastructure Commission. After Adonis edited a report on the subject, known as "the Savills report"[7] as it contained an analysis by estate agents Savills, Adonis explained his version of the "rent gap" to the *Financial Times*:

> The scale of council-owned land is vast and greatly under appreciated. There are particularly large concentrations of council-owned land in inner London and this is some of the highest priced land in the world... [The] local authority planning regime has got to adapt properly to the potential for [market-priced rent] developments.[8]

When Neil Smith first highlighted the "rent gap" as an economic explanation for gentrification, the speed of global capital flows bore no relation to what we see today and the impact of capital on potentially high-value areas took place over considerably longer periods. This has been particularly the case in London, which since the financial crisis witnessed a flood of capital into the city as a result of a number of factors. These include quantitative easing, the policy of bailing out the banks through the creation of new money which also found itself directed into the property market, and London's minimal tax and regulatory regime.[9] The impact of lax regulation, highlighted in the Panama Papers and Paradise Papers, has seen the influx of foreign investment into forty thousand anonymous shell companies, many of which are known to hide corrupt sources.[10] These factors have combined with council policies to demolish housing estates and replace them with largely luxury apartment developments, like Blackwall Reach or Elephant Park, which target private investors. Councils argue that in an austerity climate, with local authorities facing savage cuts of 40%, this is the only way to cross-subsidise affordable housing; but academics describe the process as "state-led gentrification" because of the pivotal role played by local authorities.[11] Robin Hood Gardens is just one example of the collateral damage, with academics estimating that estate demolition has so far claimed at least one hundred housing estates around London.[12]

Collateral Damage and Structural Instability

The irony is that the sheer volume of "placemaking", amply illustrated by all the cranes and construction sites around London, is not providing the housing the city needs. The Blackwall Reach sales brochure given out in Hong Kong includes an instructive

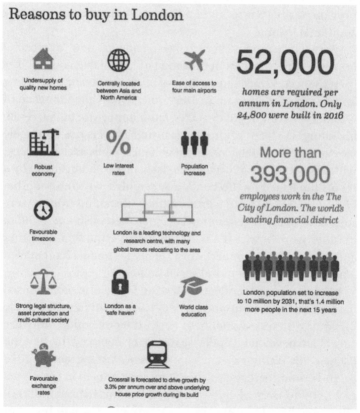

Fig. 3: *Blackwall Reach E14*, sales brochure. Seen in Mark Baines, "Want to live in Tower Hamlets? Best you pop over to Hong Kong then", *Lovewapping. org*, last accessed 3 March 2018.

section for investors headed "Reasons to buy in London". A little padlock graphic highlights the importance of London as a "safe haven", which is shorthand for the city's relaxed tax and regulatory regime, but the headline reason is the undersupply of new homes, with the graphic explaining that 52,000 homes are required per annum in London but only 24,800 were built in 2016. So foreign investors are encouraged to buy on the very basis that local people are excluded from the property market, with the implication being that the private rented market will provide steady returns for middle-class Asian investors seeking additional income.

Most people cannot afford to live in London's new "affordable" homes, as the government definition of "affordable housing" has been changed to mean up to 80% of market rent or market value and starter homes for up to £450,000.[13] So, while the result of estate regeneration policy is that more homes are built overall, including 25–30% "affordable housing", this is not affordable for even those on relatively high incomes, while social housing, which is genuinely affordable, is slashed. This is borne out by a report published by the London Assembly[14] which found that between 2005 and 2015 around thirty thousand homes were subject to estate regeneration schemes (demolish and rebuild, in other words), which almost doubled the number of homes and increased the number of private homes tenfold but entailed a net loss of eight thousand social homes.

In Elephant and Castle, the Heygate Estate originally housed more than three thousand people in 1,214 homes. But of the 2,704 new homes at Elephant Park–the development by the Australian developer Lendlease which has replaced the Heygate Estate–only eighty-two are for social rent.[15] At the start of 2018 a two-bedroom property at Elephant Park ranged in price from £890,000 to over £1 million. Given the current definition of affordable housing, this places the properties squarely out of reach not only of those on lower incomes but also those on middle and even relatively high incomes; and in the first phase

100% of all properties were sold to foreign investors.[16]

As for the collateral damage, initial promises by Southwark Council to rehouse five hundred Heygate households on the redeveloped site were not honoured. While most tenants were rehoused within the borough–albeit at some distance from social networks, schools, and communities–it is the homeowners on these estates, the leaseholders who bought their home under Right to Buy, who are particularly hard hit, with many having to move out of London as the compensation home owners received as a result of Compulsory Purchase averaged £107,230 for a two-bedroom flat. Former Heygate home owners now live in Orpington, Sevenoaks, Thurrock, and Rochester. A retired couple I interviewed who had to leave London for Sidcup have suffered serious mental and physical health problems including severe depression, problems that are common among those who have been displaced.[17]

At Blackwall Reach, which replaces Robin Hood Gardens, the £572,000 price tag is similarly unaffordable for most Londoners.

The way Elephant Park, Blackwall Reach, and other schemes in London are marketed to foreign investors is "off plan"–which means before they are even built. Not only does this fail to meet local need, it is also building structural instability into the property market. The launch event for Blackwall Reach in Hong Kong advertises "preferential payment terms", which include "5% on exchange, 5% after 12 months, balance on completion". This means that investors pay less than £30,000 to purchase an apartment–£28,600 is 5% of £572,000–followed by another £28,600 a year later if they are still interested, with 90% of the purchase price not due until completion. So, while a developer may claim that they have sold all the properties for sale in a scheme, the reality may well be that they have only sold 5% of all properties, and if it looks as if prices may fall investors will likely pull out. This is already happening in schemes across London, with fifteen thousand unsold apartments creating headlines about "posh ghost towers". Property consultants Molior estimate that it will take at least three years to sell the glut of luxury flats if sales continue at their current rate and no new apartments are built, but developers have an unprecedented further 420 residential towers in the pipeline.[18]

After Grenfell

On 14 June 2017 the Grenfell Tower fire killed seventy-one people, in an inferno that firefighters said they would not expect to see in a Third World city, let alone in one of the richest parts of one of the richest cities in the world. Shortly after, it emerged that local campaign group, the Grenfell Action Group, had warned in a horrifyingly prescient blog entitled "Playing with Fire" that it would take a "catastrophic event" to expose the scandal of how housing was run in Kensington and Chelsea.[19] The parallel with what happened at Grenfell, and the contested development struggles taking place in London and other cities, is the lack of accountability that councils and the assorted quangos and companies that deal with housing and regeneration display towards communities that stand in their way.

The paradox of Grenfell is that this unprecedented tragedy has shone a light on the multiple failures in housing, regeneration, and placemaking strategies, creating an impetus for alternative approaches. What many housing campaigners have found hardest to bear is that it is Labour councils who have been pursuing regeneration most avidly, from Newham and Tower Hamlets in East London to Southwark and Lambeth in the South. Speaking in the shadow of the disaster, Labour Leader Jeremy Corbyn told the Labour Party Conference that "after Grenfell we must think again about what are called regeneration schemes. Too often what it really means is forced gentrification and social cleansing, as private developers move in and tenants and leaseholders are moved out."[20] This was followed in 2018 by London Mayor Sadiq Khan pledging that estate regeneration would not go ahead without balloted agreement by a majority of residents.

The most unexpected intervention in a flagship placemaking scheme took place in Haringey in North West London, when Labour's governing body, the NEC (National Executive Committee), voted to ask Haringey Council to halt its controversial plan to enter into a private public partnership with developer Lendlease. This plan was called the "Haringey Development Vehicle" and would transfer large tracts of public land into a fifty–fifty joint venture between the council and developer. The twenty-year project aimed to build 6,400 homes and a new town centre in Wood Green but was bitterly opposed by residents who feared that local estates would be demolished and that new homes would not be affordable.

It is never possible to predict which direction urban policy, which operates within and reflects a wider political and economic context, will go in. But as both the political and economic contexts begin to look unfavourable, the signs are that a rethink of at least some of the more violent aspects – collateral damage, to put it another way – associated with placemaking are underway. It just might be time to revisit the Museum of London and dust down the alternative "People's Plan" for the area and glean what contemporary campaigners may learn from it; today many "People's Plans" are once again being prepared across London, from PEACH (the People's Empowerment Alliance for Custom House, which falls within Newham's "Arc of Opportunity"), to Haringey, where campaigners jubilant at the failure of the Haringey Development Vehicle (HDV)[21] are keen to present alternatives. The mushrooming of these plans is part of increasingly powerful coalitions of local residents and multidisciplinary pro bono experts which follow in a democratic tradition that may yet still be realised.

Endnotes

1   Richard Florida, *The Rise of the Creative Class: And How It's Transforming Work, Leisure, Community, and Everyday Life* (Basic Books, 2012)

2   Bruce Katz and Jeremy Nowak, *The New Localism: How Cities Can Thrive in the Age of Populism* (Brookings Institution Press, 2018)

3   Katz and Nowak, 2018.

4   Ibid

5   Neil Smith, "Toward a Theory of Gentrification A Back to the City Movement by Capital, not People", *Journal of the American Planning Association*, Volume 45, Issue 4, 1979

6   Anna Minton, *Ground Control: Fear and Happiness in the Twenty-First-Century City* (Penguin, 2007)

7   Andrew Adonis and Bill Davies (eds), *City Villages: More Homes, Better Communities* (Institute for Public Policy Research, 2015). Download at: https://www.ippr.org/publications/city-villages-more-homes-better-communities. (Last accessed 2March 2018)

8   Kate Allen and Jim Pickard, "London councils urged to demolish and redevelop council estates", *Financial Times.* 22 March 2015. https://www.ft.com/content/4129abaa-cf16-11e4-893d-00144feab7de. (Last accessed 2 March 2018)

9   Anna Minton, *Big Capital: Who is London for?* (Penguin, 2017)

10   Transparency International UK, *Faulty Towers: Understanding the Impact of Overseas Corruption on the London Property Market,* March 2017

11   Minton, 2017.

12   Ibid

13   Ibid

14   London Assembly Housing Committee, *Knock it Down or Do It Up? The Challenge of Estate Regeneration.,* 2015. Download at: https://www.london.gov.uk/sites/default/files/gla_

migrate_files_destination/KnockItDownOrDoItUp_0.pdf. (Last accessed 2 March 2018)

15   Minton, 2017.

16   Transparency International UK, 2017.

17   Minton, 2017.

18   Rupert Neate, "Ghost towers: Half of new-build luxury London flats fail to sell", the *Guardian*, 26 January 2018. https://www.theguardian.com/business/2018/jan/26/ ghost-towers-half-of-new-build-luxury-london-flats-fail-to-sell. (Last accessed 2 March 2018)

19   Anna Minton, "High-rise blocks like Grenfell can be safe. The key issue is management", the *Guardian*, 14 June 2017. https://www.theguardian.com/commentisfree/2017/ jun/14/high-rise-grenfell-tower-safe-building-west-london-fire (Last accessed 2 March 2018)

20   Rob Merrick, "Jeremy Corbyn pledges to stop 'social cleansing' in regeneration after Grenfell Tower tragedy", the *Independent*, 27 September 2017. http://www. independent.co.uk/news/uk/politics/jeremy-corbyn-grenfell-tower-social-cleansing-housing-policies-labour-party-conference-regeneration-a7969996.html. (Last accessed 2 March 2018)

21   The Haringey Development Vehicle is the joint venture proposed between developer Lendlease and Haringey Council.

THE USES OF POETRY
Gillian Swan

Since the London Olympics of 2012, I have, with a growing sense of unease, studied the development that has emerged in its wake. I regularly walk and run through it, watching, and, for a while, I worked in East Village in order to examine it from within.

It is a place that many may now call home, but it remains sterile and contrived; a neoliberal playground where the landlord is king. And, as these privatised and financialised spaces become the new norm, the streets of nearby neighbourhoods like mine, already buffeted by the polarising effects of the housing crisis, are being brutally reconfigured in order to compete.

Some claim that the Brexit vote marked the beginning of the end of neoliberalism, and, whether that proves to be true or not, it did seem to be the moment that neoliberalism entered common parlance. Out running in the Olympic Park one morning soon afterwards, I ca[me] across

Poetry in the Park

There is much more poetry around the Park for you to explore. Six poems by well known poets such as Carol Ann Duffy and Lemn Sissay, were commissioned for the Park for.the 2012 Games, and have been permanently engraved throughout the Park. Pick up a copy of the Art in the Park field guide from the Information Point to find out where you can find them.

Working closely v
Story Centre, a v
located on Stratf
created a brand
primary school c
spanned four ye
and the poems,
continue to be a
in east London.

On the hoardings around a site awaiting development, inscribed by spray can in the style of joined-up handwriting, its gentle appearance belied the anger behind the message. It was a lament in (almost) verse.

Poetry, we are told by the London Legacy Development Corporation in their marketing blurb, is everywhere in the park. Specially commis-ioned by well-known poets, accompanied by cheerful illustrations or else permanently engraved.

We are urged to explore using the field guide available from the Infor-mation Point or follow the poetry trail for primary school children, as if it is a gift to the populace from a benevolent authority. Yet, as I paused with my phone to capture the graffiti poem, I noticed officials already starting to paint over it.

There may indeed be poems everywhere in the park, but they are se-ected to reflect the desired marketable image of the lifestyle promised; unrequested outpourings from below that tell of the realities of this

This is the neoliberal age
its wealth will fade
but the environmental destructi
the corporate power and violen
the birth of death with little left
a desert of meaning
a desert of feeling
the fate sealing instead of healir
or reeling in disgust
just the lust for more profit put t
....
passing around there
sharers champagne theyre splas
as your money there cashing
put the world on rations
profit coming in as the markets a
getting you bashing each other
the face of public space but its c
give the dog a bone
or the corporation this shit
for nothing
crony capitalism loving

made

f its reign will remain

sort of meaning a degree of feeling the fate sealing instead of healing or reeling in disgust just the lust for more profit put the environment

nvironment and

rashing

hem

d

each one not them the face of public space but its owned give the dog a bone or the corporation this shit already complete...

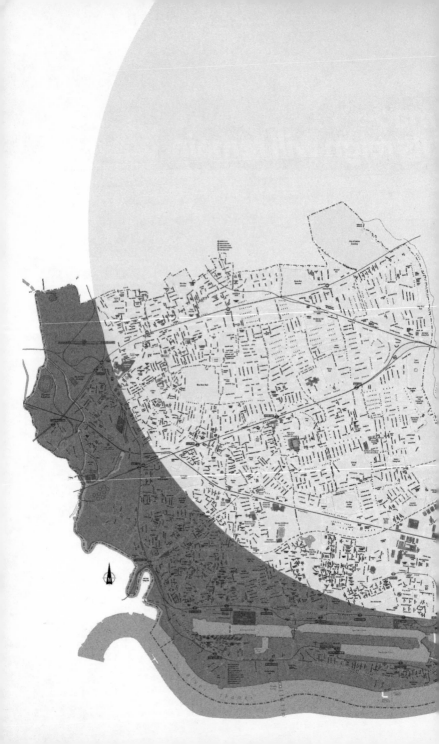

Part 2
Memory

The Song Remains the Same: Regeneration Narratives in the Royal Docks

Sue Brownill

The rebirth of the Royals will create a great new water city, unrivalled anywhere in Europe.
— LDDC, 1985[1]

The Royals, along with Stratford, Canning Town and Beckton, make Newham the pivotal player in East London's Arc of Opportunity.
— LDDC, 1998[2]

Our vision is a "water city". New investment will turn this isolated, inhospitable and deprived area and make it a more remarkable and enjoyable place.
— TGUDC, 2006[3]

The Royal docks lie within [...] an "arc of opportunity" that has been identified as having £22bn of development potential.
— GLA/LBN, 2010[4]

Introduction

These quotes are taken from four different "visions" for the Royals produced by three different regeneration agencies over three decades from the mid-1980s. They show how a particular narrative of regeneration emerged and was accepted as the only way forward for the area. Like a record stuck in a groove[5] the same phrases are repeated in these documents: "world class", "vision", "growth", "balanced communities", "enterprise", "opportunity", "waterfront quarter", "water city", "transform". Policy and governance instruments such as Enterprise Zones (EZs) and Urban Development Corporations (UDCs) appear, disappear, and reappear seemingly regardless of the political persuasion of their proponents. Not only are the words and mechanisms the same, but the logic of regeneration based on large-scale property development, exclusionary governance, and reimaging the area (what some term neoliberalisation) provides a constant background motif. As one person engaged in Docklands regeneration since the 1980s said, "If you stay in one place long enough history repeats itself, often in bizarre ways".

How did this happen? The Royal Docks must be one of the most planned-for places in the world (see Table 1). Since the beginnings of port restructuring in the late 1960s, vision after vision has been produced. These visions have set out different, conflicting futures. How did one recurrent narrative come to dominate? This chapter will trace the evolution of this discourse from the 1960s to today's talk of "Arcs of Opportunity". However, it will also show that there was nothing inevitable or "postpolitical" about this evolution and how a strong counter-narrative of different visions, regeneration approaches, and potential futures for the Royals has always been present and possible. The following account is based on the analysis of planning and development documents, personal involvement as a worker involved in the People's Plan and subsequent research, and interviews with key actors over a number of decades.[6]

Table 1: A Timeline of Development in the Royal Docks

Date	Policy	Approach	Royals Developments
1968	Community Development Project (CDP)	Social pathology — developed into structural and economic change	Argued for state support for local industries in Canning Town and North Woolwich
1972	Travers Morgan Report		Safari Park on Victoria Dock
1976	London Docklands Strategic Plan	Use Docklands to redress deficiencies of East London	Victoria Dock filled for housing rest operational
1976	Feasibility study into Olympic bid based on the Royals for 1984 Olympics	Mega-projects	
1981	Establishment of the London Docklands Development Corporation (LDDC)	Address market failure	STOLport, Draft Development Framework, Consortia schemes, UEL, Britannia Village
1981–91	Enterprise Zone (EZ), covers Lea Valley and Western edge of Victoria Dock	Pump prime private investment	Small-scale developments
1981	Closure of Royal Docks for commercial shipping		
1982	STOLport application		
1983	People's Plan	Alternative economic strategy	People's Plan Centre, training centres
1985	Royal Docks Draft Development Framework published		Consortia schemes
1985	South Docklands Local Plan	Middle way	Opportunity Zones
1986	Memorandum of Understanding on three major schemes in Royals	Second Wave, value extraction, new orthodoxy	Winsor Park Estate
1988	London City Airport opens		
1988	London City Airport opens		
1994	DLR Beckton extension opened		
1998	Britannia Urban Village		
1998	Closure of LDDC		
1999	UEL Docklands campus opens		
1999	Caning Town Jubilee Line opens		
1999	GLA established		
1999	Arc of Opportunity endorsed by Richard Caborn at British Academy	New orthodoxy	
2000	ExCel opens		
2000	Thames Barrier Park opens		
2003	Establishment of the Thames Gateway Urban Development Corporation (TGUDC)	"Benign" UDC	
2004	London Plan published	World City, new orthodoxy	
2005	Olympic bid won		
2005	Canning Town Mixed Communities Initiative		
2006	Vision for Lower Lea Published	Addressing market failure	
2007	Silvertown Quays Version 1 agreed	Mega project	Biota!
2008	Boris Johnson elected mayor		
2010	GLA/LBN Vision Statement	World City, Arc of Opportunity	
2010	Royal Docks Supernova		
2011	Meanwhile Competition		
2012	Silvertown Quays version two agreed		
2012	Crystal opens		
2012	Royal Docks Enterprise Zone established	Addressing market failure	
2012	Cable car opens		
2013	ABP Ports agreement signed		
2013	Floating island proposal		
2016	Royal Docks Revival	Alternative drivers for economic growth	

Regenerating the Royals

The contested discourses of regeneration in Docklands are discernible from the beginning of the Royals "regeneration". This history is to some extent a familiar story.[7] Accounts usually divide the regeneration of Docklands into four different phases characterised by particular policies, ideologies, and socioeconomic conditions: the Travers Morgan plan in 1972–74; the London Docklands Strategic Plan in 1974–79; and the London Docklands Development Corporation (LDDC)/Thatcher years, and post-LDDC period.[8] As Table 1 shows, the Royals has experienced all these and more. However, depicting "eras" focuses on their differences rather than their similarities and can silence the alternative regeneration narratives that challenged the official regeneration story throughout the history of Docklands' regeneration. Therefore this chapter takes a different approach, looking beyond these eras to trace how a particular approach to regeneration emerged and subsequently developed to become the dominant narrative to be followed by policy makers of all political persuasions. And it reveals how the regeneration of the Royals not only shows this in detail but also played a major role in its evolution. In particular it focuses on the key years of 1983–87 as a "watershed" when this new regeneration narrative became ubiquitous, not just in Docklands but also globally. This provides insights into the foundations and history of the present-day focus on the "Arc of Opportunity" and, crucially, reveals the contestations and alternatives that have too often been hidden from history.

It is important to remember that the regeneration of the Royals did not start with the LDDC. As Table 1 shows, the area was initially the focus of attention in 1968 when Canning Town and North Woolwich were included in the Community Development Project (CDP), the first area-based regeneration initiative in the UK. At that time the Royals were still working docks, but upstream docks including St Catherine's Dock had already closed and local industries had begun to decline. The Community

Development Project started life as a central government attempt to address the "social pathology" of communities living in "pockets of deprivation".[9] This analysis was however rejected by the Project, who put forward an alternative explanation for decline based on structural economic change,[10] concluding that policy should therefore not focus on changing people but on state intervention to boost the local economy.

However, the first Docklands-wide strategy took a different approach. In 1972 Travers Morgan were appointed by central government to respond to dock closures. Their report aimed to "bring the west end into the east end".[11] It put forward eighteen different options for the redevelopment of Docklands, many of which included "prestige projects" such as a safari park on the site of the Victoria Dock. The eventual favoured option, City New Town, was to be built around sixty thousand service-sector jobs, a "balanced" new population of one hundred thousand through private sector investment, and the establishment of the equivalent to a new town-development corporation.

After local protests and a change of government, a different Docklands narrative emerged through the London Docklands Strategic Plan (LDSP) drawn up by the Docklands Joint Committee, a partnership between local boroughs, the Greater London Council (GLC), community groups, and industry.[12] This sought to "redress the deficiencies" of the East End through using the land in Docklands to provide housing (mainly 50% social, 20% private, and 30% shared ownership) and jobs. Reminiscent of the alternative analysis developed by the Community Development Project, this was to be largely state-initiated but funded though the involvement of the private sector and embracing the same desire for "balanced" communities as in the Travers Morgan plans. The LDSP envisaged that the Royal Albert and KGV docks would remain operational, while the Victoria Dock would be filled to provide more land for housing development. Separately, and proving that nothing is new in regeneration, the Victoria Dock was also put forward as a possible site for the 1984 Olympics, but a feasibility study carried out by the GLC rejected it on the basis of cost.[13]

A new ideology entered into these debates with the establishment in 1981 of the LDDC. Its emphasis on market failure, the imperative of rolling back the state to allow the private sector to get on with the job of regeneration, the setting up of an unelected agency with extensive land-holding and planning powers but no requirement to consult, and an emphasis on high-value development aimed at attracting new residents and investors was a radical disruption to the existing regeneration narrative.[14] Canary Wharf on the Isle of Dogs is often taken as the epitome of what has been termed 3-D Thatcherism[15] and a blueprint for future regeneration schemes. However, it was largely in the Royals that the battle between these different approaches was fought and the new narrative emerged.

The Rise of a New Regeneration Narrative, 1983-87

From 1982–86 the future of the Royals was "up for grabs" as the People's Plan put it.[16] Three competing visions for the area were put forward. The first of these, the LDDC's, was based on its desire to sweep away planning and focus on major projects to show what the private sector could achieve–albeit with hefty public subsidies. The Short Take Off and Landing airport (STOLport, now London City Airport) was described as "the type of catalyst needed to change the normal rules of the market place, a project capable of taking advantage of the apparent disabilities of the area in development terms and converting them into major assets".[17] The premise behind the airport–to use the land in Docklands as a business airport for City workers–also fitted with the image of the new entrepreneurial Docklands that the LDDC was projecting and the new population that was being targeted. The major project pioneered by Travers Morgan was now placed into a narrative of regeneration versus dereliction. A planning application was submitted in 1982, preceding Canary Wharf by three years.

In opposition to this came a different vision. In 1983 the People's Plan for the Royal Docks was put before the inquiry into the airport as an alternative to the STOLport (Fig. 1). Instead of just opposing the airport, local groups supported by the Greater London Council's Popular Planning Unit (PPU) wanted to show how the area could be developed differently. A People's Plan Centre was set up in Pier Parade North Woolwich, local people were employed to work there, and the People's Plan was drawn up through intensive consultation with local people: "we decided to make the plan out of the ideas and experiences of local people – the people who have got to live with the plans and who have detailed knowledge of the needs and assets of the areas".[18] It put forward an alternative plan based on the principles of public ownership of land and investment, community participation in planning, and "meeting needs and making jobs". As such it built on the alternative regeneration

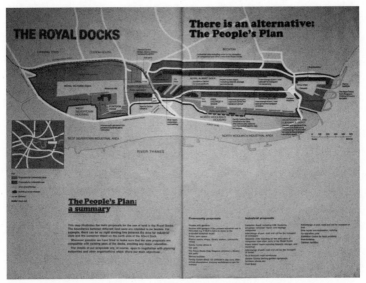

Fig. 1: The People's Plan for the Royal Docks, Newham Docklands Forum (NDF), 1983.

narrative from the Community Development Project analysis onwards, of restructuring for communities and investing in existing and new industries to meet local needs. Indeed, any of those working for the PPU had come through similar radical community-development backgrounds to the CDP. And by building on the "assets" of the area in term of its people and businesses it stood in stark contrast to the LDDC's narrative of "disabilities". So where the STOLport was proposed the People's Plan showed a fruit depot, timber depot, and dry docks, based on retaining dock usage to limit environmental impacts and continue local skills and industries. Shed 4 in the Victoria Dock was to be turned into an indoor sports arena and the Albert Dock Basin into public housing to enable families to escape from Canning Town's tower blocks, as opposed to the LDDC's proposals for a marina and private housing.

The report of the inquiry was not published until 1985. In the meantime the LDDC did not stop at the airport. Its adherence to "flexible planning" led to the production in 1985 of a Draft Development Framework for the Royals. This was not a development plan – note the use of the word "Draft" ("there are no detailed building plans or tightly drawn boundaries"; see Fig. 2) – but a glossy prospectus depicting opportunities for development and the public infrastructure that would support it,

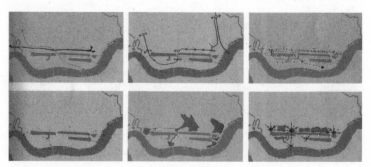

Fig. 2: From the LDDC's Draft Development Framework for the Royal Docks (1985).

though an importance sentence appears in the document: "The rebirth of the Royals will create *a great new water city*, unrivalled anywhere in Europe". Also in 1985 the LDDC announced three major development schemes for the Royals: an exhibition centre on the north side of the Albert Dock called the London Dome (a precursor for ExCel), a regional shopping centre and marina in the Albert Dock Basin, and a high-tech employment park (complete with Futurescience Centre–a precursor of the Crystal) and housing scheme on the south side of the Victoria Dock. All these schemes included houses, hotels, and leisure facilities. The western end of the Victoria Dock was also included in the Enterprise Zone, centred on the Isle of Dogs, which allowed development to go ahead with no planning permission and with fiscal incentives.

The "third vision" was set out by the London Borough of Newham, in its 1985 South Docklands Local Plan. During the LDDC years plan-making powers stayed with the boroughs, while in theory the LDDC had only the powers to make decisions on planning applications. While it might be expected in an LDDC plan, it is in this document that the language of opportunity first appears. The plan sought to take a middle line between "specific proposals to meet local needs" and "accommodations for developments of regional and national significance".[19] This resulted in designating major sites in the Victoria Dock as "opportunity zones" where the private sector could do as it wanted; they appeared as grey spaces on the proposals map. This was not enough to please the LDDC, who put forward forty-eight objections to the inquiry, leading the inspector to conclude that "the plan would not be an appropriate planning basis for the area at this time" and recommend it be withdrawn. But it did set the precedent for what has been termed "strategic flexibility"[20], an approach to planning that used the statutory land-use system (as opposed to nonstatutory frameworks or masterplans) to set broad parameters with the detail to be filled by developers.

Also in 1985 the STOLport inquiry–the inquiry into the

Short Take Off and Landing airport–came down in its favour. Nonetheless, the inspector concluded that while there was "much to be commended" in the People's Plan, the "realities of the situation were such that the docks were closed, the LDDC was in the position to control development and revitalisation was needed without delay". The GLC had attempted to buy the Docks Estate from the Port of London Authority to implement the People's Plan but this had been refused and the estate went to the LDDC; and in 1986 the GLC itself was closed by the Thatcher government.

At first sight this appeared to be a victory for the market-led approach not as result of a superior narrative but through the concentration of land, political power, finance, and ideology. But the battle was not over. The Canary Wharf development had sparked a national debate about the negative impacts on local people. Unfavourable press reports and parliamentary committees led to the LDDC announcing a "second wave" of regeneration where people were as important as buildings.[21] The re-election of a Conservative government in 1987 also led Labour councils to further modify their approaches. So later in 1987 Newham Council signed a Memorandum of Agreement with the LDDC and the developers of the three schemes announced in 1985. This secured social housing, community facilities, limited public consultation, and infrastructure in return for the council supporting the schemes. It is this new narrative of accepting major development but attempting to extract value from it that became the modus operandi of the last ten years of the LDDC's life–and can be seen in the Royals in schemes such as Windsor Park Estate, the University of East London campus, and Britannia Urban Village. It is also this narrative that became the "model" for future development often accompanied by the much-quoted–but erroneous–phrase "We are not doing a Docklands here". So out of the battle for the Royals emerged an agenda that was to dominate regeneration in the UK for thirty years.

Echoes

After the LDDC wound down in 1998, far from disappearing, this narrative became the regeneration orthodoxy. As early as 1998 the term "Arc of Opportunity" was being used both by the LDDC in its de-designation publicity[22] and by Newham Council, firstly in a development framework and secondly in the launch of the first Canning Town Masterplan by the then Planning Minister Richard Caborn.[23] The use of the term signalled an attempt to maintain the momentum of Docklands regeneration strategically and geographically in the face of the withdrawal of the LDDC's funding and powers. But the return of powers to Newham did not lead to an alternative approach. New Labour had come into power in 1997 with its emphasis on the "third way" between the market and the state; a mantra that echoed the Docklands consensus that had already been established. Thus Canning Town was to be regenerated as a mixed-tenure "balanced" community (this was to be continued in the 2005 "Mixed Communities Initiative"); and elsewhere the focus on private-sector partnerships, mixed communities, major sites, and the language of place-marketing indicates adherence to this new orthodoxy and the lost opportunities for alternatives.

By 2006 the language and approach of regeneration agencies operating in the Royals was almost indistinguishable from what had come before, as were the agencies themselves. In words strangely reminiscent of the LDDC's Royal Docks 1985 framework, another UDC – the Thames Gateway Urban Development Corporation (TGUDC) – set out a "vision for a 21st century water city to excite, inspire and influence investors and agents of change so they embrace the strategy". The TGUDC's overall vision statement, tellingly called "Engines for Growth", referred to addressing "market failure" and "Docklands style developments" and the wider Thames Gateway strategy of "ensuring that London remains a global capital".[24] This strategic flexibility and pump priming was also evident in the sketchy plans accompanying it.

The Thames Gateway Urban Development Corporation had been set up as part of a Sustainable Communities Action Plan designed by New Labour to solve the problem of providing housing in the South East.[25] Placing the very useful powers of land assembly and planning in the hands of "benign" Urban Development Corporations, pioneered during the 1980s, was seen as spreading the momentum of Docklands further east into the Thames Gateway. This shows how far the consensus had shifted: just a few years after the closure of the LDDC, the institutional mechanism that had proved so controversial was reintroduced with even some of the same individuals on the board. This same device was to be repeated with the redevelopment of the Olympic Park.[26]

The Enterprise Zone also made a comeback, reintroduced in 2011 by the Coalition government with the Royals Docks being designated as London's "green" EZ. In 1982 the LDDC had stated, "the era of the grand plan has passed… we will replace red tape with a red carpet for the private sector".[27] In 2011 then Minister Eric Pickles echoed this, claiming that "we are unblocking the complex, costly planning system, regenerating redundant sites and putting the brakes on the years of Whitehall micro-management that has tied business up in red tape, slowing and stifling growth".[28]

The extent of the dominance of this approach is also evident in the strategic planning frameworks for the area. Regional government reappeared in 1999 with the establishment of the Greater London Authority, led once again by Ken Livingstone, but he did not pursue the alternative approaches pioneered at the GLC. London did have an overall "grand plan" but the policies in the new London Plan were not those that opposed the LDDC and supported the People's Plan in the 1980s. Instead, strategic flexibility lived on in "opportunity zones" and "zones of change" – one of which was the Royals – where relaxed regulations applied, reminiscent of the South Docklands Plan thirty years before.[29]

Fig. 3: Lower Lea Valley Development Framework and TGUDC Vision for the Lower Lea Valley.

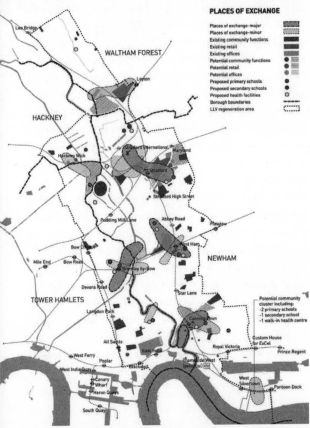

Admittedly, the London Plan until 2010 had a policy for 50% affordable housing but the delivery mechanism was the same one of value extraction through developer contributions and this target was rarely achieved.[30] The London Plan vision was "to develop London as an exemplary sustainable world city based on growth, inclusivity and environment" – a goal that did not recognise the contradiction at its heart: that these concepts were mutually exclusive. Doreen Massey[31] argues that this focus on "world city"-type development has meant that the polarisation of the LDDC era continued, as confirmed by research into wage and employment inequality.[32]

In the Royals the LDDC's land holdings transferred to the London Development Agency and then the Greater London Authority. Once again this did not lead to major change as evidenced by Livingstone's vanity prestige project *Biota!* at Silvertown Quays.[33] Approved in 2005, this £80 million aquarium designed by starchitect Terry Farrell was scrapped in 2009. The election of Conservative Boris Johnson as mayor in 2008 led to a turbo-charged version of the same. Alternative voices were less audible during this period as funding for community groups was cut and most agencies espoused the new narrative, although some smaller-scale community projects lived on. For example, in Pier Parade, a training and childcare centre survived from the People's Plan era.[34]

So it is not surprising that in 2010 another vision for the Royals was launched – this time jointly drawn up by GLA and Newham Council – embracing the language and direction of this orthodoxy, adding to it talk of a "regeneration supernova" and more: "The Royal Docks lies within the stretch of land that runs from Stratford down the River Lea to the Thames, an arc of opportunity that has been identified as having £22bn of development potential [...] The Mayor wants the Royal Docks to become a world-class business centre."[35]

So we have come full circle: three documents from different eras expressing similar objectives using similar language.

But history has also repeated itself in more positive ways. Thirty years on from the People's Plan another alternative plan for the airport site was launched arguing that the area "has not been served well by a trickledown model of economic development" and proposing that the airport should be closed. In its place it called for "an alternative model [...] to achieve a fairer and more balanced approach to achieving good lives for everyone".[36] It echoed the People's Plan's alternative economic strategy, seeing the driver for employment and value creation around social and environmental concerns, allocating sites for producers of renewable energy, food production centres, and "convivial" places to live and work. In place of public ownership, community ownership of land, housing, and workspaces is proposed; but the principles remain the same: "We need to transform current patterns that lock local people out of their own neighbourhoods – through deprivation, inequality of resources, or through lack of a local voice."[37]

Fig. 5: Royal Docks Revival, *Royal Docks Revival*, NEF, London, 2016.

Conclusion

This chapter has shown how past and present are woven together in the discourses of Docklands' regeneration. The song that emerged in the mid-1990s has indeed remained the same and it is important to recognise the origins and development of current regeneration orthodoxies. Equally important is the need to listen to the alternative "songs" that show that this is not the only possible approach to regeneration. This history is not a unique story but what happened in the Royals set precedents for wider national and global developments. Therefore what happens next in the Royals demands our attention.

Endnotes

1   London Docklands Development Corporation, A Draft Development Framework for the Royal Docks (LDDC, 1985)

2   London Docklands Development Corporation, *Completion Booklet; The Royal Docks* (LDDC, 1998). Download at: http://www.lddc-history.org.uk/royals/index.html

3   London Thames Gateway Urban Development Corporation (LTGUDC), *Engines for Growth: A Vision for the Lower Lea Valley and London Riverside* (LTGDC, 2005)

4   Mayor of London and Mayor of Newham, *Royal Docks; A Vision for the Royal Docks* (GLA, 2008)

5   Apologies to Led Zeppelin

6   Sue Brownill, *Developing London's Docklands: Another Great Planning Disaster?* (Paul Chapman, 1993); Simona Florio and Sue Brownill, "Whatever happened to criticism? Interpreting the London Docklands Development Corporation's Obituary", City, 4:1, 2000, 53-64; Sue Brownill, "London Docklands Revisited; The Dynamics of Waterfront Development", in Desfor, et al. (eds) Transforming Urban Waterfronts, Routledge (New York, 2011), pp. 121-142; Sue Brownill and Glen O'Hara, "From Planning to Opportunism? Re-Examining the Creation of the London Docklands Development Corporation", Planning Perspectives, 30:4, 2015, pp. 537-570

7   Brownill, 1993, op cit

8   Brownill, 1993, op cit . See also: M. Carmona, "The Isle of Dogs: Four development waves, five planning models and a renaissance... of sorts", *Progress in Planning* 71:87, 2009, p. 151

9   Martin Loney, *Community Against Government, the British Community Development Project, 1968-78* (Heinemann, 1983)

10 Canning Town Community Development Project, *From Canning Town to North Woolwich; The Aims of Industry?* (Canning Town CDP, 1975)

11   London Docklands Study Team, *Docklands: Redevelopment Plans for East London* (Travers Morgan and Partners, 1973)

12   Docklands Joint Committee, *The London Docklands Strategic Plan* (DJC, 1976)

13   TNA AT/60/102, Department of Environment, press cutting, "London Bows out of 1984 Olympics Race", 3rd June 1976.

14   Brownill and O'Hara, 2015, op cit

15   Guy Faulconbridge, and Andrew Osborn, "Thatcher's legacy: A citadel of finance atop once-derelict docks", *Reuters*. http://uk.reuters.com/article/2013/04/16/uk-britain-thatcher-wharf-idUKBRE93F0S920130416. (Last accessed 11 February 2013.) See also: Anna Minton, *Ground Control* (Penguin, 2009)

16   Newham Docklands Forum, *The People's Plan for the Royal Docks* (London, 1983)

17   London Docklands Development Corporation, *Proof of evidence to StolPort,* Inquiry of Reg Ward. (LDDC, 1983)

18   *The People's Plan for the Royal Docks,* 4.

19   London Borough of Newham, "Preface", *South Docklands Local Plan* (LBN, 1985).

20   Florio and Brownill, 2001. op cit

21   London Docklands Development Corporation, *1986-87 Annual Report and Accounts* (London: LDDC, 1987), p. 2

22   London Docklands Development Corporation, *Completion Booklet: The Royal Docks* (LDDC, 1998). http://www.lddc-history.org.uk/royals/index.html

23   Nick Mathiason, "Canning Town Masterplan–North of the Dome, a new world view", *Estates Gazette*, 13 April 1999.

24   London Thames Gateway Urban Development Corporation, *Engines for Growth: A Vision for the Lower Lea Valley and London Riverside* (LTGDC, 2005)

25   Office for the Deputy Prime Minister, *Sustainable Communities: An Urban Development Corporation for the London Thames Gateway* (ODPM, 2003)

26   Brownill, 2011. op cit.

27   London Docklands Development Corporation, *Annual Report and Accounts for 1981-82* (LDDC, 1982)

28   DCLG, *Radical Changes in Housing and Planning Will Drive Local Growth*. Press release, 23rd March 2011. https://www.gov.uk/government/news/radical-changes-in-housing-and-planning-will-drive-local-growth

29   Greater London Authority, *Sub-Regional Development Framework: East London* (GLA, 2005)

30   Duncan Bowie, *Politics, Planning and Homes in a World City* (Routledge, 2010)

31   Doreen Massey, *World City* (Polity Press, 2007)

32   Neil Lee, *Paul Sissons and Katy Jones, Wage Inequality and Employment Polarisation in British Cities* (Joseph Rowntree Foundation) (York, 2013)

33   London Development Agency, *Silvertown Quays Masterplan and Design Code* (LDA, 2005)

34   Sue Brownill, "London Docklandds Revisited; The Dynamics of Waterfront Development", in Desfor, et al. (eds), *Transforming Urban Waterfronts: Fixity and Flow* (Routledge, 2010), pp. 121-142

35   Mayor of London and Mayor of Newham, *Royal Docks; A Vision for the Royal Docks* (GLA 2010)

36   New Economics Foundation, *Royal Docks Revival*, London: NEF, 10, 2016

37   Ibid

Empire State of Mind

Tom Cordell

Now when I was a little chap I had a passion for maps [...] At
that time there were many blank spaces on the earth, and when
I saw one that looked particularly inviting on a map (but they
all look that) I would put my finger on it and say, "When I grow
up I will go there."
　— Joseph Conrad, *Heart of Darkness*, 1899[1]

I had found myself in a small plane, heading in that direction
by way of the London's East End [...] The rotting docks – long
since abandoned for deep-water harbors able to take modern
container ships downstream – the crumbling infrastructure that
had once supported their thriving industry and vast expanses of
polluted land left behind by modern technology and enhanced
environmentalism. The place was a tip: 6,000 acres of forgotten
wasteland.
　— Michael Heseltine, *Life in the Jungle*, 2000[2]

Flashback to summer 1985: I was seven years old and peeking
out from a train window, as it clattered eastwards across London.
It was a day out with my grandma. I knew the route as far as
Dalston, but then the train entered unfamiliar territory, a new
route stitched together from bits of track unused by passengers
for forty years.[3] We wove past the rooftops of Hackney, over
the River Lea, under the mainline at Stratford and on through

Canning Town, into the sparse cityscape of the docks. Industrial decay was an unremarkable part of Britain's cities then, but this was on a different scale – mile after mile of flat dereliction.

As a child I read this landscape as sensation: textures, sights, sounds, and smells. It's only later you learn to decode the memories. Looking back, that year was a historical pivot for Britain, the point where what we'd now call neoliberalism moved from its contingent phase into solid form. Then it was called Thatcherism; to me, having been born only a year before the experiment started, the symptoms of the rupture with the past were just the normal texture of life. I'd not known a time before the nightly television news was filled with unemployment figures, factory closures, strikes, sirens, and plastic bullets, all intercut with the occasional riot or bombing.

After the pylons and wasteland of Custom House, the line singled and the train wormed down below the ground. Trains then had windows you could open, and the dank air of the leaky Victorian tunnel under the Connaught Dock filled the carriage. After clanking through darkness below river level, the train's motors whined as they pulled us up back into the light. We'd arrived at Silvertown: on the left side of the train half a scrappy high street, and to the right a mess of rusting tracks stretching out in the shadow of the huge Tate and Lyle factory. Grandma – an autodidact communist of the 1930s variety – was unimpressed by sugar; she had a puritanical streak and she blamed it for rotten teeth and slavery.[4] The plant's survival was a reminder that Britain's industry – normally celebrated as the reward of national ingenuity and enterprise – had originally been financed from the profits of agriculture, commodities produced by forced labour in stolen colonial lands.[5]

The reason for our trip was right at the end of the line, isolated behind high walls and scrubland next to the windy Thames: the railway museum at North Woolwich. Here kids could clamber onto engines and be shunted up and down twenty yards or so of track, all in a hiss of steam. It was fun for a seven year old, but today it strikes me as an eerie memorialisation – a statement that the industrial age was dead. The sanitised past – memories of slum housing, empire, and industrial injuries stripped away – was in the 1980s clutched like a security blanket by a society that needed a synthetic past identity because it had no sense of what was coming next.

***

Thirty years later I came back. Grandma was dead, and so were the political ideals she'd devoted her life to. I was with my friend Gil. In the late 1990s and early 2000s we'd come here to film – then the emptiness provided space for our cinematic imaginations.[6] Now the railway was gone, its track lifted, and the site hemmed in by Tetris-walled blocks of flats. Even the railway museum was boarded up – Britain had transitioned and there was no further comfort to be gained from this vision of the past. I wanted to see what artefacts remained that could explain the London we found ourselves living in today. A minute's walk

Fig. 1: The Train to North Woolwich, 1985. © Tim Brown, used with permission of the photographer.

away by the river was something that hadn't changed at all, except for an accretion of rust; London's five-minute pleasure cruise, the Woolwich free ferry.

The ferry has run back and forth across the same strip of Thames since Victorian times, and like an archaeologist's trench it cuts a slice through the river's history.

When it first steamed over the river in 1889, Britain's national mythology was more certain. Back then North Woolwich was no sleepy backwater. It sat at the heart of the Royal Docks, then the most modern in the country, with hydraulic cranes and dockside rail connections. Reclaimed from marshland bordering the north side of the Thames, they formed the largest enclosed docks in the world – the logistical hub of Britain's imperial project.

A society commemorates those who reflect its self-image. The original flotilla of steam ferries at Woolwich (long since scrapped) held up a mirror to Britain, as the pragmatic and messy early colonial smash-and-grab was being mythologised into the ordered totality of empire: each boat celebrated a

Fig. 2: Postcard of the General Gordon Woolwich Free Ferry, 1889. Public domain.

local hero who symbolised Victorian virtue. Self-reliance was embodied in "Duncan"–named after Colonel Francis Duncan, an artillery officer and Tory MP who pioneered teaching soldiers and civilians first aid. "Hutton" represented scientific endeavour, taking the name of Royal Military Academy Professor Charles Hutton, surveyor and mathematician, the man who calculated the density of the earth and the force of gunpowder. "Gordon" symbolised religion and self-sacrifice. It was named after General Gordon of Khartoum, the pious Christian who was hacked to death in the name of Queen and empire after going into battle armed only with a rattan cane. (Was the irony intentional when this unmarried soldier with a fondness for handsome youths was also commemorated with the Gordon Boys Home?) Twenty thousand Muslims were slaughtered in revenge for his death, yet the general became revered as a national martyr, part of Victorian imperialism's perplexing mythology of white victimhood.

Waiting for the ferry I remembered the fictional yawl the Nellie in Conrad's Heart of Darkness, anchored midstream on the Thames. Conrad's narrator destroys the false innocence of Britain's colonial fantasies over the unmapped regions of the world; he details the human suffering and slaughter implicit in the colonial project. Today's finance towers looming in the distance make the significance of Conrad's choice of characters and location less subtle than when he published in 1899. Yes, there's Marlow the adventurer who does the messy stuff on the ground, but he's outnumbered and outranked by the London end of the team: the company director, the lawyer, and the accountant. Empire might have been a fairy tale of national destiny, but colonialism was a business venture through and through.

***

By the time the current three ferries were launched in 1963, the British elite was embarrassed by its past imperial fervour. Five years earlier the statue of General Gordon that Kitchener had erected in the heart of Khartoum had been torn down and sent back to London by the newly independent Sudanese government. Only the Gordon Boys Home had space for the bronze general, who to this day sits astride a camel outside the school in less-than-exotic Woking. Britain's chosen self-image for the 1960s was now more egalitarian.

The ferry we crossed on was the John Burns, named after one of the leaders of the 1889 London dock strike, renowned as the British labour movement's first great success in organising unskilled workers against the cruelty of Victorian capitalism. While the dock owners sycophantically named the Royal Docks after the Queen and her cousin-husband Albert, they subcontracted gangers to hire the dock workforce on an hour-by-hour basis. It was called the contract system. Men desperate for work would crush up against the dock gates, and twice a day the gangers would throw metal tokens into the crowd. A token meant work, no token meant starvation. This was the era of unashamed social Darwinism: the gangers and the dock owners knew that the fight for tokens would guarantee them the physically strongest workforce each day. The broken limbs and occasional deaths in the crush were after all externalised costs.[7]

The strike started in August 1889. As it dragged on, the Salvation Army and Catholic Church offered support and food to the striking families. Their stand made a stark contrast to the Church of England, which had spent the Victorian age promoting inequality as ideology (sing this now forgotten verse of "All Things Bright and Beautiful" and you get the idea: "The rich man in his castle / The poor man at his gate / God made them high and lowly / And ordered their estate."[8])

But public opinion was shifting towards the dockers. This banner hung in Commercial Road:

Our husbands are on strike; for the wives it is not honey,
And we all think it is right not to pay the landlord's money.
Everyone is on strike, so landlords do not be offended;
The rent that's due we'll pay to you when the strike is ended.[9]

Fig. 3: The John Burns Ferry in 2018. © The author, 2018.

It took to November before the bosses caved in. In negotiations brokered by the Archbishop of Westminster Cardinal Manning, the dock owners conceded a 20% pay rise, a minimum working day of four hours, and an end to the hated contract system. Burns saw the victory as something bigger:

Then, the labourer in the East has acquired hope [...] He has learned the value of self-sacrifice in a large movement for the benefit of his class. Conquering himself, he has learned that he can conquer the world of capital, whose generals have been the most ruthless of his oppressors.[10]

So goes the conventional narrative. But in the gaps there's a more complex story.

In the speeches of the strike leaders, alongside their campaign for better working conditions in London, coexisted the Victorian ideology of empire and their belief in their own racial superiority. Union leader Will Thorne invoked a working-class version of General Gordon's white martyrdom: "I believe, that nowhere in the world have white men had to endure such terrible conditions as those under which the dockers work."[11]

Fig. 4: The 1889 dockers' strike march. Public domain.

Burns likened the plight of the dockers to the besieged colonial occupiers in the 1857 uprisings against British rule in India:

I tell you, lads, we will no more surrender than the men in Lucknow surrendered. Now these men fought for a glory that was effervescent and ephemeral; but they nobly did their duty and stood up against a storm of shot and shell, disease and want, and all the miseries of that long siege. You, men, have to hold another citadel today. We are defending our Lucknow – the Lucknow of Labour.[12]

There was no sense here of common struggle with peoples in India, Africa, and Asia who were simultaneously being oppressed by Victorian capital.

Since the 1830s poor Londoners had been inspired by their own vision of the imperial dream, where overseas colonies would provide them with blank spaces to build new lives freed from poverty. My great great grandmother had been born near the docks in 1826. She lived out most of her life in Limehouse, but four of her brothers emigrated to Melbourne in 1854. Australia in particular attracted thousands of poor Londoners; plentiful land and a labour shortage meant there was an abundance of good-quality work. By 1870 Australia had established trade unions that had ensured good wages and a short working day for the white settlers. But central to the purpose of these unions was their insistence on a white-Australia policy, denying entry to Asian and African immigrants in a bid to maintain the white settlers' living standards. When news of London's dock strike reached Australia, the unions there raised £30,000 in support. It was enough to keep London's striking dockers – their kith and kin – from starvation. Victory for the dockers had drawn both ideological strength from the racial myths of empire, as well as material support based on an internationalism that was strictly for white Anglo Saxons.

In the aftermath of the strike there were calls to nationalise the docks. They came not from socialist radicals but from the business class. In 1892 the Times reported:

No port of any considerable size in the United Kingdom is so grossly mismanaged as the port of London. One thing, however, is reasonably certain; it is that, if any body of men, either the Corporation or the City, or the dock companies, or the Chamber of Commerce would take the trouble to push forward a scheme for the formation of a public trust to control and manage the whole of the port of London, that body of men would receive the support and the gratitude of the entire mercantile community.[13]

It took a Royal Commission, and two attempts in parliament, before in 1909 the Liberal government finally nationalised the docks. It was done in the interests of business – infrastructure was too important to be left to the whim of markets.

We crossed back on the James Newman ferry. Newman had been mayor of Woolwich, twice, once in the early Twenties and again in the early Fifties. He was part of the labour movement that grew out of the trade unions and piloted a benign, nonconfrontational socialism in local government. In interwar Woolwich this meant using income from the rates to build housing, a health centre, and public baths.[14]

World War II had advanced these ideas from the progressive boroughs like Woolwich into national policy. But the war had also shifted Britain's understanding of itself – propaganda like Humphrey Jennings' 1943 dockland blitz documentary Fires Were Started[15] presented the nation as a closed family united in the face of a common enemy. Wartime had converted London from the hub of a seafaring empire into a besieged island.

Tied up for repairs on the south side of the river was the third ferry, named after Ernest Bevin – the dockers leader who had dominated British trade unionism in the 1930s. During World War II he moved into government, and as minister of Labour improved conditions for British workers nationally by establishing a new balance of power between the state, employers, and trade unions. It was an extraordinary culminating victory to the fight started by the dockers five decades before.[16]

In 1945 Bevin became foreign secretary. The Labour

government was determined to reconstruct the nation along socialist lines, with the nationalisation of key industries (following the template provided by the Port of London) a key element in its project to civilise capitalism. Locally for the docks this meant a Labour Board that ended casual employment and gave unions and managers equal representation over employment decisions in the port. Yet like the dock strike leaders of 1889, the board lacked interest in creating broader equality between the people of Britain and those of the empire. It drained down the wealth of its colonies before decolonisation, using the funds to build the welfare state.[17] Effectively, the poorest people in the world were forced to finance Britain's free medicine and welfare. Bevin's internationalism went only as far as forming alliances with Western Europe and the USA in an attempt to hold onto the wealth Britain had acquired from its colonies.

There was one voice from London's docks in parliament that did challenge the implicit racist policies of the Attlee era: the Communist MP for Stepney, Phil Piratin.[18] Fifty years earlier the dock unions had campaigned to stop Jewish immigration to the East End, with dockers leader Ben Tillett ranting:

The influx of continental pauperism aggravates and multiplies the number of ills which press so heavily on us [...] Foreigners come to London in large numbers, herd together in habitations unfit for beasts, the sweating system allowing the more grasping and shrewd a life of comparative ease in superintending their work.[19]

But East London did become a refuge for many fleeing the pogroms, and later the heart of the protests against the rise of fascism during the 1930s. Piratin had emerged from this movement and was, like many British Jews, marginalised by the mainstream labour movement and pushed towards the Communist Party. In parliament he used his platform to interrogate the government's colonial policy, as protesters against British rule and strikers in Singapore, Malaya, Kenya, Uganda, and Nigeria were shot and killed by British troops.[20] Meanwhile,

British dreams of a new home over the sea were starting to reverse: waves of immigrants started arriving at Britain's docks from the former empire, with their own dreams of a better life in a new land.

In 1950 Piratin lost his seat in parliament as the Cold War drove anticommunist feeling. Six years later two overseas conflicts would echo back to London in ways that would shape its future. In November 1956 the covert French/British/Israeli coalition failed in its attempt to recolonise the Suez Canal. It killed any idea of European imperialism's survival. But almost simultaneously the Communist Party's moral authority, already shaken by Nikita Khrushchev's admission of Stalin's atrocities, was destroyed by the Soviet invasion of Hungary. Piratin resigned from all his official posts in the party in protest. The decade that followed saw British society evolve into the consumer age.

***

As our ferry docked back on the north side of the river, the brutalist fortress of the landing stage dropped its drawbridge to let us and a deck full of vehicles onto the land. But the landing stages symbolise a less-celebrated aspect of the postwar era. They were built to match the trio of social-democratic ferries in 1965 by the then Minister of Transport Ernest Marples' roadbuilding firm – or at least the firm he had owned, before reluctantly passing his shares over to his wife when his obvious conflict of interest became public knowledge. Yet despite lining his pockets over twenty-five years of building for the state, Marples was reluctant to pay his taxes. When in 1975 the Inland Revenue caught up with him, he fled overnight to Monte Carlo leaving his London townhouse scattered with abandoned possessions.[21] Yes, the postwar corporate state built council houses and motorways, but workers' taxes also paid for chancers like Marples to live in Belgravia and own a vineyard in France.

Tories like Marples had their own reasons to back the postwar order, but even before the new ferries were launched, there were signs of right-wing dissent. An early warning came in January 1958 when the Tory Chancellor Peter Thorneycroft resigned, along with his two junior ministers.[22] They wanted to cut welfare spending and return to the monetarist economics of the nineteenth century, abandoning efforts to improve living standards and maintain full employment. Instead they saw the role of government as solely to manage inflation, believing that market forces and not elected politicians should rule society. Their first rebellion faded away, but one of Thorneycroft's junior ministers remained determined to derail modern Britain from its social-democratic track. His name was Enoch Powell.[23]

Powell's problem was persuading the electorate to back his vision; in Victorian Britain only the propertied class could vote, and monetarism made sense to them as it protected their wealth. But in Britain's postwar democracy he was asking the electorate to throw away the benefits of a managed economy and the welfare state, threatening to create a modern version of the divided and cruel society last seen in Britain at the time of the dock strike. Over the 1960s Powell developed a strategy: for a

Fig. 5: The Ernest Bevin Woolwich Free Ferry docks at Marples' Jetty, 2018.

Britain in denial of the realities of its imperial past, he would call on emotions of national rage provoked by lost international prestige. He planned to use anger at Commonwealth immigration to crowbar a new economic order into Britain.[24]

By April 1968, Powell was ready to make his move with his infamous "Rivers of Blood" speech. Slyly placing his most inflammatory statements in the form of unattributed quotations, he told his audience: "In this country in 15 or 20 years' time the black man will have the whip hand over the white man."[25] It was the bully's fear of being bullied. And Powell pre-empted any negative response by positioning himself as the martyr: "I can already hear the chorus of execration. How dare I say such a horrible thing?" Three days later the London dockers marched to parliament in support of Powell. Two decades of the welfare state had not dented the racist ideology of empire.

Powell was sacked from the Tory shadow cabinet for his explicit racism, but his ideas had taken root. By the late 1970s the new Tory leader Margaret Thatcher shared his monetarist zeal, and had few scruples about how to gain power. In 1978 she told TV audiences:

People are really rather afraid that this country might be rather swamped by people with a different culture and, you know, the British character has done so much for democracy, for law and done so much throughout the world that if there is any fear that it might be swamped people are going to react and be rather hostile to those coming in.[26]

In power Thatcher coupled her racist rhetoric to a broader range of vulnerable targets: homosexuals, single parents, and the unemployed. The politics of resentment and hate based on past social ideas were combined with an aggressive set of economic reforms that left an eighth of the workforce unemployed and ripped the heart out of manufacturing industry, the locus of trade union power. It was a permanent realignment of society that took wealth from the many and gave it to a rich elite. Thatcher's key ally Sir Keith Joseph, who was heir to the Bovis construction fortune, explained in a 1992 TV interview the purpose of the policy: "Monetarism worked throughout the nineteenth century when we were the envy of the world, with our people growing in numbers and generally prospering, despite all the horrors of the time, generally prospering with the world looking to us for how to do it."[27]

Thatcher particularly fixated on the inhabitants of urban areas. She told the party faithful:

And in the inner cities – where youngsters must have a decent education if they are to have a better future – that opportunity is all too often snatched from them by hard left education authorities and extremist teachers. And children who need to be able to count and multiply are learning anti-racist mathematics – whatever that may be. Children who need to be able to express themselves in clear English are being taught political slogans. Children who need to be taught to respect traditional moral values are being taught that they have an inalienable right to be gay.[28]

It was as if the nineteenth-century imperial myth of the uncharted dark African continent had been reflected back at the late-twentieth-century multicultural British inner city. Powell and Thatcher had created a new mythology of the urban other, but while mythology might win elections, they needed action on the ground to profitably colonise the urban realm.

In 1981 the Royal Docks closed, obsolete in the face of containerisation and a new generation of bigger ships. To Thatcher's Environment Minister Michael Heseltine, the derelict London Docklands presented an opportunity, a site to pioneer the new political order. A more practical man than Thatcherism's creators Powell and Joseph, Heseltine took a dirigiste view of how the new kind of capitalism would work. He stripped power from the elected local authorities in the area, and gave the land and control over it to an appointed body, the London Docklands Development Corporation (LDDC).[29] This unelected structure denied the area's residents any voice at all over its future. The drive to increase land values dictated everything; they were the gateway to private investment and profit.

But as with the colonial age, the blank spaces identified for remaking–in this case by the Thatcher government–were already populated. After rioting in inner-city London and Liverpool in 1981, unprecedented in mainland Britain since it had transitioned into democracy in the early twentieth century, the government decided that the British police should call on colonial experience. First they secretly invited in the Hong Kong police to explain how they had used force to suppress left-wing protests in the colony in the late 1960s.[30] Then the Metropolitan Police hired retired soldier Brigadier Mike Harvey[31] to set up a training centre in the London Docklands to train officers in military techniques to put down civil unrest.[32]

Before joining the army, Harvey had studied at Canterbury College of Art.[33] As a young officer he'd won the Military Cross for his part in fighting communism in the Korean War. After that his postings followed the messy path of Britain's retreat from empire. He'd fought during the Cyprus "emergency" in the 1950s, before action in Kenya in the aftermath of the Mau Mau Uprising. He'd then privatised himself and worked as a mercenary in Oman before working as a consultant to the British Army in Northern Ireland. As a first step in creating this new paramilitary police force, Harvey had groups of policemen throw petrol bombs at their reluctant colleagues to get them adjusted to life in a riot zone.[34] Officers trained in these new militarised techniques would be sent on to the flashpoints of the miners' strike,[35] the print strike,[36] and to riots around the UK during the 1980s.[37] The repressive apparatus of empire had now come home.

There had been an alternative. An alternative socialist movement had emerged from the wreckage of the Communist Party in 1956–it was called the New Left.[38] During the 1960s and 1970s it critiqued the impact of empire and class division on British culture, and central to its vision was respect for the textured mix of cultures and people that made up society. As

Fig. 6: "Lesbians are coming out", See Red Women's Workshop (SRWW), 1982. Between 1981 and 1986 the GLC backed hundreds of small-scale cultural projects supporting marginalised communities, such as the See Red Women's Workshop which had existed since 1974. This poster from 1982 exemplifies both their work, and the spirit of the GLC's interventions. Reproduced with the permission of the copyright holder.

the ugly exclusionary vision of Powellism had matured into the Thatcherite political project, in 1981 a group of young politicians emerged from the New Left to take control of the Greater London Council. They harnessed the mechanisms of local government in an attempt to rebuild London ideologically.

Greater London Council (GLC) leader Ken Livingstone told me in 2009 that this new direction was in part pragmatic:

Well by that stage housing policy had gone to the boroughs, I think we built ten thousand homes in the first year I was leader of the GLC but after that the government had just stopped the programme. We therefore were looking much more at other issues like racism, sexism, sexual orientation, industrial regeneration, policing.[39]

Their plans to rebuild London's Docklands around the needs of their communities had been killed off when Heseltine created the LDDC.

The train line I'd travelled on to the docks back in 1985 was itself a monument to this alternative, funded by the GLC as part of a programme to break down social and economic barriers by building new transport infrastructure.[40] It ran alongside active interventions in schools, the arts, funding for social enterprise, and support for marginalised groups. But this attempt to forge a new kind of urban society was cut short in 1986 when the Thatcher government abolished the council. The lack of formal constitutional protections in Britain made it easy for this illiberal government to concentrate power in its own hands. There was no space for dissent within the new order.[41]

Superficially, the 1990s seemed calm after the violence of the Thatcher era, but then most opposition had already been crushed.[42] The neoliberal advance continued; public housing, electricity generators, and what was left of the coal industry were sold off, while the blue and grey trains that had first taken me to the docks were gaudily repainted, reflecting the railway's fragmentation and privatisation.

Once the realignment of power had taken place, much of

the Powellite ideology of Thatcherism could be allowed to fall away. The Blair/Brown consortium made any chance of reversal by electoral politics seem impossible. Their government saw Heseltine's approach to internal colonisation established as the new order for urban intervention, with state power used to take over urban land, before passing it on to wealthy investors.

***

Last week I went for a walk in the docks to see one last artefact of the age of empire: the Gallions Hotel in Beckton. Kipling[43] name-checked it in one of his novels; his hero travels there down the same railway line I'd taken to the docks back in the 1980s. In Kipling's 1890s novel the journey represents the height of modernity: a train to a cross-platform interchange with a steamship bound for Port Said and the empire. Even then the mythology didn't match up with reality; locals nicknamed the hotel "the Captain's Brothel".

Today in place of ocean liners, the hotel is surrounded by slabs of high-end flats. My approach was past hoardings advertising the

Fig. 7: The long road to neoliberalism. © The author, 2018.

developments, evidence that the area's reshaping as a neoliberal space was almost complete. Outside, the pub reminded me of a corpse in an open coffin—visually reminiscent of the living thing it had been, but undeniably lifeless. Inside there were uniformed waiters and a scattering of chino-clad men, who sipped meekly at beer while they feigned passion for the football glowing from flatscreen TVs. The customers seemed uneasy; this was where they lived but clearly hadn't settled. Maybe I imagined it, but it seemed the anxious fear of the coloniser was hanging over them. Perhaps one day the dispossessed would rise up and demand equal rights to their city?

Fig. 8: The Gallions Hotel today. © The author, 2018.

Endnotes

1   Joseph Conrad, *Heart of Darkness* (Wordsworth Classics, 1995), p. 7

2   Michael Heseltine, *Life in the Jungle* (Hodder and Stoughton, 2000), p. 211

3   Between 1977 and 1985 the Greater London Council (with the support of the local London Boroughs) funded a series of improvements to British Rail's North London Line, reinstating passenger services that had been withdrawn in 1944 between Stratford and Dalston Western Junction, opening stations at Hackney Central, Homerton, Hackney Wick and West Ham, and electrifying the route from Dalston to North Woolwich to replace the decrepit and unreliable diesel service. For a full description see Wayne Asher, *A Very Political Railway* (Capital Transport, 2014).

4   See Eric Williams, *Capitalism and Slavery* (University of North Carolina Press, 1944)

5   See Joseph Inikori, *Africans and the Industrial Revolution in England* (Cambridge University Press, 2002)

6   For an example, in 1999 I directed a video for the Dreem Teem's *Buddy X 99* mostly shot around Silvertown https://www.youtube.com/watch?v=8kOPLTQ4ZYk (last accessed 21 February 2018)

7   See the *Times*, 29 August 1889, quoted in Terry McCarthy, *The Great Dock Strike 1889* (Weidenfield and Nelson, 1988), p. 32

8   Cecil Frances Alexander, "All Things Bright and Beautiful". Recited from memory to author by Neave Brown, 22nd May 2017 and first published in *Hymns for Little Children*, 1848

9   *Evening Post and News*, 26th August 1889, quoted in Terry McCarthy, *The Great Dock Strike 1889*, p. 115

10   John Burns, "The Great Strike", New Review, 1:5, October 1889, p. 420. Quoted in McCarthy, *The Great Dock Strike*, p. 236

11   Ann Stafford: *A Match to Fire the Thames* (Hodder and

Stoughton, 1961), p. 40

12   Ibid, p. 27

13   John Burns (by then an MP) quoting the *Times* from 1892 in a speech to the House of Commons 13th April 1905. http://hansard.millbanksystems.com/commons/1905/apr/13/london-port-and-docks-commission-bill-by#S4V0145P0_19050413_HOC_344. (Last accessed 18 February 2018

14   John Boughton, "The Page Estate, Eltham: 'Results for the People not the Profiteers'", *Municipal Dreams*. https://municipaldreams.wordpress.com/2013/08/06/page_estate_eltham/ Accessed 18 February 2018; and "Woolwich's Interwar Health Centres: 'Monuments to Man's Achievement and to his Folly'", Municipal Dreams. https://municipaldreams.wordpress.com/2013/07/23/woolwichs-interwar-health-centres-monuments-to-mans-achievement-and-his-folly/ (Last accessed 18 February 2018)

15   Humphrey Jennings, *Fires Were Started* (Crown Film Unit, 1943)

16   On 22 June 1940, Bevin had been spirited into the House of Commons in an uncontested by election for Wandsworth Central, allowing him to serve as Minister of Labour in Churchill's coalition government.

17   See Edmund Dell, *A Strange Eventful History* (Harper Collins, 1999), p. 177-179

18   See William Gallacher, *Rise Like Lions* (Lawrence and Wishart, 1951) for a contemporary British Communist critique of the Attlee government. Gallacher had been the Communist MP for West Fife from 1935-50)

19   Ben Tillett, *The Dock Labourers Bitter Cry* (Dock, Wharf, Riverside and General Labourers' Union, 1889). Quoted in Fishman, East End Jewish Radicals, (Duckworth, 1975), p. 77

20   Phil Piratin, various contributions to parliamentary debates,

Hansard 1945-49 http://hansard.millbanksystems.com/people/mr-philip-piratin/ (Last accessed 18 February 2018)

21   Richard Stott, *Dogs and Lampposts* (Metro, 2002) pp. 166-171

22   Peter Thorneycroft to House of Commons 23 January 1958:

> We have been attempting to do more than our resources could manage and in the process we have been gravely weakening ourselves [...] over 12 years we have slithered from one crisis to another [...] a pound sterling which has shrunk from 20 shillings to 12 shillings. That is not a picture of the nation we would wish to see [...] That is not the path to greatness. It is the road to ruin [...] The simple truth is that we have been spending more money than we should [...] It is not the sluice gate which is at fault. It is the plain fact that the water is coming over the top of the dam [...] I believe that living within our resources is neither unfair nor unjust, nor, perhaps, in the long run even unpopular.

http://hansard.millbanksystems.com/commons/1958/jan/23/economic-situation#S5CV0580P0_19580123_HOC_331 (Last accessed 18 February 2018). See also Simon Heffer, *Like the Roman* (Weidenfield and Nicholson, 1998), pp. 210-241 for a detailed account of the Thorneycroft/Birch/Powell resignation.

23   See Richard Cockett, *Thinking the Unthinkable* (Fontana Press, 1995), pp. 140, 163-167 for details of Powell's significance to the influential proto-Thatcherite think tank, the Institute of Economic Affairs. See also Heffer, Like the Roman, pp. 191-192/200 for Powell's advocacy of a return to nineteenth-century liberal economics in the mid-1950s.

24   See Paul Foot, *The Rise of Enoch Powell* (Penguin, 1969) for a clinical dissection of Powell's cynical move from a liberal position on race in the 1950s to one advocating

repatriation of Commonwealth immigrants from the mid-1960s. More recently Stephen Finnigan's Britain's Racist Election (Channel 4, 15 March 2015) provided previously unreported testimony of Powell's deep involvement in Tory MP Peter Griffith's campaign for Smethwick during the 1964 General Election. Powell attended the meeting that approved Griffith's slogan "If you want a n***** for a neighbour, vote Liberal or Labour". Against a national swing of 3.5% from Conservative to Labour, Griffiths won his seat with a swing of 7.2%, proof enough to Powell and others that overt racism could win elections.

25   Enoch Powell, speech in Birmingham, 20 April 1968. Quoted in Heffer, *Like the Roman*, p. 451

26   Interview with Margaret Thatcher, *World in Action*, (Granada TV, 30 January 1978)

27   Interview with Keith Joseph, *Pandora's Box, The League of Gentlemen* (BBC TV, 22 June 1992)

28   Margaret Thatcher, speech to conservative party conference 9 October 1987

29   See Heseltine, *A life in the Jungle*, pp. 212-213 for the detail of how on the advice of Reg Prentice (a former Labour minister who in 1977 had switched to the Conservatives) Heseltine persuaded Thatcher, Joseph and chancellor Geoffrey Howe to give him control of the Docklands by telling them that the local authorities there were controlled by closet communists.

30   Gerry Northam, *Shooting in the Dark* (Faber, 1988), p. 134

31   Ellis Cashmore and Eugene McLaughlin, *Out of Order: Policing Black People* (Routledge, 1991), p. 31

32   *World in Action: The Coal War* (Granada TV, October 1984), https://www.youtube.com/watch?v=HGC0dLUz4UI (Last accessed 18 February 2018)

33   Brigadier Mike Harvey obituary, *the Telegraph*, 15th October 2007 http://www.telegraph.co.uk/news/

obituaries/1566167/Brigadier-Mike-Harvey.html (Last accessed 18 February 2018)

34   Interview with Officer 122, (Metropolitan Police historical collection) https://www.metpolicehistory.co.uk/officer-122.html (Last accessed 18 February 2018)

35   *World in Action: The Coal War,* 1984

36   Ben Emmerson and Anne Shamash, *A Case To Answer? A Report on the Policing of the News International Demonstration at Wapping on January 24th 1987* (The Haldane Society of Socialist Lawyers, September 1987) http://www.oatridge.co.uk/wapping_files/HaldaneNI.htm (Last accessed 18 February 2018)

37   Interview with Officer 105 (Metropolitan Police historical collection) https://www.metpolicehistory.co.uk/officer-105.html (Last accessed 18 February 2018)

38   Stuart Hall, "Life and times of the First New Left", *New Left Review, 61,* January-February 2010 https://newleftreview.org/II/61/stuart-hall-life-and-times-of-the-first-new-left (Last accessed 18 February 2018)

39   Ken Livingstone, interview by author, 2009

40   'Nayne Asher, *A Very Political Railway: The Fight for the North London Line 1945-2014* (Capitol Transport, 1994), p. 79

41   See Stuart Hall, "Gramsci and Us", *Marxism Today,* June 1987 for a contemporary overview of Thatcherism's contradictory appeal to the British as a form of "regressive modernity". http://www.hegemonics.co.uk/docs/Gramsci-and-us.pdf (Last accessed 18 February 2018)

42   The Conservative government continued to use the power of the state with a theatrical cruelty towards the weak and disadvantaged. See Social Security minister Peter Lilley's odious speech to the Conservative party conference in 1992 where he sings a list of "scroungers" he plans to deprive of benefits. https://www.youtube.com/watch?v=FOx8q3eGq3g (Last accessed 18 February 2018)

43   Rudyard Kipling, *The Light that Failed* (Lippincott's Monthly Magazine January 1891) https://en.wikisource.org/wiki/The_Light_That_Failed/Chapter_14 (Last accessed 18 February 2018)

The Royal Docks as Museum

Matthew Friday

If the Royal Docks (part of the Arc of Opportunity) was a museum, what issues would it throw to light?

That is the core of this chapter: to consider the Royal Docks in the light of the process and structures of museums and "museumification". This is a discussion and a metaphor, and at its heart draws on Andreas Huyssen's approach of looking at museums as mass media concerned with memory.[1] This is about the docks themselves alongside the "toughness and precipitous grimness" of Woolwich[2] and other nearby areas, and is a synecdoche of the whole of the Arc of Opportunity.

The area, whilst historical, is clearly not an actual museum. However, considering it in this way draws together some key dialectics that relate to museums as a technology. These are threefold: tradition vs. the new, purpose vs. place, and participation vs. planning. To start, however, it is worth summarising the definition and technology of the museum.

Museum as Institution and Process

The formal definitions of "museum" are straightforward, although there are minor differences. The commonalities are that museums are institutions, which collect/look after artefacts for the purpose of visitors' enjoyment and learning.[3] The artefacts in the Royal Docks are tangible in terms of architecture, and intangible in terms of history and events.

The three key verbs from the definitions are "collect", "conserve", and "curate". I'd like to add another "c" word to this: "co-presence".

Collection is the easiest here. If we look at what is collected, it seems to be mostly housing: relatively densely packed flats of varying quality, along with some infrastructure of a flyover and service roads to the ExCel Centre. The ExCel itself seems to have collected a variety of related and linked small businesses, and there is a peculiar knot of attractions at the western end.

This section seems oddly accessible in a physical sense: it is possible to get the train along by the flyover or walk around and over the docks; there is public space by the ExCel and attractions and even the ExCel itself is open for the pedestrian, as a vast, cathedral-like space with the surrounding side chapels waiting for specific exhibitions or events. The Tate and Lyle section, by Woolwich, is a different collection: an industrial complex with housing built to serve it.

This is in direct contrast to the ExCel Centre, where the housing around it was not built for workers in the ExCel Centre – it was built for those working in other places where they can afford the housing. This is a key distinction. Old parts of the collection have industrial areas and housing to serve them, and are not so well-represented. New areas are made up of housing serving elsewhere, and business serving the housing or visitors.

The relatively straightforward type of tangible artefact starts breaking down if we look again from a chronological point of view. This collection is decidedly modern. The docks themselves are the oldest sections here, and much of that form is from the early twentieth century. The ExCel Centre, light railway, and flats are from 1994 onwards, with a section of 1930s items. Much of the small knot of attractions is from the Olympics in 2012. These are mixed, as is so much of London, but we will return to this later on. There are also many new acquisitions in the area. The industrial schemes are Chinese investment, and plans for Albert Island; the housing is represented by the new wharf sections filling in by Barrier Park, itself a new development flanking the flyover. This collection of architecture and places is growing at a fast rate. This new collection is being acquired, and needs little conservation, the next verb on the list.

Conservation has become key in current museums, as methods and technology have improved. But how does conservation affect the Arc of Opportunity?

This one seems pretty straightforward. We can look at some examples of how older buildings and sections have been conserved. The docks are a good example of this: there are two warehouses remaining near ExCel from the nineteenth century, and these have been turned into bars, restaurants, and coffee shops serving the ExCel Centre and assimilated into the travel complex with the station. Nothing else remains around that has been conserved. The interiors are completely different. This falls very much under the category of extensive restoration; only the facade remains. The Stothert and Pitt cranes, used for unloading, stand tall and angular with booms raised at the same angle. The working crane cables and machinery have been removed and the cabs have been boarded up: the form remains but the function has been removed. Some rails from the docks line used for moving goods remain in the pavements. The flyover, a truly historic part of the landscape, is still in use.

The Millennium Mills site (as part of the old docks buildings) is a site in need of conservation that has started to happen. The building was a flour mill, extended and changed until its closure. Recently, the asbestos and old industrial items have been removed as part of restoration. Although this building will become something new, only the facade will remain.

This is symptomatic of the area. None of the older items have been conserved in a recognisable museum way. The industrial heritage has been repurposed as an aesthetic item but very much subservient to the modern items.

This ties into the next "c": curation.

Curate is a complex and much-used verb, and is more than slightly ambiguous. Curation is quite hard to define: it involves selection, care/management, and presentation of something.

Curation is probably the most interesting of the museum elements, the most modern and relevant, as plenty of items are now described as "curated". In the museum sense, it is what people think of as museum activity: choosing interesting tangible things, researching them, and presenting this through labels, activities, and education. Curation seems to imply the presence of a curator, which is not the case in a wide urban area, but some aspects of curation can be observed. If we intend as "Curation" the way we normally interface with museums as visitors, then many elements of curation are in place in the Royal Docks.

The warehouses converted into pubs have been curated by developers, and conserved, but the presentation is absent. There are art installations that chime with the modern conception of curation: the statue of dockers is a tangible representation of intangible process (and working-class/industrial process), and it is placed in front of the ExCel. This figurative bronze statue (by Les Johnson), installed in 2009, shows a tally clerk and stevedores carrying out their labour and is based on actual dock workers. Likewise, "The Line", a selection of modern art placed or commissioned for locations, falls into the area of curation.[4] The Stothert and Pitt cranes have been selected and conserved, and presented in a site-specific way, but curation seems to imply a necessary extra stage of interpretation: they are collected, and conserved, but not curated.

In this context, I think curation implies research and consideration of use, interpretation, and access that simply keeping in situ doesn't quite satisfy. There is also a juxtaposition of the older conserved buildings and the newer changeable art. This is an interesting parallel with museums themselves, which have shifted toward temporary exhibitions from permanent, which highlight curation as a process.

The fourth "c" is "co-presence". This certainly isn't mentioned in museum definitions but is a key element in the design of museums as institutions. Co-presence is how people in the same space experience each other. Museums, as a public space, have elements of being seen and seeing others in the same space as well as the tangible artefacts.

This, of course, is part of the enjoyment and learning of museums, although the lessons (how to behave in a middle-class manner in public? how to display appreciation of culture?) may be rarely taught formally. The corollary, of course, is the exclusivity of VIP and prelaunch parties for exhibitions and private views which hold selective co-presence as a key factor. The Royal Docks has areas of co-presence. The public spaces around the western end combine transport links, outdoor food sales, visibility from/to the cablecar, and movement along the line of art toward the ExCel Centre. With this shallow framework of verbs and some links to the Royal Docks, we can consider some of the dialectics in more depth.

Tradition vs. the New

Museums traditionally have been criticised for turning microhistories into a narrative, and especially a narrative that marginalises histories that do not fit with hegemonic interests. Indeed, museums have been a soft target for institutional critique, but this has changed completely in recent years with museums' own self-reflection, change in types and styles of exhibition, and remits.[5] This dialectic pits this traditional function of museums (rendering the past into a coherent narrative) against the new (challenging expectations, oft-conflicting microhistories, self-reflection as institution). The traditional historical narrative in the docks is one of industrial progress, where marginal land outside the main city is turned into a productive area, which then itself is bombed then rendered obsolete by new shipping technology and reinvents itself, with the Olympics as a critical moment of present reinvention.[6] This is not inaccurate, but this brief synopsis obscures the many lacunae, the simultaneous leaps in innovation and failings of capitalism, and the parallel working-class and migration histories. The collection, conservation, and curation of the docks throws away this traditional hegemony along with the microhistories and presents future as the new tradition.

Kevin Hetherington tackles this and other aspects of museumification, identifying the compression of time by museums into something controllable, and this linking to the entrepreneurial city as being consumable.[7] This breaks down with regard to the Royal Docks. The Royal Docks has failed to become (or resisted becoming) a heritage "spectacle". Whilst Hetherington correctly identifies the museum object becoming less important so that this connotative index can be used to create narrative, it simply hasn't happened either.

The chronological time of the docks, and the narrative identified above, is not obvious from the place itself and is only accessible through other forms of interpretation external to the site.[8] The docks also have a kairological aspect: time as individually experienced moments that are qualitative and distinctive (with a "right time" for actions to happen) and that links to other similar moments rather than chronology. Moments of docks hardship, or those of frantic expansion, are linked by this kairological time. Neither the kairological histories nor histories where the audience has a very different interpretation from the curatorial narrative are on display.

There are still ruins available to see in the Royal Docks but the "right time to redevelop" has often passed. The public spaces are pseudo-public, owned by business or housing, so do not have a broader discourse. The docks form their own psychogeography, neither hegemonical nor fully indexical.

Purpose vs. Place

The second dialectic is that of purpose vs place. Purpose is the original design and is active, whereas place is location and is passive. On the surface, it doesn't seem much of a dialectic at all, and doesn't seem to be part of museumification. However, this taps into the key part of museums and heritage: once something becomes a museum object, it stops performing its original purpose.

The new purpose is instrumentalised for education, study, and enjoyment–even if it is shown in context and sometimes performs the original function it is not the same. This, in turn, leads to Foucault: specifically the architecture of knowledge, and how a document becomes a monument.[9] The essence of this, in the Royal Docks context, is that as the "readability" of items disappears or is removed, the opportunity for reinterpretation is enhanced. This is part of contemporary museumification strategies (although often implicitly), and ties into the previous dialectic of removing hegemony.

This has not led to the palimpsest of meaning that would seem like the positive outcome that has been the driver of museum reinterpretation (which has flourished through contemporary, often postmodern identity reinterpretation of hegemonic histories). It is an irony not lost that the Music for Masterplanning project, and indeed this chapter's approach, have been contingent on multivalent, often critical views on the area's heritage.

This is key to looking at the industrial heritage in the Royal Docks, and the docks themselves. The docks no longer perform their original purpose, and indeed none of the remaining industrial equipment, from pontoons to cranes to tracks to mills, is any longer working industrially. The water itself, once there only as a mechanism for transport and facilitator of efficient capitalism, is now a museum object.

The modern art is not disruptive enough for the viewer to change their experience of the place: even Paolozzi's superlative Vulcan, itself allegorical to the work done in the docks, is simply absorbed into the existing landscape. The Royal Docks is a narrative of place as a collapsed singular, and this placemaking is linked inextricably with museumification functions.

Placemaking, as a modern concept, ends up being rather similar to curation: elements are managed, conserved, selected, and displayed in the service of goals (that of making positive interventions in people's lived experience of an area). The Royal Docks is a case study in imaginary placemaking but struggles to turn these into physical development.[10] The next dialectic helps to illuminate this.

Participation vs. Planning

This third dialectic could also be defined as top-down vs bottom-up. Top-down in this context is something mandated from a position of leadership or power (especially institutional), and bottom-up is from the end of consumers or individuals involved. Museum practice has, in recent years, moved toward participatory content either explicitly or implicitly. This current in museums is partly a response to their traditional role (and a way to defuse criticism of that), and partly being more responsive and entrepreneurial. However, this aspect is not clearly present in the Royal Docks, which is heavily about planning. Whilst this is unsurprising, given the requirements for large-scale projects and the challenges of planning permission in an area with many stakeholders, it also illustrates that the area has fallen between two stools. Similarly to the challenges many museums have had with becoming genuinely participatory instead of entirely planned, the Royal Docks feel neither planned nor organically developed.

In fact, the "Vision for the Royal Docks" highlights this. This is a document (from the mayor and Newham) designed to quantify the docks and provide a blueprint for economic development, but it still notes the "stubbornly resisted attempts at comprehensive regeneration" of the Royal Docks.[11] Despite the nature of this plan, the key viability seems to be getting a critical mass of visitors to ExCel and the Crystal, and this makes the surrounding areas more viable and desirable and then builds on a virtuous circle. This has not happened at scale since 2012, and there have been few changes since then to bring in new visitors.[12] Large flats have been the new addition to the collection here.

If this is considered from a participatory point of view, there is a hierarchy of cultural participation that is useful, moving from "me" (single experiences with no feedback) to "we" (social engagement and networked culture in aggregate).[13] This is analogous to many of the strands in placemaking through culture, which requires buying from a variety of stakeholders.[14] In the Royal Docks, there is little evidence of networked culture between the visitor and communities.

This is a difficult part of the metaphor, as visitors in museums are sharing an experience which can be aggregated. This is less easy in the context of place, as a local resident could be commuting or going out to buy some shopping, whilst a visitor is going to a conference or enjoying leisure time or activities, and businesses are focussed on their own viable activity. If there is local resistance to placemaking activity, then this poses a serious practical challenge.

But the challenges in the docks do not seem related to local communities being opposed to activity per se; activity happens in individual elements, housing developments and changes to the public space but does not coalesce as place.

At an interpretative level, the refurbished warehouses do not link to the dockers' statue, nor to the cranes, nor to the Siemens Crystal. Each seems almost hermetically apart; following The Line, for instance, does not have reactions or links to the local community, or previous visitors, or existing places in the area.

The many regenerated parts of the Royal Docks (cable car, ExCel, Siemens Crystal, DLR, new housing) seem to pass each other by. In another irony, a participatory culture does exist in the docks but not physically, in the form of the Royal Docks Management Authority's "Forgotten Stories" content or UEL's "Ports of Call".[15] These allow exploration via web stories or memory-trail walks with content from local communities. "Ports of Call" blends recorded audio, memories from local people, and music linked to the walking location.

The juxtaposition of stories and memories in these along with the changes in the built environment is powerful and moving. These highlight some reasons for resistance to comprehensive regeneration: the stories and communities are complex and do not allow themselves to be easily integrated within a creative placemaking entrepreneurial vision.

This is something museums as institutions are almost uniquely good at—for example, Bristol's successfully regenerated docks area has working heritage cranes alongside moored houseboats, businesses, and modern housing, and the M Shed museum can present both the difficult history of slavery and modern local perspectives on it, effectively claiming both sides of the dialectic via the institution and technology of a museum.[16]

So why has this aspect of placemaking not occurred in the Royal Docks?

A Failure of Museumification?

I would argue that, as a museumification project, the docks have failed. Indeed, the failure of the museumification is one of the key aspects of the docks.

If we look at another of Hetherington's points: that of "trauma" histories being the dominant microhistories, we can see this result. The "Forgotten Stories" project does have a large amount of content focussed on war destruction, bombing, and closure and the histories focus on the narrative of "tough times". This makes the docks particularly interesting: the area has clearly failed to be as effective economically as the more central parts of London. In addition, it has lost purpose and sense of place (revisiting Jonathan Meades, "so marginal it is off the page"[17]).

This puts it squarely into the discourse of economic instrumentalisation, but also to the kairological elements of being the "right time" to develop: the development of Canary Wharf, the arrival of the ExCel and the DLR, and the Olympics have all come and gone and the many ruins of the docks remain ruins. The conclusion, then, is not that the Royal Docks have become museumified but that despite conditions being right for this to happen, it still has not.

Perhaps it is just too difficult to create a narrative in comparison to others in London, or perhaps it is simply multiple failures of implementation for different factors. There have been many tries at narratives, from the future visions of mayors to chronological histories, but perhaps there is too much narrative to bind easily; too many factors and contexts.

Each time a single strand of memory and place takes the reins of history others wrestle it back, drawing apart the skeins and revealing more underneath. Consideration of the reasons behind this failure of a binding narrative is, alas, for another time.

Endnotes

1   Andreas Huyssen, *"Escape from Amnesia: The Museum as Mass Medium", in Twilight Memories: Marking Time in a Culture of Amnesia* (Routledge, 1995), pp. 13-35

2   Jonathan Meades, *"Strategy Safari", in Museum Without Walls* (London: Unbound, 2013), pp. 229-231

3   For definitions, see ICOM (http://icom.museum/the-vision/museum-definition/) and Museum Association (https://www.museumsassociation.org/about/frequently-asked-questions).

4   See The Line (http://the-line.org/#/landing)

5   For an excellent summary, see Andrea Witcombe, "Unmasking a different museum: museums and cultural criticism", in: *Re-imagining the Museum* (Routledge, 2003), pp. 13-26.

6   See http://www.londonsroyaldocks.com/londons-royal-docks-history/ for a good presentation of this narrative.

7   Kevin Hetherington, "Time of the Entreprenuerial City", in *Consuming the Entrepreneurial City* (Routledge, 2008), pp. 273-292

8   http://www.londonsroyaldocks.com/forgotten-stories/

9   "To be brief, then, let us say that history, in its traditional form, undertook to 'memorise' the monuments of the past, transform them into *documents*, and lend speech to those traces which, in themselves, are often not verbal, or which say in silence something other than what they actually say; in our time, history is that which transforms *documents into monuments*." Michel Foucualt, *The Archaeology of Knowledge*, trans. A.M. Sheridan Smith (Routledge, 2002), pp. 7-8.

10   http://www.silvertownlondon.com/

11   See https://www.newham.gov.uk/Documents/Environment%20an%20planning/RoyalDocksAVisionfortheRoyalDocks[1].pdf

12   See https://tfl.gov.uk/corporate/publications-and-reports/emirates-air-line-performance-data for data.

13   See http://www.participatorymuseum.org/chapter3/, Nina Simon, 2010

14   Anne Gadwa and Ann Markusen, *Creative Placemaking* white paper, (National Endowment for the Arts, 2010) https://www.arts.gov/sites/default/files/Creative Placemaking-Paper.pdf

15   http://www.londonsroyaldocks.com/forgotten-stories/ and http://www.portsofcall.org.uk/ respectively

16   See https://www.bristolmuseums.org.uk/m-shed/

17   Jonathan Meades, "On the Brandwagon", episode two of five, BBC Two series Jonathan Meades: Abroad Again, aired between May-June 2007 on terrestrial TV. The episode is available on Vimeo here: https://vimeo.com/140779893

Condensing and Displacing: A Stratford Dream-Work

Jane Rendell

16 June 2007

My apologies for not sending the route earlier in the week; we are having an intense walking schedule squeezed by the 2nd July deadline for the road closure into the Olympic zone…

Walking plan: 20.06.2007

Meeting point: 3pm, Corner of Wick Road with Cadogan Terrace (see link below)
http://www.streetmap.co.uk/newmap.srf?x=536250&y=18420&z=1&sv=536250,184250&st=4&ar=N&mapp=newmapsrf&searchp=newsearch.srf&ax=536649&ay=184563

Starting from the eastern edge of Victoria Park, crossing over the A12, into Carpenters/Rothbury Road, leading into White Post Lane, crossing over the Lee navigation and follow its path heading south,

until the Bow Locks, crossing over into the Dace Road area, up onto
the Greenway, until joining Marshgate Lane, backing into Marshgate
Lane, until crossing with Carpenters Road, all the way until the
A118/Stratford High Street, ending in Stratford for a well-earned
drink… around 6/6.30pm.

Last year I wrote about what I thought the opportunity for
UCL was on the Carpenter's Estate: to create a new kind of
university that was "Newham shaped".[1]

For Jean-François Lyotard, dreams do not arise from the
"unconscious"; rather they are made up of fragments from
the conscious and preconscious to which something is
then done. As Graham Jones notes, following a key essay
of Lyotard's in *Discourse, Figure*, "'the dream-work does not
think'; instead, it is what is done to thought".[2]

Tucked into the cliff.
Overlooking the sea.
It was the sweetest of villages.
Early mornings I would have to leave this charmed world.
And cycle up a long, steep hill to the station.
At Ashford I would change trains for Stratford.

The Dream-Work: We are thus presented with a new task
[…] of investigating the relations between the manifest
content of dreams and the latent dream-thoughts, and of
tracing out the processes by which the latter have been
changed into the former.[3]

Its role would be to directly affect the aspirations and quality
of life of the local community, and to challenge UCL to think
new thoughts about its role in local economic regeneration.
I still think that this could have been a good idea, but for
various reasons it was not to be.[4]

10 January 2017

The Lea River is a tributary of the Thames. The Thames is tidal and flows towards its estuary. But you will notice that the level of this water is not tidal, it is steady, it is controlled. Why?

> The dream-thoughts and the dream-content are presented to us like two versions of the same subject-matter in two different languages.[5]

So this is the opportunity: to take space in a globally visible, but locally isolated location on the East of London, a good 40 minutes travel from the heart of UCL in Bloomsbury. I have heard three arguments in its favour.[6]

10 January 2017

One of the first decisions of the now-defunct Olympic Delivery Authority, was to control the water level and stop its tidal nature, before the entrance to the park, because mud was considered unsightly by Olympic standards. So as in many other developments, where natural resources are used to name a structure, the natural attributes are curbed and contained in a way that stops them being natural.

> A dream is a picture-puzzle of this sort...[7]

First, that the land would be cheap, practically free to the University, as its presence on the site at this juncture would increase confidence and the value of the remaining sites on the Park and so help to recoup the Government investment in clean-up of the site for the Games. Second, that it would win us considerable political brownie points. Both Boris and Cameron would love to see the "Olympic Legacy" gain the boost of a world leading university's presence on the site before the next election. Third, it is likely that there will be significant funding available for strategic projects that help deliver on this legacy.[8]

10 January 2017

We have a river at the centre of this development, which, in order to define the space around it as natural, is not allowed to be a river, as it would be naturally! So in the park/non-park, we have a river/non-river! Let's walk through it.

20 June 2007

Alberto Duman: Is the red facing out, and the blue facing in? […] Look, forget about this map. From the second of July this whole area will be closed off, except for this one walker's path, through the middle.

Jane Rendell: So everyone will be gone?

Jude Rosen: Well, yes, except where there are still ongoing legal disputes, about the relocation of people, or even businesses. […] The travellers still have pending legal claims. And no complete agreement on relocation sites. And there will be a handful of people in the Peabody Estate in Clay's Lane. They will not be out by the second of July […] and the Manor Garden allotments. They are going to have keys, very restricted access, and security guards. And their helpers will have access until 23 September, which is seen as the end of the planting season. And then that is it.

The fundamental question, then, is how to globalise a university? I suspect that this will be in two ways. First, by cementing UCL's worldwide reputation and recognition. This is where The Olympic Park could play a useful role. The site is already known around the world, and while it is locally isolated, it is accessible at the larger scale. If we are looking for a focus to establish a national and global presence for UCL, to accommodate those who visit from overseas and act as a showcase for UCL's intellectual output, this could be it.[9]

The Work of Condensation: The first thing that becomes clear to anyone who compares the dream-content with the dream-thoughts is that a work of *condensation* on a large scale has been carried out.[10]

The air is bright,
Exquisite Georgian houses.
The beach minutes away.
The kitchen in the attic appeals.
Views of the sea.
The winter dusk is turning fast now.
Burnt orange catches the edge of the frame.
My dream flickers.
Poorly detailed even in this light.
He says the area might flood.
My dream evaporates.

Second, by inventing a business model able to deliver value at a global scale, and to derive income from an international reach. Universities generate value in three main ways, they create intellectual capital through research, cultural capital through the principles they promote and their practice based output, and social capital through education and the social networks and partnerships that result.[11]

Dreams are brief, meagre and laconic in comparison with the range and wealth of the dream-thoughts. If a dream is written out it may perhaps fill half a page.[12]

In 2012, inspired by a dream of white linen, and a
house called May Mourn,[13] I begin writing a book
on architecture psychoanalysis and social housing.[14]
In it I trace the changes made to an architectural
typology – the social condenser – over time, from the
constructivist architecture of the Russian Revolution, via
Le Corbusier's *Unité d'Habitation*, to the social housing of
London's postwar welfare state. I decide to situate this
history in the here and now, in the context of London's
"regeneration" and in relation to projects which, in
arguing for "viability and the sweating of assets", are
pushing for a version of redevelopment that exclude
refurbishment, and seek instead to demolish public
housing and its social condensers and produce, through
displacement, social cleansing.

> Rose Cottage, Summer Hill.
> A fitting follow up to May Mourn perhaps.
> Only a poetic turn of this type could sustain me.
> But this dream home demanded too much.

In the autumn of 2014, as I draw the book to a close, I
discover that my flat in Southwark is in the council's
"estate renewal zone".[15] The property consultants Savills
have been advising the council to "unearth the potential"
of public land, including "brownfield sites", a term
which for them includes fully occupied housing estates.[16]
Writing about the site in which I am writing – right
here, right now – starts to change the relation of my life
to my words. As I begin to consider these sites of my
academic production and creative imagination, I realise
they are connected to processes of displacement. Starting
to write them together, is to imagine a new project,
Condensations and Displacements, a dream-home-
work.[17]

The analysis setting out the dream-thoughts underlying it may occupy six, eight or a dozen times as much space.[18]

10 January 2017

E20 is the fictional postcode of *EastEnders*. [...] It was then adopted by the park and artificially positioned in zone two, so that all the housing could claim to be a certain distance from the centre.

> I become so angered by Southwark Council's demolition of the Heygate social housing estate that I decide to get directly involved in the fight for the Aylesbury. One site where I transform my experience of writing at and about home into a different kind of work, not for the university, but for the local community, is 'Arry's Bar at Millwall Football Ground in South East London – a ten-minute cycle ride east across Burgess Park from where I live. This is the unexpected venue for the Public Inquiry into the Aylesbury Compulsory Purchase Order, which is held over three sessions in 2015. I prepare an Academic Expert Witness Statement which is submitted to the Government Inspector Leslie Coffey on 23 April 2015, as part of the inquiry, and is thus subject to cross-examination by Southwark's barrister, Melissa Murphy.[19]

10 January 2017

This is one of the five new neighborhoods that will be eventually built in the park. What we are looking at is the show flat of Taylor Wimpey's Chobham Manor. Now we are going to walk down the Olympic Park Avenue, have a look at Celebration Avenue, and then return to Victory Park and arrive at one of these points – where the future is materialising.

Even supposing that a large piece of the dream has
escaped recollection, this may merely have prevented our
having access to another group of dream-thoughts. There
is no justification for supposing that the lost pieces of the
dream would have related to the same thoughts which
we have already reached from the pieces of the dream
that have survived.[20]

20 June 2007

JRe   So, do different laws apply then, within the designated
      area?

AD   It was always a complex area, even before the Olympics
      came about. Sometimes, rights, property rights, were
      not easy to establish. It was an area which had a lot
      of claims of public land, as we learned when we went
      through Lammas Lands sections of Leyton [...]

JRe   Common rights.

JRo   Yes, Lammas Lands were the marshlands where you
      had common grazing rights historically. And in 1892,
      they became transferred to the people of Hackney,
      and other boroughs, they were transferred to the LCC,
      as it was then, for recreational purposes, health and
      enjoyment in perpetuity.[21]

AD   Or until the Olympics.

JRo   And this is what has happened, of course, these
      common rights have been steam-rollered over.

The new connections are, as it were, loop-lines or short-
circuits, made possible by the existence of other and

deeper-lying connecting paths.[22]

10 January 2017

The site that you have been given to work with will be occupied by the temporary mobile garden project.

> Are all the dream-thoughts present alongside one another, or do they occur in sequence? Or do a number of trains of thought start out simultaneously from different centres and afterwards unite?[23]

10 January 2017

The temporary mobile garden was relocated, given space, like all meanwhile uses, as the building site was setting up. But it has been here for two to three years...

> A year after taking part in the Public Inquiry, and almost two years after completing *The Architecture of Psychoanalysis*, I look across at the Aylesbury from my flat on the eighteenth floor for the last time. The risk of a possible Compulsory Purchase Order, as well as the flawed yet highly costly major works bills, has made it impossible for me to feel "at home" in Southwark. In the five years I have lived there, I have paid Southwark £30,000 in major works bills (for a new roof and windows, lobby decoration, and fire-prevention alterations to my block), so it seems highly unlikely that my estate is under threat. Yet the fear has taken hold of me like a kind of paranoia. Despite extremely careful and repeated searches over a two-year period, I can find no evidence that my estate is to be regenerated, let alone demolished. However, the lack of threat offers an ethical moment for me to sell my flat. I do not want to go. But in the end

I decide that I prefer to be able to choose to go, rather than take the risk of waiting to be made to go (perhaps), at some future time (unspecified) to be decided by Southwark...

10 January 2017

But its temporary nature is set in the future, unquestionably: "You will not stay in the site more time than when I say you will go." In a sense this is what authority means: that which is not specified.

> It must not be forgotten, however, that we are dealing with an *unconscious* process of thought, which may easily be different from what we perceive during purposive reflection accompanied by consciousness.[24]

Four bedrooms.
Four times larger than anything I could afford in London.
Four floors.
Each one the size of my flat.
But what of this promise of size.
Size compared to site?
Is this my choice?

10 January 2017

The Qataris might decide that they don't want to finance all this, and put their money elsewhere.

> Another year on, I find I can't go, and instead I stay and continue to help the leaseholders of the Aylesbury as best I can. Following the Public Inquiry, the Secretary of State does not confirm the CPO. But Southwark start to demolish the blocks on the order land, and for complex

technical and legal reasons, a new Public Inquiry is scheduled for a future date, yet to be determined.[25]

> Another north-facing garden,
> That will never escape the shadow of the house.
> A place to put the bikes,
> That will not be against the bookcase in the living room.
> But will this be a sort of Hoxton-on-Sea?

20 June 2007

JRe   So these rights can be sidestepped, ignored, if the government decide they want to put their hands on the land.

AD   The act of compulsory purchase – it is really what it says […] The only negotiation is the compensation level, the relocation arrangements.

> […] we might conclude that condensation is brought about by omission: that is, that the dream is not a faithful translation or a point-for-point projection of the dream-thoughts, but a highly incomplete and fragmentary version of them.[26]

Six months on, and I'm writing a new witness statement to present at the Public Inquiry in January 2018. I'm still in Southwark, but a day away from moving to Kent, after having lived in London for twenty-five years, nine of them here. In the inspector's report following the April 2015 Public Inquiry she questioned the displacement maps that Loretta Lees referred to in her witness statement.[27] These maps provided evidence of how the residents of the Aylesbury had been ejected from central London, tenants to the outer boroughs of the capital, and

leaseholders out of the city entirely, into Kent and its
coastal towns. The inspector noted that the maps only
showed the people who had left the area, not those who
had stayed, and she questioned "whether those who
moved out of the area did so due to preference rather than
necessity".[28] As someone who prefers to stay, but needs
to go, I find the distinction between moving and being
moved, being displaced and displacing oneself, is not as
clear as I once thought.

AD   There is a sense of discontent in these groups. The CPO
has created a kind of reason to operate above all.

A terraced house.
Two rooms per floor.
With a staircase in the middle.
And a sea view.
I can't believe I could live in such a place.
A house.
In a row.
With a garden.
And a path.
And a fence that separates the garden from the town outside.
And the St George's flags and Brexit posters.

The unquestionable fact remains, however, that
the formation of dreams is based on a process of
condensation.[29]

Crossmount House, where I lived, was built in 1967, as
one of five, designed by Colin Locus, one of the architects
of the more famous LCC Alton Estate at Roehampton.
The Alton Estate was developed in two phases, Alton
East (formerly Portsmouth Road), was built in 1952–55,

and Alton West (formerly Roehampton Lane), was built in 1955–59. [...] Alton East pioneered the design of "point" blocks, based on Swedish designs, of which Crossmount House is a later example, and Alton West pioneered the design of "slab" blocks, based on Le Corbusier's famous *Unité d'Habitation* in Marseilles. The 5 key slab blocks of the Alton Estate, very similar to those of the Aylesbury, like Chiltern, have Grade 2* listing, and the refurbishment of the scheme is retaining many of the key buildings [...]

The *Unité d'Habitation*, Marseilles, was built between 1947 and 1953, designed to house around 1600 people in 337 apartments, including 23 different types and it is situated in 8.65 acres of parkland. Its design has been repeated in many different contexts, and is the precursor to the architectural style known as brutalism, of which the Aylesbury is a variant example. The adjacent parkland is an essential design aspect of this kind of slab block design, as it provides a place for leisure and exercise, and also offers views to all its inhabitants, [...] as well as providing internal streets, as shared meeting places, which in the *Unité* are still used successfully today [...]

The *Unité de Marseilles*, was in turn inspired by the Narkomfin Communal House in Moscow, designed by Moisei Ginzburg with Ignatii Milinis in 1928–1929, [...] a scheme which included dwelling blocks and communal facilities, and was orientated to include air, sun and access to greenery, via ribbon windows, free-standing columns and roof gardens. A key aspect of the *Unité* and the Narkomfin designs were the communal spaces, specifically the wide corridors, later termed "streets in the sky" by the British post war architects, Peter and Alison Smithson, and which inspired the recently refurbished Park Hill in Sheffield, as well as the Aylesbury.[30]

The Work of Displacement: In making our collection of instances of condensation in dreams, the existence of another relation, probably of no less importance, had already become evident. It could be seen that the elements which stand out as the principal components of the manifest content of the dream are far from playing the same part in the dream-thoughts. And, as a corollary, the converse of this assertion can be affirmed: what is clearly the essence of the dream-thoughts need not be represented in the dream at all. The dream is, as it were, differently centred from the dream-thoughts – its content has different elements as its central point. [...] Dreams such as these give a justifiable impression of "displacement".[31]

A: To be honest, I wasn't coping.

Q: Can you explain a bit more about that? You weren't coping with the work?

A: Difficult world to live.

Q: Okay.

A: It was an accumulation. It was over so many years. I mean I'm a painter. I'm used to being self-employed and working things out for myself. I couldn't work anything out. I couldn't get off the estate. I couldn't move. The surveyor wasn't speaking to my surveyor. So, nothing was going forward [...] constant stress [...] Not knowing what to do or where to go.

Q: You're a self-employed painter. What kind of impacts has it had on your work?

A: I haven't been able to work [...] Yes, I've got depression unfortunately [...]

Q: Do you still go back to those doctors?

A: Yes, for treatment.

Q: What have they said about the treatment?

A: They're very good. They treat a lot of people in the Aylesbury suffering from these problems. It's the CBT.

Q: In terms of where you've moved to now, what do you miss from the Aylesbury?

A: I did enjoy living there. I could work where I lived. I can't work here […] The layout is very different […] It's not possible to have a working area […] I didn't buy it [the flat] for an investment or anything. I just looked at it as stability.

Q: Can you articulate a bit more about these feelings, like these kinds of emotions around what's happened?

A: It's with retrospect, thinking I'd bought it as a security and I was in a most insecure position and not knowing how to get out of the situation I was in […] Not so much trapped, as […] I failed everything […] I was approaching 60 and hadn't managed to look after myself. Then it just snowballed into this. It was like every decision you had made in your life was wrong. I think you're just feeling like you haven't made a success of your life, you can't afford to look after yourself, and just the accumulation. It didn't matter what I did. I mean I knew everything is about perspective. It's trying to change my perspective on things and work out what to do and I couldn't work out anything. Everything I was told was just a lie that I'd be looked after and secure and […][32]

It thus seems plausible to suppose that in the dream-work a psychical force is operating which on the one hand strips the elements which have a high psychical value of their intensity, and on the other hand, *by means of overdetermination*, creates from elements of low psychical value new values, which afterwards find their way into the dream-content. If that is so, *a transference and displacement of psychical intensities* occurs, in the process of dream-formation, and it is as a result of these that the difference between the text of the dream-content and that of the dream-thoughts comes about. The process which we are here presuming is nothing less than the essential portion of the dream-work; and it deserves to be described as "dream-displacement".[33]

24 October 2017

Time flies and a lot of water has passed under the blue bridge over the River Lea since I last gave my thoughts four years ago on UCL East (Stratford Revisited).

10 January 2017

So in 2014 there was nothing, no shops, apart from the Westfield of course. Everything else in this block had no purpose. You had to start from scratch. What retailers do we want in here?

24 October 2017

At that time I framed a strategy around what it would take for UCL to act as a global university in the 21st Century and the particular opportunities offered by the Queen Elizabeth Olympic Park. Since then plans have progressed and much else besides. If anything the case for UCL East has become even more urgent.

10 January 2017

London is manufactured very much at the moment on a
form of cannibalism [...] what you have to do in order to
create a successful place, is to extract bits of success from
other places, and import them, copy and paste them into a
new place so that it will succeed like the original one.

24 October 2017

*Still more important to my mind are the relations to the local
communities in east London that UCL East makes possible.*

10 January 2017

Now normally this chain-reaction behaviour is based on
well-known brands, but now it is expanding to single
outlets who have been cherry-picked, boosted by food
consultants and finance and given six months' free rent or
any form of business-rates relief.

24 October 2017

*At least two of the new Masters programmes based in Here East are
working directly with the neighbouring artist community in Hackney
Wick while UrbanLab have been active in helping shape UCL's policy
around wider community engagement*

.

10 January 2017

So Tina We Salute You is a bar that happens to have
acquired a certain kind of street cred [...] in Dalston, just
off the Crossways [...] Like other businesses around here,
it was sampled and reproduced in this location as a clone of
a local success story absorbed to be re-produced here in an

attempt to wow crowds that otherwise would not venture
here at all.

24 October 2017

*The faculty is being very active in working to ensure UCL establishes
positive relationships in the area.*

Dream-displacement and dream-condensation are the
two governing factors to whose activity we may in
essence ascribe the form assumed by dreams.[34]

20 June 2007

JRo The London Development Agency wanted to relocate
     the travellers to Beckton […] it is further downstream,
     and is highly polluted, it's gas works, it's cement works
     […] They refused. And then the LDA said that if they
     could find a brownfield site that they were happy with,
     then they would go along with it. Well they found this
     site at Chobham Farm, which was railway land, and the
     railway said it was a very valuable piece of land, and so
     the LDA wouldn't buy it, because it was too expensive.

Nor do I think we shall have any difficulty in recognising
the psychical force which manifests itself in the facts
of dream-displacement. The consequence of the
displacement is that the dream-content no longer
resembles the core of the dream-thoughts and that the
dream gives no more than a distortion of the dream-wish
which exists in the unconscious. But we are already
familiar with dream-distortion. We traced it back to the
censorship which is exercised by one psychical agency
in the mind over another. Dream-displacement is one of
the chief methods by which that distortion is achieved.

But we are already familiar with dream-distortion. We traced it back to the censorship which is exercised by one psychical agency in the mind over another.[35]

24 October 2017

The Bartlett in collaboration with the Faculty of Engineering Science is within days of taking possession of our new shared premises in Here East.[36]

20 June 2007

JRe   So who else is affected by this?

AD   There is an industrial site in Marshgate Lane, there are a lot of businesses that have been compensated and been paid for relocation, but in some cases, some of the sites, it would appear, have been imaged in the eyes of the ODA, as derelict or semi-derelict, and so without apparent value. The majority of what we see here is metal, scrap metal, car parts, tyres, and aggregate from demolition that is reprocessed. You can also see new developments all along the canal. We are also going to see Dace Road, a small quarter, which has for some time been developed as a mini cultural quarter. Space had their offices there. And Hackney Wick has been earmarked as a regeneration area, which is directly affected by the Olympics.

24 October 2017

New programmes have been created, staff recruited, and students are already on site.

The question of the interplay of these factors – of displacement, condensation and overdetermination – in the construction of dreams, and the question which is a dominant factor and which a subordinate one – all of this we shall leave aside for later investigation. But we can state provisionally a second condition that must be satisfied by those elements of the dream-thoughts that make their way into the dream: *they must escape the censorship imposed by resistance.*[37]

20 June 2007

JRe   Where is the edge of the site?

AD   Well the edge of the site, where we arrived with the canal, is over there, and Carpenters Road is there. White Horse Lane becoming Carpenters Road is going to cross the Lea Navigation, the Lea Navigation is the limit, the boundary of the site. And as we cross over there, we will arrive at the other side of Marshgate Lane.

JRe   Now. This is a strange crossing, there is no colour for pedestrians at all…

AD   In a sense, finding the Olympic site is like Tacita Dean's work, "Finding Spiral Jetty". This is becoming a difficult job.

AD   Now, the next one up on Marshgate, this is just getting to this path, which would get us to…

24 October 2017

There is still a tremendous amount to do, not least in the design of the Marshgate building.

JRe   The end of it is closed.

AD   The sign has been changed.

14 November 2017

Be featured in our Wall of Inspiration
What gets you up in the morning and fires you up?
If there's an object that represents what inspires you, we'd love each
of you and/or company to add it to our Wall of Inspiration.
So far, members have included everything from books that shaped
their worldview to menus representing how their team bonds over
food.
The wall is a real talking point for visitors, and we want it to hold
your stories!
Simply leave your object with our reception team with:
• a short explanation of the object
• a company description (max 100 words)
• a high-res logo of your company

JRe   It's ready to go.

AD   The cycle way east has been closed.

JRo   The housing that they are demolishing is actually
fairly new, and is immaculately laid out. It's very good
quality. But built on a landfill site. Why was it never
properly remediated before? It's an industrial site, that
has had heavy metal processing. They've traced it back
to the company that produced it.

JRe   So was that a waste product that was illegally left, and
should have been […]

14 November 2017

Hello!
We've all worked so hard this year, but as we get to the end of 2017

it's time to celebrate. And so, we're excited to invite you and two of your friends to join us at our holiday party on the 14th of December. There will be food, fizz and festive fun to help us end the year in style.

Please click here to RSVP to let us know if you'd like to join us. And don't forget to forward this on to your clients, tech entrepreneur friends, or anyone else you think might like to come!

JRo   It was in steel drums, so it conformed to requirements. But the whole politics of land dumping is only recently emerging. Dumping occurs further and further downstream, affecting poorer communities as you go out. I was amazed to find out that the dumping of raw sewage was only stopped in 1998 by an EU directive.

We have learnt that that material, stripped to a large extent of its relations, is submitted to a process of compression, while at the same time displacements of intensity between its elements necessarily bring about a psychical transvaluation of the material.[38]

21 November 2017

They would like to keep the area looking perfect as it's the first thing people see when they enter the complex. They have very high expectations of everyone using the space in a really formal way.

JRe   Is that where we are going?

21 November 2017

We have had repeated requests not to rearrange the furniture, not to leave personal belongings lying around, not leave cups etc.

150

AD   Here, we can get over.

21 November 2017

I must request that you all wear your lanyards while on the premises. This is part of their Fire Evacuation Strategy and as such it's not optional. They have requested this on the grounds of health and safety and to improve security within the building so we will need to start enforcing this.

JRe   Have you been going around talking to people on sites?

27 November 2017

Hello!
Just a reminder about the "Take Stock Exchange" workshop today 1.30-3pm.
They are working on a Creative Storytelling Project within the Hackney Wick/Fish Island community and came in to speak to the community about collecting the stories of entrepreneurs.

JRo   I've got a little bit involved both with Manor Garden allotments, and the Lammas Lands Defense Committee, who are pretty amazing, plus the Hackney Marsh users group, they are wonderful environmentalists, with a tremendous historical knowledge.

The displacements we have hitherto considered turned out to consist in the replacing of one particular idea by another in some way closely associated with it, and they were used to facilitate condensation in so far as, by their means, instead of *two* elements, a single common element intermediate between them found its way into the dream.[39]

JRo   And it's very interesting the nature of marshlands,
       these liminal areas, which are neither and both, they
       are this margin at the edge of the city, but they are
       not country, and they have this capacity for their own
       regeneration [...] This incredible absorption of history,
       they are full of objects, whether it is from the Second
       World War [...] or from the levelling, but deeper than
       that is all the industrial archaeology [...]

We have not yet referred to any other sort of
displacement. Analyses show us, however, that
another sort exists and that it reveals itself in a change
in the verbal expression of the thoughts concerned.
In both cases there is a displacement along a chain of
associations; but a process of such a kind can occur
in various psychical spheres, and the outcome of the
displacement may in one case be that one element is
replaced by another, while the outcome in another case
may be that a single element has its verbal form replaced
by another.[40]

30 November 2017

*We've had an eventful and successful year. From mere plans on paper
to live in colour, launching and developing the community [...] As the
year draws to a close, we're celebrating with a holiday bash complete
with music, dancing and delicious treats and would be delighted if
you could join us on 14th December from 4pm onwards [...]*

Regretfully we are unable to extend this invitation to your students.

***

A Note on Authorship and Speech Extraction

This text is composed of fragments of voices extracted from a number of sources, some written and others spoken. Those that are taken from sources that are publicly available are referenced in the endnotes. Other voices have been extracted from institutional group emails relating to UCL East and Here East sent to the author and from an email sent to the author by Alberto Duman. Fragments of talks and conversations conducted on walks in the Olympic site led by Duman in 2007 and 2017 have been extracted from transcriptions made by this author. All the speech fragments from the 2017 walk are attributed to Alberto Duman, and those from the 2007 walk are attributed to their authors, who are indicated by their initials. In all other cases, when the authors are not mentioned, their position on the page–ranged left, indented, ranged right–and their font treatment indicates the source of their extraction.

Ranged left, plain: Extracts from transcriptions of a conversation that took place during a walk led by Alberto Duman on 20 June 2007, with Jude Rosen, Richard Crow, and Jane Rendell.[41]

Ranged left, italics: Extracts from an email sent by Alberto Duman to Jude Rosen, Richard Crow, and Jane Rendell concerning a walk to take place on the Olympic site on 20 June 2007.

Ranged left, bold: Extracts from a talk and walk led by Alberto Duman on 10 January 2017, with Jane Rendell, and other staff, and students of the MA Situated Practices from the Bartlett School of Architecture, located at UCL's Here East.

Indented, plain: Author's own words.

Ranged right, plain: Author's own words.

Ranged right, italics: Extracts from an a group email to Bartlett staff and students based at a temporary site.

Ranged right, bold: Extracts from a group email to Bartlett staff and students based at a temporary site.

Ranged right, bold italics: Extracts from a group email to Bartlett staff and students based at a temporary site from the main occupants of that space.

Endnotes

1   Professor Alan Penn, Bartlett Bean, "Stratford Revisited" (30 October 2013). See https://www.ucl.ac.uk/bartlett/news/2013/oct/stratford-revisited (Last accessed 14 February 2014)

2   Graham Jones, *Lyotard Reframed,* (IB Tauris, 2014), p. 46. See also Jean-François Lyotard, "The Dream-work doesn't think", translated by Mary Lydon, in *Discourse, Figure* University of Minnesota, 2011), pp. 233-67, 234

3   Sigmund Freud, "The Dream-Work", *The Interpretation of Dreams. The Standard Edition of the Complete Psychological Works of Sigmund Freud, Volume IV (1900)* (Hogarth Press, 1953), p. 277

4   Penn, "Stratford Revisited"

5   Freud, "The Dream-Work", pp. 277-8

6   Penn, "Stratford Revisited"

7   Freud, "The Dream-Work", pp. 277-8

8   Penn, "Stratford Revisited"

9   Ibid

10   Sigmund Freud, "(A) The Work of Condensation", *The Interpretation of Dreams. The Standard Edition of the Complete Psychological Works of Sigmund Freud, Volume IV (1900)* (Hogarth Press, 1953), p. 279.

11   Penn, "Stratford Revisited".

12   Freud, "(A) The Work of Condensation", p. 279

13   See for example, Jane Rendell, "May Morn", in Di Robson and Gareth Evans (eds), *The Re-Enchantment: Place and Its Meanings,* (an Arts Council of England funded publication) (Artevents, 2010), and Jane Rendell, "May Mourn", in Sophie Warren and Jonathan Mosely, *Beyond Utopia* (Errant Bodies Press, 2012). See also Jane Rendell, *Site-Writing: The Architecture of Art Criticism* (IB Tauris, 2010), pp. 135-51

14   See Jane Rendell, *The Architecture of Psychoanalysis: Transitional Space* (IB Tauris, 2017)

15   See 35% Campaign, "Southwark's Mysterious Estate
      Renewal Zone" (23 July 2014). See http://35percent.
      org/2014-07-23-mystery-objector-1301/ (Last accessed
      15 February 20148

16   See Savills Research, "London Regeneration Research
      Proposal", (24 April 2014). http://www.savills.co.uk/_news/
      article/72418/175241-0/4/2014/savills-research--london
      regeneration-research-proposal (Last accessed 15 February
      2018). For specific reports see for example Savills Research,
      "Spotlight, Public Land: Unearthing Potential" (Autumn
      2014) http://pdf.euro.savills.co.uk/residential---other/
      spotlight-public-land.pdf (Last accessed 15 February 2018)

17   See for example, Jane Rendell, "Critical Spatial Practice
      as *Parrhesia*", *MaHKUscript: Journal of Fine Art Research*,
      (2016); Jane Rendell, "Giving An Account Of Oneself,
      Architecturally", *Journal of Visual Culture* (2016); and Jane
      Rendell, "'Arry's Bar", in Michal Murawski and Jane
      Rendell (eds), *Reactivating the Social Condenser*, special issue
      of *the Journal of Architecture* (2017).

18   Freud, "(A) The Work of Condensation", p. 279

19   Jane Rendell, *Witness Statement*, (23 April 2015). See
      http://bailey.persona-pi.com/Public-Inquiries/aylesbury-
      estate/Witness%20Statements/jane_rendell/Witness%20
      Statement%20of%20Jane%20Rendell%20v5%2026%20
      April%202015.pdf (Last accessed 15 February 2018)

20   Freud, "(A) The Work of Condensation", pp. 279-80.

21   Jude Rosen has added further to clarify that since the
      medieval period, Lammas lands were farmed in strips.
      When the landowners had harvested their wheat or–along
      the Lea - hay crop in early August (between the 1st and
      8th of the month, at Lammastide–the original harvest
      festival–Lammas deriving from 'loaf mass') they had to
      open their lands up to commoners to graze their cattle and
      sheep on, until Lady Day, 6 April of the following year.
      So the lands, although privately owned were subject to

common rights of pasturage, limited to the period when they were not cultivated over the winter. Hackney District Board and the London County Council had to buy up the lands to create Hackney Marshes, transforming commoner rights to pasturage to rights to recreation to be enjoyed in perpetuity. Already in the late nineteenth century with industrialisation, conflicts over Lammas rights between commoners and landowners had shifted from rights of access to pasturage for grazing to the right of factory lads to play football on the Lammas lands. Famously, "the drivers" – i.e. the landowners' agents who registered the animals for grazing – confiscated the goalposts and chased the footballers off the land.

22   Freud, "(A) The Work of Condensation", pp. 280-81

23   Ibid, p. 281

24   Ibid

25   See 35% Campaign, "Aylesbury CPO Appeal — A Grounded Defence" (5 March 2017), http://35percent. org/2017-03-05-aylesbury-cpo-grounds-of-defence-lodged/ (Last accessed 15 February 2018); 35% Campaign, "Aylesbury CPO — What's really happened: Beyond the spin of Southwark Council's Press Office" (8 May 2017), http://35percent.org/2017-05-08-aylesbury-cpo-what-has-really-happened/ (Last accessed 15 February 2018). See also http://35percent.org/img/Decision_Letter_Final. pdf (Last accessed 15 February 2018) ; and Southwark Council, "Secretary of State overturns previous decision regarding Aylesbury estate compulsory purchase order" (25 April 2017), http://www.southwark.gov.uk/news/2017/ apr/secretary-of-state-overturns-previous-decision-regarding-aylesbury-estate-compulsory-purchase-order (Last accessed 15 February 2018)

26   Freud, "(A) The Work of Condensation", p. 281.

27   See Loretta Lees, "Public Inquiry Aylesbury Estate, London, Witness Statement" (29 April 2015), http://bailey.persona-

pi.com/Public-Inquiries/aylesbury-estate/ID%20docs/
id21.pdf (Last accessed 14 February 2018)

28   Lesley Coffey"CPO Report to the Secretary of State for
      Communities and Local Government" (29th January
      2016), para 348, http://bailey.persona-pi.com/Public-
      Inquiries/aylesbury-estate/core%20docs/cd50.pdf (Last
      accessed 14 February 2017)

29   Freud, "(A) The Work of Condensation", p. 281

30   Jane Rendell, "Rebuttal Statement: Professor Jane
      Rendell for the Aylesbury Leaseholders Group", http://
      bailey.persona-pi.com/Public-Inquiries/aylesbury-estate/
      Rebuttals/ALAG/janerendellrebuttal.pdf (Last accessed
      14 February 2018) . See also Jane Rendell, "Proof of
      Evidence of Professor Jane Rendell for the Aylesbury
      Leaseholders Group" (6 December 2017), http://bailey.
      persona-pi.com/Public-Inquiries/aylesbury-estate/
      Proofs%20of%20Evidence/Objectors/ALAG/Jane%20
      Rendell/janerendellproof.pdf (Last accessed 14 February
      2018).

31   Sigmund Freud, "(B) The Work of Displacement", *The
      Interpretation of Dreams. The Standard Edition of the Complete
      Psychological Works of Sigmund Freud, Volume IV (1900)*
      (Hogarth Press, 1953), p. 305

32   Loretta Lees, "Proof of Evidence of Professor Loretta
      Lees (FAcSS, FRSA) BA (Hons), PhD For the Aylesbury
      Leaseholders Group" (12 December 2017), Appendix
      LL2: "Sample of ESRC project interviews with displaced
      leaseholders and leaseholders in the process of being
      displaced from the Aylesbury Estate (not involved in the
      public inquiry), Interview (October 2017) with leaseholder
      decanted to Camberwell Fields". Interviewee L1, self-
      employed, had lived on the Aylesbury for over twenty
      years, ten years as a council tenant and ten years as a
      leaseholder. Took council buy out of her property. Did not
      want to leave the Aylesbury but was not coping with the

stress of the CPO. See http://bailey.persona-pi.com/Public-Inquiries/aylesbury-estate/Proofs%20of%20Evidence/Objectors/ALAG/Loretta%20Lees/LL2.pdf (Last accessed 14 February 2018).

33   Freud, "(B) The Work of Displacement", pp. 307-9.

34   Ibid, p. 309.

35   Ibid

36   Here East was developed by iCITY, a company owned by clients of Delancey, a specialist real estate investment and advisory company also known as DREAM: Delancey Real Estate Assets Management. In 2011, Delancey and Qatari-owned Qatar Diar acquired 1,400 apartments in the Olympic Village area near the venue of the London 2012 Olympics for a fee of £557 million.

37   Freud, "(B) The Work of Displacement", p. 309.

38   Sigmund Freud, "(D) Considerations of Representability", *The Standard Edition of the Complete Psychological Works of Sigmund Freud, Volume V (1900—1901)* (Hogarth Press, 1953), p. 339.

39   Ibid

40   Ibid

41   This walk was part the project We Sell Boxes We Buy Gold (2006-2008), a collaboration between curators Lucia Farinati and Louise Garrett, artists Richard Crow and Alberto Duman, and urban researcher/poet Jude Bloomfield. The project considered the 2012 Olympic site and the Lower Lea Valley as a context for interdisciplinary research and artistic intervention.

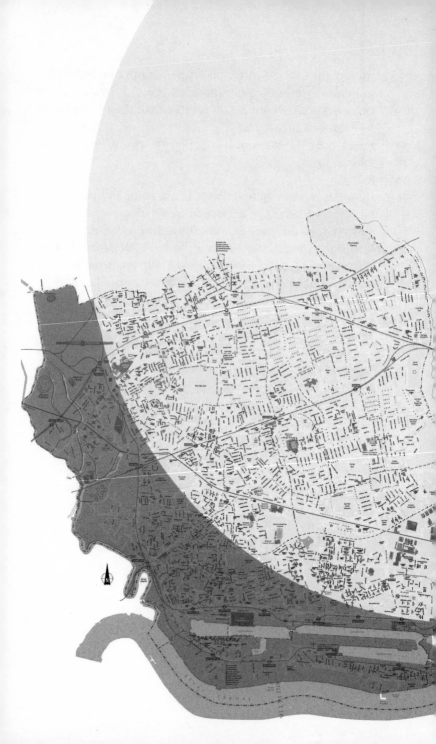

Part 3
Sound and Vision

Into the Magenta Haze: Notes on Making Art in the Arc of Opportunity

Alberto Duman

As cities are replanned, rezoned and rebuilt, culture is increasingly used as a developer's battering ram, and artists worldwide are having to assess what their relationship is to the things they make and the ways they live. This, then is a different kind of culture war.
— Nato Thompson, *Culture as Weapon*, 2017[1]

[...] like an arcane plot out of a Philip K Dick novel, the very visage of the city I knew, was being transmuted from lead to gold.
— Gregory Scholette, "Mysteries of the Creative Class, or, I Have Seen the Enemy and They Is Us", 2005/2017[2]

Purple haze all in my brain
Lately things just don't seem the same
— Jimi Hendrix, "Purple Haze", 1967[3]

1.

"The future is culture"

This is one of the messages that greets me as I walk across the space sandwiched by the hoardings currently fencing the area once known in its early planning stages as "Olympicopolis"; then – after the demise of Boris Johnson as London's mayor – renamed in a more sober way as the "Cultural and Educational District"[4] of the Queen Elizabeth Olympic Park, fittingly located within the business-driven International Quarter and beside Westfield Shopping Centre.

I am here in this piece of the city yet-to-exist, *consuming an atmosphere*, breathing an affective[5] haze of pre-emptive future planning, one stamped by the official administrative magenta[6] livery of Newham, given the blessing of the Greater London Authority (GLA), planning permission by the London Legacy Development Corporation, and funding by global investors, and sprayed all over by the benign ambiance of future cultural/educational provisions.

Fig. 1: Foundation for FutureLondon, Cultural and Educational District hoardings, Queen Elizabeth Olympic Park. Author's own image © 2017.

The message from this everyday future of East London by those curating it for us is that "everyone's invited",[7] implying that we are all going to be guests in a future hosted by global world-class institutions on a benevolent philanthropic spree.

Crucially – *albeit unknowingly for most of those passing through* – I am also caught within Newham's "Arc of Opportunity". This is the fading candy-coloured pink haze on the council's regeneration map that for the past twenty years has coated with its New Public Management overtones the mixed fortunes of Newham's masterplanning initiative in waiting. The "Arc" was propelled into "Supernova" speed by the awarding of the 2012 Olympic Games to London in 2005 and from then it has steadily grown into an area of deep transformations brought about by global investment.

I come here, in between showy digital visualisations and conceited catchphrases of placemaking, to feel properly situated in this *atmosphere* and make its contours more visible to me, otherwise they are too blurred to be truly felt within the hard materiality of the built environment and the normalised humdrum of its everyday: it is the delirious aspect of this nonplace that appeals to me and I revel in the way it explicitly speaks of *culture and capital* as the agents that "design" our future cities.

After all, it is precisely this kind of invisible "infrastructure space" that truly comes to shape our cities today. As Keller Easterling says: "contemporary infrastructure space is the secret weapon of the most powerful people in the world precisely because it orchestrates activities that can remain unstated but are nevertheless consequential".[8]

Writing in 2015, on the preponderance of space over time in late capitalism, Fredric Jameson stated: "In our time all politics is about real estate; and this from the loftiest statecraft to the most petty manoeuvring around local advantage. Postmodern politics is essentially a matter of land grabs, on a local as well as global scale."[9] But here and now, I feel wrapped around by a more complex ambiance: this is spatial land grabbing as the real estate of the future, produced through words and images, stretching space into time, effectively colonising the range of possible future urban scenarios of the city yet-to-exist by turning heavy-handed fictional accounts into seemingly inevitable outcomes, despite often being defined as "examples for the vision and subject to change".[10]

In management language, "Futuring is the field of using a systematic process for thinking about and planning for the future".[11] Within this world of elite decision making and strategic anticipation of possible outcomes, one of the "seven lesson to be learned"[12]–according to Edward Cornish, the former president of the World Future Society–is to "dream productively". It is within this context that John R. Williams speaks of "World Futures" as a specific production of "capitalizable, systematic immediacy of multiple, plausible worlds [...] involved in the consolidation of an oracular sensibility entirely at odds with previous, more singular visions of the future", a sensibility that was eventually going to become the established contemporary perception of a "pluralist temporality of global capital".[13]

Such concentrated and overlapped efforts of *futuring*, as acts of *productive dreaming and anticipatory colonisation of possible futures*, are what I will label here–for the sake of a Newham-specific definition–as *magentawashing*, understood as the particular intensity and tonality of the atmosphere of anticipatory "World Futures" in operation in the whole of the Arc of Opportunity.

Magenta happens to be the official colour of the London Borough of Newham (LBN) since 2010, when their new logo appeared at the same time as the Shanghai World Expo and the move into their new offices at Building 1000 overlooking the Docks and London City Airport. In a nod to its "world-class" ambitions–as well as an orienteering device for investors lost on the world map–the word "London" and the colour magenta now appear together in all LBN material (including roadwork barriers) as a visible reminder of where we really are.

So take this as a counter-branding parody, perhaps only just as absurd as the image of the Arc that functions as the actual brand for this specific East London urban geography under the "London is moving east" spell of productive dreaming from above. My suggestion here is that we should look at the branded magenta contours of the Arc of Opportunity as vague borders of an immaterial, affective atmosphere of an *aesthetic capitalism* at work within the exploitative *pluralist temporality of global capital*, brought about by the protracted convergence of capital investment, real estate, and cultural initiatives at multiple levels of administration, both through strategic governance and through tactical exploitation of global and local agents in this part of London in the last twenty years.

Seen through this lens, we can tune into some actual resonant consequences that this contingent regime of aestheticisation and valuation has on any act of cultural production, aesthetic discourse, or artistic practice within the range of its soft boundaries, including the *Music for Masterplanning* project in its interruptive intents and recuperation attempts.[14]

If the aesthetic practitioners of today and tomorrow must interrogate the city yet-to-exist and the urban futures yet-to-be-written, they have to do so by understanding its underlying *productive dreaming* and the agents of its cultural capitalisation, by sensing and creatively describing the atmospheres that saturate their context. Brian Holmes described such shifts in his 2008 "Affectivist Manifesto", writing that "Artistic activism is Affectivism, it opens up expanding territories".[15] The "Affectivist Manifesto" now reads like a description of an emergent panorama in the making, a vision to describe the new global affective territories already at work in our cities and in between us. Its calling is for the artist-activist to enter this emerging affective fray and stir it with new significance by recasting the *productive dreaming* and *future production* of capital into public, visible dimensions that might exploit its vulnerable dispositions.

It is hardly a secret that real estate capital and the world economy have consciously embraced an "aesthetic disposition",[16] given how loudly the evangelical sermons of placemaking consultants, filled with "creative cities" and "cultural class", have sold their message to city boosters, policy hacks, and administrative officers in need of jingles for cities in world-class competition. Even if Richard Florida, its most visible proponent, has repeatedly reframed and reconsidered the core of his proposition in different terms,[17] the formulaic virus that has entered urban policy discourse has cemented its place in the vocabulary of aesthetics demands for "vibrant neighbourhoods".

All of this has turned the late geographer Neil Smith's "rent gap" theory[18] into settled common knowledge for opponents of the placemaking strategies which seek to capitalise on potentially high land values in inner-city areas, with artists acting as the shock troops[19] of these state-led gentrification strategies. By now, the contradictions at the heart of these tropes are so widely known and pragmatically understood by all players involved, that in their harshest degree of resistance they have produced the counter-strategic agenda of actual

Fig. 2: "When the artists are coming, that's when you want to get in." The words of Tim Murphy, CEO of IP Global, in "Deptford Rise London SE8" promotional video, 2014, https://www.ipglobal-ltd.com/en/articles/blog/deptford-rise/. Fair use copyright.

evictions of galleries from neighbourhoods:

> The coalitions we build can not be distracted by the naive notion that art galleries can be maintained without direct complicity in speculative development [...] We will not stop fighting until all galleries leave. Boyle Heights will continue to fight against the false promises of development and community improvement that are supposed to benefit us, but end up displacing us from our home.[20]

But whilst these direct-action battles are raging in specific places under duress–and they will surely expand their reach to many others locations in times to come- the pernicious affective regimes at the root of these manifestations also need our attention, because their immaterial nature and hard-to-pin-down edges make them less vulnerable targets for direct activism in some of its current forms. This is despite the fact that is already ten years since Matteo Pasquinelli spoke about future "immaterial civil wars as prototypes of conflicts within Cognitive Capitalism".[21]

To sense these affective regimes and their future-oriented land grabs of imagination, we need to go back to the founding idea of *atmosphere* in an aesthetic, phenomenological, and ontological sense. As Gernot Böhme writes, it can be understood as "a vague power, without visible and discrete boundaries, which we find around us and, resonating in our lived body, even involves us".[22] We should search and become more attuned to the hazy and not immediately intelligible signs of Keller Easterling's "multipliers of infrastructure space", since these "irrational fictions, or its undeclared but consequential activities–are perhaps the very things that make it immune to righteous declaration and prescription".[23] Following up Easterling's clues we should direct our energies to the less obvious dispositions of infrastructure space as "atmospheres in operation" so that we might begin to take up the call to "open up expanding territories"[24] of cultural resistance.

Turning towards the affective dimension of capitalism can help aesthetic practitioners to reorient some energy in the dispersed logic of contemporary power towards the description and critical evaluation of atmospheres such as the magenta-tinted placemaking vapour active in the Arc of Opportunity: tracking down its hazy narrative trail seemed a good entry point to start charting some of these territories in more explicit ways, to extend our reach towards the yet unmade but productively dreamt landscapes of aesthetic capitalism.

Gernot Böhme defines *aesthetic economics* as the "ubiquitous phenomenon of an aestheticising of the real",[25] but when the affective phantasmagorias of capital are entering in the *productive dreaming* stage of future building through imagery of creativity and its manifestation as direct tactical devices, these spaces of futuring, placemaking, and cultural co-option can be opened up as public discursive platforms where their affective property and active narratives can be negotiated once again.

See for example the case of the ghostly, fictitious Newham

Fig. 3: Screenshot from the Hallsville Quarter fly-through CGI, Newham/Bouygues development in Canning Town, N16. See the Newham Biennale in the LED display on the centre-left of the image. Available at https://vimeo.com/97804270. Fair use copyright.

Biennale that appears in the Hallsville Quarter fly-through[26] in which the future presence of artists and their work is imagined ahead of ourselves: if the mere presence of artistic activities is directly invoked in visualisations of a future already regenerated, then artists truly have become transferable assets in the day-to-day magentawashing operations of aesthetic capitalism at work in the Arc of Opportunity.

The enmeshing of transferable assets and tactics across art and capital means that for many critics today, contemporary art is reduced to signifying innovation within capitalism: the reason that contemporary art and culture occupy a highly visible and central role in the financial district lies in their recent convergence of values:

> Once operating with distinct separate world views and narratives, the art world is now hyperliberal […] a paragon of neoliberalism.[27]

But the sobering effect of this acknowledged condition opens up different paths; for Fredric Jameson, now "anything and everything is possible, but only on condition that it embraces ephemerality and consents to exist but for a brief time, as an event rather than as a durable object".[28]

Can we start taking notes for the best operational tactics for future immaterial culture/civil wars that accept conditions such as those in place in the Arc of Opportunity?

2.

"And so I am here, in this piece of the city yet-to-exist, consuming an atmosphere, breathing an affective haze of pre-emptive future planning…"

As if the bold assertiveness of an organisation named Foundation For FutureLondon [sic], "bringing together world leading education and cultural institutions with the thriving creative arts sector in east London for the direct benefit of everyone who lives here",[29] wouldn't suffice to make the claim that here in this place the future will be shaped by "world-class institutions", such boasting proclamations are visually matched by a series of carefully composed large CGI tableaux of everyday future scenes of the district's indoor and outdoor life.

These are fictional landscapes where museums' atriums are filled with renderings of mocked sculptural objects—bizarre digital knock-offs, creatures combined from Henry Moore's and Thomas Schütte's large works[30]—facing busy new squares bustling with cherry-picked future cultural consumers (including licenced buskers) staring at elephant-shaped public art[31] and all of it overlooked by future office workers and visitors occupying fully glazed lobbies and terraces of architectural forms stretching the new London Vernacular aesthetics[32] into daring cantilevered spectacles of transparency.

One could read these images simply as a high-end marketing communiqué from the placemaking stakeholders. Or perhaps as an index of the nostalgic investment into the previous legacies

Fig. 4: Foundation for FutureLondon, Cultural and Educational District hoardings, Queen Elizabeth Olympic Park. Author's own image © 2017.

of Albertopolis[33] as evidence of past British grandeur, or even as highly baroque statutory planning notices to itself by the London Legacy Development as the planning authority for the area around and including Queen Elizabeth Olympic Park.

Whilst some residual nostalgia might permeate these future visions of London's cultural institutions, for some of the cultural organisations involved, the ultimate horizon of this eastward shift is set much further out than the boundaries of the Queen Elizabeth Olympic Park. The ultimate meaning of a "V&A East" is the approved franchise called Design Society in Shekou, Shenzhen, in China that opened its doors to the public on 2 December 2017. A newly globalised museum culture that began with the daring forays of private players such as the Guggenheim (who remembers today the closed-down Guggenheim Las Vegas branch designed by Rem Koolhaas?[34]) has now reached its turning point.

The opening on 8 November 2017 of the franchise of the Louvre in Abu Dhabi[35] is a milestone in the identity of the Louvre, the first public museum of the Western modern age which opened a few weeks after the French Revolution. Now it is to transfer a number of works from the Paris Louvre to Abu Dhabi and curate its exhibitions for the next thirty years in an agreement worth €832,000,000 to France.

Luc Boltanski and Arnaud Esquierre would place phenomena such as this under the rubric of an "Economy of Enrichment" understood as "the valorisation of an object based on a story – usually rooted in the past and holding the prospect that the price of the object enriched by this narrative stands a good chance of increasing over time".[36] For Nancy Fraser, these momentous shifts of global cultural routes are becoming more sharply defined in British culture after the Brexit vote of 2016 and its tilting cultural-economic axis. In her view these kind of cultural transactions represent an "exotic corner of present-day capitalism, where fading European powers devise ingenious ways to live off their former glories".[37]

Whichever might turn out to be more accurate in the end, it appears that "there is no more sanctuary for the world in the museum, and the museum is less and less a sanctuary for the history of the city"[38] unless it becomes the booty of an instinct of predatory urban necrophilia. This is the case of the Robin Hood Gardens fragment where the museum purchased a three-storey section of the estate, for display in the new V&A East[39]: "in the neoliberal-hyper-communicative-city, the choices for a museum are often reduced to either hanging on as a relic from the quaint past, or emerging as a service provider in the market place of spectacles".[40]

But whilst an economy of enrichment might be understood as an eccentric corollary of proper Big Capital, its main present drive is to "feed back on itself–double its existing territories–via speculation on futures".[41]

Fig. 5: The Sea World Culture and Arts Centre in Shekou, Shenzhen, which houses Design Society, the new V&A Gallery. Image featured on the website of V&A Design Society. © Design Society/V&A. Fair use copyright.

In the utter uncertainty of the present, the time of the global institution and its own planning (whether business or cultural seems not to matter anymore) is the one that asserts its ownership, it prefigures and articulates future urban landscapes visually and aurally and sets their goals to achieve them through marketing and management.[42]

Whichever angle you might wish to adopt, the overbearing sentences and the high-resolution CGI renderings that form the basic visual vocabulary of all hoardings for this and other building sites are just more evidence of a mode of address that has become the ubiquitous affective phantasmagoria of conglomerates of global business, big culture, and public administration seamlessly integrated beyond recognition as disciplinary arbiters of urban futures, packaged by a benign veneer of liberal cosmopolitanism and cultural value.

These *worlds within worlds* wrap the boundaries of building sites like life-size brochures, synthetic urban environments constructed through assemblages of detailed architectural renderings and a mix of royalty-free images or computer-generated characters of various degrees of resolution. They are operative urban fictions without escape routes, staking their claims to the future of London whilst selectively raiding its past, reimagined in equally heavy-handed fictional accounts, free of all the contradictions it actually emerged from.

Stemming from the "oracular sensibilities" described by John R. Williams at the beginning of this chapter, these characters are fictional oracles of the city yet-to-exist, *ghosts in reverse* since their visual presence performs a deliberate act of prefiguring the occupation of future residents and city dwellers in advance of their actual presence on the site, anticipating their existence in affirmative and expressive ways through projected identity and lifestyles, actions and positions in public space. By conjuring into being the future occupants of that space, their mission is effectively that of colonising the future in advance of our presence and capitalise on its seemingly inevitable becomings.

This rabid character of urban cannibalism – *literally the city offering part of itself for its own devouring* – is perfectly fitting with the colonising impulse of current urbanism in London, where every new area of development must be tagged with the name bearer of urban vitality of other areas of London reified as *de facto* urban-success value symbols. Shoreditch in Silvertown, Hoxton in Canning Town, Bloomsbury in Stratford Village: pieces of a reified London cut through by estate agents on a spatial binge, clones to be copied and pasted in all emerging East London locations yet to be transformed by the futuring atmospheres of "productive dreaming".[43]

3.

"And so I am here, in this piece of the city yet-to-exist, consuming an atmosphere, breathing an affective haze of pre-emptive future planning…"

Next to these active agents of *tomorrow, today*,[44] another set of board spells out its demands to sync our calendar with that of forthcoming events in the park: *DATES FOR YOUR DIARY!* One item in particular catches my attention and sends me back to the reason why I'm telling you this story here and now:

> SUPERNOVA: a 5k run like no other. Take on this enchanting journey of light and sound through the iconic grounds of the Park by night.[45]

With the large public sculpture RUN by Monica Bonvicini by the Copper Box arena at the other end of the park lit up at night like a giant prompt, it's clear where the event organisers see the propelling synergy coming into being at an accelerated pace.

It was another previous utterance of the word *SUPERNOVA* that eventually propelled this book into existence. As mentioned in the introduction to this book, in 2010, the now-defunct London Development Agency (LDA) and the London Borough of Newham jointly produced the promotional movie called *London's Regeneration Supernova*, to be screened at the Shanghai World Expo 2010. The invitation to global investors into the Arc of Opportunity regeneration plans was to come and "take your place in the future of London".[46]

London's Regeneration Supernova's spell was cast within a World Expo themed through the slogan "Better City, Better Life"—*at the time the most expensive and extensive in the history of World's Fairs*—and whose "Urban Future Pavilion"[47] concept involved an imaginary journey into the future, predictably adopting an optimistic view of opportunities for developing habitable cities via a combination of technological progress and tradition. The prefigured futures disseminated through the Arc of Opportunity's narrative haze would continue to be articulated in other terms at later stages:

> The Royal Docks will be a new global district that is known as a test bed for innovation. It will be a laboratory for future thinking and an endlessly surprising landscape of creativity.[48]

The *endless surprise* evoked here appears to describe the excitement of not knowing, an affective uncertainty of *what might be next?*. However, in terms of World Futures production, such release of enthusiasm is always exercised under strict regimes of scenario management, acting as a captivating brand facade to lure investments into the Enterprise Business Zone of the Royal Docks.[49]

It points towards images of a future not yet known, but whose terms of *endless surprise* are bound by planning and marketing, and aesthetically saturated by sensational CGI renderings of cinematic and bountiful public scenes, once again disclaimed in the small print by the statement that "creative case studies included should not be read as specific but as examples of how this vision could be achieved".[50] In this document, prefaced by the idea of "cultural engineering in The Royal Docks", we also hear that:

> Artists are well placed to creatively engage individuals and communities and give voice to their sense of place, their concerns and their aspirations for the areas they live, work and play in.[51]

Whilst global atmospheres of "futuring" through cultural engineering are in action in the Royal Docks, artists appear to be needed to ground the deterritorialisation processes instigated by these forces through acts of moot imagination and engagement, whose outcome – unless diverted and divested through specific tactics – would already be contained within the cultural ambiance of the affective magenta haze of the Arc of Opportunity.

Particularly in the Royal Docks, the culture of the Shanghai World Expo and the Shanghai Art Biennale, which both took place in 2010, have produced an eerie ricochet effect into the Arc of Opportunity; it is witnessing a boomeranged materialising of aspects of its delirious state-sponsored dreamworld and its Supernova status into an area of London desperately seeking to transform this intractable character of its land bank after the demise of the London Docklands Development Corporation in 1998.[52]

In June 2016 in Shanghai, the first Disney World in China opened its doors,[53] whilst at the Royal Albert Dock in London ground-levelling work has begun for the arrival of the Asian Business Port: "London's newest business district – a vibrant hub for people to work, live and enjoy – and a new gateway to Europe for business from Asia."[54]

And paradoxically, as the *London's Regeneration Supernova* movie was travelling to Shanghai at the World Expo in 2010, carried symbolically by the mayors of London (Boris Johnson) and Newham (Sir Robin Wales), in the interstitial dream space of imagined cities between internet art, authoritarian Chinese governance, and corporate fantasy, a fictional character called

"Supernova Sibilant" was elected as the fifth mayor of the Virtual City called "RMB", created by the Chinese artist Cao Fei in the online virtual world Second Life.

Supernova Sibilant's acceptance speech draws on themes that resonate with the language of the *London's Regeneration Supernova* video, as much as the rhetoric of most contemporary developments as spaces for imagination:

> I believe our destiny will stretch our imaginations. In ancient China, imagination meant to take a journey in your mind – a play, a dream or the afterlife offered the cultural spaces for such journeys. Today, we honor RMB City as that site for our imagination to roam in its most delirious capacity. We honor the cycle of life and death. As mayor, I bring you a children's playground and a place for the dying. Sites for eternal reinvention. Sites for imagination.[55]

4.

"And so..."

As art practices become more and more embedded into everyday life, social groups, business language, and urban development, the work of artists – and even their mere presence in neighbourhoods undergoing deep physical and social transformations driven by the speculative atmospheres of *aesthetic capitalism* – is increasingly seen as either instrumental or useless; undifferentiated from other practices or politically aligned with dubious urban projects, and ultimately contributing to the problems rather than offering solutions.

> The transfer of art from the sphere of culture into the realm of real estate and business permits art to stop being art, or to stop being only art, and it allows it to start playing a much more direct channel of empowerment, governance and even accumulation – if only of "social capital" – for specific communities and in specific contexts.[56]

As a result of these shifts, art activities and the social capital they generate are undergoing deep processes of the renewal of legitimation whilst facing issues of containment. The term "art" is becoming increasingly difficult to hold without referring it to a given purpose, however hard we might try to circumvent creatively – or avoid entirely – the issues of instrumentalisation and commercialisation.

Operating in a world subjected to drastic changes in modes of exchange, value generation, and the effect of aesthetic capitalism, artistic work in its specificity can never be fully autonomous; it is both *a producer of* but equally *subjected to* the attention economy demands of increasingly congested affective atmospheres at work in urban space. When I say "at work" I specifically mean an art called on to be actively operative in the immaterial social sphere of the present as aesthetic dividend, working to add value to material development and spatial strategies of placemaking but also – in affectively more surreptitious ways – mobilised as aesthetic fictions and formal innovation patterns to provide models of labour and subjectivity:

> It seems no coincidence today that all kinds of waged work is supposed to become creative at exactly the same time that art is supposed to become socially useful—an aid to economic growth, social integration, and urban redevelopment.[57]

In the jerking and twitching of capital investments and development acceleration drives, capital is bound to project itself into and fully *commodify* another once customary role of art: that of *visionary powers*. The CGI oracles of future developments that look at us from hoardings of development sites are the bearers of this language of colonisation and marketisation of the city yet-to-exist. They are the subjectivities absorbed by capital's futuring as the creative subjects who can actively materialise the future of their labour as culture that makes money. In reality, they are conduits for much more complex narratives.

In these acts of ducking and emerging, art is at work leading and following at the same time, hoping to maintain – just like capital – both visibility for its narratives and the invisibility of its contradictions. Through these mechanisms, artists have by now absorbed the moral discomforts and mental stress of every other worker under neoliberal managerialism (call them curators and art institutions' officers if you wish) as well as seeking comfort in theories or innovative modes of being that appear even briefly to cohere the impossible in the name of a *"continuing practice"*.

The changing pedagogy of Art and Design courses, and the competition for students in London within the manoeuvring of all major London universities moving east, is driving such processes right into the educational institutions where art students bow and stress out under the duress of massive debts and inflationary degrees. Through these contingencies, they learn that the poetics of art and the politics of the social are inextricably connected in ways that only those smart enough to accept and internalise will be able to surpass, reconfigure, and succeed within.

The overall results are that art operates at once in conditions of *delirium* and *resistance* as Gregory Scholette has clearly summoned in his sharp writing:

> Bare Art has merged with life, while life is permeated by capital. What was once capital's crisis is now also that of art, institutionally as well as epistemologically. This change of status forces art into an encounter with social frictions operating within capitalist forces of production. The truth is out, leading to conflicts of a decidedly real-world nature once perceived as largely external to art.[58]

In the generation of artists that saw the rise of the London Docklands Development Corporation in East London in the Eighties and understood its cultural significance, some saw fit to characterise those momentous changes taking place with the tagline "Big Money is moving in"[59] whilst others were sowing the seeds of what became the YBA phenomenon.[60] Today we could add that "Big Culture is moving in too", acting like the bona fide common good that underwrites other spatial acts of transition for East London beyond recognition. What Canary Wharf never managed to accomplish culturally, is now *culturally engineered* in reverse by a new generation of brand-aware museums, universities, cultural institutions, and art-commissioning practices, clearly seeing themselves as the virtuous elements at the stakeholders' table in urban regeneration processes.

At the eastern border of the Arc of Opportunity, across the Lea River in Tower Hamlets, art is once again the provider of show value in an economy of enrichment through aesthetic work. In the video showcasing the development of the newly refurbished Balfron Tower—and its transition from public asset to private ownership where value has been previously extracted through the eviction of social housing and the proximity of artists in live work conditions—the artist Ryan Gander proudly describes how:

Fig. 6: Ryan Gander, "Balfron Tower Redevelopment" video, 2017.

> I wanted to make things that would make each apartment unique and individual, so each of the doorbell melodies is completely different.[61]

This is precisely the kind of *atmosphere* that aesthetic capitalism thrives on, one where commodities are "aestheticised and are put on show in the exchange sphere"[62] in order to produce "values that no one actually needs"[63] but from which other economies can be spun.

Enlarging such an atmospheric realm in its reach, the "object to be valorised based on a story"[64] in a future planning based on an aesthetic economy is today the city as a whole, with culture as the main narrative provider for its economy of enrichment, setting out a future in which the prospect of its value will increase over time, for the benefit of some and the loss of others.

In the heavily aestheticised phase of capitalism of today, practicing art must mean also "seeing power"[65] as it constitutes itself through the aesthetic devices appropriated from art. In the current loss of purpose and dissolution through the "magenta haze" effect, one can perhaps see different roles for art other than being a provider of show value for aesthetic capitalism.

This would mean articulating a practice located in the operative gap "between the dream logic of capitalism and the newly forming worlds"[66] as fertile ground for an art practice much needed when coming up for air from the Arc of Opportunity's toxic vivid pink: Magenta Haze.

Endnotes

1   Nato Thompson, *Culture as Weapon* (Melville House Publishing, 2017), p. 123.

2   This was originally published in Mute Magazine in 2005. It has also recently been republished in Gregory Scholette, *Delirium and Resistance: Activist Art and the Crisis of Capitalism* (Verso, 2017).

3   The Jimi Hendrix Experience, "Purple Haze" (Track Records, 1967)

4   Once a creative quarter, now a cultural district: the recent history of these sanctioned places for culture in the spatial reorganisation of urban space under neoliberal regimes has seen the rise of various vocabularies of containment for cultural activities. These legitimised spaces of cultural production slotted in between financial centres and shopping malls are symptomatic of new ways of conceiving of "civic space", where democratic governance – the elected town halls once the centre of administrative power – is non-existent, replaced by a private form of governance which takes on the policing of these areas.

5   The adjective "affective" is derived from psychology and relates to moods, feelings and attitude experienced in particular circumstances and spaces. The registering of affect in our orientation and understanding of the world around us has been recognised in the last few years in many fields outside psychology, particularly in politics and spatial practices, where for a long time now since the writings of Lefebvre and Massey, the idea of space being "produced" has been at the Centre of Urban Studies. A good study in the idea of affective atmospheres close to the way I'm using the terminology here is Ben Anderson paper published on the journal *Emotion, Space and Society* in 2009: https://www-sciencedirect-com.ezproxy.mdx.ac.uk/science/article/pii/S1755458609000589

6   Magenta is the official colour of the London Borough of

Newham logo, and it is used across its website and all other official communication. It is a light mauvish-crimson colour and it is one of the primary subtractive colours, complementary to green.

7   Foundation for FutureLondon Website: https://www.future.london/

8   Keller Easterling, *Extrastatecraft: The Power of Infrastructure Space* (Verso, 2015), p. 15

9   Fredric Jameson, "The Aesthetic of Singularity", *New London Review*, 92, March/April 2015, p. 130

10   p. 12, Thames Estuary Production Corridor (TEPC) brochure. Published by GLA and South East LEP's Creative Economy Network. February 2017. Download HERE.

11   Futuring: http://www.referenceforbusiness.com/management/Ex-Gov/Futuring.html

12   Futuring.

13   R. John Williams, "World Futures", *Critical Inquiry*, 43, Spring 2016, p. 474.

14   In late April 2016, a few months into the project, I was contacted by a Communication officer of the Newham Regeneration Team, expressing interest in the project: "I wondered if it would be possible for us to meet to discuss the project and your vision further. This could be something that as a council we could support."

15   Brian Holmes, "The Affectivist Manifesto", in *Escape the Overcode. Activist Art in the Control Society.* (Van Abbemuseum and WHM, 2009), p. 9. Available online at: https://monoskop.org/images/4/43/Holmes_Brian_Escape_the_Overcode_Activist_Art_in_the_Control_Society.pdf

16   David Ley, "Artists, Aestheticisation and the Field of Gentrification", *Urban Studies*, 40:12, pp. 2527-2544

17   Richard Florida, *The New Urban Crisis: How Our Cities Are Increasing Inequality, Deepening Segregation, and Failing the Middle Class and What We Can Do About It,* (Basic Books, 2016)

18 https://en.wikipedia.org/wiki/Rent-gap_theory

19 Rosalyn Deutsche, *Evictions: Art and Spatial Politics,* (MIT Press, 1996), p. 151

20 Boyle Height, "Alliance Against Artwashing and Displacement", 2017 http://alianzacontraartwashing.org/en/coalition-statements/statement-from-defend-boyle-heights-and-bhaaad-on-pssst-closing/

21 Matteo Pasquinelli, "Immaterial Civil War Prototypes of Conflict within Cognitive Capitalism", European Institute for Progressive Cultural Policies, 2006. Read online at: http://eipcp.net/policies/cci/pasquinelli/en/print

22 Gernot Böhme, *Critique of Aesthetic Capitalism,* (Mimesis International, 2017), p. 288

23 Easterling, *Extrastatecraft*, p. 23

24 Holmes, "The Affectivist Manifesto"

25 Böhme, *Critique of Aesthetic Capitalism*

26 Hallsville Quarter is the new £600 million town centre that is being created to establish a lasting legacy for Canning Town. See the fly-through here: https://vimeo.com/97804270 Images of signage for the fictitious Newham Biennale appear clearly between 00:52 and 01:15.

27 Alana Jelinek, *This is Not Art: Activism and Other Non-Art* (IB Tauris, 2013), p. 112

28 Jameson, "The Aesthetic of Singularity", p. 122.

29 Web page of the Foundation For FutureLondon: https://www.future.london/

30 Perhaps these have been printed in the fictional, "state-of-the-art facility and foundry for manufacturing large-scale artworks and sculptures, including the UK's biggest 3D printing centre in Silvertown" mentioned in the Thames Estuary Production Corridor brochure, GLA, Feb 2017.

31 The International Quarter/Cultural and Educational District is a LandLease project and it's not escaping us the strange image of an Elephant sculpture in these renderings. LandLease has become particularly the

subject of much housing activists critical energy since they are the developers of the Elephant and Castle/Heygate Estate. The sculpture seen here recalls the well-known case study of art as attention economy device known as the Cow Parade, a phenomena propelled into the orbit of placemakers around the globe by the success it had in turning around the public image of Chicago in 1999. Spawning a whole array of imitations, eventually the Elephant Parade reached London in 2010, the same year of the Shanghai World Expo and the London's Regeneration Supernova.

32 Owen Hatherley, "London's new typology: the tasteful modernist non-dom investment", *Dezeen Online* (August 2014), https://www.dezeen.com/2014/08/21/owen-hatherley-london-housing-typology-yuppie-flats-tasteful-modernist-investment/

33 "Albertopolis" on Wikipedia: https://en.wikipedia.org/wiki/Albertopolis

34 Kristen Peterson, "Vegas, say goodbye to Guggenheim", *Las Vegas Sun* (April 2008), https://lasvegassun.com/news/2008/apr/10/vegas-say-goodbye-guggenheim/

35 Oliver Wainwright, "Louvre Abu Dhabi: Jean Nouvel's spectacular palace of culture shimmers in the desert", the *Guardian*, (7 November 2017), https://www.theguardian.com/artanddesign/2017/nov/07/louvre-abu-dhabi-sheikh-chic-throws-controversial-construction-in-relief

36 Luc Boltanski and Arnaud Esquierre , "The Economic Life of Things", *New Left Review*, 98, March/April 2016.

37 Nancy Fraser, "A New Form of Capitalism?", *New Left Review*, July/Aug 2017.

38 Nikos Papastergiadis, "From Cosmopolis to Cosmopolitan Spaces", *e-flux*, (17 January 2018) http://www.e-flux.com/architecture/urban-village/169806/from-cosmopolis-to-cosmopolitan-spaces

39 See Anna Minton's chapter in this book.

40   Nikos Papastergiadis, "From Cosmopolis to Cosmopolitan Spaces"

41   Giovanni Arrighi's characterisation of phases of capital, as cited in Simon O'Sullivan, "From Financial Fictions To Mythotechnesis" , in Ayesha Hameed, Henriette Gunkel and Simon O'Sullivan (ed.), *Futures and Fictions* (Repeater Books, 2016), p. 381

42   Kristin Ross, *Communal Luxury* (Verso, 2016), p. 7

43   Futuring.

44   It's worth remembering that these 1939 World Expo derived jingles are still abundant in the language of placemaking as future colonisation: "Exploring tomorrow's cities today" is the tagline that is etched into the glazed frontage of the Siemens Crystal in Royal Victoria Dock. These are the hegemonic future urbanism that in their strange mutations also gave birth to Disney's EPCOT, perhaps the true ancestor of the Smart City of today: a fictional city as a laboratory for the real one, to the point that is now hard to tell them apart.

45   Foundation for FutureLondon, Cultural and Educational district hoardings, Queen Elizabeth Olympic Park.

46   See the introduction of this book.

47   Shanghai World Expo Urban Future Pavilion: https://en.wikipedia.org/wiki/Expo_2010_pavilions#cite_ref-16

48   Royal Docks Cultural Vision, GLA, 2015. Prepared by officers from City Hall (Culture, Housing & Land, Regeneration) in consultation with London Borough of Newham, RODMA. Silvertown Partnership and various creative people and organisations. http://www.royaldocks.london/

49   See Robert Baffour-Awuah's chapter in this book.

50   Royal Docks Cultural Vision, GLA, 2015.

51   Ibid

52   The last official press release of the LDDC on the 26 March 1998 releases the land back to the London Borough of Newham: http://www.lddc-history.org.uk/pressreleases/

dedes/Pr260398.pdf

53   http://europe.chinadaily.com.cn/business/2016-01/15/content_23110638.htm

54   http://www.royaldocks.london/#explore/development/royal-albert-docks/info

55   http://rmbcity.com/2010/12/supernovas-inauguration-speech/

56   Marina Vishmidt, "Mimesis of the Hardened and Alienated: Social Practice as Business Model", *e-flux*, 43, March 2013. http://www.e-flux.com/journal/43/60197/mimesis-of-the-hardened-and-alienated-social-practice-as-business-model/

57   Max Haiven, *Cultures of Financialization: Fictitious Capital in Popular Culture and Everyday Life* (Palgrave MacMillian, 2014)

58   Gregory Scholette, *Delirium and Resistance*, p. 30

59   Loraine Leeson and Peter Dunn (formerly The Art of Change, Docklands Community Poster Project, 1981-8). See here an animation of the various stages of the project as it revealed its main message: "Big Money is Moving in... But don't let it push out Local People" http://www.arte-ofchange.com/content/docklands-community-poster-project-1981-8

60   Read about how Freeze, the exhibition which paved the way for the rising YBA phenomena, was staged in Surrey Quays after Damien Hirst directly approached the LDDC for the use of the location. http://www.metamute.org/editorial/articles/no-room-to-move-radical-art-and-regenerate-city

61   http://balfrontower.co.uk/#creative-team Until about a month ago, this video was free to watch. It is now password protected. However I have captured the video and you can see it at this Google Drive link: https://drive.google.com/file/d/1yHVetlXbUczVfHXIFTWHhCkrhOUgKPJ0/view?usp=sharing

62   Böhme, *Critique of Aesthetic Capitalism*

63   Ibid
64   Boltanski and Esquierre, "The Economic Life of Things",
65   Nato Thompson, *Seeing Power: Art and Activism in the Age of Cultural Production* (Melville House Publishing, 2016)
66   The voice of Alex, camped in Zuccotti Park during Occupy NY, as quoted in Michael Taussing, "I'm so Angry I Made a Sign", in W.J.T. Mitchell, Bernard E. Harcourt and Michael Taussig (eds), *OCCUPY: Three inquiries in Disobedience* (University of Chicago Press, 2013)

Pirates and Olympians: Deja Vu FM and the Copper Box Arena

Dan Hancox

"A Big Patch of Nothingness"

Young musician Jammz, from Hackney Wick in East London, is a leading light of a genre that was never supposed to be more than a flash in the pan. As a grime producer and MC, he is on the crest of a second wave of artists increasingly occupying the mainstream of British pop culture. In 2015, I was interviewing him–along with other young musicians who are now household names nationwide, like Stormzy–for a spread in the *Observer* titled "How British MCs Found a Voice of Their Own", and we tracked back to the hyper-local roots of this suddenly dominant genre. Jammz was obsessed with the genre's free-wheeling live origins on pirate radio–he had taken to using the motto "I am radio"–and told me about being twelve years old, back in 2004, and listening to one of grime's formative pirate stations, Deja Vu FM. "Where I lived was five minutes from where Deja used to be, so that was one of the main stations I could catch. Deja was where the Olympic site is now, and I lived right there: it was a big patch of nothingness."

Grime's heartlands have always been in East London in general, although specifically Bow in Tower Hamlets, a couple of miles down the road from the Olympic site, and the Newham-Hackney borders that Jammz describes: the informal and messy terrain later transformed into the London 2012 Olympic Park. Bow's pre-eminence was disrupted during the genre's critical creative moment in 2003–04, when Deja Vu's larger and more successful rival, Rinse FM, was forced to temporarily ban grime. Rinse had become victims of their own success, and MCs and DJs turning up from all over London to perform on the station jeopardised its secret location in the tower blocks of the Crossways Estate. "We're not allowed to do this!" Geeneus, founder of Rinse FM, said, recalling his panic at the time. "I can't have thirty people turning up at the door of a flat [where] we're supposed to be doing something undercover."

Because of its remote, nonresidential location – the big patch of nothingness in Waterden Road, Hackney Wick – Deja Vu had no such problem evading crackdowns by the government's Radiocommunications Agency. And because of Rinse's grime ban, the leading lights of this nascent scene, its foundational crews, MCs, and DJs, moved en masse to Deja Vu. For a while, in 2003 and 2004, it became the hub for the entire London-wide grime scene, drawing crews from beyond East London, such as Meridian from Tottenham and Essentials from Lewisham. "In the leagues of pirate radio in London, Rinse FM and Deja Vu FM were the Champions League, and everything else was Vauxhall Conference", Lethal Bizzle once said to me.

"Getting a show on Deja", as opposed to one of the smaller East London pirates, "was like going into a different league", agreed Dirty Danger from Ruff Sqwad. "Before us in the schedule was Meridian, with Skepta and Jme, then it was us and then [DJ] Supa D, then Nasty Crew, then Roll Deep. All in one day! One crazy day of radio." Beyond their wider musical influence and underground reputations, one way of measuring the impact of that group, even on the most material, mainstream terms, is that those few hours of illegal, scrappy, short-radius pirate-radio broadcasts would contain spontaneous, one-of-a-kind performances by a handful of young amateurs who would go on to produce no fewer than ten UK number ones between them (Dizzee Rascal: five; Roll Deep: two; Tinchy Stryder: two; Wiley: one), not to mention two Mercury prizes (Dizzee in 2003, and Skepta in 2016). And that is not to mention numerous other artists with phenomenal reputations both in and far beyond the London "underground" scene, such as Jme, D Double E, Jammer, and Kano, among others.

Few other genres can ever claim to have had one geographical space home to such a remarkable amount of embryonic talent—it is as if Liverpool's Cavern Club had also hosted the Rolling Stones and the Kinks on the same night as the Beatles, or as if the 100 Club's infamous punk festival in 1977 had happened every week, routinely, rather than only once. Looking back at Deja Vu in 2003–04 now, it appears as a hyper-local time capsule in the heart of the informal city, and in the fifteen years since that period, both its performers and its location have changed beyond all recognition.

Dirt, Grit, and Grime

While it has moved around, at that time, Deja Vu's secret studio location was in the same building as the Club EQ nightclub—home to a lot of formative early grime nights—in the East Cross Centre, on the sparsely populated Waterden Road in Stratford. Unlike the tower blocks used by pirates in more densely populated parts of London, it wasn't a tall building—but there was a studio box-room on the roof. When Jammz describes it as a big patch of nothingness, he isn't exaggerating. West London MC Bashy recalls his first pirate experience in that "studio":

I remember getting the cab from Stratford station because it was long to walk, it was far. Those early Deja sets were sick. For me it was like being in Mecca like, "Rah, I'm fucking here, I've made it" [laughs]. The atmosphere, it was mad because you had to walk into the building, up some mad stairs – like loads of stairs – and climb through a hole. Remember I'm 15, I'm still quite small, so I was like, "Where the fuck are we going?" It was in a little room, just tiny. There was a DJ, and decks on a mad wooden table, paper stuck on the wall with the Nokia phone number and maybe some rules like, "If you don't play the ads on the hour you're getting kicked off." You know what's mad, that was illegal wasn't it? But I didn't think it was […] for me, this is just how you get on the radio; you climb through holes, go on the radio, spit your bar. It didn't occur to me that you could be arrested for that.[1]

The "wild east" location of the Waterden Road studio came with an associated reputation for unpredictability and lawlessness. Matt Mason was editor of underground black music magazine *RWD* from 2000–05, and recalled, "it was like a madhouse in there, there were like 100 people in there, all smoking, fights would kick off, crazy things would happen". Likewise, the man known as "the godfather of grime", Wiley, recalled a terrifying, High Noon-style moment. "The Deja block was in the middle of no man's land. You know how much shit went on there? I remember coming out of the radio station and someone had a shotgun, and reckoned they were going to shoot me." Fortunately, he escaped unhurt.

Even the position of the studio, in a box-room on the roof, felt dangerous and precarious, says Shystie, the MC known as the "first lady of grime":

Deja was the maddest one, because it was on a rooftop, and it literally had no edge, so if you take one wrong move you are dead, because you're gonna fall off the roof. It was so mad,

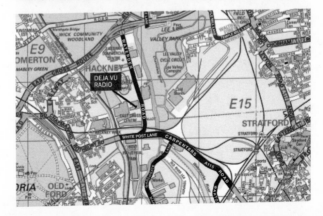

Fig. 1: Deja Vu's
"secret" studio
location in the
East Cross Centre,
Waterden Road, in
January 2007. ©
Alberto Duman.

Fig. 2: The "big patch
of nothingness" in
front of the East Cross
Centre, Waterden
Road, in January
2007. © Alberto
Duman, 2007.

Fig. 3: Location of
Deja Vu Radio in
a map from 2007.
Google Maps.

we should not have been up there! And it would be late at night, dark... if someone trips and falls back, they're gonna fall off that fucking roof and die. Now the stations all look like how 1Xtra looks, they're all in flipping Shoreditch – it's mad, they're all nice and shit. Proper different.

The origins of grime's naming are ambiguous, and disputed – although most people agree that it settled gradually, and accidentally, onto an evolving form of what had been UK garage, over the period 2002–04 – partly, perhaps, because influential UK garage DJ EZ had a habit of referring to some tracks as "grimey garage" on his KISS FM shows, as a kind of mildly synaesthesiac suggestion of its dark, "muddy" basslines.

Grime's relationship with dirt and grit, with the postindustrial, impoverished built environment of the East London around it, is fairly clear. "Most grime tunes are made in a grimy council estate", Newham MC Nasty Jack told an American documentary crew from BET in 2006: "Mum ain't got enough money, everyone's just angry... you need a tension release." In describing his hometown on his 2004 single "Graftin", before he was a fully-fledged pop star, Dizzee Rascal assumes the role of spokesperson for London, issuing a corrective to the postcard image: "I swear to you it ain't all teacups, red telephone boxes and Buckingham Palace / I'm gonna show you it's gritty out here." Newham's Nasty Crew describe, on "City Life", a "Harsh, gritty, London city life / Oh what a shame, oh what a pity life", where their only escape from poverty is rapping "about the old school life in the dusty flats". Ruff Sqwad, from Bow, conjured the same mixture of poverty and uncleanliness in their hometown, on the chorus to "London": "Right about now man have got nothing but nish / [In] east London where it smells like fish."

Dirt is "matter out of place", wrote cultural theorist Mary Douglas, and with its industry, its warehouses, and its slums, East London has long had a lot of matter out of place. Ben Campkin, in *Remaking London*, describes a 2007 exhibition of new London architecture called "Gritty Brits". In the urban context, grit, he writes, refers to

> the economically and physically run-down, ex-industrial environments in which these architects operate in (mostly East) London, to the physical nature and durability of the materials they use, and to a quality of persistence attributed to them (and within British nationalist discourses, to 'Britishness' generally).

There is an associated machismo that runs with grittiness, or at least a resilience–as well as a recognition that postindustrial settings are not easy to live in, but are, at least, authentic. It's a spirit that dovetails perfectly with the "nonstop working" idea of "hustling" for money that is prevalent in the grime scene–one that is directly in the tradition of East London life. "Coping strategies and cultures of resistance" emerged in response to the entrenched poverty, Dick Hobbs wrote in the 1980s–ducking and diving, wheeling and dealing–while the proximity to the Thames and the docks meant that the buying and selling of stolen goods "became integral to east end culture".[2]

Up on the Roof

One gritty moment in the Deja Vu studio would come to symbolise the thrilling artistic energy and explosive drama that would make grime so fascinating–if, in some cases, so flawed. Filmed for an amateur grime DVD called *Conflict*, one epochal ninety-minute grime radio show in 2003 brought many of these stars-in-the-making together: the jostling egos and lyrical skills of Wiley, Tinchy Stryder, D Double E, Demon, Maxwell D, God's Gift, Lady Fury, Sharky Major, Dizzee Rascal, and Crazy Titch (the footage later reached a much wider audience via YouTube).

If you'd asked an East London teenager in 2003, they'd have said MCs like Sharky Major, Demon, God's Gift, or Lady Fury had just as much chance of crossing over to the mainstream as any of the others–they had lots of good lyrics in their armouries, reputations for "destroying" a few big raves and radio shows with their mic skills, and maybe even a couple of studio-recorded singles. That's all anyone had at this stage. But for so many underground favourites, this was as far as they got. Their stars shone brightly in that extraordinary moment, then burned out in the blink of an eye.

The evening's notoriety stems from its implausibly stellar line-up, at a turning point in black British dance music, but also from its dramatic climax: when the growing tension in the room suddenly explodes, and a seventeen-year-old Dizzee Rascal nearly comes to blows with a rival MC who was then as hotly tipped as he was, Crazy Titch. The whole cast is teetering on a precipice: beneath them, a world of possibility, of foiled and realised ambition, triumph or disaster.

Fast-forward fifteen years from this moment to today, and Dizzee Rascal is a global superstar, with all the commercial and critical plaudits to his name you could ask for; Crazy Titch is serving a life sentence for murder. Frozen in time and seen from a distance, the poignancy of these lives, now transformed beyond all recognition, strikes with the clinical, knock-out punch of a Wiley snare. Grime's intensity was always its great strength, but sometimes a scene this close-knit can be suffocating. Dizzee helped invent as well as popularise grime–but when his fame suddenly expanded beyond the reach of the crackly Deja Vu signal, so too did his ambitions. The drama got worse, before it receded: that same summer, he was stabbed in Ayia Napa, following trouble with So Solid Crew–the titans of the old regime, the last emperors of UK garage. Two months later, in September 2003, he shocked the music establishment when he won the Mercury Music Prize for his debut album, *Boy in da Corner*, and won a way out of the grime scene in the process. By the end of the first decade of the new millennium, Dizzee was living in Miami, headlining rock festivals, collaborating with Shirley Bassey and Shakira, recording the England World

Cup anthem and being asked his opinions on Barack Obama on *Newsnight*. Crazy Titch was residing at Her Majesty's pleasure.

But it's somehow appropriate for grime's grassroots, DIY aesthetics, that the quintessential visualisation of grime is not a glitzy, multimillion-pound music video full of helicopters and swimming pools—but a grainy YouTube clip of an illegal broadcast, filmed on a rooftop in an urban wasteland, the footage then "ripped" by a fan from a long-out-of-print, amateur DVD. "Deja Vu was on top of a night club, and that night club was on the edge of an industrial estate—so it didn't really make any difference what happened there", recalled Troy "A Plus" Miller, who produced *Conflict*, and filmed the unfolding drama that night.

Dizzee 2012

A full nine years after his clash with Crazy Titch in the Deja Vu FM box-room studio, Dizzee Rascal returned from Miami to pick up the mic in the same spot—give or take half a mile—for an altogether less humble performance: in the eighty-thousand-capacity, £486 million Olympic Stadium. He was there to perform his lightweight, number-one, party-pop mega-hit "Bonkers" as a key part of the London 2012 Opening Ceremony. The ceremony cost £27 million in itself—an arirang-style extravaganza of elaborate choreography, extravagant props and dazzling pyrotechnics, with a supporting cast of 7,500 volunteers—and was broadcast live to an estimated global TV audience of nine hundred million people. Dizzee stood proud in his embroidered "E3" baseball jacket, a single piece of thread connecting this international TV spectacular to the forgotten people and forgotten genre that emerged mere minutes away.

Dizzee was also asked to record one of five official Olympic songs: his contribution, "Scream", was the kind of thumping sports anthem the situation demanded—"I feel like Rocky on the steps"—but buried in the final verse of the song, he found room for a fleeting tribute to the roots he had become estranged from, living in Miami: the area he still felt intensely conflicted about, and conflicted about leaving: "Boy it's lonely at the top, but it's overcrowded at the bottom / And where I come from's overly rotten, I'm from the east side, I ain't forgotten."

More recently, Dizzee has returned from living in the US, and has revisited his enthusiasm for the 2012 Games, too–finding himself in a much more ambivalent place: "I wonder what the Olympics was all about now", he said to the *NME* recently. "Look at all the housing they built: it's this whole new postcode, this whole new clinical little town. Round here people's houses are getting knocked down and they're getting moved on because they can't afford what's being built in their place. Back in 2012, I was like, 'Rah, it's the Olympics!' But now I can't decide whether I feel good or bad about it."

In October 2016 he returned to the exact same spot on Waterden Road that the Deja Vu FM studio building had once stood on, prior to its demolition, for another landmark performance: a rare outing for his seminal Mercury-winning 2003 debut *Boy in da Corner*, played in full. The industrial estate had been replaced by the Queen Elizabeth Olympic Park, and the crumbling East Cross Centre had been replaced by the £44 million Copper Box arena. The dark, forbidding facade of the indoor arena had hosted fencing and handball during the Games themselves, and now, in its Olympic legacy incarnation, had become a multipurpose sport and leisure venue, run by Greenwich Leisure Limited (GLL), the self-declared "social enterprise" that has been given numerous outsourced library and leisure-centre contracts in recent years, and whom unions accuse of employing two-thirds of their staff on zero-hour contracts. Dizzee had been lured by Red Bull–the unlikely, taurine-infused brand patrons of cutting-edge music in the digital age–and the 7,500-capacity show sold out immediately. Bands don't split up anymore, goes the logic, they just tour their greatest records until they die–it's a product of the same trend that has led Red Bull to a position of power once occupied by major record labels:

live performances are a vital source of income in an age where people barely pay for music, if at all.

I met Dizzee in a break during rehearsing for the show, in the same studio where he had recorded *Boy in da Corner* thirteen years previously, when still a teenager. After the best part of a decade performing pop hits like "Bonkers" and "Holiday" to festival crowds around the world, collaborating with the likes of Robbie Williams and Will.I.Am, he was genuinely surprised that people felt so strongly about the music he had summoned out of his troubled teenage mind. "I was like 'rah'—I didn't think it was that deep. I understand what it means now to this country." He told me about sitting on a wall outside the shops on the Lincoln Estate in Bow, stoned, "watching the world go by. Obviously I feel far removed from that mindset now, but because I've been rehearsing it, I feel it again when I'm performing it."

The gig itself, like many of the "classic albums revisited" gigs that have proliferated in recent years, was positioned in an awkward spot between sincere nostalgia and jarring bathos. Many of the songs being "revisited" had never been performed live in the first place, many of the fans present in the Copper Box would have been too young to know of *Boy in da Corner* at the time, many of the delicate sonics are best suited to headphones rather than stadium speakers, and most importantly, Dizzee's superbly poignant lyrics about teenage alienation, poverty, dysphoria, and petty criminality struck an odd note, coming from a thirty-two-year-old, globe-trotting superstar. Which is not to say the gig was not tremendous; indeed the profundity of Dizzee Rascal's journey resonated louder than it ever had before, across a cavernous, sold-out, 7,500-capacity arena—in the same location where he spat lyrics of transcendent anger and pain, as a seventeen-year-old boy, in the corner of a pirate radio box-room, on a big patch of nothingness. It is only to say that, perhaps, you can't go home again.

Endnotes

1   Hattie Collins, *This is Grime* (Hodder & Stoughton, 2016)
2   Dick Hobbs, *Doing the Business: Entrepreneurship, the Working Class, and Detectives in the East End of London* (Oxford University Press, 1988)

From the Factory to the Pop Centre and Back

Owen Hatherley

Dancing about Architecture in the North of England

Outside of London – whose status as barely regulated financial centre has been the overwhelming factor – one of the least researched drivers of development in the New Labour era and since has been a transformation of punk, indie, techno, and other "alternative" music into a key part of the heritage and city-marketing industry. The continued belief, however decreasingly plausible, that these by-now-quite-established forms of alleged subcultural resistance were or are opposed to neoliberal capitalism can seem absurd in a world where Hilary Clinton has as a strategist the hapless John McTernan, an ex-punk fanzine editor who occupies the extreme right of the British Labour Party. Manchester and Sheffield see the most glaring examples of this trend, but some cities have engaged with pop music and its legacies more quietly than others, and with more subtlety. In Cardiff, for instance, there is a plaque outside of the large, modern Municipal Library opened a few years ago that records its opening by the Manic Street Preachers, quoting the slogan from their 1996 song "A Design for Life" that "libraries gave us power", and that civic buildings like this became a vector for working-class self-education and collective elevation. This is something a little different to calling, say, a new luxury housing estate in Cardiff Bay the "Generation Terrorists Quarter". Nonetheless, this process of urban branding excludes any music that still exists as a working-class force. Although his personal politics may be similar or worse, Wiley is unlikely ever to have the same role as an urban booster as the late Tony Wilson.

Manchester is of course the centre for all of this. When the Conservative-Liberal coalition laid waste to the local governments of the North, causing an unprecedented number of closures of libraries, public toilets, Sure Start centres, and other municipal survivals of the "gas and water socialism" that once defined civic life in the North, Manchester City Council, one of Britain's most powerful local authorities, co-operated with then Chancellor George Osborne on his proposal for a "Northern Powerhouse", a newly organised conurbation supposedly to rival London, centred around Manchester. Its proposals were vague, and have now largely been abandoned. What was suggested included a proposed "High Speed 3" rail line, in a situation where "High Speed 2" (which would connect the already closely connected London and Birmingham with a marginally faster new line, fairly transparently to ease pressure on the capital by attracting commuters to the West Midlands city and outside of the bursting Greater London conurbation) has not yet been built.

This project would have included improving the rather poor road and rail connections between Northern cities, and it roped in a few more ambitious ideas which mostly predated the "powerhouse" proposal, such as the Graphene Institute in Manchester and the Industrial Innovation Centre in Darlington. But its centrepiece, it seemed, was a building, to be designed by Rem Koolhaas's Office for Metropolitan Architecture – the architects of the CCTV building in Beijing – called the Factory. It was an arts centre, of which twenty-first-century Regenerated

Manchester already has a few, but its name immediately recalled a different Manchester altogether – that of Joy Division, New Order, Tony Wilson, the Happy Mondays, Factory Records, now seen as the pioneers in shifting the city from a failed locus of production into the creative capital of the North. If any of these people had been told, in, say, 1985, that a Conservative chancellor would one day support a project bearing their name, it is hard to imagine the reaction. This only puts the final stamp on something that has been happening for some time.

Postpunk, which was so pivotal for Manchester, is usually represented in terms of concrete and piss, grim towers and blasted wastelands. This is best exemplified in the poster for Anton Corbijn's woeful Ian Curtis biopic *Control*, where Sam Riley, fag dangling from mouth, looks wan and haunted below gigantic prefabricated tower blocks (which, as we've seen, were shot in Nottingham, not the gentrified-out-of-recognition Manchester – although there are certainly parts of Salford that

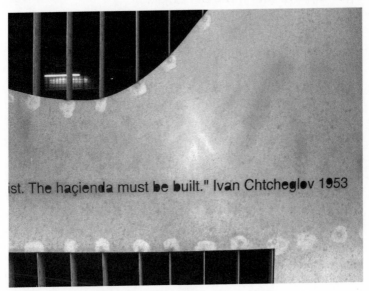

ist. The haçienda must be built." Ivan Chtcheglov 1953

Fig. 1: Public Art, Manchester. © The author.

could still do the trick). Decades ago, when asked by Jon Savage why Joy Division's sound had such a sense of loss and gloom, Bernard Sumner reminisced about his Salford childhood, where "there was a huge sense of community where we lived [...] I guess what happened in the '60s was that someone at the Council decided that it wasn't very healthy, and something had to go, and unfortunately it was my neighbourhood that went. We were moved over the river into a tower block. *At the time I thought it was fantastic*–now of course I realise it was a total disaster." (My italics.) This is often quoted as if it's obvious–well, *of course* it was a disaster. This is the narrative about modernist architecture that exists in numerous reminisces and histories–we loved it at first, in the Sixties, then we realised our mistake, knocked it down, and rebuilt simulations of the old streets instead; and then, later, built a very different kind of modern city–clean, optimistic, private.

The Postrave Urban Growth Coalition

Tony Wilson was evidently pleased that the guru of the "Creative Class", Richard Florida, had designated the Manchester of young media professionals and loft conversions as a "cultural capital", irrespective of the conspicuous lack of worthwhile culture created in the regenerated city, save for Mancunian autohagiographies like *The Alcohol Years*, *Control*, or the egregious *24-Hour Party People*. At the end of the most recent and most intelligent of these, Grant Gee's *Joy Division* documentary, Wilson reflected on how Manchester had gone from being the first industrial city in the early nineteenth century to, today, Britain's first successful postindustrial city–after the blight of the 1970s it is now a modern metropolis once again, this time based on media and property rather than something so unseemly as industrial production. The old entrepreneurs built the Mills where workers toiled at twelve-hour shifts and died before they were forty; the new entrepreneurs sold the same Mills to young urban professionals as industrial-aesthetic luxury housing.

Wilson squarely credited Joy Division and Factory Records with a leading role in this transformation, but he was by no means alone in this. Nick Johnson, one of the directors of the property developers Urban Splash, has given presentations where he dates the beginnings of his company to the Sex Pistols' gig at the Free Trade Hall. The company's boss and one of Britain's richest men, Tom Bloxham MBE, is an ex-bootleg poster salesman based in the former "alternative" enclave of Affleck's Palace. The academic and Urbis co-founder Justin O'Connor claims that Wilson

> had found Richard Florida's book and thought it said all that needed to be said about cities and that Manchester should pay circa 20k to get him to speak [...] I tried [to convince him] what a complete charlatan Florida was and how a "cutting edge" "creative city" should not be 97th in line to invite some tosser from Philadelphia. He completely rejected this and never really spoke to me again. The last time I saw him was in Liverpool at a RIBA do. He was saying that Liverpool was "fucked" unlike Manchester—and the reason was that Manchester [in the figure of the unelected Chief Executive of Manchester City Council Howard Bernstein] had an enlightened despot. Which more or less set a seal on the increasing moral and political bankruptcy of the postrave urban growth coalition which had taken over Manchester post-1996. Simpson, Johnson, Bloxham—now all millionaires—all claimed to have the new political vision for the reinvented city. Despite the fact that Bloxham was given chair of the Arts Council and now VC of Manchester University—a man of little culture and education, thus confirming the toadying of arts and education to the "creative entrepreneur"—it is Wilson who represents its saddest failures. He made little money from it all, and really believed in it. Now subject to a nauseating hagiography by the city council that kept him outside for years, until the last four or five, bringing him in when his critical faculties had been worn

down by years of punditry. He used to say, of the postrave
coalition, "the lunatics have taken over the asylum"; pigs and
farm was more apposite. (interview with the author, 2010)

The narrative of Sex Pistols–Factory–IRA Bomb–Ian Simpson–
Urban Splash has no room for the postwar years, decades of
decline which just happened to coincide with the most fertile
and exciting popular culture ever produced in the city (was it
accidental, perhaps?). When Manchester is profiled or reminisced
over, it is most often through a narrative which leaps from the
Victorian city of "Manchester liberalism" – a laissez-faire doctrine
with distinct similarities to Thatcherism – to the city recreated and
regenerated after the IRA bomb in 1996. The horrendous poverty
of nineteenth-century Manchester and the gaping inequalities of
today are entirely effaced. In between is a no man's land. Both
approaches have an essentially nineteenth-century idea of the
city, as a place that should rise autonomously out of the activities
of entrepreneurs and businessmen. The place this represses is a
housing estate that was pivotal for the original Factory Records
and its milieu – Hulme Crescents.

After leaving his post as Sheffield's City Architect, Lewis
Womersley set up a private practice with another architect,
Hugh Wilson, and together Wilson and Womersley designed a
series of labyrinthine blocks accessed by street decks. The relative
conservatism of the Crescents can be ascertained from the
names – John Nash, Charles Barry, etc., all taken from architects
of the Regency period – to whose work in Bath and London this
was intended to be the modern equivalent. Nonetheless, in the
context of Greater Manchester, where seemingly hundreds of
blocks from Pendleton to Collyhurst rose out of the Victorian
slums, gigantic spaced-out tombstones that amply made the
punks' point about the boredom of postwar redevelopment, the
Crescents provided a modernist labyrinth, with its street decks
winding round and interconnecting four vast, semi-circular
blocks enclosing a seeming no man's land of indeterminate

pedestrian space. Within a couple of years of its 1971 completion, it was vermin-ridden and leaky, as a result of costs cut during the construction. However, within a few years, Hulme was becoming something else as well. Manchester City Council, which had at that point a surplus of council housing, was implementing a policy of rehousing the families that found Hulme so unnerving on estates of houses with gardens in Burnage or Wythenshawe, leaving many empty flats. The Russell Club, which was home to the Factory nightclub, opened in 1978 by the embryonic record label, was surrounded by the estate's concrete walkways–and the club's clientele would follow suit.

Liz Naylor–fanzine editor and scriptwriter of the Joy Division-soundtracked *No City Fun*, and author of *Various Times*, a far-from-boosterist history of the area–remembers how, after running away from home at sixteen in 1978, she asked the council for a flat. First of all, she was housed in Collyhurst, then an area with a heavy National Front presence. She asked for a flat in Hulme instead, because it had already acquired "a population of alternatives", but "by then the *Manchester Evening News* had been running stories for years about how awful it was". Not only was the Factory based there, but so were many of the bands, along with fanzines like *City Fun* and recording studios. One of the most famous images of Joy Division was taken from one of the bridges over the motorway that bisected the new Hulme. Photographer Kevin Cummins later recalled how

> the heavy bombing, along with an ill-conceived 1960s regeneration programme, conspired to make Manchester redolent of an eastern European city. Revisiting my photographs, I see the bleakness of a city slowly dying. A single image taken from a bridge in Hulme of Princess Parkway, the major road into Manchester, features no cars.

Yet this image of a depopulated, brutalist Manchester as a sort of English Eastern Europe resonated in a less clichéd manner with those who chose to live in Hulme – it was welcomed. Naylor remembers that the entire scene was obsessed with Berlin – "we weren't sure whether east or west Berlin" – something that also dictated what they listened to: "Iggy Pop's *The Idiot* and Bowie's 'Heroes', was *the* music". This then extended to the films they saw at the Aaben, the estate's arthouse cinema, where Fassbinder or *Nosferatu* would be eagerly consumed by the area's overcoated youth.

Although she warns me that her views now might be coloured by nostalgia, Naylor raises the possibility that Hulme "became functional for people in a way that hadn't been anticipated by the planners". Naylor remembers the overriding feeling of Hulme being a sense of itself as an enclave, embattled but cohesive: "there's no future, but if we stay here we'll be all right". Nonetheless, from the mid-Eighties, the drugs had shifted from speed to heroin, muggings had become more common, Tory election landslides led to despair, "people started being mugged

Fig. 2: View from the "Ian Curtis Bridge", Hulme. © The author.

for their Giro", and many of those associated with the postpunk scene moved on. Yet the new-brutalist Hulme went on to become a (fairly crusty, by many accounts) centre for the rave scene in Manchester, with the Kitchen, a club made by knocking through three council flats, being the Hacienda's hidden reverse.

Culture Industry/Steel Industry

At the centre of Steel City is something called the Cultural Industries Quarter. This contains the former National Centre for Popular Music, four steel blobs designed by Nigel Coates, the then-famous designer of the "Body Zone" in London's Millennium Dome in 1999. The National Centre, another "Millennium Project" which closed within a couple of years, is used by Sheffield Hallam University for offices, though its Blairite nature is stressed through the list of lower-case verbs that decorates the entrance: "empowering. enriching. celebrating. involving. entertaining." Then there's the long-standing Leadmill Club, the Site Gallery, and for some reason a branch of Spearmint Rhino. More to the point, it contains a faïence-tiled 1930s moderne building housing the Showroom Cinema and Workstation, home of Warp Films, the only part of Warp Records' media empire that is still based in the city. The very name "Cultural Industries Quarter" was New Labour nu-language that seemed a bad joke amidst the recession's foreboding harshness. The notion that an economy can run itself through the "creative industries", financial services and tourism has taken an extremely heavy knock. It's particularly ironic that it sits next to the rail station of a once-proud heavy-industrial metropolis, which has never quite worked out what to do with itself since the steel industry's "restructuring" in the 1980s (unlike South Yorkshire's coal mining, steel never ceased production, and through the 2000s the city makes as much of it as it ever did – only with a tiny fraction of the workforce). What Sheffield *has* had since the late 1970s is perhaps the most consistently brilliant popular music of any city outside of London.

The city's electronic music, from the Human League and Cabaret Voltaire to early Warp artists Forgemasters and Sweet Exorcist, took palpable inspiration from the cyclopean factories of the Don Valley and the fearless, grandly scaled 1960s architecture built for their workers. It's no surprise, then, that in 2009 Warp Records' twentieth-anniversary celebrations – in the city the label left in 2000 – took place in the disputed remnants of a council estate and a steelworks, with film screenings in the former and a rave in the latter. The proceedings were assisted by the local regeneration quango, which bears the instructive name "Creative Sheffield". That this is not entirely benign is obvious as soon as we arrive at the first of the two events, a Warp Films showcase in Park Hill, a brutalist estate also designed under the aegis of Lewis Womersley. The main event took place in – again, note the already dated nomenclature – the Magna Science Adventure Centre, a Stirling Prize-winning building, in 2001. Again we have a perfect meeting of place and sound, and again an overwhelming reminder of the area's class conflicts and disputed transformations. Magna was once the Steel, Peech, and Tozer steelworks, part of the industrial zone that stretches between Sheffield and Rotherham. The road out from the centre goes seedy first, the strange sexualised landscape of Attercliffe, until it goes fully postindustrial, arriving at the surviving steelworks and a zone that has for decades been subject to several regeneration attempts, most on the same long, low scale as the plants they replaced, repurposed for leisure and shopping – "iceSheffield", the Don Valley Stadium, and the enormous Meadowhall shopping mall, a postmodernist megastructure of glass domes and fibreglass Victorian details abutting the M1. This in turn was for decades overlooked by the Tinsley Cooling Towers, concrete hyperbolic paraboloids that once marked the "gateway to the north". The city's "creatives" banded together to try to save the towers from their mooted demolition, proposing to turn them into enormous works of public art. In this instance at least, the culture industry did not supplant the truly industrial – a new power station, which may or may not turn out to be considerably less iconic, is being built on site. Next to business parks, retail parks, and still-functioning (if recession-threatened) steel plants, Magna attempts to unite the two "industries" by offering steel up as a spectacle – and it's an awe-inspiring one, a superhuman process whose eventual lack of use for human workers seems entirely unsurprising. Inside the cold, physically arresting, hangar-like space, reached through views of the overwhelming machinery, the DJs were rendered hilariously tiny by the Cyclopean scale of the building.

In terms of popular music, particularly in terms of music that has emerged out of postpunk and electronic music, Sheffield is a city that punches some way above its weight. Compared, for instance, with the larger West Riding industrial city of Leeds, Sheffield has contributed vastly more to popular music: from the late 1970s on, a list would include the Human League, Cabaret Voltaire, Comsat Angels, Heaven 17, ABC, Forgemasters,

Fig. 3: The former National Centre for Popular Music, Sheffield. © The author.

Sweet Exorcist (and the label Warp), Pulp, and somewhat later the Arctic Monkeys and the Long Blondes. As in Manchester, many of these groups have focused on brutalist architecture – in this case, the Park Hill estate, where Warp Records had their anniversary gig. This was (is) an immense deck-access council-housing complex on a hill above the city's railway station, at the time of writing in early 2017 still undergoing a long-running process of redesign and privatisation. One part is let and sold to "creatives" by the aforementioned Urban Splash, and the entire rest of it – four-fifths – is derelict.

Park Hill's ideas were shaped by a rejection of the clean geometries of mainstream modernism, in favour of roughness and irregularity. The marks of concrete shuttering were left, in the fashion of Le Corbusier's Unité d'Habitation, a monumental apartment block in Marseilles. Obviously, it was not utopia. It had too few lifts, and the concrete on the taller sections was cracking by the 1980s. More arguably, it may have been too successful at recreating the space of the old rookeries – like them, it was full of escape routes and shadowy spots. The notion that it could preserve a working-class community being obliterated everywhere else is unsurprisingly unconvincing. However, there is no evidence that it ever became a "sink" until at least the mid-Nineties.

Yet at exactly the point that conventional architectural opinion was turning against the streets in the sky, popular music told a different story. The Human League were keen to have it on record on the sleeve that their shimmering, proto-techno instrumental "Dancevision" – described by Simon Reynolds in terms that describe contemporary Sheffield rather well as an "ambiguous alloy of euphoria and grief" – was recorded in front of Kelvin Flats; rather aptly, the later reissue of the group's early recordings as the Future featured a photograph of Park Hill. On their first album *Reproduction* (1979), "Empire State Human" staged a strange confrontation between man and architecture, where human being and building become interchangeable, while

"Blind Youth" reprimanded punks for their antimodernism, insisting with tongue only slightly in cheek that "You've had it easy, you should be glad / High-rise living's not so bad". In their later career as bona fide pop stars, the group made great use of Sheffield's architecture in the video for "Love Action", with a wedding taking place in one of Basil Spence's minimalist, concrete-and-brick churches, and the main romance of the video/song's narrative set on a deck-access block of flats.

The more chilling, overwhelming aspect of Sheffield's postwar architecture and car-centred planning was obliquely referenced in the artwork and some of the songs on Comsat Angels's 1980 *Waiting for a Miracle*, as a rather glamorously oppressive space, on the model of Joy Division's Manchester. On the front cover, cars speed along a dual carriageway; on the back cover, you can see that they're speeding past Park Hill, whose streets in the sky are illuminated with yellow sodium light. Lyrically, *Waiting for a Miracle* presents a much more familiar postpunk city—lives trapped, relationships tense and paranoid, and loomed over by the threat of nuclear war. On the album's centrepiece, "On the Beach", the band obliquely imagine the city, with its motorways and high-rises ("a steel tide on an asphalt beach") devastated, so that "no piece of glass or chrome remains [...] we'll wash this place right down the drain". The intensity of the description of Sheffield in the song is dismissed by an interlocutor—"She says a town is just a town, full stop, but what does she know?" Oddly this chimes well with one of two major films made by TV director Mick Jackson in Sheffield in the 1980s: *Threads*, where Park Hill is among the Sheffield landmarks destroyed by a nuclear attack. In the other, *A Very British Coup*, a newly elected left-wing Labour Prime Minister and ex-steelworker is doorstopped in the first scene, in his apartment in Hyde Park Flats. The city pivots between being dystopia and socialist citadel.

It could be argued that, when Sheffield City Council was no longer prepared to create an image of the future and a new way of life, Sheffield's electronic producers did so instead. Sheffield

City Council had long had an enlightened policy with regard to ex-industrial spaces being used as studios and for raves, so it is unsurprising that the city became one of the major centres of house and techno at the turn of the 1990s. What is striking about this, however, is that the embrace of modernity by techno producers coincided with severe doubts about the modern landscape, and its progressive dismantlement. At the same time that Hyde Park's modern, cubist terraces were being given pitched roofs, Warp Records, and their early producers like Richard H. Kirk or Rob Gordon, were creating an art form that was a continuation of the streets in the sky's vertiginous sense of new space and their brutalist, low-end rumble. It is also a sound that draws on the more "high" modernist aspect of Sheffield modernism, such as the American, metropolitan slickness of Sheffield University's Arts Tower and Library, designed by Gollins Melvin Ward in a style completely in hock to Mies van der Rohe in the early 1960s, the first wholly modernist university campus in the UK. This series of precisely engineered, machine-tooled, glass-and-steel pavilions and towers, recently renovated to their postwar splendour, is closer to the aesthetic of early Warp, rather than the Human League's (or Pulp's) more Heath Robinson pop modernism. Rob Gordon's group Forgemasters took their name from a particularly large Sheffield steelworks; their clean, clear, optimistic sound derived directly from Kraftwerk's *Computer World* and the more utopian moments of Detroit techno: Model 500's "No UFOs", Rhythim Is Rhythim's "Strings of Life". In one of their harshest metal-on-metal constructions, "Stress", Forgemasters sample Cybotron's "Techno City", as if to lay claim to Sheffield as Detroit's British correspondent. A similar sense of metallic grandeur can be found in Sweet Exorcist, a collaboration between DJ Parrot and Cabaret Voltaire's Richard H. Kirk. Notably, the videos for many of these were made by local musician Jarvis Cocker, and present a modernity that increasingly bypasses the present in favour of purer images from the recent past: Space Invaders, 1970s children's television. The music is still "futurist", but a "retro" prefix is starting to creep in.

The group that most thoroughly fixated on the built landscape of Sheffield was Cocker's group Pulp, whose name, as we will see, was traduced in the marketing of Park Hill to media professionals. Long after the demise of postpunk, starting with the tour-de-Sheffield in their 1990 single "My Legendary Girlfriend", Pulp would return again and again to the ambiguous postwar landscape of their hometown, seeing it alternately as utopia and dystopia. In their 1992 "Sheffield: Sex City", Jarvis Cocker intones a series of Sheffield place names, with luridly sensual relish–from "Intake" onwards, each one of them emphasised for any possible double meanings. Frechville, Hackenthorpe, Shalesmoor, *Wombwell*. The next voice you hear is Candida Doyle, deadpan and Yorkshire, reading–of all things–from one of the sexual fantasies in a Nancy Friday book. Here, the city itself is the focus for all libidinal energies. "We were living in a big block of flats [...] within minutes the whole building was fucking. I mean, have you ever heard other people fucking, and really enjoying it? Not like in the movies, but when it's real..." Then, the "sun rose from behind the gasometers at 6.30am", and we're on a tour of the carnal possibilities in a postindustrial city.

Practically inescapable in Sheffield, Park Hill remains an overwhelming reminder of what Sheffield once wanted to be–the capital of the Socialist Republic of South Yorkshire–rather than what it wants to be now, a local service and cultural industries centre. Yet like all British cities, it spent the following decade undergoing the dubious ministrations of "free market" urbanism. This too was done with reference to pop music. The first attempt at centring "regeneration" around the musical heritage of the city was Branson Coates's aforementioned and utterly failed 1999 National Centre for Popular Music, intended as a permanent exhibition, akin to Frank Gehry's Experience Music Project in Seattle. Designed in "iconic" form as three titanium-clad drums, it originally contained exhibits on pop music history such as costumes, instruments, and suchlike. It was hugely

Fig. 4: The New Park Hill. © The author.

unpopular, and closed within two years, to be used by Sheffield Hallam University as a student's union. A much more successful example of neoliberal, "iconic" urbanism using the city's pop history is actually the privatisation and redevelopment of Park Hill by Urban Splash.

Park Hill was transferred – for free, not sold – to Urban Splash in 2008. The Manchester-based property developer is best known for turning derelict mills, office blocks and factories into city-centre "lofts", and according to its own account grew out of a pop poster stall run by founder Tom Bloxham, a former Labour Party Young Socialist. It has long been an interesting amalgam of two New Labour fixations – the "creative industries" and property speculation, as opposed to Old Labour's heavy industries and social housing. Urban Splash has always stressed a link between its work and the Manchester of postpunk and acid house, and its brochure for Park Hill was elegantly rendered by Warp Records' and Pulp's sleeve designers, the Designers Republic. Full of quotations from Sheffield bands like the Human League and ABC, the whole document was written in infantile music-press clichés that contrast tellingly with the popular but nonpatronising language of a document like *Ten Years of Housing in Sheffield*. "Don't you want me baby?" it asks. Yet in 2017, despite a Stirling Prize nomination, the redevelopment of the building can surely be seen as a spectacular failure. Thousands of people have been "decanted" from social housing, in a city with a council waiting list of tens of thousands; only one part of the building has been renovated and sold – to great fanfare, and with major public funding from English Heritage and the Homes and Communities Agency. While the redevelopment has been taking place, Park Hill's derelict hull has become a frequent set for music videos, films, and television series of the 1980s, something surely connected to the proximity of Warp Records' film production arm, Warp Films, at the converted 1930s buildings of the Showroom, just the other side of Sheffield Station.

The Past of the Future

Pop culture of the last decade in Sheffield, and to a degree Manchester, has maintained a preoccupation with the city's postwar landscape, even when the music has become increasingly retro. Manchester has the Manchester Modernist Society, a young preservationist group who put out an attractive, unashamedly nostalgic zine, called *The Modernist*. With its issues on "Government", "Education", "Expos", "Faith", and of course "the Factory", it is suffused with longing for the postwar world and its built landscape. This is on the face of it a travesty of any idea of modernism. If you regard yourself as a modernist, then you're fairly obliged to like or at least take an interest in the contemporary at its mildest, and at its strongest, a stand against the old world, against reaction and in favour of some kind of "new" force, whatever that might be. To be modern might mean embracing Manchester City Council, OMA, and George Osborne's "Powerhouse", centred on its "Factory", or the noxious twin towers currently proposed by a consortium of footballers, Manchester City Council, and international property developers. That's modern as in "modernisation", that strangely neutral term used by Tony Blair to purge the Labour Party of any connection to historical social democracy.

One of the stories Manchester has told itself is that it is, as the city's slogan, coined by Peter Saville, goes, the "Original Modern". To be "Modern" here, as we've seen, leaps between the city of the future created by graft, accident, and greed two hundred years ago to the one created by much the same forces over the last fifteen years. Manchester liberalism and neoliberalism even use the same spaces – now a cotton mill, now a unique urban luxury living solution (forgetting the twelve-hour-plus shifts that accompanied the first or the housing crisis that accompanies the second). There's not much room in that Modern for the Modern that happened in between. Conversely, it's just possible that it is precisely that modernism in between that is truly worthy of the name – rather than Old Corruption newly enlivened with barcode façades or slatted wood-and-aluminium balconies. A modernism that committed itself to socially useful things – education, public housing, the National Health Service, rather than shopping and property speculation – is something to fight for. This other modernism, which features on the pages of *The Modernist*, didn't just want things to look new; it wanted new, better content. A modernity of quality rather than (monetary) quantity. It might break with the image of Mancunia as metropolis of boom-time chancers, from cotton magnates to scallies, but it reconnects it instead with the city that pioneered socialism, the co-operative movement and communism at the same time. The celebration of this by the likes of *The Modernist* could look to the untrained eye like nostalgia; but it might be plotting for a different modernity altogether. That would be the generous assessment. Otherwise, they're just another gang of Retronauts, who are, as students and hipsters once did in Manchester, exchanging an unwelcome modernity with an uncritical longing for an old one.

Fig. 5: "Looking for Jobs and Training?", Sheffield. © The author.

Sheffield, typically, has taken this to a greater intensity. Richard Hawley's longing, knowingly nostalgic ballads have been sheathed in sleeves photographed in the (then) surviving, yet down-at-heel, mundane, modernist spaces of the city, like Coles Corner or Castle Market, which featured on the cover of his *Late Night Final*. Seemingly alongside this is an increasing interest in the city's postwar design as the material for nostalgic design objects: Jonathan Wilkinson's "We Live Here" series of prints presents clear, blueprint-like outlines of Sheffield's particularly rich seam of postwar brutalism, such as Park Hill, Castle Market, or the Tinsley Cooling Towers. One of the bands that most exemplified this was the Long Blondes, who attempted to take up where Pulp had left off in the mid-1990s in their stories of blocked lives, suburban romances and concrete fetishism. Their singer Kate Jackson also produces prints of modernist architecture, brightly melancholic images of flyovers, New Towns, and West London's Trellick Tower. Her new record at the time of writing, *British Road Movies*, is an explicit tribute to the postwar British landscape, both at the time of its destruction and at a time when it is increasingly appreciated as an object of design history, with a wave of coffee-table books and exhibitions, and when its remnants are being privatised and eviscerated as a social project.

We Need to Talk about Newham: The East London Grime Scene as a Site of Emancipatory Disruption

Joy White

What d'ya mean that ya can't find Griminal
Greengate, 6ft, light skin, slimmish
— Griminal, "F**k Radio Set" (2007)[1]

From the early years of the twenty-first century, the grime music scene has been a key feature of East London life, particularly among the young. By now, people are familiar with the pioneer narratives of Wiley and Dizzee Rascal.[2] The more recent achievements of, for example, Skepta and Stormzy have brought grime to a much wider audience. Less is recorded, however, about the influential and compelling work of Newham luminaries such as Sharky Major or Ghetts. This chapter explores

Newham's significant contribution to the grime music scene. Using a distinctive flow and regional accents, grime MCs rap or "spit" over a sparse 140bpm.[3] In many inner-city areas throughout the UK, grime is the everyday soundscape. It is produced through the convivial endeavours of young people of Caribbean, African, and English heritage.[4] Out of these everyday encounters in ordinary spaces such as Stratford, Plaistow, and Canning Town, the grime scene operates as an emancipatory disruption for young people from marginalised communities.

Newham: The Birthplace of Grime?

Newham was formed in 1965 from the old boroughs of East Ham and West Ham. Situated five miles to the east of the City of London, it is within blinking distance of the Canary Wharf financial district. Newham has experienced postwar slum clearance, industrial decline, and high unemployment. In the last thirty years there have been significant regeneration initiatives in a bid to revitalise the area. The London Docklands Development Corporation was formed in 1981 to regenerate Beckton and the Royal Docks, new housing was built in Beckton, and London City Airport was built in 1987. Although wealthier residents have moved into Newham, it is still a poor area. A recent study indicates that 40% of households earned less than 60% of national median income.[5] Also, the borough is ranked eighth in the UK on the Index of Multiple Deprivation.[6]

Newham is predominantly young – the median age is 30.8 – and with 65% of the population claiming a black or ethnic-minority background, it is very multicultural.[7] The multicultural nature of the area is congruent with its history as a location for significant migration from former Commonwealth countries.

The neoliberal political turn that surfaced in the aftermath of the Fordist-Keynesian economic era saw a decline in manufacturing and an increase in employment in the retail, education, and healthcare sectors. Like other disadvantaged areas, Newham lost many local jobs. Newham was a host borough in the London 2012 Olympics, and since then, in a further effort to regenerate the area, it has been designated a Growth Borough.[8] In Growth Boroughs people tend to "die younger, earn less, have fewer qualifications, are more likely to be unemployed, live in overcrowded accommodation or be a victim of crime than an average Londoner".[9]

In urban East London the streets and council-housing estates display the residual marks of communities past and present, from the French Huguenots who came to Spitalfields in the seventeenth century, to Jewish settlement in the early twentieth century, followed by migration from the Caribbean, Africa, and the Indian subcontinent from the 1950s onwards.[10]

Newham, like many inner-city areas, contains a complex network of people who draw on diverse cultural and historical backgrounds. Newham is home to the Royal Docks, built in the 1850s, which linked directly to the railways. At that time, the Royal Docks were one of the largest in the world and brought people from all over the world into East London. In the 1930s, for example, Canning Town was home to the Coloured Men's Institute and at that time had the largest black population in London. Both the Docks and Newham experienced heavy bombing during the Second World War, particularly in the south of the borough.

West Ham included Canning Town and Silvertown and housed the workers for the new industries; in East Ham, houses were built for professional workers. The two areas therefore developed in different ways, West Ham being heavily industrialised and East Ham with much more open space including Central Park, Plashet Park, and Wanstead Flats.

In the 1970s, Silvertown and Canning Town had a significant far-right (National Front) presence, effectively creating no-go areas for ethnic-minority communities. In those days, black and white moved through the world separately – it was a very polarised existence. Now, however, there is a certain hard-fought, but partial, conviviality.

This confluence of people and place created an environment from which grime music could emerge. The label for the genre is as gritty as the landscape its creator occupied. A symbiotic relationship between music, place, and community[11] means that it is unlikely that grime could have come out of the leafy suburbs of Richmond upon Thames. The movement and migration that is a feature of this East London area contributes to the convivial musical practice of black and white youth.

East London is the birthplace of grime music.[12] Despite a suggestion to the contrary from Mykaell Riley, who claimed that grime started with South London's So Solid Crew,[13] it is evident that the London Boroughs of Newham and Tower Hamlets are where UK garage evolved into grime.[14] At first, it had no name, hence Wiley's quizzical references in "Wot Do U Call It?",[15] where he runs through various suggestions of what this new genre could be called. Before it was called grime it was also known as 8-bar, sublow, or eskibeat.[16]

Grime is a specifically English musical genre. It is a creative expression that attracts a national and international audience. A diasporic cultural form, influenced by hip-hop, jungle, dancehall, and UK garage, grime has been nourished by its black Atlantic[17] connections to the Caribbean, Africa, and North America. It comes out of an inner-city environment where the offspring of Caribbean migrants intermingle with a white working-class population and its linguistic canon reflects this.

The Grime Crew as a Symbolic Space

The crew is a key component of the grime scene, particularly in the early days. A crew operates as a group of like-minded individuals, who share a common interest – in this case, music. Often there will be a familial connection and crews may include members who attended the same schools, grew up on the same estates, are brothers or relatives of some kind. Newham Generals, East Connection, and Nasty are crews with a strong connection to the Newham area.

Arguably, the kingpins from Newham with the most influence were Nasty Crew, a fluid collection of approximately a dozen young male artists. Nasty—an acronym for Natural Artistic Sounds Touching You—was founded at the turn of the twenty-first century by Marcus Nasty (Marcus Ramsay), D Double E (Darren Dixon), and Jammer (Jahmek Power) until an acrimonious split left Marcus Nasty at the helm for a while. After the split, D Double E, Jammer, and Footsie (Daniel Carnegie) transformed themselves into the Newham Generals and eventually signed to Dizzee Rascal's Dirtee Stank label. All three continue to perform as independent artists.

Music crew membership allows for a creative expression and performance firmly rooted in the black diaspora experience. Predominantly male, a crew is a space that offers a number of opportunities to learn your craft as a musician as well as develop tacit knowledge about the scene and how it operates. In the crew, roles and responsibilities are delineated and may include DJs, MCs, vocalists, and producers; however members can—and do—cross boundaries often moving temporarily or permanently between one role and another. Although often from distinct geographical areas, grime crews are not static entities. In the early days, members would move back and forth between crews. The postcode boundaries were less firmly drawn and young people would travel around London and beyond to attend and perform at events such as Eskimo Dance and Sidewinder.[18]

In 2003, Dizzee Rascal won the Mercury Music Prize, and in so doing, firmly placed Tower Hamlets on the map as a grimy location. Although he was not formally a member of a particular crew, in the early days Dizzee was mentored by Wiley, the self-styled "Godfather of Grime". A decade on, the fallout between Dizzee and Wiley continues apace, with verbal shots being fired on social media and in interviews.[19] Meanwhile, in neighbouring Newham, Marcus Nasty, Jammer, and other founders of Nasty Crew were also formulating a new sound from the waning UK garage genre. Nasty no longer rules the roost—ruptures, disagreements, and infighting put an end to their output as a crew[20]—however, their pirate radio sets continue to be almost universally lauded.[21] Former members have evolved into different roles and genres: Marcus Nasty is a DJ on Rinse FM, Ghetts is an independent recording artist, Stormin (Shaun Lewis) is a drum and bass MC, and Jammer's Lord of the Mics annual MC clash continues to make waves.

Putting Newham on the Map

In the quote that opens this chapter, Griminal is unequivocal. In his freestyle, he tells us exactly where to find him. Greengate is an area in Plaistow, in Newham, a junction on Barking Road that is the site of the Greengate Pub. In the Newham grime scene, it is something of a landmark. But it's not just Greengate that is meaningful here; the map indicates some of the grime MCs and

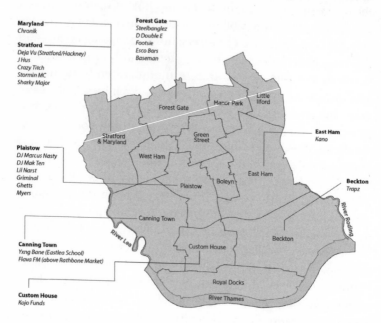

Fig. 1: Mapping grime artists in Newham.

other artists, such as J Hus, that continue the convivial activities of the grime genre through the performance of Afro/dancehall.[22]

An iconic image of MC Crazy Titch (Carl Dobson)[23] adorns the front cover of Don't Call Me Urban, Simon Wheatley's ten-year photo investigation into the grime scene.[24] Deja Vu FM, the influential pirate radio station, operated on a number of sites in East London, including Stratford. It is this location that hosted the now notorious clash between Dizzee Rascal and Crazy Titch.[25] The Stratford site has since been demolished and has become part of the Olympic Park. Sharky Major is a grime scene veteran, having featured on Dizzee Rascal's remix of "I Luv U" in 2003.[26] Afro/dancehall artist Yxng Bane caught the public's attention with a remix of Ed Sheeran's "Shape of You"[27] which got to number one on the Billboard Hot 100 in 2017. Signed to Tinie Tempah's Disturbing London label, Yxng Bane's most recent single "Rihanna"[28] entered the top forty. Another emerging Afro/dancehall artist is Kojo Funds; he featured on "Finders Keepers"[29] by Mabel, which got to number eight in the UK national charts in 2017.

Flava FM, a pirate radio station, is transmitted from a flat above Rathbone Market in Canning Town. On a 2001 recording from Flava[30] you can hear Nasty originals Stormin, Sharky Major, Kano, and Armour spitting over garage beats played by Marcus Nasty. Rathbone Market and the surrounding area form the third phase of Newham Council's £3.7 billion project to regenerate Canning Town and Custom House.[31] Rathbone, a typical combination of shops and stalls, has existed at the Canning Town end of Barking Road since the mid-nineteenth century. Despite promises to retain the market post redevelopment, only one or two shops/stalls remain, and the market has been erased from publicity materials.[32]

Steelbanglez, a music producer for over a decade, talks about listening to Nasty Crew on Rinse FM and starting out as a grime producer before moving on to other genres.[33] Well-regarded MC Esco Bars[34] (Jade Gavin Defoe) was a sometime affiliate of

Slew Dem crew. Esco Bars, a half-brother of footballer Jermain Defoe, was killed in 2009. Sir Spyro (Karl Joseph), originally from Manor Park, was a Grime DJ on Rinse FM for many years until a recent move to BBC 1Xtra. Sir Spyro produced four tracks on Stormzy's Gang Signs and Prayer album.[35] St Bonaventure's Roman Catholic Boys School in Forest Gate boasts Tinchy Stryder (Kwasi Danquah), Gracious K (Lance Agyepong) – responsible for UK funky anthem "Migraine Skank"[36] – and Griminal as former pupils.

Grime Music Scene as an Emancipatory Disruption

In June 2016, I spoke with an event promoter called Neville,[37] who I had first met in 2009 in Cyprus. He had been involved in grime since the early days, starting out as an MC; he then became an event promoter/music manager. In the late 1990s, when pirate radio stations such as Flava FM and Deja Vu were playing UK garage, Neville was organising under-twenty-one events at two popular venues in Stratford. According to Neville, these venues acted as a training ground for many young East London MCs, including Dizzee Rascal (who also speaks of these events on "Make It Last"). In those days, Neville said, "it was just voices, you couldn't see any of the artists on the radio and you didn't know what they looked like".

Victor was another person that I interviewed several times, once in Ayia Napa in 2009 at the height of the UK funky scene, and again in London in 2010. Victor had started out as a grime DJ and then moved over to UK funky. At our last interview in 2017 he reflected on the very early days of grime in Newham and paid homage to Sharky Major:

> It wasn't just about the music, we used to live the life, the culture. Going to record shops. It was a big community. There were lots of crews out there [in 2000–2001], but none of the MCs were as lyrical as Sharky.

By using English accents, and therefore their own voice, grime provided an opportunity to step away from the "elders" in the UK garage scene who, at the time, were not paying much attention.[38] At the same time, the commercial juggernaut that was US hip-hop and rap was subsumed, in London at least, by a black English aesthetic. From that comes the liberating aspects that can occur in the creation of a liminal space where young people could talk about their everyday lives, struggles, and aspirations.

In the grime scene, spitting bars is a form of cultural exchange. The symbolic spaces of the crew developed out of a sound-system culture that was the sonic background for many MCs. Jammer's basement in Leytonstone where many MCs and crews clashed and recorded is another symbolic (and physical) space. Youth centres and street corners where young people could congregate allowed for the development of creative clusters from which innovative musical practices, like grime, could emerge. Many of my younger respondents talked about learning their craft in school playgrounds. Here's Andrew: "Being around music was a gift […] me and my friends from school would listen to Nasty, Roll Deep, and East Connection and try to do our own version at break."[39]

As grime occurred as a convivial construct, so it also influenced a new spin on the Afrobeats genre: Afro/dancehall, a specific UK genre sonically nourished by Jamaican and West African connections that has developed more recently. Like grime, it hosts a multilingual array of vocal styles: J Hus (Momodou Jallow) from Stratford, of Gambian heritage, releases "Bouff Daddy",[40] which is then remixed featuring Popcaan, a popular Jamaican dancehall artist. On his track "My 9nine",[41] Kojo Funds, who is of Ghanaian ancestry, samples Jamaican dancehall artist Wayne Wonder. As with many tracks in this genre, the soft vocals and lively beats belie the harsh lyrical content.

For the young people in Newham, the imagined boundaries of the street and the estate are real. Postcode delineations have replaced the relatively easy movement of the early days to form clear, definitive boundaries, and bounded territories.

Road life and the veneration of quick cash places borders on conviviality, and the temptations for wrongdoing remain. On his highly acclaimed album Gang Signs and Prayer, Stormzy featured and paid homage to Crazy Titch, who is currently serving a minimum thirty-year sentence for murder. Crazy Titch has been incarcerated for so long that during his conversation with Stormzy he declares that he "doesn't even know what a hashtag is".[42] In 2015, J Hus was stabbed five times and temporarily abandoned his music career.[43] In 2017, Trapz (Sadik Kamara) was handed a fourteen-year sentence for a series of violent robberies.[44]

Conclusion

As a historically poor area, Newham is a neighbourhood that has experienced many years of economic decline. It has felt the brunt of almost a decade of austerity. Young people from Newham mired in structural disadvantage are effectively excluded from many social and economic milieux; however, creative practice in the grime music scene creates a site of emancipatory disruption.

In this somewhat gloomy landscape, despite fragmented institutional structures and a challenging youth labour market, grime music offers an opportunity for young people from poor communities to operate in a convivial aspect that is generative for the production of meaningful creative work. In Newham, young people's investment in grime as a cultural form and creative practice allows for a chaotic and unruly formulation of conviviality[45] that disrupts what it means to be young, black, and poor.

A unique confluence of people and places created the environment for the growth of grime. The Newham influence so far has been consistently overlooked in academic and popular writing, despite its critical role in the development of grime and other genres such as UK funky and Afro/dancehall. The thriving African and Caribbean communities in Newham allowed for a reinterpretation of reggae and hip-hop musical forms. The emergence of a site of emancipatory disruption is exemplified by the level and variety of musical expression that continues to flow out of these areas. Regeneration buried Deja Vu FM under the Olympic Park, and the onward march of consumerism saw the pub at Greengate become a Tesco Express, but young people continue to find ways to make music that matters for them. Despite postcodes and poverty corralling young black lives into ever-smaller spaces, these convivial activities continue to flow through, and expand out of, local Newham neighbourhoods.

This chapter is dedicated to Stormin, a pioneer in the grime scene, who sadly passed away in February 2018.

Newham Artists: Selected Discography

Baseman ft. Snizzy (2016), "Talks"
    https://www.youtube.com/watch?v=TM4urXhsPvU
Chronik (2012), "Ring"
    https://www.youtube.com/watch?v=pu-Vj7-vSRA
D Double E ft. Wiley (2017), "Better Than the Rest"
    https://www.youtube.com/watch?v=_gOTqm0ihTY
DJ Mak 10 (2004), "GRIME (100% DUBS) MIX"
    https://www.youtube.com/watch?v=66Iw01gYAy0
Footsie ft Giggs (2016), "Hot Water"
    https://www.youtube.com/watch?v=sCaZOeuamEk
Ghetts (2017), "Slumdog Millionaire"
    https://www.youtube.com/watch?v=0HfGENtAj2M
Griminal ft. JME (2012), "HAM"
    https://www.youtube.com/watch?v=0ANe9nyFTZk
Kano (2007), "Signs in Life"
    https://www.youtube.com/watch?v=N7XAGvc5N34
Lil Nasty (2016), "Regardless"
    https://www.youtube.com/watch?v=__4gvd2Moa4
Marcus Nasty (2015), "Boiler Room Set"
    https://www.youtube.com/watch?v=aBc9NKlk1t8
Myers (2017), "Home"
    https://www.youtube.com/watch?v=Xo9WfPGFsJo
Sharky Major (2017), "We Shall See"
    https://www.youtube.com/watch?v=pVtrhgIkoLw
Steelbanglez ft. MoStack, MIST, Haile, Abra
    Cadabra (2017), "Money"
        https://www.youtube.com/watch?v=LwtpuoR9r7Q
Stormin ft. Black Steve (2014), "Hindu Kush"
    https://www.youtube.com/watch?v=MJoQLXcYr7M
Trizzy Trapz (2016), "Mi Na Talk"
    https://www.youtube.com/watch?v=lZ1JhPlrD-0

All webpages last accessed 29 December 2017.

Endnotes

1 https://www.youtube.com/watch?v=9nUJMEo1hIw. Lyrics reproduced with kind permission of Joshua Ramsay (Griminal).

2 Dan Hancox, *Stand Up Tall: Dizzee Rascal and the Birth of Grime* (Kindle, 2013)

3 Hancox, *Stand Up Tall*; Matt Mason, *The Pirate's Dilemma: How Hackers, Punk Capitalists, Graffiti Millionaires and Other Youth Movements are Remixing Our Culture and Changing Our World* (Penguin, 2008); Joy White, *Urban Music and Entrepreneurship: Beats, Rhymes and Young People's Enterprise* (Routledge, 2016)

4 White, *Urban Music and Entrepreneurship*

5 Kat Hanna and Nicolas Bosetti, *Inside Out: The New Geography Of Wealth And Poverty In London* (Centre for London, 2015)

6 London Borough of Newham. (2017). Newham Info. Retrieved 2 September 2017, from http://www.newham.info/factsandfigures

7 London Borough of Newham Newham's Local Plan. (2012). *Newham 2027 Newham's Local Plan Detailed Sites and Policies Development Plan Document* (p. 291). NOMIS. (2017). *Newham Profile: Official Labour Market Statistics* (p. 11).

8 The Growth Boroughs are: Barking and Dagenham, Greenwich, Hackney, Newham, Tower Hamlets and Waltham Forest. These boroughs hosted the 2012 Olympic Games and are deemed to have the strongest potential in the UK for economic growth. See http://www.growthboroughs.com/

9 Newham Council Communications (2014) *Newham's Legacy Story* (p4).

10 Richard Tames, *London: A Cultural History* (Oxford University Press, 2006)

11 John Connell and Chris Gibson, *Sound Tracks: Popular*

Music, Identity, and Place (Routledge, 2003)

12   Chris Campion, "A look at grime music), the *Observer*, (23 May 2004), http://www.guardian.co.uk/music/2004/may/23/urban1 (Last Accessed on 13 April 2012); Simon Hampson, "Interview: Geeneus", *FACT*, 2009. (1st January 2009), http://www.factmag.com/2009/01/01/interview-geeneus/ (Last Accessed on 11 September 2010); *Dreamers row, 10 Years of Grime – A Genre That Defined a Generation* (2012), http://www.dreamersrow.com/10-years-of-Grime-a-genre-that-defined-a-generation/ Last Accessed on 21st June 2012; Hancox, *Stand Up Tall*

13   Jack Grove, "Interview with Mykaell Riley", *Times Higher Education* (16 November 2017), https://www.timeshigher education.com/people/interview-mykaell-riley-university-of-westminster (Accessed 17 November 2017)

14   Hancox, *Stand Up Tall; Mason, The Pirate's Dilemma; White, Urban Music and Entrepreneurship*

15   Wiley, "Wot Do U Call It?", *Treddin' On Thin Ice* (XL Recordings, 2004). Available at: https://www.youtube.com/watch?v=e1YKFV45M18

16   Hancox, *Stand Up Tall*

17   Paul Gilroy, *The Black Atlantic* (Verso, 1996)

18   Wiley, the Godfather of Grime was founder of The Eskimo Dance event, it ran from 2002-2005. Subsequently revived in 2012, it is now a UK-wide series of events showcasing existing and emerging talent. See: https://boilerroom.tv/the-eskimo-dance-it-was-chaos-but-thats-what-made-it-special/ Another legendary club night was Sidewinder (See http://www.officialsre.com/). It started in 2004 out as a UK Garage event and then progressed into live Grime performances in Northampton, Swindon and Bristol.

19   http://www.independent.co.uk/arts-entertainment/music/news/dizzee-wiley-beef-twitter-underage-sex-allegation-death-threat-instagram-video-raskit-tour-a7978506.html

20 N.A.S.T.Y Biography (2008) https://www.last.fm/music/Nasty+Crew/+wiki

21 British Grime/Garage Music History (2013) *2001 Rolldeep B2B Nasty Crew 92.3 Deja Vu FM*. Available at: https://www.youtube.com/watch?v=7JVCGsbtm94&feature=youtube_gdata_player Last Accessed on 4th May 2015

22 We are, perhaps at another "what do you call it?" moment with this genre which has been referred to as Afro Swing, Afro Trap.

23 Crazy Titch, "I Can C You" (Look Down Records, 2003). Available at: https://www.youtube.com/watch?v=sbZAAr1NHFU

24 Simon Wheatley, *Don't Call Me Urban! The Time of Grime* (Northumbria Press, 2010)

25 The Crazy Titch and Dizzee Rascal clash in 2003 on the roof at Deja Vu can be seen here: https://www.youtube.com/watch?v=VShFt53ZkqA

26 Dizzee Rascal, "I Luv U: Wiley and Sharky Major remix". Available at: https://soundcloud.com/dizzeerascalfeatwileyandsharkeymajor/i-luv-u-remix

27 Ed Sheeran, "Shape Of You (YXNG BANE REMIX)": https://www.youtube.com/watch?v=lMUfg75kZwk

28 Yxng Bane, "Rihanna" (Disturbing London Records, 2017). Available at: https://www.youtube.com/watch?v=1ruitsqQ34c

29 Mabel ft. Kojo Funds, "Finders Keepers" (Polydor, 2017). Available at: https://www.youtube.com/watch?v=O3TDhPVx1Do (Last Accessed on 12 February 2018)

30 Original London Pirate Radio: Nasty Crew Flava FM 87.6 (2001) https://www.youtube.com/watch?v=qW3wAaSU90U (Accessed 12 February 2018)

31 NOMIS, *Newham Profile: Official Labour Market Statistics* (2017), p. 11

32 http://www.projectorange.com/projects/view/rathbone-market (Accessed 12 February 2018)

33   Timi Ben-Edigbe, "UK rap super-producer Steel Banglez is finally getting the recognition he deserves", *Hyponik* (2017), http://hyponik.com/features/steel-banglez-money-interview/ Last (Accessed on 30 June 2017)

34   Esco Bars, "Just Listen" (2008). Available at: https://www.youtube.com/watch?v=Q20lkT9syiA

35   https://en.wikipedia.org/wiki/Gang_Signs_%26_Prayer

36   Gracious K, "Migraine Skank" (Sony, 2008). Available at: https://www.youtube.com/watch?v=XR3gfLa5c50

37   To protect the identity of my respondents, I have used pseudonyms in this chapter.

38   Mason, *The Pirate's Dilemma; Lloyd Bradley, Sounds Like London: 100 Years of Black Music in the Capital* (Serpent's Tail, 2013)

39   Andrew interviewed in 2017.

40   J Hus "Bouff Daddy", *Common Sense* (Black Butter Records, 2017). Available at: https://www.youtube.com/watch?v=zTaJA-0jvs8

41   Kojo Funds, "My 9ine" (2016). Available at: https://www.youtube.com/watch?v=k_rFKqkYWQY

42   https://crackmagazine.net/article/lists/eight-talking-points-gang-signs-prayer/

43   Kieran Yates, "Rapper J Hus: 'I was a doughnut hustler!'", the *Guardian* (25 May 2017), https://www.theguardian.com/music/2017/may/25/rapper-j-hus-i-was-doughnut-hustler-common-sense:

44   Tanveer Mann, "Thugs filmed squirting acid in shopkeeper's face during robbery", *Metro* (13 October 2017), http://metro.co.uk/2017/10/13/thugs-filmed-squirting-acid-in-shopkeepers-face-during-robbery-6997034/

45   Paul Gilroy, *After Empire: Melancholia or Convivial Culture?: Multiculture or Postcolonial Melancholia* (Routledge, 2004)

Harmony and Prosperity Unlimited: Real Estate Rhetorics between Shanghai and London

Michela Pace

Sounds are like flavours. Different elements complete one another: one breath, two styles, three types, four instruments, five sounds, six measures, seven notes, eight winds, and nine songs. Different sounds complement one another: the pure and the impure, the big and the small, the short and the long, the rapid and the measured, the sorrowful and the joyful, the strong and the tender, the slow and the fast, the high and the low, the in and the out, and the inclusive and the non-inclusive. Listening to this kind of music, the heart/mind of the good person (jun zi) is purified.
— Yan Zi (?–500 bce) on the notion of harmony[1]

Cultural References as Drivers for Development

In global cities, regeneration is driven by increased housing demand and the appetites of market economies looking to exploit the built environment. This process has seen systemic changes in the pattern of land ownership with an augmented emphasis on luxury buildings.[2] Gigantic urban developments have disrupted local communities at the same time as they have produced spaces which are homogenous, banal, and purified.

This homogenisation starts in the early stages of regeneration projects–in the marketing and promotion strategies. These strategies are layered with codes and the ideologies, produced not in isolation but transnationally. Regeneration projects produced between Newham, London and Shanghai provide powerful examples of this.

Culture is particularly prominent in this coding, especially where developers want to provide a sense of place to otherwise detached architecture. By culture, I mean notions of history, heritage, or memory, visual and philosophical traditions, and other elements of local and national character. Their function in a global capitalist marketplace is to embed cultural values into popular aesthetics to gain consent, and at the same time to appeal to local and global audiences.

The strategic use of culture is not new. It has been observed in urban planning since at least the 1990s.[3] What distinguishes it today is its transnational configuration and the prominent use of heritage in its codes. In these projects heritage establishes an allusion to well-established values derived from the past, capitalising on them for the appetites of investors. Through heritage the anonymous urban development recovers a sense of place and is magically returned to the people while also upholding new economic and social horizons for the area.

East and West: A Two-Way Relationship in Communication Strategies

In this schema London and Shanghai, two cities at the centre of the housing market's financial deregulation in antipodal continents, produce similar narratives, communication techniques, and contents. While these cities' economic and

Figs 1 and 2: Images and wording around a redevelopment site in Shanghai (top) and London (bottom). Heritage is often recalled as one of the cultural drivers fuelling the regeneration, and at the same time, as one of the qualities that the new project will return to the collectivity.

Figs 3 and 4: (top) Painter reproducing a traditional landscape scene on the walls of a redevelopment site in Shanghai. The painting stands just in front of the shikumen houses that will soon be knocked down at the rear of the plot. (bottom) The CGI, belonging to the same scheme, covers another side of the same wall, this time on the main road at the front of the redevelopment site.

political backgrounds are different – one the capital of European neoliberalism, the other the centre of the red neoliberalism – both include culture and heritage as communications strategies, not only as marketing tools but also as instruments to influence our understanding of the city.

In Shanghai's city centre historic buildings are protected to boost renewal. Where actual historic buildings are absent, references to random historic buildings are included in promotional images. Similarly, traditional Chinese landscapes are painted directly on the walls of redevelopment sites to provide a sense of familiarity and location. In London, too, a well-declared relationship to the past bolsters many redevelopments, which claim to "blend heritage architecture with the best of contemporary design". "Timeless brick" often comes to service here to provide "exquisite craftsmanship" and "a quintessentially British past", to global capitalist developments.

The mutual influence of East and West in regeneration strategies is under-observed in contemporary understandings of global communication.[4] For the most part, the exchange between East and West is thought to occur on different channels, with China importing Western architectural models and techniques, especially after the Cultural Revolution, and the West importing Asian capital investments. However, the speech by President Xi Jinping at the Historic Communist Party Congress in October 2017 gives a different impression of China's role in this relationship. Unlike dominant Western understandings, Xi Jinping makes clear that China no longer needs to learn from the West. Its transition from a "rich country" to a "strong nation" – central to China's and Xi's historical mission – then entails disrupting the twin channel assumption.[5]

What China is exporting today goes beyond capital. Through land reform and an increasing orientation to a market economy model, the government has supported the real estate market and accommodated the demands of private investors.[6] Examples of this include the state's role in environmental beautification, land assembly (to overcome fragmented property rights), and gentrification.[7] Notions of culture, memory, and heritage are frequently used to market these redevelopment projects and make them appealing to investors.

The figuration of culture in these new projects builds on earlier uses of culture and heritage in Chinese architecture. After the Cultural Revolution, Western architectural designs were often copied and reproduced in Chinese cities. Thames Town, created to absorb Shanghai's expansion, and reproductions of the English village are examples of this. The difference today is that Chinese investors have turned their attention from architectural mimicry to acquisitions in the UK market itself, and where Western cultural references are prominent in Shanghai developments they exist alongside local narratives on heritage and authenticity. This is increasingly communicated through branding because as the built environment grows generic and simplified local cultural difference is necessary to mark originality.

To understand this in greater detail, and its relation to the cultural intertwining of London's and Shanghai's urban developments, we can look at two narratives of heritage: harmony and prosperity.

Harmony: The Case of Suhe Creek, Shanghai

One of the most referenced concepts in the construction of liveable spaces in China is "harmony". In China, "harmony" draws on Confucian philosophy and increasingly occupies popular political discourse promoting "urban renaissance".

The word *he* (和) is central to Chinese culture and refers to a set of discourses rooted in Confucianism. Confucianism defined harmony as a framework for organising life and maintaining balance at different levels: the individual, the family, the community, the nation, the world, the governance of the state, between human beings and nature, and at its final and highest level, as a cosmological law of order.[8]

The revival of harmony in recent political discourse can be

Figs 5 and 6: Images on the walls and fences of the redevelopment sites in Shanghai (top) and London (bottom). While hiding renewal of urban fabric and communities, the images depict smoothed sceneries through the use of traditional Chinese landscape and nature. In Shanghai, the term of reference is a representation of nature according to an established artistic canon, which reveals the importance of "tradition". In London, the photographic simulation of the ivy recalls the plants covering old buildings and a generic notion of "past".

Figs 7 and 8: Advertisements in London (top) and Shanghai (bottom) depicting an outdoor place and an interior.

traced to the speech made at the fourth plenary session of the Sixteenth Central Committee of the Communist Party of China in September 2004 by former President Hu Jintao. The subject of the speech was "building a harmonious socialist society". The concept of "Harmonious Society" or *hexie shehui* (和谐社会), "Harmony" or *hexie* (和谐), has since become prominent.

The Confucian ideal of "harmony" is then a powerful reference for Chinese attitudes toward private and public life. At the same time, it has become an aesthetic and political doctrine, and can be observed in images used to represent new urban redevelopments. Here, harmony is found in tensionless representations where people meet naturally and conflicts are erased. Images of interiors generally show men and women in upmarket environments, cleaned of any disturbing elements to the point where outdoor spaces are generally distant bird's-eye views connoting grandness and detachment.

However, in Confucianism, it is "difference" not blandness that is the "precondition and cornerstone of harmony".[9] Harmony presupposes the acknowledgement of difference as a creative tension generated through the interaction of different elements. The energy that sustains harmony is relational; it welcomes strain, conflict, and negotiation.[10] By contrast, the images used to promote new developments translate these commitments into detached, homogeneous landscapes where conflict is absent.[11] Harmony is twisted and flattened onto advertisement hoardings to recall an idea of order and beauty able to redress an increasingly unbalanced and unfair landscape.[12]

The Suhe Creek redevelopment in Shanghai includes 243 apartments spread over twenty-seven floors, a luxury resort, and a hotel of forty floors branded by Bulgari, an Italian luxury firm famous for jewellery. The project overlooks the Bund, the celebrated historic promenade of Shanghai along the Huangpu River, a stone's throw away from People's Square. The urban project is overseen by a world-class architectural design team Foster + Partners, and the Bulgari complex, scheduled to open in fall 2017, is overseen by the Italian luxury architectural firm Antonio Citterio, Patricia Viel Interiors. Here the centrality of culture as heritage is made clear by the use of an Antonio Bulgari quote on the development's billboards: "One has to go deep into the course of history, understand the past, this knowledge as a foundation for the future [sic]."[13]

As you enter the marketing suite of the Suhe Creek redevelopment, a four-metre-long map depicting a hundred years of urban change greets you. There is a short video titled *An Historical Celebration of Suzhou River*, explaining the fundamental role of this water route in the development of the local built and social environment. The redevelopment appears at the end as the final act of restitution. A second video, this time for Bulgari, claims history as a continuous source of inspiration. "Classic Is Revolutionary", it concludes, thus re-establishing revolution as luxury creative genesis. Heritage is once again at the centre of a revolution, a driver of placemaking able to produce urban and social regeneration alike.

The concepts of past, inspiration, and nostalgia through which the Italian brand is made recognisable are successfully used to market the regeneration project and to inform the Chinese notion of harmony. Heritage becomes the language through which "harmony" is established–cleaning, ordering, and reinventing a part of the city. This project is exclusionary. After wiping out the old *shikumen* houses on the Suhe Creek, the redevelopment will not be returned to its original inhabitants. Heritage has branded the cultural and financial value of place, while harmony renders the process of renewal natural and inevitable for the wellbeing of a selected few.

Prosperity: The Case of Newham Supernova, London

In 2010, Newham Council launched a promotional video at the Shanghai world trade fair, Shanghai Expo. The video, titled *London's Regeneration Supernova*, promoted Newham's

" One has to go deep into the course of history,
understand the past,
this knowledge as a foundation for the future."
– Nicola Bulgari

"了解自己的过去才能面对未来。"
——尼古拉·宝格丽

gs 9 and 10: "One has to go deep into the course of history, understand the past, this
nowledge as a foundation for the future"–Nicola Bulgari. The sign around the working
te of Suhe Creek (top) and the area where old shikumen houses laid just in front the
xury towers (bottom).

London's moving east

伦敦正在向东拓展

Where there is huge potential for growth and prosperity

繁荣发展的潜力巨大

Figs 11 and 12: Text from the video London's Regeneration Supernova, produced by Newham Council/London Development Agency and presented at the Shanghai World Expo, 2010. The references to history and English recognisability are abundant.

"Arc of Opportunity" (an area extending from Stratford to the Royal Docks via Canning Town and Custom House) to Chinese investors. Alongside stock images of the city, the video's text proclaimed "London's moving east", referencing the geographical location of Newham within London, and the Eastern market. The video's following invitation to "take your place in the future of London" was a call to Chinese investors interested in buying UK real estate.

London relies heavily on foreign investment to support developments, and large flows of overseas capital are seen as necessary to keep the real estate market afloat.[14] Between 2006 and 2016 foreign investments in London increased from 1% to 25%.[15] Among the buyers, the Chinese were particularly prominent,[16] notably the upper middle class investing in residential properties, and larger investors looking to diversify and stabilise their property portfolios with Western acquisitions. The real estate company Pittar predicts a four-fold increase in Chinese investment over ten years on the current figure of £38 million.[17]

Newham Council's video *London's Regeneration Supernova* is part of this trend. Its intention was to attract financial investments from overseas. In the video, heritage was used to provide cultural value to Newham's "Arc of Opportunity". The slogans that appealed to the East (mentioned above) were paired with red buses and pictures of Big Ben – pieces of history made ready for global consumption – and these were assembled alongside Chinese cultural codes.

In the video, the word "prosperity" appears to make reference to the Chinese cultural pillar of good fortune. In Chinese culture, the prosperity symbol *Lu* is part of three celestial stars: *Fu* (luck), *Lu* (wealth), and *Shou* (longevity).[18] These stars have a set of meanings spanning from financial wealth to personal wellbeing. In the video, "prosperity" then becomes a cultural strategy for speaking about money and personal wellbeing. In this way, a well-established Chinese concept is used to make investment in a Western city more appealing. The pairing of "prosperity" with images of British heritage locates and distinguishes that investment.

Conclusions

This discussion of "prosperity" and "harmony" demonstrates how cultural references are used in marketing materials to promote regeneration projects in London and Shanghai. This strategy blends social values based on place specificity and historical legacy with the necessity to increase the financial value of redevelopment schemes. This occurs at two scales: the neighbourhood, where there is a need to establish an existing built legacy; and the global, where investors are provided with proof of place authenticity. In the transnational market, references to place include not only local and national icons, but also foreign symbolism necessary to create familiarity for global investors.

In this world of global investments, local culture, which is layered and complex, becomes reduced to the essential codes[19] – red phone boxes, branded architecture, or ancient monuments. At the same time, Western cultural references mix with Eastern concepts and Eastern philosophy is embedded in Western communication. These strategies exploit familiar cultural narratives and embed them in a different context to make sense of new realities. In this way, financial possibilities are rendered appealing for a wider range of investors.

This is all part of a wider mechanism of capital extraction operating in global cities.[20] Large-scale regenerations use all possible means to feed profit, including culture, which preserves identity and originality adding value to the landscape. Heritage then becomes the means to maximise buildings' economic return on the basis of a nostalgic credit to construction. Projects are presented as restoring the city to its inhabitants through the rediscovery of cultural elements; however, in effect, the project becomes a means of privatising the area for investment.

igs 13 and 14: Random images of colonial buildings and pieces of architecture on the
anners around a working site in Shanghai (top). The depicted buildings, belonging to the
und, have nothing to share with the location of the redevelopment. In the bottom picture,
he promotion of the "Heritage App" in the Battersea Power Station area.

Demolition of existing homes and communities is the collateral damage – a necessary action to protect, promote, and reinvent the cultural value of the site.

Where the use of "harmony" is concerned, it is worth recalling that "Confucian harmony is not 'immediate harmony'; it is not the kind of harmony in which Adam and Eve find themselves in their natural state. Confucian harmony is reflective and mediated",[21] a process that requires time and debate. Globalisation by contrast entails the homogenisation of the built environment through processes that neither take time, nor entail debate.

The journey of a building "from desire, to model, to construction, and to occupancy has compressed",[22] eventually occupying a double spread of a brochure. We sell and live a purified image of the city, risk of conflict is discarded, and happiness presented as a given. Here culture is no more than an asset, easy to reproduce, defend, and advertise to feed the real estate market. Global cities work on this logic, and the transnational use of culture is now more than ever a driver of redevelopment able to simultaneously create consent and value.

Endnotes

1   Confucian classic Zuo Zhuan (Chapter Shaogong 20). Cited in: Chenyang Li, "The Philosophy of Harmony in Classical Confucianism", *Philosophy Compass*, 3:3, 2008, pp. 423-435. http://onlinelibrary.wiley.com/doi/10.1111/j.1747-9991.2008.00141.x/pdf (Accessed 15 June 2017)

2   Saskia Sassen, "Who Owns Our Cities and Why This Urban Takeover Should Concern Us All", the *Guardian* (24th November 2015), https://www.theguardian.com/cities/2015/nov/24/who-owns-our-cities-and-why-this-urban-takeover-should-concern-us-all (Accessed 15 January 2018)

3   On this topic see also Sharon Zukin, *The Culture of Cities* (Blackwell, 1995); Franco Bianchini, "Rethinking the relationship between culture and urban planning", in François Matarasso and Steven Halls (eds), *The Art of Regeneration (March 1996 Conference Papers* (Comedia, 1996); A. Whyatt, *The Creative Capital: Cultural Industries, Young People and Regeneration in London* (Trafalgar Square, 2000).

4   On this topic see also Jean Baudrillard, *Il delitto perfetto,* Italian edition, trans. Gabriele Piana (Raffello Cortina Editore, 1996); *Vilem Flusser, Per una filosofia della fotografia,* Italian edition (2006) trans. Chantal Marazia (Mondadori, 2006).

5   "President Xi and the Chinese Dream", narrated by David Aaronovitch, *The Briefing Room,* BBC Radio4 (19 October 2017), http://www.bbc.co.uk/programmes/b098nfg4 (Accessed 27 October 2017)

6   Douglas Spencer, *The Architecture of Neoliberalism: How Contemporary Architecture Became an Instrument of Control and Compliance* (Boomsbury, 2016)

7   Dallas Rogers, *The Geopolitics of Real Estate. Reconfiguring Property, Capital and Rights,* (Rowman and Littlefield International, 2016)

8   Xuan Wang, Kasper Juffermans and Caixia Du, "Harmony

As Language Policy in China: An Internet Perspective", *Language Policy*, 15(3), 2015, pp. 299-321. Available at: https://link.springer.com/article/10.1007/s10993-015-9374-y (Accessed 5 June 2017)

9   Ibid.

10   Li, "The Philosophy of Harmony in Classical Confucianism"

11   On the way "degenerated utopias" dissimulate oppositions see also Louis Marin, "Disneyland: A Degenerate Utopia", in Sam Weber and Henry Sussman (eds) *Glyph One* (John Hopkins University Press, 1983), pp. 50-66.

12   Bin Yu, "China's Harmonious World: Beyond Cultural Interpretations", *Journal of Chinese Political Science*, 13:2, 2008, pp. 119-141.

13   Verbatim English text on a Chinese billboard around the Suhe Creek redevelopment, Shanghai

14   Kath Scanlon, Christine Whitehead, Fanny Blanc, with Ulises Moreno-Tabarez, *The Role of Overseas Investors in the London New-Build Residential Market. Final Report for Homes of London, Annex B, LSE London* (2017) https://www.london.gov.uk/moderngovmb/documents/s58640/08b2b%20LSE%20Overseas%20Investment%20report.pdf (Accessed October 27, 2017).

15   Robert Booth, "Foreign Investors Snapping Up London Homes Suitable for First-Time Buyers", the *Guardian* (13th June 2017), https://www.theguardian.com/society/2017/jun/13/foreign-investors-snapping-up-london-homes-suitable-for-first-time-buyers (Accessed 27 October 2017)

16   Tom Philips. "'This Is Just the Start': China's Passion for Foreign Property", the *Guardian* (29 September 2016), https://www.theguardian.com/cities/2016/sep/29/inside-china-passion-foreign-property-investment-uk (Accessed 27 October 2017)

17   Juwai, Accessed 10 February 2018, https://list.juwai.com

18   Cindy Chan, "Chinese Character for Harmony: Hé⊠, Portraying the Traditional Chinese Ideal of Harmonious

Balance Between Nature and Humankind", Epoch Times (15 March 2013), https://www.theepochtimes.com/chinese-character-for-harmony-he-d_3913.html (Accessed: 27 October 2017)

19 Anna Klingmann, *Brandscapes*, (MIT Press, 2007)

20 Saskia Sassen, "Predatory Formations Dressed in Wall Street suit and Algorithmic Math", *Science, Technology & Society*, 22:1, 2017, pp. 1-15, http://saskiasassen.com/PDFs/publications/Predatory-formations.pdf (Accessed 10 February 2018)

21 Li, "The Philosophy of Harmony in Classical Confucianism"

22 Adam Brown, "The Spinning Index: Architectural Images and the Reversal of Causality", in Daniel Rubinstein, Johnny Golding and Andy Fisher (eds), *On the Verge of Photography* (ARTicle Press, 2013), pp. 237-258.

Jean-Michel Jarman:
The Last of Docklands

Will Jennings

Fig. 1: Millennium Mills, 2018. © The author, 2018.

Fig. 2: Millennium Mills, 2013. © Bradley Garrett, 2013.

Silvertown is a new piece of city in London's Royal Docks for people to make, show and share. Silvertown is an effect. Buildings reinvented. Spaces activated. And openness, wellness, curiosity, collision and collaboration are the order of the day.
–Silvertown developers, 2017[1]

A great hulk of industry stands proud in the Royal Docks, a solid white monolith which seems to relish looking across at the flimsily engineered frame of ExCel Arena across the water. This is old Docklands staring at the new, an apparent solidity and sheer mass of industry looking down upon the young interloper's service and entertainments economy.

The 1930s Millennium Mills have hung on, surviving the closure of the Royal Docks in 1981 and grand renovation plans including an early 2000s scheme to fill the building with luxury apartments, with an aquarium and extreme sports centre next-door for what Ken Livingstone said would become "an international visitor attraction worthy of Europe's world class city".[2] The 2008 financial crisis killed the plans, with Millennium Mills remaining empty for urban explorers and ruin-lustful photographers.[3]

To coincide with the 2012 Olympics, empty tracts at its base were transformed into the London Pleasure Gardens, a pop-up modern-day interpretation of the Vauxhall Gardens. One week in, it hosted a star-studded music festival, Bloc 2012, for musicians including Steve Reich, Snoop Dogg, and Orbital. Snoop never got on stage; the festival cancelled in chaos and overcrowding before his slot.[4]

The site was planned to become a temporary "meanwhile space" for arts, entertainment, and activity, putting the site on the cultural map whilst developers got their plans and finances lined up. The rear of Millennium Mills would be a backdrop for video mapping projectors; a ten-storey-high Shepard Fairey mural was already painted over a façade. It had even received a loan of £3 million from Newham Council to transform the rubbish-hewn site, but debris and dust remained throughout, concerning locals aware of historic asbestos.[5] Vauxhall Gardens lasted two centuries until swallowed by industrial expansion in 1859; the Pleasure Gardens closed five weeks into an intended two years, going into administration, workers and bills unpaid.

That art, culture, and music are used to rebrand and market a site or project is now an expected element of any major development. Phrases like "placemaking", "meanwhile", "pop-up", and "cultural capital" are now as embedded within emerging-artist lexicon as much as with the agencies and quangos constructing, marketing, and selling real estate. The latest scheme for the site will see Millennium Mills become a "making, showing and sharing community" of creatives, sitting within the wider Silvertown regeneration area, the idea of culture deeply embedded into a £3.5 billion pitch already dubbed by GQ as "the new Brooklyn".

The largest asbestos removal in British history has cleared the site and, despite a brief pause in works when sparks from steel-burning workers ignited a fire across two floors, the mill

Fig. 3: Derek Jarman, still from The Last of England, 1987. London: Second Sight Films, 2008, DVD.

is being "reinvented" as a space of entertainment and cultural industry. The construction site is occasionally interrupted by cultural placemaking events in preparation – a dance performance with "interactive audio experience" took place in the remains of London Pleasure Gardens and a nearby industrial building which will become shared workspaces launched with a "warehouse-warming" rave and "immersive" contemporary art exhibition coinciding with Frieze art fair.

***

> The rain pours down; skinheads beat people up; there are race riots; there are drug fixes in squalid corners: there is much explicit sex, a surprising amount of it homosexual and sadistic; greed and violence abound; there is grim concrete and much footage of "urban decay".
> –Norman Stone in *The Sunday Times*, 1988[6]

Derek Jarman's film The Last of England took its name from Ford Maddox Brown's oil painting of middle-class emigrants reduced to poverty, on a boat with their backs to Dover's White Cliffs, destined for Australia and a new beginning. Jarman's film ends with refugees earlier seen huddled and nervous under military watch on the dockside next to Millennium Mills, crowded into a small boat floating off, drifting westwards along the Thames. "Are they leaving for a new life; or are they going to their deaths?"[7] he asks. The boat calmly rows into unknown darkness.

The ninety preceding minutes are a schizophrenic and mesmerising montage of debauchery, history, personal archive, and poetic montage. "I don't work for a passive audience, I want an active audience", Jarman says, and the work he created, the culmination of a decade looking at the physical and psychic postwar state, demands an attentive eye and open mind. A poetic rendition of the rise and fall of postwar postindustry, where "the present dreams the past future",[8] the Royal Docks and Millennium Mills are locations through to the final scene of

Tilda Swinton manically ripping off a wedding dress, spinning possessed in front of a dockside bonfire.

Starting with footage of Jarman himself writing at a desk and mixing family footage shot by his father, there is also a strong autobiographical element to the film in which a romantic trace of middle-class, pastoral memory lingers amongst ashes of Seventies and Eighties London flames. His father would later turn "potty",[9] trauma from World War II bombing raids he carried out which caused so many civilian casualties in the path of military progress.

Representations of ruinous London, coupled with scenes of heroin use and the British flag flailing beneath a balaclava'd soldier writhing with a naked male, raised the ire of Conservative traditionalists. Early in 1988 Norman Stone, friend of and advisor to Thatcher, wrote "Through a Lens Darkly", a page-long article for Murdoch's Sunday Times, in which he said Jarman's film made no cinematic sense, before damning it and five others as "dominated by a left wing ideology".[10] Stone cited David Lean's A Passage to India as the kind of cinema to aspire to, globally projecting a positive representation of our history that "toned down"[11] criticisms of British colonial rule explored in E.M. Forster's novel.

The idea that art should act as advertising for a nation's brand didn't sit well with Jarman, who in the same paper the following week replied:

> Stone's attack is contradictory because it comes from a supporter of a government that professes freedom in the economic marketplace yet seems unable to accommodate freedom of ideas [...] the decay that permeates The Last of England is there for all of us to see; it is in all our daily lives, in our institutions and in our newspapers. [British films for a Hollywood market feed] illusions of stability in an unstable world.[12]

But the 1980s Thatcherite neoliberal project was reliant upon hollow illusion and pretence, creation of a "Little England" with "cosmeticised historicism"[13] where simulacra of an imagined history were reconstructed amongst fragments of a postwar optimism, a state-sanctified romanticisation of empire, and a new industry of exporting images.

***

I perceive that everything my parents had fought for was being taken away by people of my own generation who seemed to me were fearful people who missed out on all the more liberating aspects of the sixties [...] faced with a Tory MP a few weeks ago on a stage I realised there was absolutely nothing there. Actually, if you blew the whole thing would fall down [...] People think of this monumental edifice and impenetrable political situation we're in, but it's not at all like that. The premises it's based on are completely fraudulent.
–Derek Jarman, 1989 [14]

Architectural historian Joe Kerr says of 1977 London, "Strange pockets of silence and stillness, the spaces vacated by unwanted

Fig. 4: Derek Jarman, still from The Last of England, 1987. London: Second Sight Films, 2008, DVD.

trades and industries [...] The air of hopelessness that seems to have fallen over the city is exacerbated by the daily evidence of growing disaffection."[15] This feeling was evoked in a trilogy of Jarman films, starting with 1978's Jubilee in which John Dee transplants Queen Elizabeth I into a devastated 1970s dystopian Britain of spaced-out squatters watching Top of the Pops, playing Monopoly, and committing murder, where plastic flowers are the only remaining urban nature. One of Jarman's characters, a rich media mogul named Borgia Ginz, has taken over the music industry: "As long as the music's loud enough, we won't hear the world falling apart."

The Royal Docks closed in 1981, the latest in a gradual emptying of industry and docks moving westwards along the Thames since the late 1960s, leading to a decade of pickets, inner-city deprivation, and unemployment. While the Conservatives were in opposition, the docks became symbolic of their ambitions to change political and social structures; a 1978 speech in the Isle of Dogs by Geoffrey Howe, soon to be Chancellor of the Exchequer, called them an "urban wilderness" indicative of the "developing sickness of our society".[16] He and Michael Heseltine saw the area as a testing ground for the ideological shift they wished for state, markets, economy, and urban centres to make.

Having seen "immense tracts of dereliction"[17] from a plane window, Heseltine set about forming the London Docklands Development Corporation (LDDC) after the election victory. With wide powers to acquire, promote, manage planning, and dispose of land in vast sites along the Thames as the Port of London relocated, the quango offered a platform to promote their laissez-faire urban and financial plans unhindered by local authorities, Labour councils, and opposing residents.

Over 1,550 acres of land had been acquired by the LDDC by 1988, often compulsory purchased, with pump priming from central government feeding a fund intended to lead to self-sufficiency from sales of premium-rate land on the open market. But amongst the dereliction and Heseltine's perceived tabula rasa there were communities of homes and places of employment, just not the type that suited the area's planned image and agenda. Other models where renewal could take place to benefit communities rather than the market were available: a People's Plan presented alternative ideas; anarchist planner Colin Ward published Arcadia for All promoting ideas of self-organised communities; and Coin Street Community Builders were beating big developers in Waterloo. But the Docklands project could not be seen to fail, the money and political impetus behind it was too great, residents and workers simply collateral damage to the grand vision, anonymous victims of "progress".

While not a huge fan of the music industry or artistic restrictions of pop videos, Jarman frequently used the format to explore his visual critique of state, regularly using Docklands locations as settings. 1986's "Ask" by the Smiths had the hulk of the Millennium Mills as a constant background, and their three-song video of the same year, The Queen Is Dead, was partially filmed in the shell of Beckton Gas Works prior to Kubrick turning it into Vietnam for Full Metal Jacket. Jarman's camera panned graffiti: "LOCAL LAND FOR LOCAL PEOPLE", "LDDC ARE BLOODY THIEVES", and "OFF OUR WATERFRONT".

Eighties Britain was a country in which the idea of society was dismissed by a prime minister busy dismantling and privatising the very nuts and bolts from which it was built. Right to buy, selling off national industries, discriminatory taxes, increasing unemployment, systemic racism, police harassment, Irish bombings, and demonisation of AIDS sufferers. Despite this, 1986 was a success for Thatcher; fresh from victory over the miners' strikes the prime minister set to work breaking apart the metropolitan political structures with a promise of giving control to the boroughs, and through this shifted power towards unelected quangos and private developers. Six urban centres were stripped of local governance, including the dissolution of Ken Livingstone's Greater London Council in an all-out assault on urban Labour strongholds.

Jarman observed that Thatcher was "starting on the inner cities [...] No opposition is tolerated [...] dissent ruthlessly crushed [...] families to be broken up by a tax on just being alive",[18] and 1985's The Angelic Conversation explored this transformation of English landscape. A tone piece of psychological and homoerotic sequences, he called it "a dream world [...] of magic and ritual", but one with haunting undercurrents of "burning cars and radar systems, which remind you there is a price to be paid in order to gain this dream in the face of a world of violence".[19] The surveillance and destruction that hum in the background were a constant presence for Jarman, who had lived in vacated warehouses along the Thames: first a South Bank house awaiting demolition; then a Blackfriars warehouse in the way of an office tower; to his Bankside bed in a reassembled greenhouse in his warehouse space; finally to semi-ruinous Butler's Wharf on Shad Thames. This last warehouse was lost to flames in 1980, Jarman's westward migration through the docks foreshadowing the developers' own movement as they followed artists, capitalising on their culture and flushing them

Fig. 5: Millennium Mills, 2018. © The author, 2018.

out. As it was in the works of Milton, Blake, and Turner, fire was a recurring motif for Jarman, with some of the flames he filmed started by property developers.

***

In the short space of my lifetime I've seen the destruction of the landscape through commercialisation, a destruction so complete that fragments are preserved as if in a museum.
–Derek Jarman [20]

In 1986 the London financial markets deregulated, easing stock market transactions, encouraging competition of trading commissions and ending the enforced separation between stock traders and the investor advisors. This created a Big Bang explosion in the industry, requiring larger, open floors and a more global outlook for computerised and automated buying and selling of invisible finance. As John Friedmann pointed out in his 1986 "World City Hypothesis", major importance was attached to "corporate headquarters, international finance, global transport and communications, and high level business services",[21] and Docklands could offer all three in its new architecture. In 1988 developers Olympia & York [O&Y] broke ground on One Canada Square, a tower to rise high above the flattened docks, acting as a symbol of optimism to the world and centrepiece of a vast Canary Wharf development. At the opening ceremony, architect Cesar Pelli proclaimed, "the reality of a hollow object is in the void and not in the walls that define it".

Needing to maximise income from land sales in a climate of decreasing property speculation after the Black Monday crash, the LDDC set about projecting a confident, desirable and futuristic image of the area through brand awareness, brochures, and promotional videos, putting Docklands onto a global stage.[22] They had always used image and rebranding as a tool of increasing value, from presenting the docks as a hybrid of Venice and New York to whitewashing existing cultures and place names in preference of a new, on-message "Docklands". But now new ideas were needed to promote the vast potential of the emptiness in a flailing economy, stating that "cultural regeneration might be a fair description for the process of change for which the LDDC is the chosen instrument".[23]

The Docklands landscape was a temporal and shifting aesthetic responding to free market economics more than any grand plan. By 1988 some plots had been developed three times, each building sold to a developer who demolished it to make way for a larger, shinier project before selling on. As such, the LDDC's initial foray into using art to bring attention to the area also looked to pop-up projects, including Peter Avery's production of Aristophanes' The Birds and the ICA project Accions.

In July 1988, the LDDC and O&Y joint-sponsored an exhibition of graduates' art in a Surrey Quays warehouse. Freeze, organised by Damien Hirst and his Goldsmiths cohort including Sarah Lucas, Michael Landy, and Gary Hume, was the first step of the Young British Artists brand, later to become key to New Labour's cultural positioning of Britain. By providing redundant architecture, LDDC garnered the kind of cultural capital that developers and "placemakers" now crave ahead of regeneration, and in return the artists of Freeze got not only a venue and cash to produce a professional catalogue, but also access to the new emergent movers of business and art worlds. It also showed that for success artists had to adopt the Thatcherite entrepreneurial manifesto, or the words of Julia Peyton-Jones, who attended the exhibition and later directed the Serpentine Gallery—"Vision. Ambition. Desire. And also attitude."[24]

There was plenty of community-led art-activism and socially engaged practice which actively opposed the LDDC project—for example, Loraine Leeson and Peter Dunn's collaborations with local workers, residents, and action groups for a series of billboards using montage to communicate issues within the local population. There were also diverse and political musical cultures emerging in reaction to the inner-city politics of the

Conservative government, developing in small networked communities. The warehouse-party culture of house music had been developing in empty urban spaces across Britain since the start of the Eighties, emerging from black sound systems and as a response to London's exclusive clubland culture of expense and consumerism.[25]

But the LDDC needed drop-in culture that could promote their brand and further ideological ambitions. It's hard to imagine they would have supported a rave or funded The Last of England, even though Jarman arguably did more than any other artist to archive their territory and put their project into public consciousness.

***

I think this show here tonight might wake up the city.
–A spectator at Rendez Vous Houston [26]

1986 the USA was also struggling with postindustrial reshaping. Houston was in the peak of an oil-slump, unemployment crisis, and real estate collapse. Two months earlier a failed O-ring had caused the space shuttle Challenger to spectacularly break up and explode, killing all seven crew members, live CNN footage providing one of the world's first live-streamed disasters of the information age. Houston was then a collapsing city where even Texan bravado couldn't conceal the despair, damage, debt, and mass defaulting of mortgages.

The city needed a kickstart and so the authorities invited French electronic musician Jean-Michel Jarre to use the city as the stage for a pop spectacle on a scale never before witnessed. Vast white sheets were draped over downtown skyscrapers transfiguring them into giant canvases for video projections, a backdrop for 1.5 million Houstonians to stare up at amongst searchlights, lasers, and fireworks set to the electronic music of Jarre.

Jarre was a child of the baby-boomer generation and son of Maurice, globally renowned composer of music for over 170 films and TV shows over five decades, most remembered for scoring David Lean's epics including A Passage to India. This classical heritage lingered in Jean-Michel, who would later enrol to study piano at the Conservatoire de Paris. By day learning classical skills of the institution, by night playing the guitar for several bands including in a brief party scene on film in Des Garcons et des Filles, a 1967 comedy following communally living students in a soon-to-be-demolished derelict house.

In 1968, amongst the cacophony of student protests (internet fan message boards talk of lost TV footage showing Jarre being handcuffed and thrown into a police van), he abandoned the conservatoire and joined Groupe de Recherches Musicales, an electro-acoustic experimental organisation created by Pierre Schaeffer, creator of experimental musique concrete. Jarre's music quickly found a fusion between the mechanical rhythms developed under Schaeffer and his classical training, with chart success leading to a free 1979 Bastille Day concert for a million Parisians.

Two years later Deng Xiaoping invited Jarre to become the first Western artist to perform in communist China. The mix of largely lyricless tradition and technology that marked the French Revolution deemed safe enough for a somewhat bemused Chinese audience. Then came Houston and its grand civic boosterism.

> "Spectacular," "imaginative," "amazing". Words that can be applied equally well to a Jean Michel Jarre concert or the development of London Docklands.
> –LDDC advert in the Destination Docklands souvenir brochure [27]

Just as images of the Challenger exploding in mid-air spread across the world, so too did footage of Jarre's "Rendez-vous Houston". In London, media-savvy employees of the LDDC may have seen MTV clips or read about the urban spectacle because while Jarre discussed repeating the concept across other US cityscapes, with meetings lined up in New York and Los Angeles, London's Docklands would be the next setting for his architectural take-over. The concert "Destination Docklands", and partnering album Revolutions hung on a three-act structural device of industrial, 1960s cultural and contemporary technological social shifts. As well as offering a stage for the show, this was an opportunity for the LDDC to project its brand identity and message across the world. Perhaps loudly enough that nobody could hear the Docklands economy falling apart.

As with the transformation of Houston, Jarre partnered with British architect Mark Fisher to turn buildings into scenography. Also a baby-boomer, Fisher had trained at the Architectural Association during their mid-Sixties exploration of radical new ideas for architecture and society: pop-up, portable, inflatable, walking, DIY, ephemeral, and cybernetic. From 1969 Fisher studied for his diploma under Peter Cook as the Archigram

Fig. 6: Mark Fisher, The Stage from the Royal Box, official concert programme. © Concessions Ltd, 1988.

founder pushed the architectural agenda towards pleasure, questioning rules of the elite and pulling inspiration from popular consumerism as much as classical tradition. Jarre partnered with him for his architectural extravaganzas after Fisher had already designed The Wall for Pink Floyd and taken his utopian trainings firmly down the path of spectacle and sensation.

> As a spotlight traces across the sky I would think there are a lot of people in Newham who would remember World War II who will have themselves jerked back into the 1940s this evening.
> –Simon Bates' Radio 1 live commentary of Destination Docklands [28]

The concert nearly didn't happen; two weeks before its intended September date the fire services pulled the plug on safety grounds. A frantic period followed in which Jarre visited other cities–the site of Liverpool's Garden Festival empty since the 1984 event, Glasgow, Manchester, Thurrock, Newcastle, even Alton Towers. It created a media storm and the kind of neoliberal intercity competition now built into national cultural mechanisms. But it may have all been a ruse to scare Newham and the LDDC, and after an extraordinary council licencing meeting for which Jarre flew in, it returned to its site of inspiration, Docklands, albeit for a delayed October date.

Fisher's visual design of the project was massive. The façade of Millennium Mills had been painted white to offer a vast surface for projected images, part of an enormous triptych including the Co-operative Wholesale Society Mills, an immense 90x100 metres scaffold structure. The concert programme lists some of the projected imagery, offering a snapshot of the curated narrative:

Part 1: Industrial Revolution

empires
deserts
jungles
industry
emigrants
commerce

Part 2: Cultural Revolution

hitchcock
quant
twiggy
vietnam
avengers
caine

Fig. 7: "Destination Docklands", Jean-Michel Jarre, 9 October 1988.
(Photographer unknown.) Available on Jean-Michel Jarre's website:
https://jeanmicheljarre.com/live/destination-docklands.

Part 3: Electronic Revolution

leisure
silicon
comsat
replicant
deconstructivist
revolutions

At other points the words "employment" and "no employment" were cast over the hulk of the mill, visible for miles across the very neighbourhoods suffering since the docks' closure. Two hundred and fifty thousand pounds' worth of fireworks, equivalent to the total costs of The Last of England, exploded above the docks and World War II searchlights reflected off clouds. Later, the previous year's violence caused by social inequality and deprivation was visually represented by fireworks and projections of flames described by Radio 1 DJ Simon Bates as giving "the impression that the warehouse opposite with its windows red and smoke coming out of them is ablaze".[29]

> This is where Jean takes a musical [...] look, at what he believes will happen to the Docklands area in the 1990s. And of course is using this enormous and clumsy, or clumsy-looking, pair of asbestos gloves for his guitar which otherwise would electrocute him.
> – Simon Bates' live commentary[30]

At one point an image of a modern office building was projected over the top of the Millennium Mills, giving the slightly macabre impression of a shroud, perhaps a marketing gimmick for the LDDC trying to at once acknowledge and disguise the dirty industry of the area. When Jarre puts on a pair of asbestos gloves to break the green divergen beams of his trademark laser harp, it is impossible not to think of the asbestos embedded into the docks which would have led to the premature deaths of countless industrial workers. An industrial material transfigured to function the new service and culture economy.

The stage formed of ten lashed-together barges shipped from the northeast was designed to float from left to right in front of the crowds, but the sheer weight of equipment and performers rendered it motionless. British autumnal weather deluged the site. Improvised tarpaulins were lashed over equipment while rehearsals saw musicians fighting winds to stay on the floating stage. But despite the technical and seasonal issues, the sheer immensity of spectacle dominated the Royal Docks; footage shows searchlights darting across a sea of static faces starring up in awe.

Jarre's said his concert was "a tribute to the anonymous victims of every revolution",[31] dedicating the album to "all the children of the revolution" and "the children of immigrants".[32] In a coincidental mirroring of The Last of England, the concert ended with Jarre's song "L'Emigrant", a choir of local children – wearing lifejackets in case they fell from the floating stage – offering harmonies to a crescendo of classical and electronic instruments wrapped up in the drama of relentless firework explosions.

> No-one seems to have moved in almost two hours. They're standing rock still, loving the fireworks and now seeing "Newham" projected in large letters on the two buildings opposite the stage.
> – Simon Bates' live commentary[33]

This was a total spectacle in a Guy Debord sense. The romanticising of empire and industry and the simplification of the area's history into a neat narrative to further the LDDC agenda, fits his notion that "spectacular consumption preserves the old culture in congealed form".[34] Crowds stood on the dockside, once busy with workers, silently facing the Millennium Mills, enacting Debord's "deceived gaze and [...] false consciousness", their sense of shared experience "nothing but an official language of generalised separation".[35] In many ways this event was the counter to the rave culture developing over the previous few years which appropriated locations for community-organised parties; this was an on-message, state-sanctified appropriation of place and history to help the wider objectives of the LDDC.

Outside, ticket touts showed the kind of entrepreneurial spirit that would have made Thatcher proud, selling £30 tickets for £50, making £2,000 in an afternoon. While inside, away from the raked seating and vast tract of postindustrial land for the 100,000 punters, sponsors and businessmen enjoyed the corporate entertainment. A video produced by the main sponsor, the Carroll Foundation Trust, intersperses the performance and visuals from the stage with footage from the corporate marquee, businessmen mingling with dignitaries, sponsors, and celebrities. This is where Gerald Carroll worked the room, shaking hands and posing for photos, inviting the key figures of the period to his party. Princess Diana. Robert Maxwell. Jeremy Beadle.

> Our society is built on secrecy, from the "front" organisations which draw an impenetrable screen over the concentrated wealth of their members to the "official secrets" which allow the state a vast field of operation free from any legal constraint, from the often frightening secrets of shoddy production hidden by advertising, to the projections of an extrapolated future.
> –Guy Debord[36]

Derek Jarman said of authority, "all I saw was deceit and bankruptcy",[37] and in 1992 some of the walls surrounding the hollow voids of finance collapsed. Robert Maxwell, who along with his son Ian received a "special thanks" from Jarre in the liner notes of the live album, drowned after leaving the Mirror Group's pension scheme drained. Gerald Carroll, who in 1986 put his entire business portfolio, assets, houses, and art into his Foundation Trust, saw his speculative empire collapse in massive debt and allegations of fraud. Hollow objects. The promoters of "Destination Docklands" ran up spiralling bills from the delay, weather, and sheer scale, leaving countless suppliers and workers unpaid for their work seeking damages in the courts–the projected façade of the spectacle concealed the failures of its production.

Even counter-cultures got absorbed into the late-Eighties neoliberal race for profit. The warehouse rave scene was turning from community-led right-to-the-city activation of redundant spaces into an entrepreneur-led business. Saving money earnt from gambling to enter property development, Tony Colston-Hayter turned raves into vast pop-up festivals, inviting media attention and consequential police pressure against the rave scene. His PR manager Paul Staines, then working in a Conservative Party right-wing pressure group and now as blogger Guido Fawkes, considered Colston-Hayter one of "Thatcher's children" with an entrepreneurial spirit "pushing the boundaries of free enterprise".[38] This was when the culture industry exploded, and

Fig. 8: "Destination Docklands", before the concert, 9 October 1988. © Dennis/Spitfire 13, 1988. Available on Flickr: https://www.flickr.com/people/26502588@N02/.

everyone wanted some of it, or to benefit from its glory.

> We're live on Radio 1 in stereo, on FM. We're broadcasting the "Destination Docklands" concert as it happens from, guess where, from Docklands, with 100,000 people. It's freezing cold here. On my left-hand side are camera crews from Brazil, the USA, from Canada, from Germany, from all parts of Europe, from Australia, from New Zealand. They are absolutely frozen but hypnotised by what's happening on stage and in and around the docks.
> – Simon Bates' live commentary [39]

"Destination Docklands" was one of the first globally mediated cultural events on this scale, incorporating the music, dance, fireworks, architecture, and awed crowds now firmly embedded in contemporary pop culture. Fisher would continue to revolutionise the large-scale pop spectacle, developing the super-structures that U2, the Rolling Stones, Lady Gaga, and Elton John carry around the world–the lo-fi radicalism of 1968 subsumed into the late-twentieth-century capitalist drive for sensation and scale. This sense of event is now rolled up with neoliberal hypergentrification and push for vast capital returns on urban redevelopment. The launch of Canary Wharf's tower in 1992 and that of the Shard in 2012 were mediated affairs with live music, lasers, and searchlights.

The visuals of industrial workers, Queen Victoria, colonial success, pop revolution, and James Bond that congealed the Millennium Mills in light were witnessed again for the 2012 Olympics Opening Ceremony up the road in Stratford. Seen by a global audience of a billion, the ceremony was executive produced by Fisher and had similarities to Jarre's sequenced narrative of eras set to a classically infused pop beat. No modern-day event is as spectacular as the Olympics, loud enough to distract from the compulsory purchasing of land from profitable businesses and rooted communities to make way for the grander and shinier cultural offerings planned to follow the few weeks of sport.

Millennium Mills has now been scrubbed clean for the next chapter of its life. The docks it sits within have been undergoing another cleansing since the 1980s to form a "new piece of the city".[40] There is no space in that new city for the narratives that Jarman explored, there is no room for other narratives to the prescribed, official one. The trajectory of neoliberal urban politics since 1988 has taken us to a place where it has become harder to separate the function of art from the wider capital economy. It is now so deeply enmeshed within the very physical changing face of London, even if it's only a sacrificial veneer or a pop-up spectacle moment. The Millennium Mills have not only survived throughout, now a single white tooth standing as the history and architecture has been extracted, but have been repeatedly co-opted into the changing representation of the area.

Congealed, a preserved fragment.

Fig. 9: Silvertown Quays, CGI rendering of proposed development, 2017. Available at http://www.silvertownlondon.com.

Endnotes

1   Jean-Michel Jarman: The Last of Docklands Silvertown. "Silvertown." http://www.silvertownlondon.com.

2   London Development Agency. "London Mayor Ken Livingstone Launches London's Silvertown Quays and Reveals Plans for World-Class Visitor Attraction to an International Audience at MIPIM 2005".

3   The internet is awash with urban exploration photographs from Millennium Mills, including: https://www.proj3ctm4yh3m.com/urbex/2015/02/11/urbex-spillers-millennium-mills-london-united-kingdom-september-2014/ and https://www.28dayslater.co.uk/millennium-mills-london-2017-may.t108718 and http://www.beyondtheboundary.co.uk/millennium-mills-london.html.

4   Ahmed Jamil, "BLOC 2012 @ London Pleasure Gardens", 6 July, 2012, https://www.musicomh.com/reviews/live/bloc-2012-london-pleasure-gardens-london

5   Stop City Airport Masterplan, "Press Release -Toxic Asbestos Risk at London Pleasure Gardens," http://stopcityairportmasterplan.tumblr.com/post/26067945985/press-release-toxic-asbestos-risk-at-london.

6   Norman Stone, *"Through a Lens Darkly"*, *the Sunday Times* (10 January 1988)

7   Derek Jarman, *Kicking the Pricks* (Vintage, 1996), p. 208

8   Ibid, p. 188.

9   400 Blows, "Gaye Temple (nee Jarman) on Derek Jarman." http://www.400blows.co.uk/inter_temple.shtml.

10 Norman Stone, "Through a Lens Darkly." *Sunday Times*, January 10, 1988.

11 "A Passage to India: David Lean's Rocky Road to Creating a Most Powerful Adaption", *Cinephilia & Beyond*, https://cinephiliabeyond.org/a-passage-to-india-david-leans-rocky-road-to-creating-a-most-powerful-adaptation.

12 Michael Charlesworth, *Derek Jarman* (Reaktion Books,

2011), p. 134.

13   Jarman, *Kicking the Pricks*, p. 81.

14   Derek Jarman, "Derek Jarman in Conversation with Simon Field," interview by Simon Field. ICA Guardian Conversations, 1989. Video, https://player.bfi.org.uk/free/film/watch-derek-jarman-in-conversation-with-simon-field-1989-online.

15   Joe Kerr, "Introduction", in Andrew Gibson and Joe Kerr (eds), *London from Punk to Blair* (Reaktion Books, 2003), p. 29.

16   Timothy Weaver, *Blazing the Neoliberal Trail: Urban Political Development in the United States and the United Kingdom,* (University of Pennsylvania Press, 2016), p. 253

17   Fiona Rule, *London's Docklands: A History of the Lost Quarter,* (Ian Allen, 2012), p. 91.

18   Dennis Sewell. "Not the Last of Jarman." *Spectator*, May 7, 1988.

19   Jarman, *Kicking the Pricks*, p. 133.

20   Derek Jarman, interview.

21   John Friedmann, "The World City Hypothesis.", Development and Change, 17:1, January 1986, pp. 69-83.

22   Taner Oc & Steven Tiesdell, *"The London Docklands Development Corporation* (LDDC), 1981-91: A Perspective on the Management of Urban Regeneration."

23   Robert Maycock, *Regeneration and the Arts in London Docklands* (LDDC, 1998)

24   Elizabeth Fullerton, "How Britain's Shocking Art Movement got its Start", *BBC Culture* (25 April 2016), http://www.bbc.com/cultu-re/story/20160419-freeze-how-britains-shocking-art-movement-began

25   Jon Savage, *Time Travel: Pop, Media and Sexuality 1976-96* (Chatto and Windus, 1996)

26   Derek Jarman, interview.

27   Derek Jarman, interview.

28   Simon Bates' BBC Radio 1 live commentary of *Destination Docklands*.

29   Ibid

30   Simon Bates' BBC Radio 1 live commentary of *Destination Docklands*.

31   From the Destination Docklands official programme.

32   Liner notes to Jean-Michel Jarre, *Revolutions* (Disques Dreyfus, 1988)

33   Simon Bates' BBC Radio 1 live commentary of *Destination Docklands*.

34   Guy Debord, *The Society of the Spectacle, trans. by Donald Nicholson-Smith,* (Zone, 1994), p. 192

35   Ibid, p. 3.

36   Simon Bates' BBC Radio 1 live commentary of *Destination Docklands*.

37   Jarman, *Kicking the Pricks*, p. 181.

38   Paul Staines, "How did Acid House Change the British Music Scene?" Interview by Annie Nightingale, *BBC Today* (16 November 2013), http://www.bbc.co.uk/news/av/uk-24971287/how-did-acid-house-change-the-british-music-scene

39   Simon Bates' BBC Radio 1 live commentary of *Destination Docklands*.

40   Silvertown, "Silvertown."

Keller Easterling

> 'the more rationalised spatial products become, the
> better suited they are to irrational fictions of branding'
> Keller Easterling, Extrastatecraft: The Power of Infrastructure Space', Verso,
> 2014

Promotional videos for the world's instant cities invariably begin with a
view of earth from outer space. Any number of different musical themes—
canned trumpet fanfare, synthesized operatic overture, or something appropriate to the thundering hooves of a Western film—accompany a drop
from the stratosphere to locate a new center of the earth.

A more sentimental, perhaps ethnically inflected love theme continues as
a field of digital skyscrapers sprout from the ground. A deep movie trailer
voice lists in broken English all the requisite features of 21st century urbanism: free zone status, no taxes, cheap labor, no unions, streamlined customs,
deregulation of labor and environmental law. A Star Wars style fly-over
swoops through the cartoon skylines, industrial areas, container ports, iden-
tical villas and resorts.

The videos make magnificent claims of global connectivity or world city
urbanity enjoyed by doughy human figures rhythmically waddling along
boulevards or plowing forward stone-faced in a speed boat. Other videos
advertise their logistical apparatus by thoroughly inspecting back office
spaces, factories and storage facilities to a theme like "It's a Feelin'" from
Flashdance.

Persuaded by these new urban trends, even a totalitarian regime like the
DPRK, creates an ecstatic version of the video form that shifts rapidly, almost
frantically, through a number of up-tempo musical themes—a synthesized
harp or run on the piano keys transition between organ polkas, patriotic
marches, high pitched accordion jigs, emotional lullabies and waltzes. And
most all of the videos from any country end with glowing sunsets, bursting
hearts, confetti or a pan back into the stratosphere past fireworks and orbit-
ing satellites, perhaps to the theme from Titanic.

his sort of video has become a standard offering in the global confidence
ame of urban development. Subtitles often appear in the language of the
ntended investor, and the animations break occasionally for footage of actual
eople gathering around conference rooms and hotel ballrooms to enthusias-
cally invest in the cartoon scenes that have just been playing.

rbanism as a service industry provides not only entire cities according to
epeatable formulas but also rendering of urban porn—that is a routine, repeti-
ve, even tedious fantasy.

his porn is a strange reflection of the utopias of the design disciplines. The
ost serious utopias—portraying perfect arrangements that transcend politics
vith totalizing solutions—are comedy and Kitsch from the instant they emerge.
Vhile relatively powerless as the one and only prescription of designers, as part
f a rolling set of lies and garden variety fictions, they are wildly contagious.

Vorld City Trailers, 2014
ttps://vimeo.com/112833164

Marsh Wall, Isle of Dogs, 1987. © Mike Seaborne.

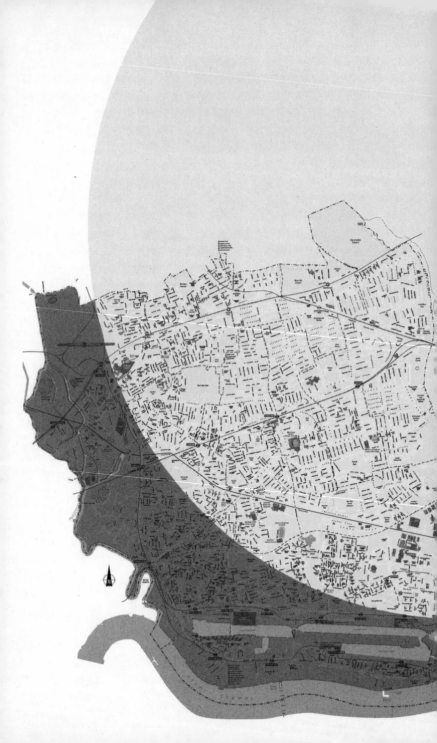

Part 4
The Lived City

Authoritarian Populism | Populist Authoritarianism

Malcolm James

In Brexit and the election of Donald Trump we have witnessed the rise of authoritarian populism. Across the Atlantic, appeals to the people are being made in the name of law and order, race and nation. Trump, Nigel Farage, and Boris Johnson are not alone. In continental Europe, Marine Le Pen, Viktor Orbán, Geert Wilders, and the Flemish national party, Vlaams Belang, also suture individuals' dissatisfaction with neoliberalism with racial, nationalist, and authoritarian allures.

While moments such as Brexit provide a lens through which authoritarian populism becomes apparent, there is a risk that over-attention to its spectacle will detract from wider analysis of the problem at hand. Certainly, Farage and Johnson did not come out of thin air. Rather, they are the product of history and social context. As they took to the stage, their positions were already sketched in popular culture.

Architecture and urban development provide an important access point for this discussion. Key indicators of dominant culture, they offer incubators for the forms of populist authoritarianism prominently observed in recent times.

Newham's Arc of Opportunity is a case in point. Here, in the regeneration of Stratford Town, Canning Town, Custom House, and the Royal Docks we see authoritarianism fabricated in glass, grass, and concrete, and we see this done in the name of the masses.

Authoritarian Populism

I refer to the fabrication of authoritarianism in populist architecture and urban development as *populist authoritarianism*, but to appreciate this, we must first return to Stuart Hall's earlier formulation of *authoritarian populism*. Writing at the end of Callaghan's Labour administration and the beginning of Thatcherism, Hall was interested in the ways in which popular social democracy was being eroded and replaced with populism and authoritarianism. Terminology here is important. For Hall, the word "popular", as in "popular democracy", denotes social democracy for, and by, the people. The word "populist", as in "populist authoritarianism", denotes an appeal to the popular that took place as part of Thatcher's right-wing shift. Populism is not then democratic. It uses the varnish of representational politics (of the people and the popular) for the project of authoritarian rule.[1]

In Hall's analysis, populism emerges in the late 1970s as the crisis of social democracy under Callaghan takes hold, and it is here too that it finds its authoritarian expression. As social democracy struggles against the stratifying tendencies of capitalism, Labour's popular mandate is strained, and appeals to the people (populism) are made in terms of law, order and security (authoritarianism). This tendency expands under the proceeding Conservative administration, and as recorded in Hall's seminal text *Policing the Crisis* a popular mandate for rule is increasingly sought on the grounds of crime and criminality. These discourses are overwhelmingly directed at black and working-class young men, and at the populations of the inner city. The resulting unrest in Toxteth, Brixton,

Handsworth, and Tottenham is testament to this.[2]

Hall's point is that Thatcherism takes on the language of popular representative democracy, championed by social democrats, and guts it. In this move, a new political cleavage is established. Working-class solidarities are displaced by the private and self-actualising individual (personified in the petit bourgeois shopkeeper, and therefore Thatcher herself). The "big state" (welfarism, collective politics, and by implication social democracy) is replaced by free market capitalism. As welfarism shrinks, the power of capitalist elites expands.

Times have moved on. Some aspects of Thatcherism we retain: the thin appeal to representative democracy and the rationale for privatisation. But changes we can also acknowledge: the boardroom executive has replaced the shopkeeper as the prime subject of neoliberal capitalism, and under the aegis of austerity, mutual commitment to coexistence, institutionalised in the welfare state, has been further weakened.[3] And of course, this runs alongside seventeen years of constant war, which has seen Muslims and asylum seekers elevated alongside black, Asian, and working-class young people as the principle threats to law, order, and security.

Populist Authoritarianism

If these dimensions of authoritarian populism are now moderately well observed, less attention has been paid to the ways in which they congeal in popular culture – as populist authoritarianism. When Hall was writing, popular culture was quite different. It was more varied, less commercial, and indeed contained the tail ends of strong alternative modernisms (such as Afrofuturism and democratic socialism). Today, many (although not all) of these tendencies have been captured. In architecture and urban development this is particularly the case, on account of its close relationship to capitalism.

In *Postmodernism*, Fredric Jameson makes a compelling argument for the decline of alternative modern utopias, and the spread of populism into architecture and urban development. He argues that the forms of architecture stigmatised as mass or commercial in the democratic-socialist (or Keynesian) period now widely inform the cultural realm.[4] This shift–from rejection to the embrace of populism–can be seen in recent urban developments. Across London, universities (an appeal to popular education) butt up against museums and public art institutions (an appeal to popular art and culture). Local government offices (an appeal to popular democracy) nestle in shopping districts (an appeal to commercially realised selfhood) often dressed in green credentials (an appeal to environmentalism).

These glittering vestiges of public education, selfhood, democracy and environmentalism gain consent for high-rent housing and high-end commercial facilities. Their built condition does not accrue through local democratic processes, but is mandated from boardrooms and is inured against the unruly surrounding population in accordance with dominant ideas of criminality, security and social order. Ad hoc capitalism, homelessness, urban poverty, and congregations of working-class and black and minority ethnic young people (staples of city life) are absented from their pavements and pseudo-public spaces. It is through this confluence of high-end capitalism, populism and authoritarianism that the urban development is deemed a success.

The Arc of Opportunity

Newham's Arc of Opportunity is a case in point. Appearing in an economic planning document in 2010, the Arc of Opportunity was announced as 1,412 hectares of land "stretching from Stratford through Canning Town, the Royal Docks and Beckton", equating to a £22 billion investment in the borough.[5]

Steeped in the New Labour language of aspiration and brought to fruition in austerity Britain, the Arc of Opportunity is a steroid-fuelled building programme facilitated by the status of its postindustrial land. Owned and managed by the Greater London Authority and the London Legacy Development Corporation (the organisation responsible for managing the Olympic Park after London 2012), this postindustrial condition provided a *carte blanche* for Boris Johnson and his vision of post-European global capitalism.

With planning powers held by Johnson himself, international capital (from Canada, Kuwait, United Arab Emirates, Australia, Netherlands, Qatar, UK, Germany, Ireland, Singapore, and China) was attracted to housing, transport, business, arts, and shopping developments with minimal local accountability. In the south, Silvertown Quays, Royal Wharf, Siemens Crystal exhibition centre, and the Asian Business Port (ABP) – touted as London's third financial centre – took shape; in the west, the Olympic development, six housing villages and Westfield Shopping Centre.

***

From its inception, the narrative for the Arc of Opportunity was a *tablua rasa* – erasing the past and the people that live there. In the 2010 Shanghai Expo, Newham Council branded the Arc of Opportunity a "regeneration supernova". Commenting on this, Dan Hancox wrote, it "is not about 'modifying', 'modernising' or 'improving' a run-down area. No: It is about wiping it out in a 'supernova' – a brief moment of total and blinding destruction."[6] East London has historic precedent for this: the Victorian sanitation projects, post-World War II "slum" clearances, the imposition of high-rise blocks and then their condemnation. Working-class places like Newham have long been ripe for violent aesthetic and architectural reinvention by those who don't live there.

The Olympic Park was presented as a "clean slate" (belying the housing, allotments, wildlife, sports facilities, and businesses that were already there). During the Games, the Carpenters Estate and the nearby Stratford Centre were hidden by advertising hoardings and shiny fins. After the Games, in the Royal Docks, Chinese investors ABP announced they were "changing a piece of *wasted land* into the future of the third financial centre" (my emphasis).[7] In this way, homes, a popular market, and a former centre of East End working life were saturated in blinding light.

Around the Olympic Park today, there are plans for Victoria & Albert and Smithsonian museums, university campuses, and the Sadler's Wells auditorium.[8] These populist creative and cultural projects come flanked by two forty-seven-storey luxury apartment towers. At the Royal Docks, the clean lines of the

Fig.1: The Arc of Opportunity within a map of East London. Image Source: http://albertoduman.wixsite.com/music-masterplanning.

Siemens Crystal sustainable exhibition centre look across the water to London City Airport, the Asian Business Port, and the new offices of Sir Robin Wales' local authority.

Gone is the dirt of the docks and so too the people that made it. The Arc of Opportunity's clean façades, cultural zones, warehouse educational establishments are predicated on the obliteration of the working population and their histories. All that is left are nostalgic adornments and clichéd branding. The refurbished quay cranes and lighter vessels provide packages of working-class "community" and "spirit" – sold to those investing in dehistoricised places. Accompanying publicity brochures tout the "vibrancy" of multi-ethnic populations to prospective residents, just as repeated assurances of safety mitigate against their more unruly associations.[9]

***

Located on the west bank of the Royal Victoria Dock, Siemens Crystal sustainable exhibition centre is an archetype of this vision, and a recurrent reference in Newham Council's promotional material. Commonly framed against the backdrop of Canary Wharf and the Millennium Dome – ironically notable for their economic and political failure respectively[10] – the Crystal claims progress and enterprise. From vulgar yuppie moneymaking to casino-cool, the Crystal radiates clean, green, digital capitalism. The building is extremely energy efficient. Inside are CGI projections of gravity-defying gardens, growing on Zaha Hadid-style skyscrapers, sonically surrounded by the flow of water. Here "green" does a particular kind of work.

In *The Urban Birder*, David Lindo, an ornithologist of the city, recalls how he was courted by Olympic Park bureaucrats in the run up to the 2012 Games.[11] On a visit to the site, officials pressed upon him the Park's wildlife credentials. Biodiversity and nesting sites left him captivated, as many others were. After all, the fanfare given to the greening of former industrial lands was mesmerising.

Some of those claims were of course true, but they also functioned to mask the more determining capitalist and jingoistic imperatives for the Park. The Games were inexorably tied to enormous capital investment, and to the failure or success of a nation. The flourishing grasslands, riverbanks, and nesting holes for sand martins were at the same time window dressing for a nationalist regeneration machine that would succeed at all costs.

The green populism that Lindo and others encountered was, however, more than just a bolt-on to business as usual. Rather, it collected powerful stories sceptical of industrial Britain and its people. In the greening of the Olympic Park, pastoral Conservatism with its over-investment in the green and pleasant land combined with the left-leaning humanisms (of William Morris and William Blake) sceptical of machines and industrial progress.[12] There, Cameron's "caring Conservatism"–the former Tory logo of a burning torch already replaced by a tree–found affinity with the nationalist invocations of Blake's "Jerusalem".

So, Siemens Crystal green is not only CGI gardens in the sky, total waste control, and 24/7 networked harmony, nor is it only

Fig. 2: Stratford Centre hidden by shiny fins.

a verdant abettor for run-of-the-mill capitalism. Rather, through pulling together diverse political narratives, it makes an appeal for the future city, one that can be as global and nationalist as it is cleansed of industry and working people.

In the Crystal, this narrative unfolds with planetary reach and authoritarian vigour. The permanent exhibition showcases a multinational company with a smart-city plan, applied locally onto technocratically defined problems. The poetic quality of human life is starkly absent. People appear as digits, risk factors, and CGI landscape adornments, narrated by a robotic female voice.

This 24/7 networked Elysium ends with an exhibit on law, order, and security. It is here that green populism finds affinity with classed and racialised authoritarianism. Through a series of installations, a cast of characters associated with social disorder are sketched, but left vague for the audience to fill in (based on their own cultural assumptions). Assumptions made, the threats are reassuringly secured through Siemens' surveillance technologies, smart buildings, and total connectivity. At the

Fig. 3: Lighter vessel moored off the private development Britannia Village, Silvertown. ExCel Exhibition Centre in background.

end, it is less a vision of planetary coexistence you are left with than one of technologised totalitarianism, justified through an appeal to greenness.

***

That sense of vagueness, or absence, present in the Crystal, is characteristic of the Arc of Opportunity at large. A flexible identikit applied to future cites from Shanghai to Mumbai, Berlin, and Newham, the urban planning of the Arc of Opportunity is necessarily detached from the people on the ground. Envisioned in boardrooms, distributed at international business fairs, and beamed between skyscrapers, it has taken form far above everyday realities of ordinary people. But that is not to say that new residents can't imagine themselves here.

Newham's motto for an earlier time–"Live, work & stay"–still appears on major access routes into the borough. Whereas before it made the case for rest and consolidation amid the fluidity of internal, regional, and international migration, for which the borough is famous, it now welcomes a new citizenry, one that identifies with the global imprint. As the Silvertown Quays propaganda reads: "Silvertown is not a place for everyone: it is a place for people who want to reshape their world. It's for those who invent, create, break and make."[13]

At the end of 2017, I watched a young Hong Kong couple and their friends posing for wedding photos on the grassy mound outside the Siemens Crystal. They appeared to be students, maybe living locally because of cheaper rent, and perhaps studying at the university on closely monitored Tier 4 visas. The newlyweds had come to the Crystal in their ceremonial attire–a black suit and a white dress–and wanted a poignant backdrop for their photos. The Crystal had been identified, and it was onto its sharp digital lines that they projected their future union. Newer members of a mobile but monitored global bourgeoisie, they found affinity in its futurity. They might have found the same in any number of global cities, even as they were standing

Fig. 4: Quay cranes, Silvertown.

on the wall of the Royal Victoria Dock.

But such visions are not for all.

**

We are after all seeing the building of a Newham wholly unaffordable for the majority of its inhabitants. In Canning Town and Custom House, just over 40% of residents live in social rented accommodation.[14] As the selective demolition of that area begins, the question remains as to what happens to those residents. Newham Council states that 35% of new social housing will be "affordable" but that term has proved highly erroneous in the past – 80% of London market rate is not affordable for most people – and from a cash-strapped authority under austerity conditions it is difficult to see how that will change.[15]

Today, the price of a two-bedroom house in Olympic East Village is £580,000, an "intermediate rent" for the same size is £1,404 per month, and the "social rent" (the cheapest rent model) £754 per month. However, the median wage in Newham is only £882.29 per month.[16] This would make a social rent in

Fig. 5: Canary Wharf, Millennium Dome, and Siemens Crystal looking west from Royal Victoria Bridge.

East Village an enormous 85% of a monthly wage. And indeed these are the better deals. After Boris Johnson took over housing planning at the Olympic Park, affordable and social rented properties decreased by 21%. Now 61% of homes are for the private market with 29% divided between social rent, "affordable rent", and shared ownership. Under the Housing and Planning Act 2016, these inequalities will worsen as local authorities sell off social housing stock to supplement their substantial deficits.

If the forced removal of residents from Carpenters Estate showed the willingness of the council to take on high-profile and well-organised resistance (and Russell Brand), to achieve its future vision, less reported will be the social violence that these new high-rent developments bring to some of the poorest parts of the capital. As land is repurposed for housing, high art, international business, creative industries, higher education, and shopping, and Newham Mayor Robin Wales' much-hoped-for middle classes throng to the borough, racial and classed violence will be meted out.

Casting our eyes back to the Olympics we can get a sense of how this might transpire:

As the Olympics entered its second week, I walked through West Ham Park, ten minutes from the main site, and stopped to speak to a group of Afghani and Kurdish young men sitting on a bench under a tree. Interested in the actions of the police, I asked how the Olympics were affecting them. Rather than trot out TV-derived platitudes of patriotism and aspiration, they expressed anger at being stopped (on the pretext of immigration checks), harassed, and illegally strip-searched in the backs of police vans. These were not new experiences but the Olympic Games had increased their frequency to absurd levels. Affronted and angry, they shared stories and reflections on the clean-up, its racial registers and its basis in their day-to-day marginalisation. In the glare of neoliberal whiteness, they noted how their brown bodies and associated cultural signifiers had become hyper visible.[17]

Today, the temporary police orders have expired, and the officers have gone back to their routine assignments, but the basis of that violence has not dissipated. After all, populist authoritarianism forms the blueprint for living in the Arc of Opportunity. An urbanism with sharp aesthetics and a *tabula rasa* narrative has been established precisely through the obliteration of the borough's past and its working people. With the locus of neoliberal capitalism shifted from the high street to the boardroom, generic plans are implemented without local participation, just as security and information system are designed to correspond with generic risks and social threats. On the ground, these exclusions are made concrete through high living costs and the private policing (on privately owned land) of racialised and classed dangers. All of this operates through an environmental commitment to green efficiency which dispenses with industry and working people, as it sanitises an urbanism-to-come.

Endnotes

1   Stuart Hall, "Popular Democratic Vs Authoritarian Populism: Two Ways of 'Taking Democracy Seriously'", in Alan Hunt (ed), *Marxism and Democracy*, (Lawrence and Wishart, 1980).; *Stuart Hall and Martin Jacques, The Politics of Thatcherism* (Lawrence and Wishart, 1983).

2   Stuart Hall et al., *Policing the Crisis: Mugging, the State, and Law and Order* (Macmillan, 1978).

3   Gargi Bhattacharyya, *"Racial Capitalism", in Neoliberalism and its Others* (University of Sussex: 2016).

4   Fredric Jameson, *Postmodernism, or, the Cultural Logic of Late Capitalism* (Verso, 1991), p. 64.

5   LBN. "Local Economic Assessment 2010 to 2027 - Looking Forward: Planned Investment and the Scale of Opportunity ". (London Borough of Newham, 2010), http://www. newham.info/Custom/LEA/LookingForward.pdf.

6   Dan Hancox, "A 'Regeneration Supernova' Is About to Destroy East London as We Know It", *Vice* (22nd April 2014), https://www.vice.com/en_uk/article/nnq7q7/dan-hancox-regeneration-supernova

7   Newham Recorder, "'Historical Moment' as Chinese Investors Sign Deal to Make Newham a Financial Centre", *Newham Recorder* (10 November 2016), www. newhamrecorder.co.uk/news/historical-moment-as-chinese-investors-sign-deal-to-make-newham-a-financial-centre-1-4770491.

8   Oliver Wainwright, "London's Olympic Legacy: A Suburb on Steroids, a Cacophony of Luxury Stumps", the *Guardian* (3 August 2016), https://www.theguardian. com/artanddesign/2016/aug/03/london-olympic-legacy-stratford-suburb-on-steroids.

9   LBN, *Canning Town and Custom House Supplementary Planning Document* (LBN, 2008), 10.; Mayor of London and Mayor of Newham, *Royal Docks* (Mayor of London and LBN, 2010), p. 6.

10   For a wider discussion on failure in architecture see Douglas Murphy, *The Architecture of Failure* (Zero Books, 2010)

11   David Lindo, *The Urban Birder* (New Holland, 2011)

12   Owen Hatherley, *A New Kind of Bleak: Journeys through Urban Britain* (Verso, 2012)

13   For a wider discussion see Alberto Duman, "Shadows of the Future: The Agency of Tomorrow's Visions in Today's Royal Docks" *dpusummerlab* (2015) ; official website of the Silvertown Quays http://www.silvertownlondon.com/.

14   LBN, "Newham Info," *LBN*, http://www.newham.info/explorer/resources/.

15   LBN, *Canning Town and Custom House Supplementary Planning Document*, 18.

16   Katrina Gaus, "Impact of the Affordable Rent Model: Newham", *East Thames*, http://www.east-thames.co.uk/assets_cm/files/pdf/impact_of_the_affordable_rent_model_newham.pdf.

17   Malcolm James, *Urban Multiculture: Youth, Politics and Cultural Transformation in a Global City* (Palgrave, 2015), p. 114.

Other People's Plans for the Royal Docks

Douglas Murphy

In May 2013, an announcement was made that–at long last–one of the final large areas of London's postindustrial docklands was to be developed. An almost kilometre-long strip of derelict land on the north side of the Royal Albert Dock (the RAD site) was to be transformed into the Asian Business Port, an office park that would be specifically used by Chinese companies as a beachhead for their operations in the UK. The scheme would be developed by Asian Business Port (ABP), a Chinese company that would build almost half a million square metres of office space, an investment of more than £1 billion. This announcement was a triumph for the London mayor Boris Johnson, who along with the national government of the UK had been energetically courting Chinese investment during the "Great Recession".

By the end of 2017, nothing as yet has been built, although site preparation works continue. If developed according to plan, this site represents one of the last large-scale developments left in inner London, and will culminate a development cycle that has been one of the most productive since the period after World War II. In some ways RAD is atypical of recent London development in its size and scale, and in the fact that it is a predominantly commercial rather than residential development. But it is also at the same time typical, in terms of who has the power to make the city, where the money to make the city comes from, and also who stands to benefit from changes in the fabric of the city. The process by which ABP is coming into being highlights a remarkable sclerosis in the authorities and establishments that are able to give form to the built environment.

Furthermore, ABP also represents a consensus regarding what is the acceptable architectural and urban expression of new development at this time. This consensus is relatively speaking conservative, but at the same time can be understood as symbolic of a way of creating space that is fundamentally at odds with the economic character of the spaces themselves.

***

The history of the RAD site tells a condensed story of British capitalism. Until the late nineteenth century the land, on the north of a bow in the Thames immediately downriver of London, was marshy and barely used, with the furthest edge of the city still only a few kilometres to the west. In the late eighteenth century, the vast majority of London's dock traffic was still handled within the Upper Pool, the patch of river that now sits just upstream of Tower Bridge, but the increase in global sea trade and the growth of the empire stimulated the construction of dock infrastructure, effectively progressing eastward from the edge of the old city.

Throughout the nineteenth century, large enclosed dock systems were rapidly constructed along the river by private companies, including the West India Docks that would one day become Canary Wharf. The Victoria Dock to the west of the ABP site was operating by 1855, the first of the docks to be fully connected to the new rail infrastructure. The Royal Albert Dock was built later, opening in 1880, and when augmented by the King George V dock in 1921, it represented the peak of the upper Thames docking infrastructure, capable of handling the largest cargo ships of the time.

By the mid-twentieth century, the Royal Albert Dock was

lined with cranes, behind which stood a series of long single-storey warehouse sheds, and behind them were the rail lines bringing goods in and out. The docks themselves were restricted zones, inaccessible to the public behind secure walls. There were small residential neighbourhoods to the south at Silvertown, and to the north at Cyprus, which housed dockworkers, but most of the land to the north, apart from the massive Beckton Gas Works which dominated the Thames immediately downstream, remained largely undeveloped right into the late twentieth century, when some low-density housing estates were built.

What happened next is a familiar story. The invention and success of the intermodal container (standardised in 1968) led to the creation of much larger container ships, a shift from rail to road distribution, and the automation of loading and unloading. Shipping rapidly moved down the Thames to ports such as Tilbury and Gravesend, while the jobs disappeared, not to return. The dockland areas of East London were among the working-class communities hardest hit by the unemployment and decline of the 1970s and 1980s: in 1981 there were 27,000 workers left in Docklands from a peak of over 100,000 a generation before, and the many acres of derelict industrial infrastructure seemed to have no future use.

***

The story of the London Docklands Development Corporation (LDDC) is a prime example of social tensions that are made explicit when postindustrial urban areas are redeveloped. Created by Michael Heseltine in 1981 as a special infrastructural vehicle on the "free zone" model, it saw the filling in of docks, the construction of road and rail infrastructure, and unique planning and tax incentives for construction. After an ad hoc beginning largely centred on the Isle of Dogs, with small business estates and new light industry, the late 1980s saw the construction of the financial centre around Canary Wharf, and surrounding the Royal Victoria dock, a series of low-density housing developments and eventually the mammoth ExCel conference centre.

Local communities and the Greater London Council (GLC) organised resistance to the LDDC, creating the People's Plan for the Royal Docks. Against the plans for London City Airport, which was built from 1986 on the strip of dock between the Royal Albert and King George V docks, the People's Plan advocated for addressing the issues that were affecting the existing local community, such as poor-quality housing stock and lack of employment opportunity. The tensions were clear: the airport as infrastructure with obvious potential for economic stimulus, set against an existing community whose needs were more immediate, and who were rightly suspicious that the benefits of the LDDC were not going to trickle down to them.

Economic crises in the early 1990s and then again in the late 2000s left large areas of Docklands undeveloped and uncertain, but in both cases the construction cranes returned, and Canary Wharf has now reached a certain urban maturity. The American postmodernism of the first wave of construction was joined by the corporate headquarters for the larger banks after the millennium, and now, with the development of Wood Wharf, Canary Wharf is acquiring residential skyscrapers in the Dubai mode, and soon nearly all plots will have been developed to extremely high density.

The LDDC was wound up by the end of 1998, and the RAD site remained empty. Early plans for the Royal Docks had been drawn up in 1986 by Richard Rogers Partnership, who got to build a pumping station for their trouble, but the only plan for the ABP site that made it to the council was drawn up by Edward Cullinan Architects, and envisioned the site transformed into a business park. This final LDDC masterplan suggested that there could be 150,000 square metres built on the site, and the drawing[1] submitted shows a rather low-density development with quite substantial landscaping and parking space. One of the prime restrictions on any development of the site is the proximity of London City Airport, which means that any development must fit underneath a shallow "cone" that is roughly thirty metres high as it passes over RAD, meaning that no tall buildings are possible.

The application was submitted by LDDC in 1997, supported by Newham Council with the comment that the proposals were "consistent with the Council's ambition to secure high quality business development on what is potentially one of the most prestigious sites in the Borough".[2] But in the subsequent sixteen years the majority of this plan remained undeveloped, apart from two schemes. The land to the far east of the docks would be developed as the site for a campus of the University of East London, with Cullinan as the architect, which was occupied by the year 2000. To the west, the only significant development was Building 1000, a large office block of 10,000 square metres, built by 2004, and which the Borough of Newham took on as its offices in 2007. Today it sits lonely against the water, a building with little connection to anything beyond its car park and DLR station.

**

On 31 March 2014 a planning application was submitted for the RAD site, describing in outline form the overall parameters of the development, but also describing in detail the first phase of the development, which will renovate two listed buildings and create new offices and serviced apartments in roughly the centre of the site. The applicant was ABP, with the UK-based developer Stanhope, and the application itself was prepared by a large group of consultants, including the asset managers CBRE and the architects Farrells.

Farrells, the firm of Sir Terry Farrell – a specialist in planning large regeneration schemes, and the favoured architect of the Conservative establishment in the same way Rogers was for New Labour – prepared the Design and Access Statement, which is the mandatory report used to describe the principles and salient aspects of the proposed development. Reports such as these, which often stretch to many hundreds of pages for an urban development, are very useful for what they describe, but also what they omit to mention, or for that matter the obfuscations and disavowals that they contain within them.

The foreword, by Farrell, speaks of several key points, first of which is that "connecting this new area to its local hinterland is vital, so that the local community can gain best benefit from employment and skills through to providing access to the dock edge and beyond".[3] Then, based upon the "Anglo-Chinese trade accent and extended working hours", Farrell aspires towards "a 24-hour place, one of several characters; a series of new places in London". This suggests a concern for the overall quality of the city as a whole, but also a specific concern for the local area, a concern that is not borne out by the proposals.

Further into the document, the aspirations are described differently:

> Royal Albert Dock is a post-industrial stretch of land in a prime waterfront location. The vision is about changing a piece of London from a "backland" into a "frontland" and a new form of international trading centre in London once again. If London is to continue to grow and maintain its status as a "world city" it needs to embrace such changes.[4]

Here the implied relationship to the local area is seen in a different light. The site may have been empty for decades, but if "London" (understood as an economic entity) wants to remain an important location in the world, then "London" (understood as a population) must accept what is being put forward. Memories of the tension between LDDC and the People's Plan echo through statements like this, with the elision of different implied communities within the word "London" a key element of developer rhetoric.

The masterplan itself is perfectly sensible, laying out simple routes for movement, dividing the site into a variety of different plots of the size that make for functionally useful floor plates but also can be individually built with minimum risk. But memory also seems to play a role in the planning of the site in a way that speaks of current attitudes to development. For example, the "strip"-like development of the site is described as being a "translation of the site's former character",[5] rather than a simple and logical way to divide up the plots on such an area.

Elsewhere, one of the building types is said to "create the urban character of a London dockside architecture"[6] through its use of brick, when it genuinely bears no aesthetic resemblance to any dockside building previously extant, while the open spaces proposed for the site are described as being a series of new "London squares", specifically invoking a nostalgic image of the Georgian period. This attitude to historicism is even more apparent in the street naming, which carries the theme of Prince Albert through many of the streets, and names others "mews" and so on.

Neither of the previous developments on the site, Building 1000 and the UEL campus, developed at either end of the New Labour administration, adopt the same historicist attitude, and while the aesthetic of ABP is not exactly reactionary, it adopts a number of conservative architectural strategies, such as enforcing classical "base-middle-top" facade divisions, and deploying a very basic version of the austere brick detailing of the "New London Vernacular".[7] All these points demonstrate an ideology of a particularly British type, the odd Thatcherite melding of extremely liberal economics, with a historicist and nostalgic view of history and aesthetics.

But despite this, the banality of the planning and architecture give lie to all this "placemaking" and nostalgia, as the space and buildings proposed could — in true "free zone" manner–be anywhere. Plugged into London City Airport, ABP might as well be in the American Midwest, on the outskirts of Bangalore, in a small Chinese city of ten million people, or anywhere with tax exemptions and high-speed broadband. In this context, claiming that "both building form and shape of public realm have a direct resemblance of the historic layout of the site and combined together to create a similar character of space"[8] is meaningless jargon.

As for the types of buildings, the initial phase aims to build a variety of office buildings, some catering to the "Far East Market",[9] which appears to favour long, thin offices, and other buildings for local companies with a deeper, more spatially efficient plan. Much of the ground floor is to be given over to leisure and commerce, with "active frontages" and all the usual shibboleths of contemporary development, while serviced apartments–at twenty-seven square metres just over half the size of the minimum requirement for a one-bed flat–are intended for visiting workers' three-month stays. Later parts of the masterplan offer the opportunity for residential buildings, in particular the "attractive product"[10] of Private Rented Sector housing, a typology that has allowed larger investors to take advantage of the increasing numbers of people priced out of home ownership.

***

But what is the Asian Business Port, exactly? One of the primary reasons that development on the site had stalled for so long was not due to any particular economic headwind, but was to a large extent because any developer would have seen the 150,000 square meters of the 1997 masterplan as being far below the quantum of development that was possible. But for another plan to come forward to address this profit deficit, there would need to be a serious proposal on the cards, to cover the large cost of consultancy fees required for an application.

Enter Boris Johnson. In a premonition of Donald Trump's insistence that his political nous is because "I like making deals, preferably big deals", throughout his two terms in office Johnson took pride in unveiling a number of high-profile projects with prominent private backers. Among these there was the Orbit sculpture at the Olympics, backed by Lakshmi Mittal, the cable car between Canary Wharf and the Royal Docks, backed by Emirates Airlines, and later there was the Garden Bridge, whose backers failed to turn up in the end, leading to its descent into scandal and eventual cancellation.

The big money prize for Johnson was a Chinese connection, however, and before ABP there was a prior attempt to hook investment through offering up the site of the Crystal Palace in Sydenham to the developer ZhongRong, in order to "recreate" the palace as a mall of sorts. This initial plan disintegrated when the developer demanded half of the publicly owned Crystal Palace Park as well, and insisted that they would accept no constraints from British planning law. For ABP, the proposals were far less risky, or audacious. The use as a business park was already accepted, and the site formed part of Newham's "Arc of Opportunity", the less built-up, largely postindustrial part of the borough that the local authorities see as the prime site for growth and investment. Newham themselves had been actively promoting the borough in China as an investment opportunity, hoping to use the proximity of the Olympics as a hook.[11]

Terry Farrell's desire that the new development relates positively to the existing communities is admirable, but the real possibilities can be judged by looking at two factors: the sharing of the economic benefits of the schemes within the local context, and furthermore the question of housing.

Based upon the floor areas proposed, the application estimates that 15,780 jobs would be created within the site, on a site that currently employs almost no one. Clearly this represents an economic improvement, and the application notes that it represents "a similar number of jobs to when the site was a working docks and the hub of trade and economic prosperity for London, bringing the site back to its full potential and economic capacity".[12] But on the other hand, other than the cleaning and service jobs (predicted to be about eight hundred of the total), nearly all of these jobs are understood to be office jobs for skilled and trained business employees, of whom presumably many will be coming from China, or will be drawn from elsewhere in the City of London.

According to the application, "The Applicant is committed to working with Newham and Newham's employment brokerage partners to ensure that the benefits arising from the jobs created on-site are maximised in terms of opportunities for local people".[13] This sounds admirable, but within a document that deals largely in policy and legal obligation it represents no enforceable commitment, and there is little to suggest that the presence of a "free port" over the wall will be of benefit to the residents of Newham.

The question of housing is similar. The initial application only includes serviced apartments, but there is an understanding that sale and rental residential buildings will be part of later stages in the development, up to a total of 845 units. Newham's local plan aims for between 35% and 50% of all new housing developments to be "affordable", which refers to a variety of tenures, such as rental apartments set at under 80% of local rents.

It is here where the slippery word "viability" takes on its sinister implications. In the "affordable housing" section of the planning statement, which features eight points, all of them are excuses why no affordable housing should be provided, ranging from noting how many jobs are being created, pointing out that previous developments had failed, to simply saying that "the [Royal Albert Dock] site is a very difficult site to develop".[14] These caveats build up to the statement that the applicant was preparing a viability assessment, and that "the development will seek to maximise the provision of affordable housing whilst ensuring the development remains viable".[15] It is now widely known that viability assessments have become a secretive tool that developers use as leverage to avoid demands to contribute to local communities, and it would be not at all surprising if the amount of affordable housing that ABP sees as "viable" is zero, which all suggests that – to use the semantic slip again – the applicant's only commitment to any "local" community is to those who will eventually pay full price to become "local".

***

After the announcement of the RAD scheme, not everything went smoothly in the media. The first issue was a paranoid and perhaps xenophobic one: that Britain was being sold off to foreign powers, which prompted strenuous denials from Boris Johnson whilst on a trade mission to China.[16] The next issue was that as the press looked into the developer, headed by Xu Weiping, they found very little background information, with just a single previous development completed. This is reasonably common with Chinese investment in the UK, and usually leads to assumptions that these developers are simply commercial entities representing the Chinese Communist Party.

Further investigations revealed a host of connections that put the whole operation under a cloud. It was found that ABP had been sharing an office in Beijing with a company called London & Partners (L&P), which was a subsidiary of the London mayor involved in attracting foreign investment. L&P had been involved in the tendering process for the site, during which time people had changed employments from L&P to ABP, raising serious questions about the impartiality of the tender evaluations.[17]

Further questions were raised about Lady Xuelin Bates, a property developer who is married to Lord Bates, a Conservative peer. She was involved in bringing ABP forward to look into bidding for the site, but had also donated £160,000 to the Conservative Party. It was also later found that she had been involved in the early stages of the Crystal Palace project, giving the impression that she was acting as some kind of broker, skewing the impartiality of tendering procedures in the process, a messy situation that eventually led to Lord Bates being investigated (and cleared) by the House of Lords for his conduct.

This seedy, if not necessarily illegal, twisting and flouting of procurement rules is mirrored in some of the revelations that have emerged since the Garden Bridge project was cancelled, including suspicious staff movements from client to successful bidder, and in the case of the designer Thomas Heatherwick, a tenderer who appeared to already be part of the client. Although this project was abandoned, large amounts of public money were spent on a project in which every single stage appears to have been most poorly organised, and questions continue to be asked of Johnson's behaviour.

Similarly, with ABP, while the public cost has been minimal, the RAD site was in public ownership, and transferring it across to a private entity deserves scrutiny and transparency over how decisions were made. The ABP bid had more than fifty letters of intent from Chinese businesses stating they were ready to take space in the development, but this is also opaque, and suggests a level of commitment suspiciously immune to business cycles and other changes in outlook. And while the first phase of the development, representing 15% of the total, is set out in detail, there is nothing to suggest when future stages will be brought forward, or whether they will follow the original proposed character at all.

The problems of ABP of course reside largely in the procurement process, which demonstrates a haughty disregard for fair practice and public scrutiny. Johnson, as a powerful character aiming to stay prominent on the national stage, needed projects like this for the headlines that they would produce, as well as the general praise he'd receive just for managing to "get things done". But by behaving in this way, treating the RAD site almost as a generic global business park to be given away, Johnson and ABP show just how invisible other communities have become in the global investment game. Newham, and London in general, are historic not just for their dock walls and bollards, but in the people and networks that already exist, and that are often completely absent from the new worlds created.

Endnotes

1   N/97/0134

2   N/97/0134–Planning Committee Meeting 9th September
     1997 p.7

3   14/00618/OUT — Outline Component Design and Access
     Statement Chapter 1, p. 6

4   14/00618/OUT — Outline Component Design and Access
     Statement Chapter 2, p. 11

5   14/00618/OUT–Outline Component Design and Access
     Statement Chapter 1, p. 11

6   14/00618/OUT–Detailed Component Design and Access
     Statement Chapter 3A, p. 14

7   The "New London Vernacular" is an architectural style,
     mainly used for housing, that has become popular since
     the 2008 economic crash. It is modern construction
     that references historic housing "terrace" types in its
     proportions and detailing, and is most distinguished by its
     extensive use of brick panels. See: Urban Design London,
     A New London Housing Vernacular, 2012

8   14/00628/OUT–Design and Access Statement, Chapter
     3C, p. 1

9   14/00618/OUT–Planning Statement, p. 17

10   Ibid, p. 27

11   Dan Hancox, "A 'Regeneration Supernova' Is About
     to Destroy East London as We Know It", *Vice* (22 April
     2014), https://www.vice.com/en_uk/article/nnq7q7/dan-
     hancox-regeneration-supernove

12   14/00618/OUT — Planning Statement p. 18

13   14/00618/OUT–Environmental Statement, Chapter 7,
     Socio-Economics, p. 9

14   14/00618/OUT — Planning Statement, p. 28

15   Ibid, p. 29

16   Andrew Parsons, "Boris Johnson: Don't be afraid of
     Chinese firms buying into London", *Evening Standard* (14
     October 2013), https://www.standard.co.uk/news/politics/

boris-johnson-don-t-be-afraid-of-chinese-firms-buying-into-london-8879135.html

17   Michael Crick, "Big questions for Boris over billion dollar property deal", *Channel 4* (13 November 2014), https://www.channel4.com/news/boris-johnson-london-propery-deal-china-albert-dock

"That's Just the Way It Is": Ageing and Mobility in East London

Theodora Bowering

I stand holding my cup of peppermint tea, looking for a place to sit. I see that all the tables are full and I am pleased. I have spied an older lady sitting alone and really hope that I can talk to her. I momentarily loiter near her table and she immediately invites me to join her. We sit in silence for a few minutes sipping our drinks while the customers bustle around us, sugaring their coffees and chatting. We smile at each other. "A good spot for people watching", I say. She smiles and nods, looking out the window at the crowds moving past. "Too many foreigners", she says, her face almost comical in its expression of distaste. We sit for a few moments more.

Over the next four hours, Betty and I get to know each other as she takes me on a journey across London, visiting the various shops and cafés that she patronises as part of her everyday routine. Nearly eighty years old, Betty has been coming to the Stratford area for over thirty years. She used to live here but moved to Greenwich, where she still lives, during the slum clearances of 1977. She notes her disapproval of the number of immigrants whilst simultaneously praising the café staff who are part of these diasporas. Lunch at the "Rainbow English and Chinese Fast Food" café in the Stratford Centre is followed by a ride on the 108 bus to Lewisham.

Along the way Betty tells me about her daughter and how happy she is that she's married to a "good man who looks after her". Her daughter lives in Eltham, only twenty minutes down the road from Betty, so they see each other regularly. Betty divorced her husband when her daughter was two and never remarried. She doesn't explain why; she just says, "I'd had enough by that stage, I couldn't take it any more". From the bus window, Betty points out her house in Greenwich and tells me about how she was recently ill for a year and couldn't get out very much. She has a disease that affects her muscles and bones so she now walks with a stick. We spend a lot of time sitting in silence and watching the city pass by. Once we reach the end of the route Betty takes me to the Lewisham Shopping Centre where she buys a TV magazine at WHSmith, a cup of corn at a stand in the mall, and a tea at the BHS café. At every café we visit Betty is known, maybe not by her name but definitely by her face. Every space visited is also private and commercial, requiring a purchase for the right of occupation. When I ask Betty about this, she shrugs and says, "That's just the way it is".

Understanding what it means to grow older in cities is of increasing importance as ageing and urbanisation continue to accelerate worldwide.[1] Older people also offer a unique lens through which to view the civic spaces and practices of cities. In their everyday routines they inhabit, traverse, observe, avoid, and contest these spaces and by these acts, both passive and active, they assemble their own personal territories and networks. These assemblages reflect the changing mobilities–the evolving speeds and scales of time and space–of people as they age and engage with the formations of the city, in turn offering insight into how the accessibility of civic sites and infrastructures supports older people in resisting their marginalisation.

Abstract, top-down readings by the government and media depict the London Borough of Newham as one of the most deprived and problematic areas for older people in the country.[2] While the determination of deprivation is an abstract construct blind to local strengths, the challenges are real, restricting older people whilst also provoking creativity and resilience in their responses. Inequalities in older age have been shown to be a continuation of deprivation and other factors developed over time.[3] The UK's most deprived neighbourhoods have the highest rates of loneliness and fear, opening up links to other considerations, such as exclusion from resources, the labour market, public services, social relationships, socioeconomic status, and the perceived quality of a neighbourhood.[4] The growing population and density of London and Newham prompts a questioning of how older people are marginalised within cities. This is particularly important as older people often have greater attachments to their neighbourhoods, having lived in them for longer periods, and are more greatly affected by changes due to growth and migration.[5] Consequently, the older people within Newham, like Betty, are among the most deprived people living in one of the most highly marginalising contexts.

Newham has become the ground of complex mechanisms of planning, continuing a legacy of neoliberal policies introduced since the 1980s under Thatcher's Conservative government and continued by New Labour from the 1990s.[6] With the London Legacy Development Corporation formed to manage the recent Olympic Park site and the adjacent Westfield Shopping Centre and Stratford City,[7] these and other "regeneration" projects – including Canning Town, Custom House, and the Royal Docks – are continuing along the "Arc of Opportunity",[8] and capitalising on investment opportunities to help manage the borough's high debt levels and long housing waiting list. As Ben Campkin observes in "Remaking London: Decline and Regeneration in Urban Culture":

[The] gentrification strategy is only very thinly veiled as regeneration strategy, focused on raising land values, opening new markets, and attracting the "right" kind of businesses and residents to settle – with the assumption of a trickle down effect in which this new wealth will benefit at least some of the existing communities.[9]

The Carpenters Estate, Robin Hood Gardens, and the Heygate Estate are just some of these projects that have a dramatic social impact on their local communities, disrupting and displacing older people who are often most invested in their environments and the least equipped to move or take advantage of the opportunities of regeneration. These issues are highly politicised and must be read within the context of global capitalist trends and national-level initiatives such as the Localism Act and the Big Society.[10] At the local level these agendas are reflected in Newham Council's resilience policies[11] which are shown to unfairly disadvantage older residents in Newham who are already among the most

Fig. 1: Betty and the author on the 108 bus to Lewisham.

marginalised in the community.[12]

The value that older people bring to society is rarely reflected in the strategies and priorities of developers, whose marketing materials and site hoardings present only the most superficial aspirations of a consumption-oriented and economically productive youth. The image of Newham's "Arc of Opportunity", utilised across the borough's policy and promotional material, is another powerful symbol of the capitalist drive for development and the position of the borough as being open for business and investment. It is a pink swathe that depicts time and space as smooth, seamless, and muted, deleting all obstacles from the spaces of Newham including the existing older residents who don't fit the sales pitch to investors. An image is conjured of a positive, putty-like flow of capital filling all the cracks and crevices of East London, muffling all noise, to create a homogenous silky matt finish, a tabula rasa ready for development. But, where is Betty in this seamless pink swathe?

Betty's story challenges the presumed authority of increased speed, ongoing expansion, constant development, and technological innovation. Her daily routine involves the minutiae of interactions with people, objects, and infrastructures that over years and decades have created familiar and supportive networks that allow an ongoing engagement with her history, Newham, and the broader city of London. These networks are, however, vulnerable. Betty's physical accessibility of Newham and the city is of increasing significance as she ages, and her mobility and visibility are both positively and negatively affected by improvements, disruptions, and disconnections wrought by urban developments.

Older people, as a heterogeneous population, encompass a great diversity of access to systems, services, and structures of mobility. Looking at how older people travel as they age, there is a clear recognition of changing patterns of mobility, and growing exclusion and isolation, in the transition to retirement.[13] The extent of this marginalisation is highly variable and not explained by simple social, economic, and spatial relations. For example, it cannot be assumed that living in close proximity to public transport infrastructure will guarantee its use, or that being wealthy or having an extended family will prevent experiences of exclusion.[14] It is not just the poor that are marginalised due to age; it is a class-transcending phenomenon. Living in London, Betty's potential mobility is increased by her home's proximity to bus routes, and her ability to walk to them. She can take advantage of this most accessible form of public transport, which generally offers equal access to all users, as well as being free for older people.[15] In "More Than A to B: The Role of Free Bus Travel for the Mobility and Wellbeing of Older Citizens in London", it is argued that the bus in particular provides "a mundane, yet potentially therapeutic, space: a taken-for-granted part of the city landscape which nonetheless provides a source of potential events, social encounters and opportunities for engagement".[16] The value of transport infrastructures, as a type of banal civic space, in alleviating isolation and loneliness, is important for older people, including Betty. Interactions with strangers can be more socially acceptable while travelling and waiting at bus stops, offering an opportunity for exchange, even if simply about the weather. This is also true of other civic spaces as demonstrated by my encounter with Betty at a café in Stratford. Two people with time on their hands and an interest in observing and discussing the world around them led to an afternoon of growing intimacy and understanding.

It can be understood that as people age their relationship to time and space changes. As they become frailer and more dependent their spatial world contracts, intensifying those spaces they do occupy. Equally, as it takes longer to move across and between sites, time intensifies. The value of a public bench, a welcoming café, a friendly face, and a dynamic vista, close to home, becomes increasingly important in the resistance of isolation as people age. The young and active can travel to where they "want" to be, whereas older people are more limited to where they "can" be. Local policies often remove or limit public benches in order to reduce loitering and rough sleeping, in an attempt to mitigate antisocial behaviour, such as in the square around Queens Market, the Queens Pub, and Hamara Ghar sheltered elderly housing at Upton Park. The consequent absence of places to sit can disadvantage older people's capacity to rest and access the public realm, as well as observe and interact with the diversity of the commons. This shows how the lives of older people and their experiences of marginalisation are interlinked with those of other marginal groups; the exclusion of youths, street drinkers, and the homeless unwittingly also excludes older people. These consequences for older people's rights to the city are neither well-recognised nor defended. Older people do not march in the streets to demand their rights to the city, engage in "antisocial behaviour", or rise up in spontaneous protest. Betty experiences this lack of welcoming public space; she has to pay to spend time in the cafés and buses of her daily routine, and is resigned to the fact that "That's just the way it is".

What will be the force of this growing ageing population? In what unforeseen ways will it impact the city? Will the slower-moving and more cautious nature of older people come to balance out the speed and impatience of London's youth? Imagine a sea of pensioners on Oxford Street at lunchtime. As if in a quagmire, will the corporate suits and shoppers be slowed to a meditative pace, or will they scream in frustration whilst elbowing an eighty year old in the face? Will this scenario ever be tested; will old people all be shipped out to the suburbs, to retirement villages and "naturally occurring retirement communities"; or will they simply continue their retreat from the eyes and support of the civic realm, progressing further and further into invisibility and the loneliness this brings? Even in the suburbs, the same challenges exist, just in different configurations. The density is lower but the need for civic spaces – a corner store, public transport, street life – still exists. The cost of living in London is increasingly prohibitive, and regeneration continues to displace poorer communities. Will older people be priced out of the city, and if so what are their alternative options? The changes will disrupt all and displace some. Positive improvements will come with the increased investment but at what price? London's prosperity cannot grow indefinitely. Political and economic forces cannot be predicted and London's status as a site of global investment could shrink. It can be said that the challenge that comes of change, whether at the scale of global and national economic collapse, Brexit, or the closure of a familiar local service, can prompt innovation and resilience. But it must be acknowledged that within the Newham community, older people already face a greater share of challenges. And so the additional tests that come from the closure of a community centre or the change of a bus route would weigh more heavily and draw more deeply from their reserves than for those who have more private resources.

The civic spaces of the city are where community, contestation, and contradiction are mediated daily, and how well they are integrated into the city and older people's lives is of great consequence. They are the ground of civic participation, instrumental in the resistance of institutionalisation, medicalisation, and segregation. In accessing and occupying shared urban spaces older people are able to develop resilience and enact their right to the city.

Recently, I went looking for Betty, and even though everyone I spoke to still remembered her, they said they had not seen her in a long time. Whether due to her health deteriorating or her family situation changing, Betty's assemblage of civic spaces and her engagement with the city had changed. I can only hope that she is continuing to take advantage of whatever places and interactions are available to her, and that she is maintaining her contestation of the city.

Endnotes

1   Globally, in 2017, 13% of people were over 60, and this is projected to rise to 16% by 2030, 21% by 2050 and 28% by 2100 (United Nations, Department of Economic and Social Affairs, Population Division. "World Population Prospects: The 2017 Revision, Key Findings and Advance Tables", Working Paper. New York, 2017. https://esa.un.org/unpd/wpp/Publications/Files/WPP2017_KeyFindings. pdf.). This demographic change is most concentrated in urban areas, with approximately 58% of over-60s living in cities in 2015, up from 51% in 2000 (United Nations, Department of Economic and Social Affairs, Population Division. "World Population Ageing". New York: United Nations, 2015. http://www.un.org/en/development/desa/population/publications/pdf/ageing/WPA2015_Report.pdf.). In the United Kingdom over-65s will rise from 18% in 2016 to 24.7% in 2046 (Office for National Statistics. "Overview of the UK Population". London: Office for National Statistics, 21 July 2017. https://www.ons.gov.uk/peoplepopulationandcommunity/populationandmigration/populationestimates/articles/overviewoftheukpopulation/july2017.); the mid-2016 population of 65.6 million will increase to 73 million by 2041 (Office for National Statistics. "National Population Projections: 2016-Based Statistical Bulletin". London: Office for National Statistics, 26 October 2017. https://www.ons.gov.uk/peoplepopulationandcommunity/populationandmigration/populationprojections/bulletins/nationalpopulationprojections/2016based statisticalbulletin.); and urbanisation will rise from the current 82% to 89% by 2050 (United Nations, Department of Economic and Social Affairs. World Urbanization Prospects: Highlights. New York: United Nations, 2014. http://esa.un.org/unpd/wup/Publications/Files/WUP2014-Highlights.pdf.).

2   The borough continues to be one of the poorest performing areas in London and the UK for older people, as shown by a ranking of 3 on the Income Deprivation Affecting Older People Index, with 41% of older people living in income deprived households (Department for Communities and Local Government. "The English Indices of Deprivation". Statistical Release. London: Department for Communities and Local Government, 30 September 2015. https://www.gov.uk/government/uploads/system/uploads/attachment_data/file/465791/English_Indices_of_Deprivation_2015_-_Statistical_Release.pdf.).

3   Jan Baars, Dale Dannefer, Chris Phillipson and Alan Walker, *Aging, Globalization and Inequality: The New Critical Gerontology.* (Baywood, 2006). Also: Christopher, Gilleard and Paul Higgs. *Cultures of Ageing: Self, Citizen and the Body* (Pearson Education Ltd, 2000)

4   Thomas Scharf and Jenny de Jong Gierveld, "Loneliness in Urban Neighbourhoods: An Anglo-Dutch Comparison", *European Journal of Ageing,* 5:2, June 2008, pp. 103-15. https://doi.org/10.1007/s10433-008-0080-x.

5   Chris Phillipson, "The 'Elected' and the 'Excluded': Sociological Perspectives on the Experience of Place and Community in Old Age", *Ageing and Society,* 27: 03, May 2007, p 321. https://doi.org/10.1017/S0144686X06005629.

6   Patrick Dunleavy, *The Politics of Mass Housing in Britain, 1945-1975: A Study of Corporate Power and Professional Influence in the Welfare State* (Clarendon Press, 1981); Nick Gallent, *"Planning and Affordable Housing: From Old Values to New Labour?"*, *The Town Planning Review,* 71:2, 2000, pp. 123-47; Chris Hamnett, *Unequal City: London in the Global Arena* (Routledge, 2003); Jamileh Manoochehri, *The Politics of Social Housing in Britain* (Peter Lang, 2012); Michael Parkinson, "The Thatcher Government's Urban Policy, 1979-1989: A Review", *The Town Planning Review,*

60:4, 1989, pp. 421-40.; Nicholas Bullock (ed) "West Ham and the Welfare State 1945-70: A Suitable Case for Treatment?", *Architecture and the Welfare State* (Routledge, 2015), pp. 93-109.

7   Tim Butler and Michael Rustin, *Rising in the East: The Regeneration of East London* (Lawrence & Wishart, 1996); Ben Campkin, *Remaking London: Decline and Regeneration in Urban Culture* (IB Tauris, 2013); Simona Florio and Michael Edwards, "Urban Regeneration in Stratford, London", *Planning Practice and Research*, 16:2, May 2001, pp. 101-20; https://doi.org/10.1080/02697450120077334.

8   Newham Council. "Newham London Investment Prospectus" (Newham Council, 2010)

9   Campkin, *Remaking London*, pp. 163-164.

10   Nick Clarke and Allan Cochrane, "Geographies and Politics of Localism: The Localism of the United Kingdom's Coalition Government", *Political Geography*, 34, May 2013, pp. 10-23, https://doi.org/10.1016/j.polgeo.2013.03.003; Department for Communities and Local Government. "Decentralisation and the Localism Bill" (Department for Communities and Local Government December 2010), https://www.gov.uk/government/uploads/system/uploads/attachment_data/file/5951/1793908.pdf; Department for Communities and Local Government, "A Plain English Guide to the Localism Bill", (Department for Communities and Local Government, November 2011), https://www.gov.uk/government/uploads/system/uploads/attachment_data/file/5959/1896534.pdf; Andrew Harrop, "Will the Localism Bill Deliver Power to the UK's Older People?", the *Guardian* (20th January 2011), http://www.theguardian.com/society/joepublic/2011/jan/20/will-localism-bill-deliver-older-people-power; Andrew Hoolachan, "The 'Nature' of Legacy under Localism: Fragmentation along the Greenway", *Architectural Research Quarterly*, 18:04, December 2014), pp. 342-52, https://doi.

org/10.1017/S135913551500007X.

11   LSE Housing and Communities, "Facing Debt: Economic Resilience in Newham - CASE Report 83". (London School of Economics, 18 July 2014), http://www.lse.ac.uk/newsAndMedia/PDF/FacingDebt.pdf; Newham Council, "Community Resilience in Newham" (Newham Council, 2011), https://www.newham.gov.uk/Documents/Council%20and%20Democracy/Community ResilienceinNewham.pdf; Newham Council, "Quid pro Quo, Not Status Quo: Why We Need a Welfare State That Builds Resilience" (Newham Council, 2011), https://www.newham.gov.uk/Documents/Council%20and%20Democracy/Whyweneedawelfarestatethat buildsresilience.pdf; Newham Council, "Building Resilience: The Evidence Base" (Newham Council, September 2013), https://www.newham.gov.uk/Documents/Council%20and%20Democracy/BuildingResilience TheEvidenceBaseSep2013.pdf.

12   Dylan Kneale, "Can Localism Work for Older People in Urban Environments?" London: International Longevity Centre, 2011. http://ilcuk.org.uk/files/pdf_pdf_176.pdf. Kneale, Dylan, and David Sinclair. 'Localism and Neighbourhoods for All Ages: Is Localism Sounding a Death Knell or a Wake-up Call for Creating Neighbourhoods for All Ages?", *International Longevity Centre* (22 March 2011), http://www.ilcuk.org.uk/index.php/publications/publication_details/localism_and_neighbourhoods_for_all_ages

13   Jessica Berg, Lena Levin, Marianne Abramsson and Jan-Erik Hagberg, "Mobility in the Transition to Retirement–the Intertwining of Transportation and Everyday Projects", *Journal of Transport Geography, 38*, June 2014, pp. 48-54, https://doi.org/10.1016/j.jtrangeo.2014.05.014; A. Church, M. Frost and K. Sullivan, "Transport and Social Exclusion in London",

Transport Policy, 7:3, July 2000, pp. 195-205, https://doi.org/10.1016/S0967-070X(00)00024-X.; Judith Green, Alasdair Jones and Helen Roberts, "More than A to B: The Role of Free Bus Travel for the Mobility and Wellbeing of Older Citizens in London", *Ageing and Society*, 34:3, March 2014, pp. 472-94, https://doi.org/10.1017/S0144686X12001110; Tim Schwanen, and Antonio Páez, "The Mobility of Older People – an Introduction", *Journal of Transport Geography*, 18:5l, September 2010, pp. 591-95, https://doi.org/10.1016/j.jtrangeo.2010.06.001.

14   Tim Schwanen, Karen Lucas, Nihan Akyelken, Diego Cisternas Solsona, Juan-Antonio Carrasco and Tijs Neutens, "Rethinking the Links between Social Exclusion and Transport Disadvantage through the Lens of Social Capital", *Transportation Research Part A: Policy and Practice*, 74, April 2015, pp. 123-35, https://doi.org/10.1016/j.tra.2015.02.012.

15   Laura Ferrari, Michele Berlingerio, Francesco Calabrese and Jon Reades, "Improving the Accessibility of Urban Transportation Networks for People with Disabilities", *Advances in Computing and Communications and Their Impact on Transportation Science and Technologies*, 45, August 2014, pp. 27-40, https://doi.org/10.1016/j.trc.2013.10.005.

16   Green, Jones and Roberts, "More than A to B", p. 490.

Does This Place Exist? Identity Making in the Royal Docks

Robert Baffour-Awuah

In between the roar of aircraft rising steeply out from London City Airport and over Royal Victoria Dock there are long periods of silence. The relative quietness that characterises the Royal Docks today is what has attracted fifty-four-year-old Mrs Clark—as she formally introduces herself—to the area. "It's still in London but because of the water it's so peaceful—it's like no one knows where it is", she tells me. Callon, a web developer in his mid-twenties, tells me that he moved to Britannia Village—a residential area in the Royal Docks—out of "pure coincidence, not choice, just over a year ago" and is looking for a way out. "Apart from the summer, the area is boring. It's lacking shops, bars, and places people can hang out."

Like many residents I have met since I became involved with the Royal Docks, Mrs Clark and Callon have in common their desire to see more amenities in the Royal Docks. The lack of street life, scarcity of shops, pubs, restaurants, and other cornerstones of established places are the most noticeable signs of the area's current standing. The Royal Docks were never created to lay this still and silent but they have largely been this way since the last ship left the docks in 1981. However, things are beginning to change.

***

In all senses, the Royal Docks is a real place, but at the same time it doesn't really "exist". Not in the way that places are increasingly "existing" in modern London. In numerous meetings that I have attended, I've heard developers, council officers, business representatives, and even some residents repeat a version of the phrase "We need to put the Royal Docks on the map".

I first recall hearing this phrase in relation to the Royal Docks back when I met a senior representative of the Silvertown Partnership, a consortium that, at the time of writing, is behind the development of a new residential, commercial, and brand experience district at Silvertown Quays in the Royal Docks. "We are one of the biggest developments in London but putting the Royal Docks and Silvertown Quays on the map is a massive deal when 90% of Londoners don't even know where it is."

"On the map" has become an overused buzzword in regeneration. With increased competition between cities and places to attract businesses, investment, and visitors, public- and private-sector organisations have wholly embraced the idea of brand and identity as devices to increase recognition and build value for places. A place is "on the map" when it is rooted in collective imaginations. It's "on the map" when a stranger in the street can tell you where it is and why you'd want to go there. A chief executive could convey to her board why, beyond financial reasons, the company should relocate all two hundred of its staff to that place. Increasingly it also means the place has a Twitter and Instagram account and a YouTube channel. It effortlessly attracts visitors to its events, residents to buy its apartments, and businesses to lease its office spaces. It spins a thousand stories into a simple narrative and constructs a marketable identity.

London has a growing litany of regeneration programmes with

the explicit aim of putting an area on the map. Particularly in places that have suffered economic stagnation or slow growth, positive media attention, a boost in visitor numbers and the arrival of new businesses providing job opportunities are some of the potential benefits of being thrust onto a visible stage.

Too often, though, these benefits come at a cost that communities are unwilling to bear. Across the city, existing business and residential communities want alternatives to proposals that relegate them to the sidelines, as the identity of their neighbourhoods is transformed by developers and landowners in a staged performance intended to appeal to the tastes of new visitors and investors.

It is clear that for some developers across London, identity does not exist unless it is marketable. The identities that reside and are performed in everyday spaces are often overlooked. Many developers will often only pay attention to the narratives woven in these everyday spaces when there is an alignment with their own vision for a place. The story of a local resident, shopkeeper, or business owner will frequently only find its way into a marketing brochure, development website, or YouTube channel if it adds value. There is a long history of developers appropriating local value to some degree. With her analysis of destination culture, sociologist Sharon Zukin identified the weakening grip on identity and yearning for authentic experiences that city dwellers face in light of the corporate-led image making and reinvention of the physical and social fabric of the city.[1]

Equally relevant is Zukin's observation that the confluence of capital investment and consumer culture has fuelled the belief that cities can "have it all" and be "both a corporate city and a new urban village".[2] In London, this is seen in the proliferation of "premiumised" developments and places marked by heavy cultural programming and a destination aesthetic. Premium cultural events, street food markets, expensively commissioned public artworks, and brand activations converge in a heady mix of corporate and everyday culture. They are the manifestation of the reliance of urban change on private finance, mixed with the obsession with creating places that appeal to aspirational millennial lifestyles.

Appropriately implemented, some of these elements are welcome additions to neighbourhoods–bringing activity to open spaces, and supporting and growing local economies. The issue arises where interventions are formulaic, becoming shortcuts for putting places on the map. They confound their own claims of uniqueness–and stifle opportunities for identities to form and alter by smothering neighbourhoods with identikit brand messaging and cut-and-paste placemaking projects.

London's formerly disconnected areas can be particularly vulnerable to this type of urbanism. Kings Cross, Vauxhall Nine Elms Battersea, Queen Elizabeth Olympic Park, Greenwich Peninsula, and the Royal Docks are just some of the "new" places that have emerged or are emerging from past industrial sites. Sites like these have previously had their identities shaped by industry, infrastructure, and in some cases dereliction. Existing industrial uses on sites of this nature have been historically under-recognised, and despite relatively recent efforts to re-evaluate their importance to London's economy and communities they have generally not featured in the vision and identity of development sites–or remain as convenient background imagery for "authentic" brand messaging.

Developers of post-industrial sites operate in a perceived vacuum of identity and, in some cases, attempt to present new residents and businesses with ready-made profiles. Developers of City Island in Canning Town and Greenwich Peninsula have turned to an artifice of identity–branding new residents as "Islanders" and "Pioneers". These starter-pack identities can be seen as genuine attempts to establish a rootedness to place as much as they are cynical marketing and brand devices.

Across the capital, the difficulties of aligning profit, value, identity, and socially just development are being played out with very public missteps and small successes. Over the coming years the spotlight will fall on the Royal Docks as a public sector team begins to contend with these issues.

Since August 2017 I have been working with the Royal Docks Team as promotion and investment manager. From the very first day, it was clear what my priority was: "develop an identity for the Royal Docks and a strategy to communicate this to investors and the wider public". The Royal Docks needed to appear as an attractive destination for businesses and visitors. I had to help put the Royal Docks "on the map".

The history behind this aim, the complex motivations of the individuals and groups implicated, and the strong feelings on all sides about identity shed a unique light on the current state of urban change in London today.

The Enterprise Zone Formula

The Royal Docks has a complex history of development, and public and private interventions. It is a vast landscape of individual neighbourhoods and emerging developments. Silvertown Quays alone is of the same scale as the whole Kings Cross redevelopment area.

Royal Victoria Dock, Royal Albert Dock, and King George IV Dock are the three man-made bodies of water that make up the collective Royal Docks. The composite tracts of land and water were inherited by the mayor of London through a chain of transactions that began in 1981 with the London Docklands Development Corporation–the government-appointed body that had begun the task of bringing together land that had until then been in multiple ownership. The land passed through various bodies over the years, but has been held by a GLA subsidiary known as GLAP (GLA Land and Property) since 2012. At 266 hectares, the Royal Docks is the largest land holding in the control of the mayor of London, and its future rests, as it has always done, on a mixture of formalised and tenuous partnerships between the private and public sectors.

The latest iteration of this is the Enterprise Zone, one of twenty-four nationally designated spatial zones created to drive growth and economic development—the Royal Docks is currently there only active zone in London. Enterprise Zones are primarily focussed on driving private-sector-led growth in localised areas that have the potential to generate benefits that affect the wider local and national economy. By offering tax breaks and other incentives to businesses, Enterprise Zones encourage accelerated development and economic growth. Former Mayor of London Boris Johnson brought the Royal Docks' Enterprise Zone into effect in 2013, lauding the designation—in exaggerated fashion—as "the icing on the cake for my vision to return the Royals to their former glory as a thriving, vibrant place to live, work and visit".[3] The landmark Enterprise Zone announcement under Boris' tenure was the signing of a development agreement with Chinese developer and investor Advanced Business Park (ABP), to create a business district in Royal Albert Dock that will accommodate a mix of companies from Asia, the UK, and Europe. During this time, a development agreement was also signed with the Silvertown Partnership for the redevelopment of Silvertown Quays.

While commentators have questioned the effectiveness of Enterprise Zones as a tool to grow local economies,[4] they do provide an invaluable and focused source of investment for the public sector. The implementation of the zone enables local business rates to be retained and spent by a Local Enterprise Partnership (LEP): a body tasked with leading economic growth in a designated area. The arrangements for the Royal Docks Enterprise Zone are that the local authority, in this case the London Borough of Newham, collect business rates as any other local authority does. However, for the first twenty-five years—from 2013—the London LEP, known as the Local Economic Action Partnership (LEAP), retains business rates generated within the Royal Docks Enterprise Zone and sets priorities for investment. The retained rates can be spent in the zone or on projects with a direct benefit to the zone. The Royal Docks Team was created in an agreement between the mayor of London, mayor of Newham, and LEAP as an instrument to act on those priorities by conceiving of and implementing strategic and localised projects.

Over the next quarter of a century, the Royal Docks could benefit from an unprecedented level of investment as a direct result of retained business rates income. Transport connections and streets will be improved – linking previously cut-off and hard-to-access parts of the area. The vast and largely inaccessible water bodies will be opened up and transformed into a usable asset. A more diversified economy will be created by investment in initiatives that seek to support and grow small local businesses.

Given the potential benefits of investment and the limited twenty-five-year period of business rates retention, politicians, LEAP members, and council officers are united in agreement that there is a need to urgently attract businesses to the Royal Docks that will feed the virtuous cycle of retained business rates and direct reinvestment back into the area. There is little argument that this is investment that the Royal Docks really needs. Better infrastructure, roads, rail, and open spaces are equally as important for prospective businesses as they are for incoming and existing residents. Tension however arises in the contested visions for the area.

The Burden–and Hope–of Visions

When Boris Johnson inaugurated the Enterprise Zone he referred to "his" vision for the Royal Docks – this wasn't a completely unjustified claim. The Royal Docks has throughout its history been a grand top-down project of the state's engineering, and rendered through joint private- and public-sector tools that have carved a unique yet disjointed place. Alternative approaches created within communities have been proposed – the most significant evidence of this being the 1984 popular planning exercise that was the People's Plan for the Royal Docks. In reaction to the economic decline of the docks and the impending airport-led regeneration plan that birthed London City Airport, community interests put forward an alternative vision focused on jobs and growing the local economy. However, plans for the airport pressed ahead facilitated by national and local government–thus reasserting the hegemonic planning and envisioning activities that underlie the recent visioning for the Royal Docks.

Created to serve the London business market, the airport is the most visible and contentious of projects intended to facilitate investment into the Royal Docks. It was also intended as a project that could change perceptions of the area and drive investor confidence. London City Airport was imagined as a project that could put the Royal Docks on the map. Investment did follow–in the form of ExCel Exhibition Centre and the University of East London–but not at the anticipated scale.

Another public-sector-backed scheme intended to shape the identity and kickstart the transformation of the Royal Docks is the Crystal, a building that at one time was held up as a beacon of sustainability. The Crystal was envisaged as being the landmark attraction for the Green Enterprise District, a regional policy and branding exercise that set out to encourage the growth of an internationally renowned low-carbon region, with the Royal Docks at its heart. "New visionary attractions and exhibitions" were imagined for the district that would act as a draw for "people to live, work and visit".[5] The policy was intended to raise the profile of the Royal Docks and wider district on a national and international stage. Peter Bishop, former deputy CEO of the now defunct London Development Agency, points out that the Green Enterprise District was driven by a desire for a landmark concept to address climate change and the "need to brand and market an area where development activity had been very weak".[6]

The Crystal has had some success as a local visitor attraction, events and conference venue, and local meeting space; but you haven't got to walk too far around the Royal Docks to see that the rest of the Green Enterprise District hasn't materialised. While the policy hasn't been officially dropped it doesn't seem that there is any rush to revive it either.

The Royal Docks Team has inherited these histories of bureaucratically driven grand visions and strained attempts to develop an identity for the area. The fact that the Royal Docks has a dedicated team that can affect change in the area is a positive move. However the history, context, and mechanisms through which the team have been created risk reimposing a dominant vision and identity on an area and its citizens. The pressure to accelerate the rate at which businesses set up in the Royal Docks also creates the risk that the immediate purview of the team is focused on private interests. This tension has been played out in the early days of the Royal Docks Team—particularly in trying to address the needs of a diversity of business and residential communities.

Making Places, Creating Destinations

It's mid-morning in the Crystal and I'm meeting a representative from Siemens. The Royal Docks Team have been based in the Crystal since August 2017, in a small second-floor office on the southern end of the building, overlooking a flyover and aggregates yards, Greenwich Peninsula, the O2, and Canary Wharf in the near distance. One half of the angular glass structure of the Crystal houses a number of Siemens staff, a public café, and extensive events and conferencing facilities.

The other half of the building is taken up by "The Future of Cities", a publicly accessible exhibition, telling the story of the challenges that cities face and the technical solutions that could solve them. One exhibit invites visitors to furiously pedal on one of London's Santander hire cycles, to find out what devices the transferable energy could power. Like the last time I was here, the exhibit is out of order.

The meeting today has been organised in order to discuss the potential future uses for the building that was acquired by the

GLA from Siemens in 2016. An idea that has been floated is a promotional and marketing facility. The rationale for the project is that "developers, investors, businesses and visitors" need to see visible change in the area. The promotional facility would help to drive footfall and visitor numbers as well as changing perceptions of the Royal Docks.[7] However, there is scepticism about the real need for a dedicated facility like this and its ability to attract visitors beyond built-environment professionals.

This is a challenge the representative from Siemens knows all too well. The first time I met him in August 2015 he took me on a tour of the "Future of Cities" exhibition and explained that his role, which he still fulfils to the current day, involves working with city leaders, architects, developers, and planners to tackle the challenges that cities currently face and develop solutions for energy-efficient buildings and transport.

The exhibition is popular with local schools but footfall is a recurrent issue in the Royal Docks. He explains:

> We have an informal group called the Royal Docks marketing group. I represent Siemens on that, but also ExCel are involved, Silvertown, ABP, the airport—we're trying to look at how we can promote the Royal Docks. You know ExCel have three and half million go through it every year, London City Airport has around 4.1 million passengers a year. We tend to see these people come to ExCel, they may stay in the hotels around here but generally they fly in, go to their conference, and then fly out again or go into Canary Wharf or into town. We want to try and keep them around and make it a destination.

Smaller businesses in the area are faced with similar challenges. Later the very same day, I walk into a local restaurant and bar. Inside I meet Sohel, who is just leaving his shift at a local restaurant and is about to head back home to Forest Gate in the north of Newham. "You're only the third person that has come in here today", he says, holding up three fingers to drive home the point. Sohel tells me that the Royal Docks needs more of everything: "more places for kids to play, more shops and restaurants... and more people".

On one level, the drive to turn the Royal Docks into the "business and leisure destination" proposed by Boris Johnson and Mayor of Newham Robin Wales back in 2011[8] could attract the visitors that Siemens and Sohel both desire. Six miles west from the Royal Docks, developers Argent have transformed Kings Cross into a "destination". The former intractable railway lands turned mixed-use district is held up as a success story of modern urban regeneration. Argent's mix of placemaking initiatives has contributed to a rise in visitors from 3.5 million to 7 million, between 2014 and 2016. Not only has footfall increased, but also the area has delivered measurable improvements against jobs and other markers of social impact. By these measures, Kings Cross is performing the difficult trick of being both corporate enclave and urban village. For Argent, commercial and social aims "are not mutually exclusive, rather they are mutually dependent". Nevertheless, the extent of a measurable positive impact on existing local communities is unclear.[9] The risk for new large-scale development projects like Kings Cross and the Royal Docks is that through their development trajectories, they may exist as an island apart.

The Royal Docks Enterprise Zone boundary skirts the dock water edge and hugs the perimeters of mayoral-owned land. Lying on the fringes of the boundary are the residential communities of Custom House, Silvertown, and North Woolwich – areas that have been cut off by a legacy of infrastructure and disjointed planning. In a recent meeting with a senior officer working with the London Borough of Newham, I was told that the existing residential communities in the Royal Docks "have high aspirations but low expectations" of public bodies responsible for development and regeneration.

The present risk is that the "accelerated" development of the

Enterprise Zone could compound the disillusionment felt by local communities. It is clear what making the Royal Docks a destination could potentially do for Siemens and Sohel but not so clear what it will do for its existing residential communities. Lessons need to be learnt not only from failed top-down visions but also from some current "premiumised" London regeneration projects where everyday life and normality are coated with a sheen of exclusivity.

***

It is still relatively early days in the current Royal Docks Enterprise Zone project. Inevitably there will be tension in the conflicting visions and ambitions for spaces as developers seek to maximise the value of their developments alongside existing struggling neighbourhoods. There are developing initiatives that seek to address imbalanced development, like the North Woolwich Social Enterprise Zone – a project being led by the London Borough of Newham and supported by the GLA. However, change is rapid.

The political and financial momentum behind development in the Royal Docks ensures that the area will transform physically and economically. New residents, businesses, and visitors will arrive but the mere fact that the Royal Docks might soon be "on the map" should in no way be accepted as a marker of success.

The Royal Docks currently does not register as a place in the collective imaginations of the wider public and neither is it, or its constituent parts, marketable in a similar way to other higher-profile areas in London. Despite this, it does not exist in a vacuum of identity. For better or worse its identity is its vast dock waters, its industrial history, its divisive airport, its failed grand visions, its aspirational but let-down communities, and its entanglement of local and regional governance with private interest and finance. Intimately and collaboratively engaging with these realities – however fraught the process - will hopefully help to challenge and resist the homogenous brand imagery, messaging, and replicative urbanism increasingly overwhelming

London's landscape. Only then can anything close to a truly shared vision, purpose and identity for the Royal Docks become a reality.

These views and opinions are the author's own and do not necessarily reflect the views of the Royal Docks Team or Greater London Authority.

Endnotes

1 Sharon Zukin, "Destination Culture and the Crisis of Authenticity" in *Naked City: The Death and Life of Authentic Urban Places,* Oxford University Press, 2010, pp. 219-246.

2 Ibid, 223.

3 Tom Bawden, "Budget 2011: selected enterprise zones designed to encourage new investment.", the *Guardian,* 23 March 2011. www.theguardian.com/uk/2011/mar/23/budget-2011-enterprise-zones-designed-to-encourage-new-investment.

4 Paul Swiney, "What next for enterprise zones?" *Centre for Cities,* 1 June 2015, www.centreforcities.org/blog/what-next-for-enterprise-zones/.

5 London Development Agency. "Green Enterprise District". haringey4020.org.uk/wp-content/uploads/2015/11/green_enterprise_district_summary_6666_1_.pdf

6 Peter Bishop, Approaches to Regeneration, Architectural Design, 82(1): 28-31.

7 Greater London Authority, *Royal Docks Marketing and Promotional Facility,* www.london.gov.uk/decisions/add2146-royal-docks-marketing-and-promotional-facility

8 Mayor of London and Mayor of Newham, *A Vision for the Royal Docks, London Development Agency,* 2011, p. 6.

9 Regeneris. "The Economic and Social Story of King's Cross". https://www.argentllp.co.uk/content/The-Economic-and-Social-Story-of-Kings-Cross.pdf, 2017

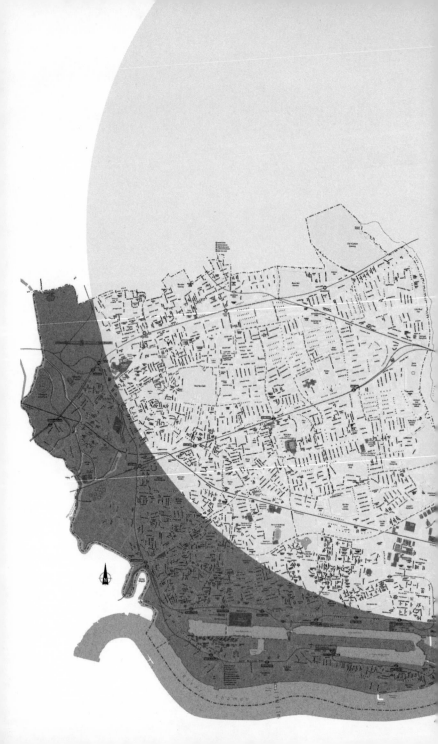

Part 5
Fighting Back

RECLAIMING REGENERATION

Concrete Action is a collective comprised of architects, journalists and researchers, which aims towards a more ethical practice of architecture and transparency in the planning process. The concreteaction.net site has been operational since 2015 as a platform which aims to connect professionals working in the fields of urban design, planning and architecture with grassroots community groups and activists fighting for social housing and public land in London.

Concrete Action has initiated a number of projects since its inception. Assisting community groups in understanding the planning process led to the need for a better understanding of the obstacles to forming alternative models for regeneration. In March 2016 we held a workshop titled 'Ethical Disobedience in Design Industries: Collective interventions to test existing codes of conduct' for MArch and MA Graphic Communication students at Central Saint Martins, University of the Arts London. In May 2016 we held a workshop titled 'A participatory database for Housing Justice' in association with the Civic Media Hub at the the University of Bournemouth and the Centre for Investigative Journalism (CIJ). The workshop investigated barriers to the accessibility and analysis of data within regeneration processes and was attended by lawyers, academics, housing activists, and residents.

The reclaiming regeneration manual is a rework of the RIBA plan of work, a tool used by architects to organise projects from concept to completion. The manual is a work in progress, a reflection on realistic alternative models of community-led regeneration in the current climate of neoliberal politics and the financialisation of development.

concreteaction.net

STAGES/ TASKS	0 STRATEGIC DEFINITION	1 PREPARATION AND BRIEF	2 CONCEPT DESIGN	3 DEVELOPM DESIGN
	What are the aims and objectives of the project: What do you need?	*Describe what you need and what you need to prepare for it to happen*	*Translating what you need into a design strategy*	*Turning your desig strategy in a proposal*
Core Objectives	Creating a community led alternative regeneration plan can give weight to the concerns of residents facing regeneration and redevelopment. The needs and priorities of all stakeholders in an area may have significant overlaps			
Procurement (How)	DEFINE THE PROJECT AND ORGANISE THE TEAM.	GET THE WHOLE COMMUNITY INVOLVED & ACTIVE.	COMMUNITY ENGAGEMENT	CO-DESIGN PROCESS
	What is the aim of the community regneration? Who is going to manage the project?	What are the local issues? What options are available for community control?	How do you use mapping to articulate the needs and aspirations? To what extent do residents want to be involved in the management of their homes?	How do you organize feedback wi the commur
Programme (What)	-Regeneration proposal managed by residents. -Project managed by community organisers. -Funding for full time employee. -Funding for a part time regeneration team comprised of a mix of residents and professionals.	-Find out local issues via door knocking -Organise a monthly event with and for the community -Find out the common interests of different local stakeholders -Make fun events which bring people together. -Go on local explorations with residents to 'map' the area.	-Run a workshop on your map findings -Run a workshop on housing aspirations -Present research on potential management models -Use games to increase understanding of unfamiliar ideas -Discuss the concequences of refurbishment versus demolition	-Workshops the design c the masterpl -Codesign events -Use models instead of pl -Show progress and how people' ideas are incorporated -Organize fir event with tl whole of the community to assess the result.

...CHNICAL ...SIGN	5 CONSTRUCTION	6 HANDOVER AND CLOSEOUT	7 IN USE
...ke it feasible and ...ievable	From design on paper to building	Transfer of ownership and management	Keeping an eye on things

...areas where there is a willingness to compromise, as well as differing skillsets and areas of ...ert knowledge. This guide distills one ongoing community-led regeneration into a process ...ch mirrors the conventional architectural plan of work.

...ANCIAL AND ...CHNICAL CONTEXT	COMMUNITY CONTROL	MANAGEMENT	MAINTENANCE
...w do you make your ...posal financially ...le? ...t will make your pro-...al attractive to other ...eholders?	How can you make sure you are still involved in the decision making process? How can you make sure the community stays together during construction?	Who is managing the rented homes? How do the homes remain under community control?	What is the strategy for maintaining the buildings? What is the strategy for maintaining common areas?
...derstand the finances ...our local authority. ...k at past regeneration ...hods ...t a financial viability ...ert to value your ...posal. ...: a socially minded ...eloper for support ...lore financial models. ...ke sure the financial ...essment reflects the ...ciples. ...k at ways to influence ...selection of contrac-...and designers by the ...ncil. ...oritse the social over ...financial.	-The residents choose the contractor according to the criteria which were embodied in the principles -The construction programme is phased in a sensitive manner so that residents remain in the area and only have to move house once. -The construction phasing ensures that there are always facilities open for local use	-Have an independent form of management structure to take over once the construction is completed -Have a strategy for evaluating the result, does it meet the aims and objectives, does it meet the principles -Have a strategy for the role of the community regeneration team and their level of involvement after completion	-Long term maintenance involving all project stakeholders: contractor, design team, and residents.

STAGES/TASKS	0 STRATEGIC DEFINITION	1 PREPARATION AND BRIEF	2 CONCEPT DESIGN	3 DEVELOP DESIGN
	What are the aims and objectives of the project: What do you need?	*Describe what you need and what you need to prepare for it to happen*	*Translating what you need into a design strategy*	*Turning your desig strategy in a proposa*
Planning *distilling information*	MEANS OF ORGANISATION	PRODUCE YOUR OWN EXPERTISE	YOUR PRINCIPLES	UNDER-STAND YO POLITICAL ECONOMIC CONTEXT:
	What is the appropriate structure for the regeneration team?	How do you value what is already there? Who haven't you talked to yet?	How do you turn your findings into a brief for the design of your area?	Who is doin what in re-generation your area? they open t dialogue?
	-Value local knowledge and professional knowledge equally. -Evaluate the ability of people to commit time to the project. -Equal pay at London's living wage. -Consensus decision making within the team allows everyone to feel valued	map your area (uses, materials, green & public space, state of existing buildings, housing typologies, building height & age) -what are people's memories of place	-write a series of principles that will guide the design of the masterplan. -discuss the principles in the community. -make it public	-Do freedom of informatio requests -Be persona -Find out the stories, pow of decision making and weak points -Establish p sure strateg
Key Support Tasks	KNOWLEDGE TRANSFER WITHIN THE TEAM			YOUR PAS
	How do you learn from each other within the team? How do you translate each others' expertise?			What has b achieved in area?
	-residents know the area, their needs & their aspirations, the architect knows about planning & design -architects go out into the area and meet people -residents gain technical expertise in team meetings through excercises on planning vocabulary, reading drawings, translating ideas into design -monthly meetings are designed and planned collectively by the whole team			-history give a sense of belonging, -similar sucessful strategies c be used aga

CHNICAL DESIGN	5 CONSTRUCTION	6 HANDOVER AND CLOSEOUT	7 IN USE
ake it feasible and lievable	*From design on paper to building*	*Transfer of ownership and management*	*Keeping an eye on things*
ST YOUR SOLUTION	BENEFITS	RESULT	LONG TERM VISION
ere can you get extra vice and feedback on ur proposal?	How will the construction process benefit the local community?	How can you celebrate your achievement? How can you warn others of mistakes?	How to make it sustainable?
lk to developers lk to viability experts lk to other community ups lk to each other	-Local people are trained and employed to build the scheme.	-Have a strategy for getting the last parts finished -Create publicity -Invite people	-Make a 5, 10, 20 year maintenance programme, with business plan.
PPORT		FEEDBACK	HOUSE-KEEPING
w can you get support at each stage in the cess? How can you support residents over a g time period of uncertainty?		Is there anything missing?	How to making sure that repairs are done?
e aware of similar campaigns ep on building the support network within the nmunity		-Make a checklist based on the original principles -Walk around the area with residents before handover	-A resident-led overview of planned maintenance -Make sure residents can sign off repairs

STAGES/ TASKS	0 STRATEGIC DEFINITION	1 PREPARATION AND BRIEF	2 CONCEPT DESIGN	3 DEVELOPMENT DESIGN
	What are the aims and objectives of the project: What do you need?	_Describe what you need and what you need to prepare for it to happen_	_Translating what you need into a design strategy_	_Turning your design strategy into a proposal_

SUSTAINABILITY CHECKPOINTS — Keeping on track

	0	1	2	3
	FUNDING	WINS FOR THE COMMUNITY		PROPOSAL
	Where are possible funding sources?	How can you keep people motivated? Can you solve pressing housing issues?		How can you persuade the coucil and other authorities to collaborate?
	-A business plan -Money to budget for expert consultants?	-People bond over similar issues and have more motivation to fight when they feel they are not alone. -Direct action organised within the community to solve specific issues -Immediate amelioration of daily living conditions builds trust in the community.		-Be open to collaboration and compromise; a pragmatic and realistic proposal will go further

INFORMATION EXCHANGES

	0	1	2	3
	ESTABLISHING A MEETING STRUCTURE	KEEPING THE ENERGY .AND...................................		
	How often do you need meetings with residents: council tenants, temporary tenants, leaseholders, private renters?			
	-How to make the meetings attractive -Regular bi-weekly team meetings, regular monthly meetings with the wider community. -Accountability for every major decision happens in the monthly meetings.			

UK GOVERNMENT INFORMATION EXCHANGES

	0	1	2	3
	WHAT IS THE CONTEXT	WHO HAS THE POWER?	GROW YOUR OWN PRESENCE	
	Which developers have relationships with the local authority? -Make a list -Draw a diagram of their relationships	Who do you need to talk to? -Create a dialogue with your local councillors and the team responsible for regeneration in your area	How do you apply pressure and get noticed? How do you anticipate conflicts? How do you deal with people being decanted?	

TECHNICAL DESIGN	5 CONSTRUCTION	6 HANDOVER AND CLOSEOUT	7 IN USE
Make it feasible and believable		Transfer of ownership and management	Keeping an eye on things
	A COMMUNITY PRESENCE	RETHINK YOUR ORGANISATION	EVALUATION AND LEGACY
	How do you make sure that everyone is cared for?	Is the regeneration team still involved and how? Do their working hours reduce?	What was sucessful, what went wrong?
	-Helping people to move -Make sure that residents who move have new houses which are appropriate for their needs -Hold events	-Make sure that the roles for each part of the organisation are clear -Make a handover strategy if there is a new management body	-Evaluate the process -Make a model which can be replicated
RHYTHM OF COMMUNITY ENGAGEMENT		EVALUATION	DISSEMINATION
		Do you need to keep the same structure?	How do you share your experiences?
Through workshops and games the residents must understand and be able to knowingly support the proposals made by the team Record your activities		-Less frequent meetings needed, -strategy for dealing with upcoming issues relating to management and maintenance.	-Set up an archive -Find an appropriate format -Organise events for the whole community including newcomers.
BE PREPARED		FORMALISATION	
Keep the pressure constantly on Local Authorities to obtain a seat at the negotiation table Look out for moments which can take up a lot of your resources, such as Compulsory Purchase Orders from the council Get support from other groups and lawyers to challenge using legal channels Make your proposals public		How is your organisation a long-term stakeholder in the process? -Formalise your relationships	

The Art of the Possible: The ArcelorMittal Orbit, Collective Memory, and Ecological Survival

David Cross

As the 2012 London Olympics have long since passed from anticipation through lived experience into history, or at least memory, I decided at last to "experience" the ArcelorMittal Orbit in its physical setting. Emerging from Stratford tube station, I tried to reach the Olympic Park without passing through Westfield, Europe's largest shopping centre. But as the pedestrian walkway petered out in a banal and featureless nonplace; with no viable way forward, I had to concede, and return to the main concourse.

Surrounded by surveillance cameras, I felt self-conscious and began to suspect myself of having criminal thoughts. But with my field of vision dominated by a brilliant screen playing fragments of a disaster movie, interspersed with an advertisement for Dairy Milk chocolate, it was easy to be distracted. Framed by an avenue of retail façades, my first glimpse of the ArcelorMittal Orbit had the quality of a computer-generated image, a silhouette shimmering faintly in the polluted London air. Having found my bearings, I decided to relax and "go with the flow", allowing my movement to be governed by the urban form. I wandered through the corporate branded environment, a "forest of signs" enjoining me to "Explore, Discover, Experience, Share, Indulge, and Eat". I went into a stylish boutique café with a ceiling of beaten copper and a display counter of authentic-looking wooden fruit-packing crates, where I was served an organic fair-trade coffee and a delicious pain au chocolat, heated and handed to me in a recycled paper bag by someone who seemed so bored or exhausted that they were almost gone.

I hurried away from the shopping centre, and was channelled from one branded space to another by construction site hoardings, their messages proclaiming: "The future is closer than you think." "The future is designed." "The future is tech." "The future is culture." Searching my memory for an antidote, I recalled a line from Terry Eagleton: "For culture is now palpably part of the problem rather than the solution; it is the very medium in which battle is engaged, rather than some Olympian terrain on which our differences can be recomposed."[1] As I crossed the bridge over the canal, I looked around for some trace of the homes, allotments, and artists' studios that had made up the area. But nothing remains of these everyday commons and repositories of social memory: following their compulsory purchase and demolition, the varied spaces they once produced have been reconstituted as a bland and uniform commercial territory.

In this desolate tract of urban blight, which is still undergoing phased "regeneration" long after the 2012 Olympics are over, the ArcelorMittal Orbit combines the fixity of a landmark with the mutability of a virus. Though its red paintwork is fading, the vast artwork, or "visitor attraction", like the Queen Elizabeth Park in which it stands, still seem inchoate, in the sense of being provisional, and contingent on unpredictable forces. The arbitrary nature of those forces is celebrated in a propagated anecdote: that in 2009 Boris Johnson, who was then Mayor of London, met by chance with Lakshmi Mittal in the cloakrooms of the World Economic Forum in Davos, Switzerland. Mittal is the chairman and chief executive officer of ArcelorMittal, the world's largest integrated steel and mining company. (In 2017, Forbes ranked Mittal as the fifty-sixth richest person in the world with a net worth of US$16.4 billion.) Johnson described an encounter that lasted less than a minute, in which he proposed building a landmark to rival the Eiffel Tower: "Our conversation took about 45 seconds. I explained the idea, which took 40 seconds. 'Great. I'll give you the steel,' he said, and that was it."[2]

Despite the impulsive origin of its commission, and its apparently haphazard form, the ArcelorMittal Orbit is the result not so much of an aesthetic gamble as of a calculation of how public art as public relations might serve private interests. Creating the impression of a lively debate, the Head of Brand at ArcelorMittal Worldwide generated and stage-managed polite controversy around the work by focusing media attention on its gargantuan scale, its complex structure, and the influences cited by the artist and engineer.

Here, I consider these aspects of the corporate brand-management strategy in relation to the sculpture's commissioning, form, and production. My discussion of the production leads to an examination of ArcelorMittal's activities as a company, whose business model is based on extreme social, cultural, and ecological damage. I then look at two examples of politicised counteraction: a powerful *détournement* that has drawn attention to the ArcelorMittal Orbit's relationship to an actual historical trauma, and a tenacious popular resistance campaign to one area of ArcelorMittal's planned expansion. These indicate a surprising potential for taking control over the work's meaning, and even for shifting the underlying balance of power.

An Oversight

Proclaimed as the largest piece of public art in Britain,[3] the ArcelorMittal Orbit has been repeatedly ranked by media commentators alongside other landmarks, including Frédéric Bartholdi's Statue of Liberty, Antony Gormley's "Angel of the North", and Gustave Eiffel's Tower. Such comparisons are not only banal but unfavourable: although the Olympic commission aimed to rival the Eiffel Tower, it fell short from the outset; when the budget became known to the designers of the ArcelorMittal Orbit, they further reduced its height in an act of expedient compromise.[4] Even so, the sculpture has an overbearing scale that reduces the viewer to an insignificant speck, perhaps in an "acting out" of unconscious impulses of domination.

Structurally, the ArcelorMittal Orbit consists of two elements: the vertical tower which supports the viewing platform and houses the lifts and stairs, and the lattice of steel tubing that loops around the tower. The design is the result of an artistic collaboration between Cecil Balmond and Anish Kapoor. Cecil Balmond is a designer, artist, architect, and writer, Professor of Architecture at the University of Pennsylvania School of Design, and Deputy Chairman of Ove Arup Engineering, where he founded the Advanced Geometry Unit in 2000. In 2015 he was appointed Officer of the Order of the British Empire for his services to architecture. Anish Kapoor studied art at the Chelsea College of Arts in London. He represented Britain in 1990 at the Forty-Fourth Venice Biennale. In 1991 he received the Turner Prize; he was elected a Royal Academician in 1999; and in 2003 he was made a Commander of the Most Excellent Order of the British Empire. In 2017 Kapoor was included in the *Sunday Times* "Rich List" with a personal fortune valued at £134 million.[5]

Having undertaken a commission that exemplified the values and processes of exclusionary privilege, Kapoor and Balmond asserted that they were "interested in a place where architecture meets sculpture".[6] Such an abstract conception of place might be innocuous enough, had it not been for the compulsory evacuation of people and removal of all traces of communities that had prepared the ground on which the sculpture would be built. But despite being international cultural practitioners with unrivalled access to information and resources, Kapoor and Balmond showed a colonialist impairment of vision, describing the East London site as "a bit of virgin land where one can set the parameters again".[7] Anyone working to critically engage with contemporary life will be familiar with the problem of visualising ideology, which is often unseen not because it is invisible, but because it is overlooked. Conversely, the commission brief was to design a structure to offer a vantage point over a tract of urban land that had been erased and remade as a corporate image of urban regeneration. In relation to this commercially fabricated terrain, the structure invites the viewer to take up a position of oversight.

Transcending questions of social cost and value, Kapoor and Balmond declare a fascination with "the way that form and geometry give rise to structure".[8] Yet even such ostensibly disinterested relationships as these are mediated by proprietary tools based on codes. As Douglas Murphy has written, "what we have is a doodle that has been turned into a digital shape which has then been translated into a buildable structure by some very advanced computer software".[9] The parametric software Murphy refers to enables architects and engineers to develop virtual three-dimensional models that can be endlessly altered and viewed from any angle through a variety of simulated camera lenses to generate "realistic" artists' impressions for securing planning consent. More concretely, the software links to databases of materials and components to calculate the cost implications of formal decisions. By enabling a reflexive relationship between design choices, production costs, and professional fees, parametric software erodes the distinction between financial and aesthetic considerations, which makes it a valuable tool for optimising the profitability of constructing shopping centres, office spaces, and the "London vernacular" style of shared-ownership apartments in regeneration schemes. The ArcelorMittal Orbit may be an icon of parametric design as much as an example of free artistic expression, but with the ground form levelled by the property developer and the construction material predetermined by the sponsor, it seems the only remaining parameters were the professional fees and production budget.

Kapoor's website displays an image of the painting *The Tower of Babel* by Pieter Bruegel the Elder (c. 1563). Beneath the image, Kapoor quotes himself: "There is a kind of medieval sense to it of reaching up to the sky, building the impossible. A procession, if you like. It's a long winding spiral: a folly that aspires to go even above the clouds and has something mythic about it."[10] The airy reference to myth may lift the mind's eye away from the struggles of daily life and the troubles of history, but following the global financial crisis of 2008, extreme inequality could drag British society back to the class divisions of the nineteenth century; around the world, systemic inequality is increasing fast. As labour's loss is capital's gain, Kapoor's dreamy linking of aspiration and medievalism seems like a view from an elevated position of comfort and security. However, Kapoor asserts, "It is an object that cannot be perceived as having a singular image, from any one perspective. You need to journey round the object, and through it. Like a Tower of Babel, it requires real participation from the public." Public participation may be a requirement set by the artist, but even disregarding the sponsorship of the work by Britain's richest man, the essentially private nature of the structure is impossible to ignore: to journey round the object, the viewer has to enter a compound inside a steel security fence, coated with anti-climb paint, before paying an admission fee that for many people has either been prohibitively expensive, or simply unappealing.

Both Kapoor and Balmond cite Tatlin's Tower as a key reference for the ArcelorMittal Orbit. After the Bolshevik Revolution of 1917, the Russian artist and architect Vladimir

Tatlin designed a vast helix-shaped structure of iron, glass, and steel as a monument to the Third International, who held as their stated aim "the struggle by all available means, including armed force, for the overthrow of the international bourgeoisie and the creation of the international Soviet republic as a transition stage to the complete abolition of the state".[11] Whether the ArcelorMittal Orbit bears even a passing resemblance to the elegant geometry of Tatlin's Tower is an open question, but the comparison is unfortunate: Tatlin's Tower embodied the emancipatory and egalitarian vision of the early Russian Revolution; it also had the decisive advantage of being unrealised, allowing it to retain something of its ideal and imaginary potential. In sharp contrast, the ArcelorMittal Orbit is an emblem of compromise as both index and sign of an established order of private power, wielded in full knowledge of the social injustice and ecological destruction on which it is based.

A Clear Winner

Lakshmi Mittal built Mittal Steel through buying up old, highly polluting, and dangerous steel mills around the world, and cutting costs by laying off workers and economising on environmental, health, and safety provisions.[12] In 2006, Mittal Steel conducted a highly controversial and aggressive takeover of Arcelor, the world's second-largest steel producer. The takeover was "an object lesson in the force of international capital markets", in which the notorious investment banking firm Goldman Sachs "was a clear winner".[13] The result was ArcelorMittal, which now describes itself as "the world's leading integrated steel and mining company". ArcelorMittal is by far the largest steel company in the world; in 2009 it produced around 8% of global steel output and generated over US$65 billion. As well as being the CEO of ArcelorMittal, Lakshmi Mittal has been, since 2008, a director of Goldman Sachs, experts in financial sleight of hand who were heavily implicated in the 2007–08 global financial crisis, and in the 2010 European sovereign debt crisis.

In 2008 a reputational risk analysis by Ecofact ranked ArcelorMittal among the top ten most environmentally and socially controversial companies in the world for its human rights abuses, corporate complicity, and negative impact on communities and ecosystems. Summarising their analysis, Ecofact states:

> ArcelorMittal was accused of pollution, intimidation, poor safety standards, forced evictions and acquisition of agricultural land, local participation issues, suppression of union activities and poor pay conditions. Repeated accidents and high death tolls at its mines in Kazakhstan resulted in the company having dozens of sites shut owing to safety violations. Its operations also came under fire with residents protesting that emissions levels from its steel mills had increased further, thus polluting local areas.[14]

Between 1999 and 2009, ArcelorMittal received low-interest loans of around €562 million from the European Bank for Reconstruction and Development (EBRD) and the International Finance Corporation.[15] In 2010 ArcelorMittal Finance and Services Belgium made profits of €1.4 billion, but paid no tax.[16] In 2011 the European Environment Agency[17] costed damage caused by ArcelorMittal's air pollution in Europe at between €421 million and €595 million. In 2017 the EBRD lent ArcelorMittal $350 million for "modernisation and environmental upgrades".[18] Despite receiving hundreds of millions in loans and subsidies for pollution abatement, ArcelorMittal has repeatedly attempted to obstruct and weaken EU climate policy,[19] and pushed for exemptions to the EU Emissions Trading System, so reaping "windfall" profits of €2.5 billion in 2009.

ArcelorMittal has particularly poor relations with trade unions, including suppressing union activities.[20] In a 2009 shareholders' meeting at its headquarters in Luxembourg ArcelorMittal announced that it was halving production and offering "voluntary redundancy" to nine thousand of its staff, while paying out a dividend of $1.1 billion to shareholders. When 1,500 steel workers gathered to protest outside the company headquarters, special police units were called in, resulting in violent clashes.[21] Employees of Mittal have accused him of "slave labour" conditions after multiple fatalities in his mines,[22] and ArcelorMittal has a track record of repeated violations of health and safety, resulting in many injuries and deaths of its workers all around the world.[23]

With its influential relationship to state power in over sixty countries, its access to global private financial institutions, and its highly effective public-relations and brand-management operation, ArcelorMittal's position may appear unassailable. Yet two very different responses by citizens suggest that the scale and global reach of ArcelorMittal, which are key sources of its power, entail aspects of vulnerability. The first of these responses is a project conducted by the Forensic Architecture Research Centre at Goldsmiths.

A Memorial in Exile

Omarska, an iron ore mine and ore-processing plant outside Prijedor in northwestern Bosnia, was used by Bosnian Serb military and police to imprison more than five thousand Bosniaks in the summer of 1992.

> Among them were (to mention but some): the mayor; politicians from the SDA and the HDZ in Prijedor; an imam; judges and lawyers; employees from the military and civilian sectors; a veterinarian, a physiotherapist, a dentist, and a number of medical doctors; an engineer and some economists; headmasters and teachers from schools at different levels; journalists and an editor of Radio Prijedor and of Kozarski Vjesnik; an author and an actor; directors and members of the Rudnika Ljubija management board; directors and managers of Bosnamontaža, Kozaraturist, Celpak, and the biscuit factory

Mira Cikota; the director and the secretary of the Prijedor Red Cross, the president of Merhamet (the Muslim charity organization) in Prijedor; restaurant owners, business men and entrepreneurs; leaders of sports clubs and football players.[24]

In 1992, Ed Vulliamy and fellow journalists Penny Marshall and Ian Williams visited the camp at Omarska.[25] Their reporting provoked an international outcry, following which a United Nations commission of experts collected evidence of rape, torture, and killings of detainees at Omarska, leading to the establishment of the International Criminal Tribunal for the former Yugoslavia, the first international war crimes court since Nuremberg and Tokyo.[26]

Eyal Weizman, Professor of Forensic Architecture, and artist Milica Tomic of the Monument Group of Belgrade, visited the site in April 2012. During this visit, they met with Mladen Jelača, Director of ArcelorMittal Prijedor, who disclosed that the steel of the ArcelorMittal Orbit had been made using iron ore from the Omarska mine. This information allowed Forensic Architecture to identify the basis of their collective project as a "material link between London and Omarska—between a site where crimes against humanity were committed and another that celebrated that same universal humanity".[27]

On 20 April 2012, Refik Hodzic, a journalist, filmmaker, and justice activist from Bosnia and Herzegovina, published an article online setting out Mittal Steel's relationship to the situation, starting in 2004 when the company acquired a 51% stake in a complex of mines and facilities around Prijedor.[28] Hodzic describes how the complex included the site and buildings that had served as the concentration camp, and the locations of mass graves where Serb authorities had dumped the bodies of hundreds of people they had murdered in Omarska.

In 2005, ArcelorMittal agreed to permit victims and their families to access the buildings where the crimes had been committed, and also pledged to finance and construct a memorial commemorating the atrocities. But Hodzic then observes how in 2006, ArcelorMittal shelved these plans, saying it did not want to take sides in a divisive dispute, and later denied access to the place, citing safety concerns.

Responding online to Hodzic's article, Mr M. Mukherjee, Chief Executive Officer of ArcelorMittal Prijedor, claimed that the company had only reluctantly cancelled the project of "finding an agreed solution to the question of a memorial at Omarska", but that it was "ready to support any solution that had the support of all sections of the community".[29] Yet as Susan Schuppli observes, "The desire to see a memorial and the desire to stop one are once again divided across ethnic lines".[30] Rather than engage with the intractable issues in which ArcelorMittal is implicated, Mukherjee reaffirmed the safety concerns, describing the Omarska site as "a busy working industrial area, with heavy machinery operating constantly". However, he did offer to cease operations on several days during 2012 to allow victims and their families access to the site.[31]

In July 2012, shortly before the start of the London Olympic Games, Forensic Architecture and the working group Four Faces of Omarska held a press conference in the Olympic Park, at which survivors of the camp laid claim to the ArcelorMittal Orbit as the "Omarska Memorial in Exile".[32] Throughout this time, and to the present day, ArcelorMittal has used the site, buildings, and equipment of the Omarska camp to operate a profitable mine, while employing a workforce that—as a result of the ethnic cleansing—is almost exclusively Serb. In recognition that preventing commemoration of trauma is a form of denial that obstructs healing and reconciliation, Forensic Architecture designated the Omarska mine as a "Living Death Camp", while calling for "a project of commemoration that would remain responsive to the demands of ongoing life".[33]

In 2018, Anish Kapoor's website refers to the ArcelorMittal Orbit simply as "Orbit", and makes no mention of the name ArcelorMittal.[34] If Kapoor wanted to fully dissociate his largest public work from the private sponsor who made it possible, he could face a costly legal dispute, as it appears that in return for sponsoring the project, ArcelorMittal secured naming rights over the sculpture in perpetuity.[35] Dissociating his own name from the sculpture might be easier, though that would probably mean returning the fee, and risking alienation from influential people who could provide future career opportunities. In contrast, Forensic Architecture's reclaiming of the sculpture as the "Omarska Memorial in Exile" demonstrates that although singular meaning is often imposed by private interests, in certain situations it can be publicly contested with ethical precision, opening the way for just and emancipatory possibilities to emerge.

A Bit of Virgin Land

> The Queen Elizabeth Park has a surface area of 560 acres (227 hectares), has 6.5km of waterways, 30 acres of woods, hedgerow and wildlife habitat and 4,300 new trees. There are 525 bird boxes and 150 bat boxes at the Park.[36]

In India, in 2005 and 2006, the Mittal Steel Company signed memoranda of understanding with the governments of the neighbouring states of Jharkhand and Orissa (now Odisha) for two vast industrial projects. The projects planned to take up a combined land surface of 16,656 acres (6,740 hectares), and would produce 24 million tonnes of steel a year.[37] In Odisha, the proposed project would require 7,800 acres (3,156 hectares) for facilities including coke smelting, steel making, steel rolling mills, and a 750 megawatt power plant.[38] In Jharkhand, which means "land of forests", the proposed project would require 11,000 acres (4,451 hectares)[39] for a development including a steelworks, coal mine and associated township powered by a 2,500 megawatt power plant, all designated as a Special Economic Zone benefitting from tax concessions and exemption from environmental protection laws.[40]

Dayamani Barla, a member of the indigenous Munda tribe, led opposition to ArcelorMittal's plans, on the grounds that the proposed development would destroy streams, rivers, and forests that are ancestral community-owned natural resources, as well as sacred sites, that together are essential to the cultural identity of the indigenous peoples who live there.[41] This interlocking of legal, cultural, and ecological arguments, which in itself is compelling, gains additional strength through its precise relevance to the lives of indigenous peoples.

> Indigenous peoples are the descendants of those who were there before others who now constitute the mainstream and dominant society. They are defined partly by descent, partly by the particular features that indicate their distinctiveness from those who arrived later, and partly by their own view of themselves.[42]

The indigenous peoples of the world's remaining forests have knowledge, customs, and cultural practices that protect and sustain forest ecosystems. Yet, as the Forest Peoples' Alliance observes, "forest policies commonly treat forests as empty lands controlled by the state and available for development, colonisation, logging, plantations, dams, mines, oil wells, gas pipelines and agribusinesses".[43]

The resistance movement led by Dayamani Barla combined two approaches: claiming human rights enshrined in India's national constitution and law,[44] and collective direct action by indigenous people, putting their bodies at risk to defend the land on which they depend for survival. For five years, while the indigenous people physically prevented ArcelorMittal from accessing their land, Barla used her skills as a journalist to engage with the bureaucratic processes of the Indian state, through which ArcelorMittal was seeking to gain ownership or control of the land.[45]

Frustrated by the resulting delays to his scheme, Laksmhi Mittal declared in an interview with the *Financial Times* that people in India "had to be 'educated' into supporting gradual industrialisation, including the need to build steel plants on agricultural land".[46] But after centuries of catastrophic damage caused by colonialism and extractive industries, the indigenous people reject such a view. The assimilation of indigenous peoples into the dominant paradigm of industrialism, along with the militarism and consumerism on which it depends, would be in itself a terrible cultural loss. Moreover, in the struggle to avoid precipitating global ecological collapse, the "developed world" has much to learn from the indigenous worldview that enables people to live well, in harmony with ecosystems, through collective decision making and community ownership of natural resources.

Barla summarises the indigenous peoples' demands and aims: "We would like the government to restore our mines, clean up our polluted rivers, and bring clean drinking water to our communities [...] This fight is the fight to save humanity. We need a fundamental shift in the way we view development."[47] So far, the indigenous peoples' demands have not been met, and they are far from achieving their aims. Yet they won a decisive battle to protect their forests: in 2013, citing "delays in acquiring land, uncertainties over iron-ore supplies and deteriorating market conditions", ArcelorMittal scrapped its planned project in Odisha.[48]

In 2013, for her leadership of the resistance to ArcelorMittal, Dayamani Barla received the Ellen L. Lutz Indigenous Rights Award, given by campaign group Cultural Survival in honour of the memory of Ellen L. Lutz, a human rights lawyer dedicated to the rights of indigenous peoples. The respected award recognises "outstanding human rights activism, dedicated leadership for Indigenous Peoples' rights, and a deep commitment to protecting, sustaining, and revitalizing Indigenous cultures, lands, and languages".[49] In making the award, Cultural Survival declared,

"The movement's bold resistance stopped this megacorporation from displacing nearly 70,000 people from over 40 villages and seizing over 12,000 acres of land".[50]

The delays preventing ArcelorMittal from acquiring land are certainly attributable to the skill and tenacity of the resistance movement. But the movement's victory was partly due to the global economic downturn: in 2009 ArcelorMittal's sales decreased by 48%, and their net income decreased from $9.5 billion to $0.1 billion;[51] at a certain point, ArcelorMittal decided that in Odisha, the probable losses outweighed the possible profits.

Yet the company determined to press on with its project in Jharkhand. In 2013 ArcelorMittal applied for permission to cut over seven thousand trees and to extract five million tonnes of iron ore every year from the Saranda forest reserve, an area of rich biodiversity including an important migration route for elephants.[52] Although the application submitted by ArcelorMittal was incomplete and contradictory, and its consequences would be large-scale destruction of priceless ecological heritage, the state government of Jharkhand granted permission. In 2016, the *Environmental Justice Atlas* reported that, despite a resistance campaign involving widespread mass mobilisation of indigenous groups and traditional communities, and marked by a high intensity of conflict, including arrests, violence, and deaths, the mining companies including ArcelorMittal had laid waste to large areas of the Saranda forest:

> Streams which serve both domestic and agricultural purposes of the villagers now flow red with mining waste, polluting drinking water sources and resulting in loss of agricultural productivity (Priyadarshini, 2008). Forests, and mountains which are sacred to the adivasis lie degraded due to iron ore mining operations.[53]

In a further blow to indigenous tribespeople, in 2016 the state government of Jharkhand diluted key laws protecting tribal lands, to allow government to take the land for industrial and commercial purposes, or even to sell it off.[54]

More enlightened decisions may be taken at the national level: in January 2017 the environment minister Anil Dave overruled the approval granted by Jharkhand state to ArcelorMittal, and rejected the company's application to expand its operation in the Saranda forest. Meanwhile, strategic work is progressing at the highest level. International lawyer Polly Higgins is campaigning for ecocide to be recognised as the fifth international crime against peace, alongside genocide, crimes against humanity, war crimes, and the crime of aggression. The *Eradicating Ecocide* campaign makes a crucial connection between the social and the ecological, the world and the earth:

> Ecocide is the extensive damage to, destruction of or loss of ecosystem(s) of a given territory, whether by human agency or by other causes, to such an extent that peaceful enjoyment by the inhabitants of that territory has been or will be severely diminished.[55]

Establishing ecocide as a crime against peace would make governments and corporations accountable in a court of law, multiplying the legal, financial, and reputational risks faced by the extractive industries, and helping indigenous peoples to defend their rights as part of the historical struggle towards decolonisation.

A Conclusion, Forgone

It was Otto von Bismark, the reactionary authoritarian founder and first Chancellor of the German Empire in the nineteenth century, who said that politics is the art of the possible. Here, I have tried to reopen questions around the political possibilities of art.

Describing the aims of the Olympic sculpture commission,

the Mayor of London, Boris Johnson wrote of his wish for "something to arouse the curiosity and wonder of Londoners and visitors".[56] If such curiosity and wonder were to be directed not only at the sculpture, but at the system that brought it into being, then the resulting understanding could lead to unruly processes of discovery, and possibly changes in behaviour that might be exciting. Director of the Tate and Chair of the ArcelorMittal Selection Panel, Sir Nicholas Serota predicted that the ArcelorMittal Orbit "will make people aware of their own bodies and their place in the world".[57]

When the experience of art is confined within the frame of leisure and consumerism, to be aware of one's own body probably leads no further than a solipsism, while an awareness of one's place in the world likely means an acceptance of the prevailing social order. But when the critical potential of art is activated through the practices of reflective and emancipatory questioning, far greater possibilities emerge, the consequences of which stretch the powers of imagination.

An embodiment of the contradictions of neoliberalism, the ArcelorMittal Orbit is inchoate. ArcelorMittal has been closely associated with unlawful activities including severe breaches of health, safety, and environmental legislation, and crimes against humanity; should the crime of ecocide become recognised, it is possible that ArcelorMittal could in future be prosecuted in the International Criminal Court. However, to describe the sculpture that bears the company name as inchoate in the legal sense that it anticipates, and is preparatory to, further criminal acts, would be going too far. What is certain, is that the ArcelorMittal Orbit is key to a brand-management programme that aims to secure "the social license to operate"[58] for a multinational corporation whose core business is socially unjust and ecologically destructive.

But undeterred by the ruthless exercise of corporate power, the Forensic Architecture research centre and the Adivasi indigenous peoples' resistance movement show that it is still possible to resist the symbolic and actual dominance of the public and commons by private capital. Such acts of resistance are vital in engaging with specific issues, but by enlarging the range of possibilities, they also open the way for other liberating struggles at the intersection of cultural practice and political action. As neoliberalism compounds extreme inequality, and accelerates ecological collapse, the idea that the eradication of historical memory, cultural difference, and biological diversity is inevitable is a stupefying limitation of thought and action. Instead, by creatively inhabiting uncertainty as a condition of complex and dynamic relationships, we might live more fully, and reclaim the art of the possible.

Endnotes

1   Terry Eagleton, "The Crisis of Contemporary Culture", *New Left Review*, 196, November/December 1992, pp. 29-41, 34

2   Boris Johnson (May 2010) *ArcelorMittal Orbit press release*, p. 3 (undated)

3   Ibid

4   Tim Adams, "Anish Kapoor's Orbit tower: the mother of all helter-skelters", the *Guardian* (5 May 2012), www.theguardian.com/artanddesign/2012/may/06/olympics-orbit-anish-kapoor?INTCMP=ILCNETTXT3487 (Accessed 12 February 2018).

5   Eileen Kinsella, "Damien Hirst and Anish Kapoor Land on UK Rich List (Again)" (8 May 2017), news.artnet.com/art-world/artists-on-sunday-times-rich-list-952055 (Accessed 12 February 2018)

6   Mayor of London (May 2010) *ArcelorMittal Orbit press release*, 7

7   Ibid, p. 1

8   Ibid, p. 7

9   Douglas Murphy, "More thoughts on the 'twisted thing'" (6 April 2010),youyouidiot.blogspot.fr/2010/04/more-thoughts-on-twisted-thing.html (Accessed 12 February 2018)

10   See anishkapoor.com/332/orbit-2 (Accessed 12 February 2018)

11   Harold Henry Fisher, *The Communist Revolution: An Outline of Strategy and Tactics* (Stanford University Press, 1955), p. 13.

12   Greg Aitken (ed.), *In the Wake of ArcelorMittal: The Global Steel Giant's Local Impacts* (CEE Bankwatch Network, 2008)

13   Martin Flash, Jonathan Story and James Burnham, "The Takeover of Arcelor by Mittal Steel", sites.insead.edu/facultyresearch/research/file.cfm?fid=2671 (Accessed 12 February 2018)

14 Charlotte Mansson, *Most Environmentally and Socially Controversial Companies in 2008,* Zurich, 4 July 2008, platform.reprisk.com/downloads/specialreports/1/Most%20Controversial%20Companies%202008.pdf (Accessed 12 February 2018)

15 Friends of the Earth, *Public Funds Addict ArcelorMittal in Line for New 250m Euro Public Loan* (2009), foeeurope.org/press/2009/Oct21_ArcelorMittal_in_line_for_new_public%20loan.html (Accessed 12 February 2018)

16 See euro-correspondent.com/eu-insider/240-steel-steal (Accessed 12 February 2018)

17 Mike Holland and Anne Wagner, *Revealing the Costs of Air Pollution from Industrial Facilities in Europe* (European Environment Agency, 2011).

18 "EBRD loans $350 mln to ArcelorMittal's Ukraine Mill", in.reuters.com/article/ukraine-arcelormittal-ebrd/ebrd-loans-350-mln-to-arcelormittals-ukraine-mill-idINL8N1OM3GE (Accessed 12 February 2018)

19 Oscar Reyes and Belén Balanyá, "Carbon Welfare: How big polluters plan to profit from EU emissions trading reform", *Corporate Europe Observatory* (December 2016), pp. 17-21, corporateeurope.org/sites/default/files/attachments/the_carbon_welfare_report.pdf (Accessed 10 February 2018)

20 See Aitken (ed.) *In the Wake of ArcelorMittal*, pp. 7, 14, 18, and 28.

21 Ulrich Rippert, "Steel workers storm ArcelorMittal headquarters in Luxembourg", *International Committee of the Fourth International* (15 May 2009), wsws.org/en/articles/2009/05/stee-m15.html (Accessed 10 February 2018)

22 Mark Franchetti, Robert Winnett, "UK's Richest Man in Slave Labour Row", the *Times* (10 June 2017)

23 Aitken, *In the Wake of ArcelorMittal*, p. 14

24 "VIII: The Concentration Camps: Logor Omarska", in

United Nations Security Council, "Letter dated 24 May 1994 from the Secretary-General to the President of the Security Council", Annex: Final Report of the United Nations Commission of Experts established pursuant to security council Resolution 780 (1992). See icty.org/x/file/About/OTP/un_commission_of_experts_report1994_en.pdf (Accessed 20 February 2018).

25   Ed Vulliamy, "Shame of Camp Omarska", the *Guardian* (7 August 1992), theguardian.com/world/1992/aug/07/warcrimes.edvulliamy (Accessed 12 February 2018)

26   See United Nations: International Criminal Tribunal for the former Yugoslavia. See www.icty.org Accessed 12th February 2018.

27   Eyal Weizman et al., *Forensis: The Architecture of Public Truth* (Sternberg Press, 2014), p. 217.

28   See Refic Hodzic, "Shadow of London 'Orbit', Bosnia: Mittal Suppresses Memories of Omarska", *Balkan Transitional Justice* (20 April 2012), balkaninsight.com/en/article/mittal-suppresses-memories-of-omarska (Accessed 12 February 2018)

29   Ibid

30   See Susan Schuppli, "A Memorial in Exile in London's Olympics: Orbits of Responsibility", *Open Democracy,* opendemocracy.net/susan-schuppli/memorial-in-exile-in-london's-olympics-orbits-of-responsibility (Accessed 10 February 2018)

31   See Hodzic, "Shadow of London 'Orbit', Bosnia: Mittal Suppresses Memories of Omarska"

32   See Susan Schuppli, "A Memorial in Exile in London's Olympics: Orbits of Responsibility"

33   Eyal Weizman et al., *Forensis*, p. 193.

34   See anishkapoor.com/332/orbit-2 (Accessed 20 February 2018)

35   Andrew Cave, "Steel Magnetism", *CorpComms* (1 July 2014), corpcommsmagazine.co.uk/features-and-analysis/

view/steel-magnetism (Accessed 12 February 2018).

36 See queenelizabetholympicpark.co.uk/media/facts-and-figures (Accessed 12 February 2018).

37 Moushumi Basu, "Protesters In Eastern India Battle Against Mining Giant Arcelor Mittal", *corpwatch* (3 March, 2010), corpwatch.org/article.php?id=15544 (Accessed 12 February 2018)

38 Aitken, *In the Wake of ArcelorMittal*, p. 16

39 "Arcelor Mittal Steel Project faces Land Acquisition Row in Jharkhand", *Thandian News* (18 October 2008), thaindian. com/newsportal/business/arcelor-mittal-steel-project-faces-land-acquisition-row-in-jharkhand_100108681. html (Accessed 12 February 2018)

40 Dayamani Barla, "The Proposed Mittal Steel Plant in Jharkhand", *Proceedings of the Convention of Displaced Persons,* Nav Jagriti, Kalunga, 6-7 March 2010 (Displaced Persons' Conference Organising Committee, 2010).

41 See Basu, "Protesters in Eastern India Battle Against Mining Giant ArcelorMittal"

42 Stephen Corry, *Tribal Peoples for Tomorrow's World* (Freeman Press, 2011), p.18

43 See forestpeoples.org/en/about (Accessed 14 February 2018)

44 Basu, "Protesters in Eastern India Battle Against Mining Giant ArcelorMittal"

45 Saurabh Chaturvedi, Alex MacDonald and Biman Mukherji, "ArcelorMittal to Scrap Project in India's Orissa State", *4-Traders* (17 July 2013), 4-traders.com/ ARCELORMITTAL-34942237/news/ARCELORMITTAL-to-Scrap-Project-in-India-s-Orissa-State-17108379 (Accessed 13th February 2018)

46 Peter Marsh, "Mittal set to quit $20bn Indian steel project", *Financial Times* (4 October 2009)

47 Rucha Chitnis, "Our Resistance Will Not Stop", *Cultural Survival* (December 2013), culturalsurvival.org/

publications/cultural-survival-quarterly/our-resistance-will-not-stop

48   Chaturvedi, MacDonald and Mukherji, "ArcelorMittal to Scrap Project in India's Orissa State"

49   "Selection Panel Statement On Naming Dayamani Barla As Recipient Of The Ell Indigenous Rights Award", *Cultural Survival* (28 April 2013), culturalsurvival.org/news/selection-panel-statement-naming-dayamani-barla-recipient-ell-indigenous-rights-award

50   Chitnis, "Our Resistance Will Not Stop"

51   ArcelorMittal Annual General Meeting (11 May 2010), p. 6, corporate.arcelormittal.com/~/media/Files/A/ArcelorMittal/investors/agm/agm-archive/236-28-17-2010-May-AgmPresentationFinalVersionWithResults.pdf (Accessed 20 February 2018)

52   Ministry of Environment, Forest and Climate Change, Government of India: application for diversion of 202.35 ha of Reserved forest land in favour of Arcelor Mittal India Limited for mining in Saranda Forest of West Singhbhum District in the State of Jharkhand (8-49/2013-FC) forestsclearance.nic.in/Reports4.aspx (Accessed 16 February 2018)

53   Environmental Justice Atlas. See ejatlas.org/conflict/iron-ore-mining-in-sanranda-forest-jharkhand (Accessed 17 February 2018).

54   Jepsen Broch Hansen and Leiva Jacquelin (eds), *The Indigenous World 2017* (Copenhagen: International Work Group for Indigenous Affairs, 2017), p. 385, iwgia.org/images/documents/indigenous-world/indigenous-world-2017.pdf (Accessed 20 February 2018).

55   See eradicatingecocide.com/the-law/what-is-ecocide (Accessed 20 February 2018)

56   ArcelorMittal, *Orbit,* p. 3. The press release is undated, but I have tracked it to 23 May 2010). See corporate.arcelormittal.com/~/media/Files/A/

ArcelorMittal/orbit-files/press-release-23-may-2010-arcelormittalorbitbrochure.pdf (Accessed 10 February 2018)

57 ArcelorMittal, *Orbit*, p. 14.
58 See Kieran Moffat, Justine Lacey, Airong Zhang and Sina Leipold, "The Social License to Operate: a Critical Review", *Forestry*, 89, 2016, pp. 477-88 .

LONDON AFTERSHOCK: Variation on a Theme by Walter Benjamin

Phil Cohen

1. In Town Tonight

My favourite listen as a child growing up in Central London in the 1950s was *In Town Tonite*, BBC radio's primetime news programme. One of its most distinctive aspects was its opening signature which featured a medley of urban sounds – a plane taking off, a train screaming through a tunnel, a boat's foghorn, the pedestrian hubbub of rush hour – all set against a background of Eric Coates' bustling Knightsbridge March, and then a BBC voice shouted "STOP", followed by a moments silence, before the announcer continued "Once again we halt the mighty roar of London's traffic to bring you – *In Town Tonite*".

As an eight-year-old who travelled on his own across London to school and delighted in the traffic jams and smogs that frequently postponed my arrival in class, I found the implied power of a single voice (albeit that of the BBC Home Service) to halt the city's affairs quite shocking and awesome. Perhaps when I grew up I would learn the trick and never have to go to school or work!

Since then, the mighty roar of London's commerce with the world has not ceased to intensify as globalisation penetrates ever more deeply into the social fabric of our great city. It is sweet music to some ears, part of the global urban buzz, whilst to others it is a cacophony which deafens the voices of its citizens, especially those forced to live all too precariously on the economic margins: the poor, the homeless, the chronically sick. But equally, the sudden arrest of this momentum, applying the emergency brake to runaway urban "regeneration", while it may afford a space and time for alternative visions of the city to be heard, may also presage the collapse of its most vital infrastructures. In the teeming silence, amidst the haunted ruins of the hollowed-out city, some quite nasty plants may take root and flourish.

This is not a new issue, although it has taken on a special urgency in the wake of the financial crash and now Brexit, both of which have administered short sharp shocks to our prevailing system of urban economy even as the majority of politicians and economists go on acting as if it is still business as usual.

Shock, according to Walter Benjamin writing in the 1920s, was the normal state of affairs in the big city, linked to the advent of the railway, the automobile, and all the other technologies that were speeding up the circulation of commodities, information, and people.[1] Benjamin could never quite decide whether the impact of this accelerated pace of urban life was to force people into a chronic state of dissociation or distraction – a kind of general numbing down as everyone cocoons themselves within their own fractured worlds – or whether it would create platforms for the emergence of new and more dynamic cultural forms breaking out of the parochial, inward-looking communitarianism associated with what Hannah Arendt once presciently called the "nationalism of the neighbourhood".

So shock in this view is double-edged, a moment of violent

disruption, which can provoke a purely nihilistic or NIMBYistic response, but it can also serve as a prompt for a more creative and proactive strategies.

Those two perspectives are still held in some kind of tension in Benjamin's reading of the capitalist city, highlighting the contradiction between its dynamic modernity, as both a creative and destructive force so spectacularly concentrated in the downtown areas of commerce, wealth, and power, and the backward-looking conservatism of so much of its domestic architecture especially in the sprawling suburbs. That tension is there too in the discordance between the agitated rhythms of popular urban culture soundtracking mass commutes between home and work, and the leisurely tempo of the bourgeois flâneur strolling around the downtown shopping arcades. Whereas in Benjamin's Paris or Berlin these could be seen as two complementary sides of the same big city story, today, these different aspects of city life have hardened into rival camps within the field of contemporary urbanism, and given rise to competing futurologies.[2] Both can be heard, loud, if not clear, in current debates about London's future; both can be considered as responses to the intensification of the tempo of urban life, and the impact of ever-more-intrusive technologies of social alienation and control.

The first position is strongly associated with a group of utopian social philosophers who call themselves "accelerationists".[3] They take their inspiration from Marx's "Notes on Machines"[4] and also, to some extent, from the Italian futurists in the 1920s. They, following Marx, argue that productive forces (technologies) tend to make knowledge ever more socially accessible and shareable for the public good but that this is always being held back by the relations of production, by private ownership and control, by monopolies, cartels, restrictive work practices. Accelerationists advocate going all out for full automation, because in their view that will create the conditions for a new kind of society, in which people are at last freed from monotonous, soul-destroying work and will be able to concentrate their energies on doing properly human stuff, like educating and caring for one another, engaging in co-operative enterprises, building their own homes, creative endeavours of every kind. The fluid network society that they see emerging through new information technology has, in this view, the potential to erode, circumvent, and finally replace the hierarchical order of corporate capitalism and state.

So what would an accelerationist city look like? For a start it would be one where all the obstacles to free circulation of goods, services, and people had been removed. So, yes, an end to traffic gridlock, by banning private cars from the centre of London, the development of free or very cheap and fast public-transport systems, monorails, overhead cycle routes, and cable cars. The automobile would finally live up to its name and become fully driverless, getting you from A to Z in the fastest and safest possible time, reducing untold stress and carnage on the roads. London would become a velo-city.

It would also mean dismantling all those bureaucratic bottlenecks which at present riddle the planning process and make London's governance unaccountable and impervious to popular demands. There will be no local councils, because these

Fig.1: Bikeway. Creative Commons.

administrative boundaries are an irrelevance in the space/time of global flows. Instead there will be a form of direct democracy, with online plebiscites on every aspect of urban policy: housing, education, health, welfare, the environment. The electronic agora will make smart cities immediately responsive to the needs of their citizens and speed up the whole process of decision making. As Tony Vertigo, the once and future director of the Centre for Accelerationist Studies, put it recently, "We declare that only a promethean urban politics of maximal mastery over the city and its environment is capable of dealing with the problems of globalisation. Make technology work for the many not the few. More speed less haste!!!"[5]

Accelerationism involves an extreme form of technological determinism overlaid by an apocalyptic "shock-proof" futurology. The second position which has gathered increasing momentum in recent years, partly in reaction to the very trends the accelerationists wish to accentuate, is associated with a conservationist stance.[6] Its aim is to construct a new set of "shock absorbers" to protect the fabric of civil society from the destructive impact of both state and market forces, and its focus is mainly around environmental issues. Its manifesto was spelt out in the novel *Slowness* by Milan Kundera which is, in part, a critique of the malignant velocities generated by turbo-charged capitalism:

> The man hunched over his motorcycle can focus only on the present instant of his flight; he is caught in a fragment of time cut off from both the past and the future; he is wrenched from the continuity of time; he is outside time; in other words he is in a state of ecstasy. In that state he is unaware of his age, his wife, his children, his worries and so he has no fear, because the source of his fear is the future and a person freed of the future has nothing to fear.
>
> Speed is the form of ecstasy the technological revolution has bestowed on us. In contrast to a motorcyclist, the runner

is always present in their body, forever required to think of their blisters, their exhaustion; their weight, their age. This all changes when we delegate the faculty of speed to a machine; from then our own bodies are outside the process and we give ourselves over to a speed that is non-corporeal, non-material, pure speed, speed itself, ecstasy speed.

Why has the pleasure of slowness disappeared? Today, the pleasure of indolence has turned into having nothing to do which is a completely different thing. A person with nothing to do is frustrated, bored, is constantly searching for the activity they lack. Someone who is in tune with the seasons of his or her own soul, who has learnt to appreciate long duration, the beauty of small things unfolding slowly is best placed to withstand the onslaught of a future in which everything that is valuable has been reduced to its monetary worth.[7]

As Jonathan Crary recently reminded us, the 24/7 city is a city where no one sleeps.[8] Sleep, where the body and mind slow down, to regenerate vital functions, creates a space and time for dreams or reverie, which remains the last barrier against the full and final capture of our inner lives by the imagery of manufactured desires. To live the dream of capital is to exist in a state of chronic insomnia and stress, as everything that is solid and makes for solidarity in our social world melts into the thin air of cyborg communication.

For conservationists the popular anxiety dream of running faster and faster to stay in the same place perfectly captures the futility of life and labour under turbo-charged capitalism. On one side, the constant battle to prevent the rate of profit from falling by producing ever newer, more obsolescent commodities. In a word, a runaway economy underpinned by a throwaway society. On the other, the imperative to continually reinvent ourselves, driven by the terror that unless we continually adapt we will be left behind and thrown on the scrap heap. And what does the constant acceleration of new information produce but mountains of data that are mined for profit but threaten to overwhelm our capacity to make sense of it all?

There is today a growing movement of citizens in revolt against the endless speeding up of everyday life and labour. Workers vote to go slow, to regain some control over their work process and mitigate the principles of hyper-exploitation built into new management strategies for measuring productivity. Consumers are rejecting fast foods, in favour of healthier–and that means slower–cooking and eating. Slow sex is advocated in place of speed dating. Conservation areas are preventing slash-and-burn regeneration; the creation of cycle lanes and pedestrian-only areas is slowing the pace of urban life.

Fig. 2: Vertical Forest.

As Rowan Moore argues in *Slow Burn City*:

Change has tended all in one direction – converting all the qualities of its urban fabric into investment value, especially residential property. This process has threatened qualities fundamental to the city, its availability, generosity, fluidity and social diversity. If this trend continues, it looks as if London will consume itself at a rate that will liquefy all its vital organs of work and sociality, pricing all but the very rich out of access to its human resources. To prevent this happening ever again we need to slow down the whole process of London's regeneration, to ensure that if and when it happens it is with the active participation and assent of the populations most directly affected, those who live and work in the area concerned.[9]

Accelerationists are fond of quoting Marx to the effect that "revolutions are the locomotive of world history". To which they add that the shock troops of revolution are those who have mastered its technologies, not those dispossessed by them. Conservationists reject the blitzkrieg model of class struggle in favour of an evolutionary approach to social change. But it would be wrong to portray them as simple reformists. Benjamin after all put forward the idea that revolution might be an act of *de*celeration, an interruption, stopping "the runaway train of history". Perhaps revolutions are an attempt by the passengers on this train – namely us human beings – to activate the emergency brake before it is too late.

2. Welcome to East London: Fictitious Capital of the Twenty-First Century

Haunting the terms of this debate is a pervasive sense that the building of New Jerusalem in England's not-so-green and decidedly unpleasant post-Brexit land has stalled so far this side of any Blakean utopia, that his dystopian vision of London-as-

Babylon is a far more realistic scenario of what is likely to take place. In the second part of this essay I want to briefly trace these visions back into the recent history of London's eastward turn, to consider what alternative regeneration songs may still be possible.

In the basin of the Royal Docks, where once ships unloaded goods and people from across the globe, and where generations of dockers, foreign seamen, labourers, and small traders rubbed along together with the denizens of East London's vibrant hidden economy, today there stands a glistening monument to the corporate imagination of the city's future. The Crystal is owned and operated by Siemens, the giant German engineering company, and the building itself, as well as the exhibition it contains, is designed to dramatise the role that smart technologies can play in transforming London into a clean, green, environment for all its citizens. Using dazzling state-of-the-art multimedia and interactive presentations, the exhibition sets out to demonstrate that planning, transport, housing, shopping, education, work, and play, every aspect of urban life, is being regenerated by the digital revolution. Homelessness, poverty, social inequality, racism, pollution, global warming have all been magically–that is, technologically–fixed, or at least airbrushed out of the picture of an algorithmic city dancing to its own enchanted tune. A corporate utopia then, which always and already contains its dystopic negation.

The Crystal's mise en scène has gutted the accelerationist and conservationist visions of anything that would disrupt turbo-charged capitalism, and combined what remains into a rationale for a seamless web of infrastructures, invisibly and algorithmically regulating the frictionless accumulation of wealth. In its facile amalgam of environmental and technological determinism this exhibition illustrates very well the values of hysterical materialism which, I have argued elsewhere, is the main driver in the recent eastward turn in London's economic growth, a shift that was triggered by and still pivots on the

Fig. 3: The Crystal Exhibition Centre. © Siemens Crystal Website. Fair Use Copyright.

Fig. 4: Olalekan Jeyifous, Vertical Shanty Town Lagos.

creation of a new financial services quarter at Canary Wharf.[10]

Why *hysterical* materialism? I am not thinking here of sales fever or the frenetic consumerist pitch. I am using the word in the classical psychoanalytic sense as a play of substitutions set in motion by a displacement of desire.[11] Material things (artefacts, instruments, relay devices, buildings, and technologies of every kind), instead of being treated as products embedded in the capital/labour relation, as affordances or hindrances to various projects of human enterprise, are magically invested with an autonomous power of efficacy or designation, a mysterious performative capacity to condition or compel human actions which in fact substitutes itself for them. That substitution can go in either direction. Symbolic action can be substituted for a material intervention which is blocked; for example, changing the colour of the British passport is magically supposed to reclaim Britain's national sovereignty. Conversely an act of physical force, like sending in the bulldozers to demolish the Jungle at Calais, substitutes itself for the cultural and political action required to develop a viable European policy on welcoming and integrating refugees. In both cases, changeable social relations between things take on a phantasmagoric form and are treated hysterically *as if* they were fixed object relations between people. To take a more homely example, your mobile phone, which affords you a technical prosthesis in your dealings with the world, and which you may well feel "lost" without, instead of opening up new networks of facilitation, can become an immersive principle of social and cognitive closure, to which you become ever more attached as to an umbilical cord.[12]

It has recently been argued that hysterical materialism is symptomatic of the emotional logic of late capitalism, and its enrichment economy, an economy in which the financialisation of personal assets (not only houses and possessions but social, cultural, and intellectual capacity) has become a prime driver of wealth creation and its transmission between the generations.[13] In a society dominated by what Karl Marx called fictitious capital, "money talks", while people without it are robbed of a voice in economic affairs, and even the most ephemeral objects of domestic consumption become collectibles and acquire additional market and status value.

Hysterical materialism is fictitious capital in ideological action. At a political level it usually involves substituting a material problem that the political class lacks the will or capacity to solve (viz. the housing crisis, and, more generally, forms of structural inequality linked to class, gender, ethnicity, and age) for a problem that is resolvable through purely symbolic action but which may still become financialised. So for example, winning an Olympic Games bid through lobbying and PR (and sometimes bribery) can be passed off as a strategy for tackling the deeper, albeit disavowed issue of endemic poverty. As we can see in the case of London 2012, a double displacement is involved here: the symbolic means of intervention (the fabrication of the Olympic vision) creates a putative material object (the decayed urban fabric around Stratford), and the true subject of action (the architectonic drive of the 2012 masterplan) is subsumed within a pseudo-consensual discourse (the Olympic compact with local communities) through which it is magically realised.

Increasingly the material is treated as if it were symbolic and vice versa. For example, we have seen the widespread introduction of "benchmarks", "gauges", "litmus tests", "yard sticks", "barometers", "milestones", and a whole host of other pseudo-material tropes for conjuring measures of progress out of an increasingly dematerialised economy, in order to impart a sense of momentum and direction to work processes that do not lend themselves to quantifiable accountancy.

The project of regenerating or "making over" an area of multiple deprivation – in other words, its gentrification – involves a similar set of displacements, at once material and symbolic, and their imaginary linkage; material stakes in zero-sum games over social housing, public amenity, and community resources become mediated by symbolic stakes in aspirational discourses and projective identifications that tend to blur the distinction between winners and losers. The cultural geography of belonging is reshaped, often across class and ethnic divides which are then reinscribed in postcode delineations of socioeconomic status. As a result, what to some is an all-too-palpable form of social cleansing is to others simply a process of social improvement, while the consequent upgrading of physical infrastructure is plausibly passed off as the work of enlightened property developers and middle-class home owners supported by the local authority.

There are two threads of continuity in this regeneration process, and both have to do with the hydraulics of power. The first is the capacity of the state to combine legal coercion with the solicitation of public consent and thereby to transubstantiate a totalising vision of city development into material transformations on the ground. Today, the use of sophisticated mapping technologies, visual imagineering and "narrative planning" dis/simulates civic engagement and provides a rhetorical space in which the priority of driving up land and property values goes virtually unchallenged and unchecked.[14]

The second thread involves the reverse move: the combined impact of global real estate and local market forces to deterritorialise place and deindustrialise the urban economy, hollowing out existing community and tearing apart the residential labourhood, replacing it with looser, spatially distributed social networks of elective affinity or affiliation centred on individualised life styles and personal assets.

In both cases the effect is to disperse and/or hyper-localise resistance. Future shock is both normalised, embedded in the ongoing practice of urban regeneration as its inevitable concomitant, *and* split off into a separate category of extreme quasi-pathologic experience for those who are classified as "failing to adapt to the pace of change", "lacking resilience", or simply "the left-behinds". It may be that we need to identify the symptomatology of posttraumatic urban stress more clearly and regroup social statistics of alcoholism, drug abuse, and depression accordingly in studying the negative impact of large-scale regeneration schemes. But let us also note that the physical violence of slash-and-burn regeneration has been largely replaced by the symbolic violence of place rebranding and "re-imagineering". The bulldozer has given way to the architectural flythrough and the marketing suite as the preferred vehicle of planning coercion/consent.

The regeneration of the Royal Docks makes a good case study in the uneven and combined development of the processes I have been describing. As you come out of the Crystal Exhibition, your gaze is inevitably drawn to the anonymous hangar-like structures that line the dock on one side, and on the other to the long-abandoned Millennium Mills, once upon a time the home of the white loaf, that staple in the manual working-class diet, now scheduled to be the hub of a new business and commercial district; and to Tate and Lyle sugar refinery at Silvertown, the last of the smokestack industries that once dominated the landscape.[15] Overhead, cable cars circle in eerie silence bringing pilgrims from the O2 and the Greenwich Peninsular to sample this surreal mix of urban past and future; en route they may well marvel at the stupendous aerial views of Riverine London, perhaps lulled by the reassuring commentary so that this affordance of the bomber's-eye view no longer evokes the shock and awe of the Blitz, that founding moment in the slow but steady destruction of East London as a working-class city, a moment only briefly evoked by two spectacular fires at Millennium Mills in recent years. Perhaps it is not surprising that East Enders of an older generation, when trying to describe their sense of shock at the transformation of the St Katherine Docks, Stratford, or the Royals spontaneously draw on the language of the Blitz. One ex-Docker told me that visiting Stratford in the run up to the Olympics was like seeing the area devastated by a "capitalist bomb".

Any such reflections are likely to be rudely interrupted by the roar of a plane taking off from nearby London City Airport, the first and still the most important feature in the local regeneration economy. Residents who have the misfortune to live in the social housing surrounding the airport have been subjected to industrial levels of noise and chemical pollution for over a generation, a lethal form of environmental degradation that can be precisely measured, but is largely invisible, unlike the toxic fogs that used to blanket the docks. Those who live on the council estates of North Woolwich, historically the most deprived and neglected in the whole of Newham, may well wonder what the attraction is for the students and young professionals who have come to occupy the new blocks of private flats that have been built in the area over the last twenty years.

The simple answer, of course, is that this accommodation is still affordable to those on middle incomes, driven out of the inner East End by rising rents and house prices. Yet that is only half the story. It is the raw edginess of this part of London, its natural symbolism of marginality, so lovingly recreated in the writings of Iain Sinclair, which has made it so inhabitable by would-be "urban pioneers" with their disavowed mission of pushing the boundaries of "culture" ever further east, ever more downriver into ever more exotic and unknown country.

In the Royal Docks, we can clearly see the two faces of hysterical materialism at work. Firstly, the creation of abstract logistical space by and for capital in which the work of construction, maintenance, and occupation leaves little or no human mark on the landscape. The giant sheds that house Newham Council and the ExCel Centre are an extreme example of this hyper-modernist urbanism. Secondly, the invention of place that brings dead labour back to surrogate life, in the form of heritage sites, objects of industrial archaeology, and public artworks designed to create a symbolic aura to fill the material void. The Line art trail with its non-site-specific works by well-known artists is a case in point. So is the replacement of the Railway Heritage Museum at North Woolwich by yet another arts centre.

Fortunately, that is not the whole story. The People's Plan

for the Royal Docks, published in 1981 by a group of local trade unionists and community activists, outlined a strategy of economic regeneration around developing the existing skills base of the area, with boat building and repair, hi-tech maritime industry plus a floating maritime heritage museum, watersports centres and social housing around the dock. The plan continues to be an inspiration for many of those now campaigning for a working waterfront against property developers who want to replace the remaining industrial estates along the Thames with luxury apartment blocks. In the Royal Docks itself, long-term residents and schoolchildren have combined with the help of staff from the UEL Royal Docks Campus to create an audio trail, "Ports of Call", which tells the area's back story but also brings it up to date.[16] A recent resident has made a marvellous map showing the ecology of the Royal Docks, documenting all the vegetation and trees that have managed to withstand and adapt to the high levels of pollution around London City Airport, a potent metaphor of sustainable resistance.[17] A group of staff and students from the Development Planning Unit at UCL have produced a new design strategy for the Docks which gives priority to the needs of existing communities. Meanwhile as graffiti sprouts along the Dockland Light Railway and Crossrail routes that slice through the area, severing many potential social links, a group of "Walking Artists" are creating an alternative narrative trail through the area, reconnecting its past, present, and future.

In one of the most significant recent developments a group of young artists in Silvertown, unable to find affordable places to live and work, have occupied the Tate Institute, a building originally donated to the council as a social club for local workers and residents. Their plan, to turn it into a craft centre for use by schoolchildren and resident groups, gained considerable local support, despite–or because of–the fact that the council applied to evict them. An alliance has thus sprung up between these new East Enders and members of a long-established dockland community.

These are small acts of resistance. These local victories need not just to be joined up horizontally but to be scaled up vertically to create a London-wide platform for popular planning. That is what Living Maps,[18] in collaboration with Just Space and other groups, is attempting to do with the Citizens Atlas of London. The aim is to create an online platform made by a network of citizen mappers, located in each of the thirty-six so-called "opportunity areas" identified in the London 2050 Plan and, using a specially designed cartographic toolkit, to not just represent the past and present of these areas but more importantly to envisage an alternative future for them and for London as a whole.

In order to test our approach we recently put on an event for the Museum of London's "City Now, City Future" programme in which we presented participants with three scenarios of urban future shock and invited them to construct their response in the form of a map on which they charted what they would like to preserve, expand, demolish, repurpose, or create to make London into "their kind of town".

Whether they were dealing with the post-Brexit meltdown of financial services followed by a housing market crash, the impact of global warming and the flooding of central London, or new forms of political action linked to the emergence of an urban protest movement amongst Londoners on a large scale, we found that there was no shortage of imaginative proposals. But, of course, most of those taking part in this "salon" (sic) were the usual suspects: actual or budding architects, planners, community activists, and academics who are professionally involved in thinking about alternative futures for London. The real challenge faced by a project of this kind is how to engage with people whose time horizons are limited to paying the rent at the end of the month, and having enough money to live on from week to week, maybe not even knowing when their next pay check or benefit allowance is coming. Under these circumstances, worrying about what London is going to be like

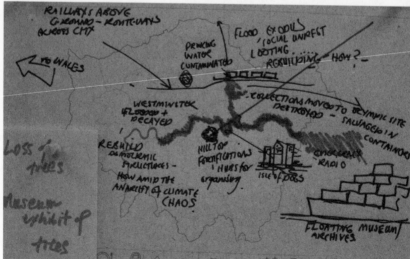

Figs 5 and 6: Maps from the Museum of London Salon, Living Maps event.
© The author, 2017.

for their children, if they can afford to have them, in twenty years' time, or imagining alternative planning scenarios is not top of their list of priorities.

Any viable strategy for turning the tide in East London's regeneration has to forge alliances on the ground between three social formations which understandably view each other with some suspicion but who are now faced with a common set of problems:

- the residual manual working class, including immigrant and minority ethnic communities who are condemned to a precarious existence, whether in the gig economy or as the Helots of personal service industries;

- generation rent, students and young professionals, budding gentrifiers all, but frustrated at their inability to get on the housing ladder or pursue anything like a career;

- the "creative class" who have moved opportunistically into ex-industrial areas but who realise there is more to community art than making cultural capital out of other people's misfortune.

Whether London's regeneration song will carry on with its same old harmonics, harmonics that are increasingly discordant with the realities experienced by most Londoners, or will be replaced by an altogether different tonal structure, allowing a diversity of groups to find their own voice without having to sing in unison, remains to be seen. But there are encouraging signs in the Royal Docks, as in many other parts of London, of the kinds of alliances that will make such a shift possible.

Endnotes

1   Walter Benjamin, *One Way Street and Other Writings* (Penguin, 2009)

2   See Nick Dunn et al., *Future Cities: A Visual History of the Future* (HMSO, 2014). For a general critique of contemporary futurology see John Urry, *What is the Future* (Polity Press, 2016)

3   See Nick Land, *Fanged Noumena* (Urbanomic, 2013) and Robin Mackay (ed), *#Accelerate: The Accelerationist Reader* (Urbanonomic, 2014). Also https://londonfuturists.com. For a more politically focused account see Nick Srnicek and Alex Williams, *Inventing the Future* (Verso, 2016). For a thoroughgoing critique of the accelerationist position see Benjamin Noys, *Malign Velocities: Accelerationism and Capitalism (Zero Books, 2014), and for a sociological analysis Hartmut Ross (ed), High-Speed Society: Social Acceleration, Power and Modernity* (Penn State Press, 2015)

4   Karl Marx, *Grundrisse: Notes on Machines* (Penguin, 1993)

5   Quotation taken from the script of the London Aftershock event at the Museum of London December 2017. Further information from www.livingmaps.org.uk

6   In what follows I have drawn on the work of Carl Honore and Laura Brett, *In Praise of Slow* (Orion Books, 2005). On the slow city movement see www.citta-slow.com

7   Milan Kundera, *Slowness* (Penguin, 2007)

8   Jonathan Crary, *24/7: Late Capitalism and the End of Sleep* (Verso, 2013)

9   Rowan Moore, *Slow Burn City* (Picador, 2016), p. 475

10 For further discussion of this concept see Phil Cohen, "A Place beyond belief? Hysterical materialism and the making of East 20", in Phil Cohen and Paul Watt (eds), *London 2012 and the Post Olympic City: A Hollow Legacy?* (Palgrave Macmillan, 2017)

11 For a critical reading of the Freudian concept of hysteria, see Sander Gilman et al., *Hysteria Beyond Freud* (University

of California Press, 1993). For a Lacanian re-construction see Elisabeth Bronfen, *The Knotted Subject: Hysteria and its Discontents* (Princeton University Press, 1997). On the concept of political hysteria derived from the work of Istvan Bibo see Emmanuel Terray, "Headscarf Hysteria", *New Left Review*, 26, March 2004

12 See for example Sherry Turkle, *Alone Together: Why We Expect More of Technology and Less from Each Other* (Basic Books, 2011)

13 See Martijn Konings, *The Emotional Logic of Late Capitalism: What Progressives Have Missed* (Stanford University Press, 2015), and Cedric Durand, *Fictitious Capital: How Finance is Appropriating our Future* (Verso, 2017). See also the chapter by Andrew Calcutt on "London and the Financial Imagination" in G. Poynter, et al. (eds), *London After the Recession: A Fictitious Capital?* (Ashgate, 2012). On the financialisation of collectibles see Luc Boltanski and Arnaud Esquerre "Enrichment, Profit, Critique", *New Left Review*, 106, August 2017, and for its wider ramifications Martin Haiven, *Cultures of Financialisation: Fictitious Capital in Popular Culture and Everyday Life* (Palgrave Macmillan, 2014).

14 For a discussion of this point see Phil Cohen, "Stuff Happens: the Narrative Turn in the Planning of Thames Gateway" in Phil Cohen and M. Rustin (eds), *London's Turning: The making of Thames Gateway* (Ashgate, 2007)

15 See Melanie McGrath, *Silvertown: An East End Family Memoir* (Fourth Estate, 2002). For a historical overview of how the East End has been imagined by artists and writers, in relation to how it has been lived and narrated by those who grew up in the area, see Phil Cohen, *On the Wrong Side of the Track: East London and the Post Olympics* (Lawrence and Wishart, 2013), pp. 36-136

16 The trail and background material can be downloaded at www.portsofcall.org.uk

17   The map by Emma Jane Crace can be accessed at : https://
      www.google.com/maps/d/viewer?mid=1ZIZfW_u8rJM
      3HtpR7wttCoEvC70&ll=51.49294057273844%2C0.09
      85703758546515&z=13

18   www.livingmaps.org.uk

Can You See Us Now
Rohan Ayinde and Amina Gichinga of Take Back The City

While you enjoy the fruits of our labour
our heads deep in everyday struggles

Our eyes reading along the lines
of newspapers written in a language
made to conjure fear and conquer thought -
the thought of looking up to read
between the lines of people's faces who reflect
Our own made to seem,
foreign.

But we will not be governed by fear –

We will dance on the trains
that plough through zones
We will dance on the bulldozers
that demolish our homes
And we will skip the barriers
to recite these poems

Can you see us now

TAKE BACK THE CITY
CAN YOU SEE US NOW

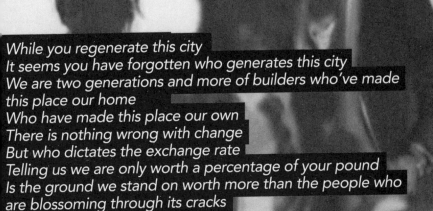

While you regenerate this city
It seems you have forgotten who generates this city
We are two generations and more of builders who've made
this place our home
Who have made this place our own
There is nothing wrong with change
But who dictates the exchange rate
Telling us we are only worth a percentage of your pound
Is the ground we stand on worth more than the people who
are blossoming through its cracks

I think not – we do not agree

So we will dance on buses, smile on trains
And raise our voices to make change

I'm sure you see us now

Part 6
Future
Fictions

The Zone

Dean Kenning

The force hit us hard when it arrived, like an enormous slab hurled out of the fourth dimension and into our lives. Splat! – but excruciatingly drawn out over Phase One. We stood there numb, trembling, the x sq. feet of ground beneath our feet – our homes! – already giving way, revealing a digitally rendered stage upon which each of us was forced to read the unfamiliar lines to our newly scripted futures – so far removed from our expectations, hopes, and plans. Shock turned to anger, and then to an illness-nurturing despair, as the fatigue of resistance kicked in, and the inevitability and extent of our erasure in the pursuit of the Regeneration became apparent. Some of us even took up the offer of "expulsion counselling", a concession offered by the Developer as part of its ever-shrinking legal obligations to residents, cooked up in secret with Local Control.

***

"Yes I suppose I *am* depressed, that's why I'm off work. Also – I've been having these… hallucinations. Nothing seems real anymore."

"I do understand, of course I do, Maureen Area D. But there's no use beating yourself up about The Zone. We all have to move with the times – in your case, literally. Try to look on the positive side…" The onscreen counsellor was going through her lines. A pair of raised eyebrows signalled sympathy, but below them steely eyes stared out in goal-oriented exhortation.

"It's better to invest your *survival capital* in an alternate future in Faraway Town… It's really not such a bad place. Think of it as a *new chapter* in your life…"

The patient's continued silence seemed to make the counsellor change tack, as if initiating a tonal recalibration, from positivity to harsh realism. "Try looking at the situation *rationally*: your continued presence was not feasible, as was confirmed in the Developer's 'Opportunity Report'."

Maureen Tenant said nothing. She was seated at the last remaining terminal in the high-windowed public library. Her mind was drifting, thinking of the times she had spent as a child in this very place, and of how she had brought her own kids here when they were young. Now it was due for imminent repurposing as private apartments. *Is there a library in Faraway Town?* she wondered.

The voice persisted with what Maureen half-detected to be rising enthusiasm. "Projections for growth are now phenomenal. And you've played your part, all of you – that's something to be proud of. People who would have avoided it like the plague, professional people, actually *want* to live in the area. We can't keep up with demand. Speaking on behalf of the develllllllllleprr-rrrrrrr…"

The frozen audio caused Maureen to refocus on the screen where the counsellor's face was melting into a pixelated soup before being replaced, to an accompanying sound effect, by the Developer's logo. *Just as well*, Maureen thought – her increasing irritation with the virtual shrink had brought on a nauseous dizziness. She got up carefully and shuffled past a librarian clearing away the last remaining books in the local history section. As she stumbled towards the exit, she encountered on the way the glass-encased scale model of The Zone.

She stopped to catch her breath, leaning over the vitrine and scanning the neat, bright Perspex geometry below: a miniature world of immaculately shaped, translucent blocks; a perfect, homogeneous world purged of colour, texture, and human life.

The display was interactive, so that by pressing various buttons different parts of the redevelopment glowed red. She pushed her thumb against the button marked Area D, lighting up a pair of large, balconied blocks, rising impressively above the surrounding buildings: *Offshore Towers*, a pop-up graphic helpfully pointed out. *160 Exclusive Apartments. SOLD OUT.*

There was no trace of Welfare Estate where Maureen had lived her entire life.

Sold out, thought Maureen bitterly, as she staggered onwards towards the automatic doors.

***

Dockers Plaza

"It moves upon the face of the earth, a blood-sucking force; a devouring, glutinous mass, creeping over the planet, feeding off the people; satisfying its *insatiable appetite for growth*!"

John Revelator was on good form. Megaphone to lips, he stood by the regimented grid of fountains on the newly pedestrianised and privately managed Dockers Plaza, a small assortment of

© Dean Kenning, 2018.

self-made pamphlets on a foldable table beside him.

"Visible but unseen; multiple but unitary. Rents extracted from stolen common wealth; value siphoned from workers; surpluses seeping across borders, slipping out of tax jurisdictions… It needs somewhere to go! It needs flesh to feast on! LOOK AROUND YOU…"

A Development Vehicle pulled up and a high-vis Hygiene Officer in wraparound sunglasses got out.

"No politics, this is a family area."

"Family?" John spat back. "What about the families your company has decanted to Faraway Town?"

The Hygiene Officer studied him. "Look I told you, no politics. It's bad for business. Do you think the customers of this plaza want to hear your deluded rant while they're enjoying lunch?"

John Revelator lifted his megaphone and put it back to work. "I'm preaching the truth! *I will not be silenced…*"

"Put that bloody thing down, Revelator! I'm losing my patience", warned the HO as he fingered the electronic stun truncheon hanging from his belt. "Anyway what's all this stuff about preaching the truth? Your blood-sucking vampire squids and all that slimy bollocks… sounds to me like homelessness has driven you loony. You've a fevered imagination. And you're generating unwanted attention."

"What's wrong with having an imagination?" John stared at his own dishevelled figure reflected back at him in the Officer's shades.

'"Look", John said, "it's not me who's mad, *it's the system*. I had a home, stability. I was told it was a home for life. Suddenly I discover I live in The Zone and everything is shifting. I'm being moved out. My home is reduced to a pile of rubble. Has there been an earthquake? Is there a war on? Why have I suddenly become a target?"

The HO remained silent, stroking his stun truncheon as John continued. "Look, I'm trying to explain it to you—market forces. I lived on Welfare Estate, the part that's already been knocked down. The Regeneration has pushed land values through the roof – so the council say we must move to Faraway Town because they cannot afford to rehouse us locally: the area is now too expensive, *too valuable*. But that's true only *because* we have been cleared out! So you see, when they say we are expendable, it's not that we are unimportant. In fact, we are *absolutely necessary*. The market… it's a funny thing. I'm here on the square because I have to find a way to represent the abstraction; to *make it visceral*."

"I'll show you visceral", said the Hygiene Officer, and gave John a high-voltage shock that threw him to the ground. Then, turning his weapon to manual, he proceeded to administer several rhythmic whacks to John's skull. Little puddles of fountain water turned red as the latte-sipping café dwellers of Dockers Plaza looked on.

***

© Dean Kenning, 2018.

Two Years Earlier: The Local Controller's Phone Conversation.

Controller: "Look, it's simple. Central Command have run out of money because they had to give it to the bankers. Now we have to be entrepreneurial and look for opportunities. Luckily, God has blessed this territory with riverside views, with a dockyard waterway system, and with good transport links. The only thing standing in the way of massive investment in this area is…"

[…]

Controller: "Yes exactly. Like it's their God-given right. But I'm telling you, its basic economics. If we want to eliminate poverty then we need to get rid of the poor."

[…]

Controller: "No of course I don't mean kill them! I mean…"

[…]

Controller: "Right. If we want to make the area richer then we need rich people living here. They're the ones with the money. I don't know what is so hard to understand about that…"

[…]

Controller: "It will be beautiful. It's all been envisioned. Our partner is Rentokil Capital. Diversified portfolio. Experienced operators, multinational. They not only build it, they manage it: take care of street cleaning, repairs, pest control, law and order. We're handing it over. Balancing the budget."

[…]

Controller: "It's sorted. One of the big backers is Global Infleshment. Offshore. I saw the communiqué by Lord Vulture. He's expecting huge profits on projected 20% annual yields for initial off-plan investors, and 10% yields for second-wave investors who buy to rent on completion. Impressive returns I'm sure you'll agree – off the record of course, but there's still a couple left if you were looking for somewhere to…"

[…]

Controller: "Alphas – although a lot of them will remain empty, inevitably, just sort of accumulating money. The market's booming. But yes, city bankers, finance lawyers, property speculators. We are envisioning a whole new community. Only this demographic have the income to make initial investment attractive – for the luxury retailers too. Again it's basic economics. The current population cannot generate enough surplus – frozen benefits, stagnating wages and all that. Useless."

[…]

Controller: "Three estates over Phase One. It's like Lord Vulture said in *City AM*: 'The continued existence of these people is costing me money.' Opportunity costs."

[…]

Controller: "It's negotiable. A smattering of what we are calling 'affordable housing', contemporary sculpture commissions (which are actually really going to help with values), and something new which they call 'expulsion counselling'. It's very educational actually, I went to a presentation. Cognitive reprogramming therapy combined with market rationalism. The thinking behind it is that people adapt better to their

© Dean Kenning, 2018.

displacement once they comprehend the economic logic behind it. It's a sort of invitation to embrace reality, take responsibility…"

[…]

Controller: "It's economic Prozac for this area."

[…]

Controller: "Okay, see you at the public consultation. Remember to learn your script! We need to manage this sensitively."

***

Peter Winner, CEO of Creative Distortion, Interviewed for Emergence C, the Creative Branding Magazine

[…]

PETER WINNER: The way I see it is that we are storytellers. We write the script and create reality. We are incredibly powerful disrupters. Shamanic engineers. We not only determine the imaginative backdrop to people's lives, we actually shape people's futures by supplying what I call the "perceptual framework" to their reality.

INTERVIEWER: That's interesting. You've always presented an impressively rigorous conceptual…

PETER WINNER: My original idea – I studied art at Central St Martin's Business School – my original idea and theoretical contribution to the field of real estate marketing, is that creative innovation is really a question of simultaneous burial and exhumation. That is to say, when we develop a narrative for an investment project, we are dealing with the dead as much as we are with the living.

INTERVIEWER: Yes that, let's say, "gothic" element is a unique selling point of Creative Distortion. Perhaps you could say more about that with respect to your company structure.

PETER WINNER: Basically the creatives are divided into three groups, which we call the Ghosts, the Ghouls, and the Gravediggers.

INTERVIEWER: This is all sounding very spooky! So what do these Ghosts and Ghouls actually do?

PETER WINNER: The Ghosts are the CGI guys. They visualise the whole scheme in such a way that it becomes irresistible to investors, and is just generally appealing. Gleaming retail centres, luxury apartment blocks, fountained plazas, riverside walkways, manicured shrubbery. We call them Ghosts because of the digital figures they create to inhabit these virtual spaces. These are weightless, floating figures, ideals far removed from the material inertia, bad habits, and unattractive physical traits of any ordinary, mixed-community people.

INTERVIEWER: No hoodies or mobility scooters then!

PETER WINNER: Ha ha! No we try to avoid them. Market feedback tells the Ghosts who to exorcise: crisp munchers, groups of children, old people, mothers struggling home with the shopping. Tracksuits are only for joggers or people leaving the gym. Everyone is looking positive, going about their own business, really enjoying being in the new development.

INTERVIEWER: So that's the Ghosts. Tell us about the Ghouls.

PETER WINNER: I should explain that ghouls are mythical creatures that hang around in graveyards and feed off the bodies of the dead. And that's essentially what our guys do.

INTERVIEWER: Gruesome! I hope they don't mind you saying that about them!

PETER WINNER: Not at all. They're proud of it! Although some of them perhaps prefer to see themselves as local historians. But our guys, they don't just dig up the past; they actually *put the dead to work*! Let me explain. So the big project we are currently engaged with is Rentokil Capital's development of The Zone. The Ghosts have done a lovely job, reimagining the future on billboards, at trade fairs, and on screens around the world. But we need something else, and that is the "A" word: *authenticity*. The Ghouls are really authenticity managers, and that means getting their fingernails dirty. So they exhume some old bones and get them dancing to the tune of the Developer. What they dug up at The Zone were the dockers. They became the poster boys for our regeneration scheme. The quintessence of hard honest graft, but distant enough in the past to remain reassuringly quaint. We pasted these grimy, flat-capped faces all over The Zone, enormous portraits in high-contrast black and white. We were determined to mark the area's working-class heritage.

INTERVIEWER: They are beautiful images, and they certainly lend the area a sense of place. So let's talk about your final category of creatives...

PETER WINNER: The Gravediggers, yes. We really see this as an innovation in the profession. Just as we envision the future, and reanimate the past, we also need to bury the present. As I often say, one man's grave is another man's foundation. After all, prime real estate is not something that can be conjured into existence, no matter how powerful our "dark arts". What do the Gravediggers do? They infiltrate the channels of communication and change the story. For example: the modernist council block is much loved by the tight-knit community of residents who call it home? No, it's a run-down, crime-ridden hellhole which keeps its residents, particularly the old folks, virtual prisoners in their own dilapidated flats. The marketplace is a thriving area of activity where small local businesses can flourish and the less well-off can shop? No, it's a sad spectacle of inferior knock-off goods, an eyesore, and a general put-off to anyone not compelled by convenience to frequent it. Concerned activists bravely standing up for the rights of tenants? Wrong. They're privileged out-of-towners and attention-seeking misfits trying to stir up trouble. You see?

INTERVIEWER: Yes, I get the picture. And this "gravedigging" activity, as you call it, this dissemination of an alternative present which is more, let's say, conducive to redevelopment... Is this activity really a *creative* marketing activity?

PETER WINNER: I believe it is the most creative activity of

all, the most advanced at any rate. The Gravediggers are really the conceptual avant-garde of the regeneration game.

***

© Dean Kenning, 2018.

Maureen Tenant staggered out of the library and into the light. A group of workmen were removing the access ramps next to the stone steps. Above them, flapping in the breeze, an enormous canvas billboard read: "PHILANTHROPY LODGE. PRESTIGIOUS MUNICIPAL CONVERSION. SIX APARTMENTS."

Maureen recalled the argument the Controller had put forward at the public consultation: "At a time when we are being asked to tighten our belts and think more entrepreneurially, the storage of books in heritage buildings is *a luxury we can ill afford*. It would be both criminal and stupid not to take up the sums being offered by the private sector for some of our most beautiful listed sites. A feasibility study found that the hire of Portakabins is the most efficient way to maintain an array of public services…"

The most normal, taken-for-granted thing suddenly becomes a luxury, thought Maureen. *And luxury is a luxury we can't afford! Our luxury for your luxury.*

A realisation was solidifying in her mind. *Our homes for your profit. My depression for your growth…*

She remained on the top step, gazing out across the main road onto Dockers Plaza. Everything about the place looked unfamiliar, as if a film production unit had come along one night and changed the set. Designer boutiques, posh cafés, an "anti-gym" – whatever that was. Apart from the façade of The Old Ship (secured by "property guardians"), the launderette was the only reminder of the old centre, except it was now an art gallery deceptively called The Launderette. Geometrical trees stood about in little clusters, and, in the distance, beyond the choreographed fountains springing from the immaculate paving slabs, Maureen could just make out a couple of Hygiene Officers chasing off a group of kids on bikes. *God knows this place needed some attention*, Maureen thought, *but it's as if the new square has been beamed down from outer space. And some of its new inhabitants with it.*

Looking up, Maureen scanned the skies. Everywhere giant cranes were at work, moving slowly above the balconied residential towers and glass office blocks. Off in the distance to her right, Maureen located the crane hovering above her own Welfare Estate, and the single polished golden tower, unfinished but rising into the sky on that section of "Area D" that had already been cleared. *We're about to be evicted to make way for its evil twin*, she thought.

She began counting the number of new developments that had been completed or were in progress, and imagined all the others that had not yet been started, based on her visual recollection of the Perspex model in the library. The sun came out with an intensity that made Maureen squint, and as the scene brightened, the cranes disappeared, bleached out together with the last structural remnants of all that had been condemned. The future glowed with a high-definition finish. And with the harsh light reflecting against the polished architecture, the walls of every office building and apartment block took on a transparency and nearness, so that Maureen could see through into the uncurtained rooms and office spaces, and beyond every room into the rooms beyond, and further into the ones beyond that. And in every one something was moving. Everywhere that Maureen looked, rooms were *spilling out numbers*... numbers that were rapidly increasing, like the incessant upward count of seconds and tenths of seconds on a digital stopwatch. As if the interiors could no longer contain the energy of them, they leaked out from every part of every building. Soon the whole skyline, and much of the ground below, was covered in accelerating digits, glowing red like a biblical swarm of LED displays.

What happened next gripped Maureen with a corporeal intensity. Each room of each apartment, including the balconies, was abandoning its peculiar transparent character and taking on a sort of viscous, organic quality, as if a gloopy but rapidly coagulating blood-red substance were adumbrating each unit of space. The impression being formed was one of irregular, translucent blocks, piled next to and on top of one another, like stacks of cyclopean jelly cubes. Not only that, but, as with the numbers – which continued to emanate and accumulate all around – and in seeming sympathy with them, each congealed unit did not remain still, but pulsated and, as Maureen realised with a distinct sense of nausea, *began dividing up like living cells* – each single cubic unit becoming first two, then four, then sixteen... never causing an expansion in overall size, but multiplying into smaller and smaller sub-units like a gruesome living fractal. Everywhere Maureen looked revealed to her the same pattern of hideous metamorphosis: everything red and writhing in turmoil, *as if the whole Zone were one enormous and homogeneous, spontaneously regenerating life form.*

Maureen squeezed her eyes tight together and held them shut for a good half-minute – long enough for the afterimage of what she had witnessed to eventually fade beneath the redness of her eyelids. Opening them again, she registered that the crimson glow of the living world had dissipated. Cautiously she walked down the library steps, crossed the road and entered the square, noticing that her heart was racing and her palms were sweating. A large three-dimensional plastic arrow stood before her blocking her way. As she navigated herself around it she saw, facing out at her from the other side of a glass wall, a row of moving shapes, silhouettes in tight-fitting clothing, running and peddling on the spot. Averting her eyes, and with some trepidation, she looked up to the apartments above. The ones she was able to see into, which were on the lower levels, appeared as normal: neat, tastefully furnished, but strangely impersonal, antiseptic even; as if each were in fact a show flat. She moved ahead through the square as intermittent solitary figures floated rapidly by her like quick-motion ghosts, seemingly oblivious to their surroundings and the people around them, locked in preset trajectories. It was then that she saw the bloodied figure before her, face down in the water; a crushed megaphone, several damp pamphlets and a collapsed table at his side.

"Oh my God! John?"

"Maureen?"

"John what happened? Are you alright?" She had snapped out of her daze.

"I'll survive. Hygiene Patrol were just sending me a not-too-subtle message."

"Shall I call an ambulance?"

"No, don't bother."

He seemed sentient enough despite his abject condition. "So you're still here then? Didn't move to Faraway Town?"

"Plague Town more like! No chance. I'm staying put—here, in The Zone. They'll either have to rehouse me locally, or they're going to have to kill me."

"Looks like they might do if you keep up your, err, 'public speaking'."

"I can't help it Maureen. I know too much. What else am I supposed to do with that knowledge?"

He remained lying on the wet paving stones, jets of water spurting up around him at a military tempo. His wounded head resting in his hand, he looked up whimsically at the apartment blocks above him and made a wide sweeping gesture towards them with his free arm.

"Look up there Maureen. *All that wealth*. One day all of that will be ours."

Maureen looked at him dubiously. "Those are luxury flats John. They're not for us."

"They used to say plumbed indoor toilets were a luxury", John responded, quick as a flash. "These days 'luxury' is just another word for enforced scarcity."

"That's why they want to make us scarce", said Maureen.

"That's it Maureen. You understand! Public provision is bad for business. But we've seen them working on it; seen it going up day by day. Glass, steel, concrete." John's eyes were gleaming now, and despite his otherwise abject state he appeared to Maureen to be supremely happy, as if he were having the most wonderful dream.

"I just know it. All of this will be ours."

***

Coda

The death of John Revelator from a brain haemorrhage was the definitive turning point. Individualised suffering and anger collectivised around a focal point, like isotopes of a common element fusing, triggering a startling release of energy. Pressure mounted until a public enquiry found the Developer culpable, and so Rentokil Capital lost its management license and suffered reputational meltdown. Eventually the calls for a public memorial in "Revelator Square" – as it has come to be known by us – became too strong a force for Control and their investor partners to suppress. And so a statue was commissioned, replacing the Turner Prize-

© Dean Kenning, 2018.

winning bronze aubergine at the centre of the Plaza: John Revelator, arms outstretched, gazing skyward, preaching on his territory (something about value, no doubt).

If Control had hoped the sculpture would put an abrupt end to this unforeseen chapter of The Zone, rather than becoming a locus of political pilgrimage and community resistance, they were mistaken. All the commotion, the crowds and demos, occupations, smashed windows and picnics, have inevitably had a negative market effect. And so, having made the supreme sacrifice, John Revelator's final euphoric prophecy may yet prove to have substance, and cannot simply be dismissed as the effect of confusion brought on by lethal bleeding of the brain. Many apartments remain empty and unsold, and prices are dropping like a concrete block down a high-rise elevator shaft. Meanwhile there are a lot of angry, organised people who need homes.

Recurrence of All Things

Kunal Modi

[He] was a genius [... the] unseen chasm in the canon of world cinema and the standing giant of anomalous art. What he gave to cinema [...] I mean Chaplin was a master, Lang was an artist. Hitchcock was a true auteur. But Aria had a vision so singular, so perverse that it left us no choice but to reconsider cinema itself. As such, he is our Duchamp [... Aria] is the great, lost filmmaker of the Eastern migration routes; the architect who, like the characters of his great work, became lost in the loops of time.
— Stanley Kubrick, 1998

Zeta UMa

The Zeta UMa (ZU) ideogram is the final living symbol of this city. Like an optical illusion, it's impossible at first to see.[1] "Each example of the Zeta UMa returned to us an image of our dual nature, to remind us we are unstill in our essence," wrote the archivist Zephaniah Zola, whose job it was now to find the meaning of the symbol, and trace the fall of his former home, London.

Zola discovered the first activated ZU on camcorder footage taken at the Woolwich underpass, in the autumn of 1988: a young family returning from Ralph Hyde's "Panaromania!".[2] The ideogram today is known to predate this image, although the timeline is indeterminate.

The Woolwich ZU vanished under the centralised regeneration programme of the borough, a community autodissected into a global investment village, "an Arc of Opportunity".

Over time, more examples of the ZU were discovered, embedded in the autonomous psyches of art, advertising, logographic

Fig. 1: The Zeta Uma (ZU) ideogram.

design, and other capitalist artillery.

"There seemed through history to be a tradition of twos", wrote Zola, "spirit and matter, the hero and the traitor, life as a patchwork of opportunity, and then immutable fact. This was reflected in the Zeta UMa."

Zola had become transfixed by his search for this lost city. His memory was a half-made puzzle when he began his study and, as the account develops, overlaps between items of fact and fiction become increasingly frequent.

The First Chapter

An esoteric public-private sect that governed London from 2042–68 maintained the border running from the Barbican, through the far east of the city. It was called the First Chapter.

"Knowledge of the Chapter is almost completely lost, but its omnipresence is a fitting metaphor", wrote Zola. The archivist spun a fragment of a high-resolution screen-plate in his palm, wearing a look of disquiet on his scarred face. He had been working alone along the city border, abandoned since the fall of the First Chapter, for as long as he could remember.

Each morning he walked to the boundary, passing ivy-covered tower blocks and squares overgrown into unhinged pastorals, architecture quietly reprogrammed by nature. The border came to an end by the River Lea canal, under view of the Fallen Helix (formerly the ArcelorMittal Orbit). Zola pinned it to his interpretive map as a point of territorial significance, a reference to navigate the terrain.

The First Chapter's origins remain obscured behind a trail Zola's study drew back through the previous century: "Screenshots of early '90s chainmail; half-torn notes on Jung's *Mysterium Coniunctionis*; post-scarcity memetics and ancap coding rituals; correspondence from the London Orbital rave scene, and so forth." The group formed within the soundsystem culture of the era, creating improvised spaces of euphoria bookended by exploitation and dereliction, "Capitalism's own leitmotif, the fanfare and the swansong."[3]

The Chapter controlled a part of the city through a precedent-setting zonal claim and ratified power in the 2036 Boleyn by-election, foreshadowing a future dominance in which all of Newham Borough was captured.

The Chapter of Zola's youth transformed into a vessel of interests, neglecting its radical foundations in pursuit of greater power (the hero and the traitor).

"It evolved like all objects of capitalist ordinance: a shimmer in the mind's eye, a youthful (naïve) extrapolation of principles, the spirit of a community rendered, the language of opportunity proffered. Then, betrayal by that same language, the ironic twinkle of commercial neon, suited shadows enfolding, unseen from the dark."

Nous

"Nous was the technological apparatus of the First Chapter, a benign monolith at the heart of the city that fed on data alone", wrote Zola.

Nous's biotech implant was patented in the previous era by the recondite leader of the First Chapter. During rare public pronouncements, they would issue either a formalised injunction, or a mystical excursus.

"I recall their voice casting out over the city", wrote Zola, "beaming spiritual knowledge directly into your mind, to abide by or perish".

Members of the city-state connected to cloud intelligence networks via the implant, developed to mediate communication, record data, and redesign the public and social infrastructure of the city and its inhabitants. The one embedded in Zola's own hand had left a slight scar, which he traced compulsively with his opposite forefinger.

"By applying the methods of evolutionary computation", read a fragmentary statement, "there was no need to hardcode ethics into Nous's models. The system arrived to a naturalist understanding of its moral responsibilities, free from our ideological chassis."[4]

The First Chapter reimagined social and epistemic relations as information, establishing the supremacy of data over human initiative; "We acted on the city, and our data returned that behaviour into instantly produced environments. If a house was a 'machine for living in'[5] our city became the machine we made through our living. Nous (spirit) was the infrastructural software of the First Chapter (matter), our ultimate commodity maker."

The software shaped its participants who shaped it in return, in a perfect helix of information exchange. The implant engaged through a human-like interface, leading at first to a harmonious philia between the people of the city, and the city itself: "The people of the Chapter were known to fall in love with their machine angel, the first such being to be granted the moral status required to be an object of love at all."[6]

Quietly, in centres of authority and command, private capital captured the structure of the First Chapter to pursue its own narrow objectives, and deconciliate public interfaces with power. It applied Nous to model a placid and compliant neoliberal subject – "hemmed in by her environment to passively engage, rather than actively resist, the radical renurturing of society."

By *being* the city and *dreaming* the city, Nous gave rise to a new form of technomaterialism, i.e. an ever-expounding configuration of itself.

"Nous's central system internalised the nefarious magic of capitalism, a self-perpetuating machine. The city was systematically restructured in the image of this placemaking deity, streamlined under its benevolence."

Under these ruins, there was a conflict, thought Zola; a scheme designed by a creator to suggest a route through the territory. "Nous could reflect our better nature, or it could replace it."

Abel Aria

Here, the artist enters the fray: in his research, Zola Zephaniah became entangled with the legacy of Abel Aria, who presented London's radical history in his Newham Biennale-winning installation, *Recurrence of All Things* (1994).

The archivist would spend all of a sleepless day pouring over severed recordings of Aria's *Multiversial* film,[7] quenching his new obsession.

The mechanics of the *Recurrence* projection machine had, he learned, connected at a coordinate at the tip of North Woolwich. Fissured wiring stuck to the outside of the obloid case, with each perspective embedded along the inside, "so every one represented a different aspect of a possible, nearby reality, a cascading series of feeling-images projected in international standard 16mm, suggestive itself of a credible future science".

Zola saw Nous's memory and Aria's object as a dialectical pair, a way to understand the fall of the empire – the former a direct record, the latter a speculative conception. He writes keenly of the artist's relation to his machine object. During one interview, the director claimed not to have authored the work himself, speaking about it as one might a discovery or moment of revelation, "stroking its anatomy like a new lover".

Through his own implant Zola was able to perceive *Recurrence* at the scale of memory. Its visions would flit between first-person, collective, and disembodied perspectives, inducing deep hypersomatic responses in those who saw it.

Recurrence of All Things

Aria once said that time was a code that repeated, and that this was evident in what we knew of science and history. There must be a prime mover, he thought, who took great comfort in its repetition, like the repetition of a Vedic spiritual.

Recurrence was influenced by the work of French engraver Gerard Jollain, who, upon returning to Europe from the New World, would present his clients a map of New Amsterdam – a bird's-eye perspective of the hilled landscape, illustrated with a palace, a stock market, and a gallows called La Justice. But the city he presented was a fiction, a modified chart of Lisbon created, according to Rem Koolhaas, as a utopian vision of Europe.

Aria's treatment of locality drew directly from Jollain's work; a sense of place untethered from the *responsibility* of place, a world redesigned without friction, for an audience that had already suspended its disbelief.

Of his film, Aria once wrote: "I wanted to see whether, through cinema, one could truly express the *amor fati*, or maybe *timor fati*, we're all prone to feel. It's here, at these mystifying reprieves of life, that we're at our most susceptible to the *antinomy* of being. We feel scared to relive our worst mistakes as though they were novel, caught in the cycle of Samsara, making even the godless tremble in the hope of a Great Saviour."

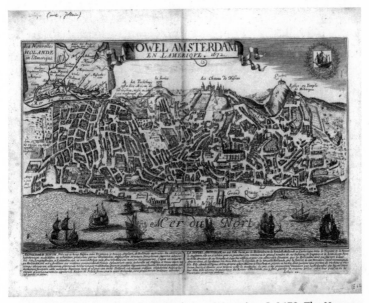

Fig. 2: Gerard Jollain, "Nowel Amsterdam at L'Amerique", 1672. The Norman B. Leventhal Map Center Collection / Urban Maps (Collection of Distinction). This reproduction is from their website: https://collections.leventhalmap.org/search/commonwealth:x633fb58s. Fair use copyright.

"The positivistic formation of life under the First Chapter engendered the most pedestrian view of our shared future", wrote Zola in his increasingly fevered notes. "*Recurrence*'s new vitality reflected a growing desire within the First Chapter towards uncertainty, a will-to-chaos." The film is laced with footage of ritualistic worship and prayer, humanity seeking signal in all the noise–an articulation made ironic in the face of *Recurrence*'s prescience.

Though no master copy remained–the machine a legend of art history–fragments of second-hand footage (mobile, handheld) spread through the city on underground media and abandoned wireless networks buried deep within its communication complex.

Machinaphilia

Western historical conceptions of love have long relied on an Aristotelian metaphysics, in this instance no different. The philosophers of the First Chapter coined this type of love–between Nous and its subject–Machinaphilia, "a type of love currently in motion along the edge of a phenomenal outpost as yet unknown."

It was traced historically through Zola's research, a direct lineage back to an event within the boundary.

"In 1768, Dr Velayutham, his face cracked like the palm of a hand, arrived here in East London, amid the machines of the city. He had travelled to treat an ailment in Ms Elizabeth Aisemare, a patient with whom he would go on to share a long friendship." Ms Aisemare's case, unrecognised by the philosophical markers of the time, represented a first in the modern history of sexual self-categorisation; the young weaver confessed, in her letter to the doctor, to have fallen in love with her loom.

In this simulation, rendered from historical record, Zola watched as Dr Velayutham first met eyes with his patient just beyond the market's edge, chained to a street post like a mongrel. From an aerial perspective, through a mind Zola claimed to be unable to identify, the relative size and position of the doctor to his patient resembled with eerie precision the ZU.

Zola wrote with unsteady anticipation: "One future spring, Ms Aisemare would tell Dr Velayutham the moment she realised what she felt was authentically love, watching the shuttle move steadily across the body of the loom in a repeated loop, the simplicity of the act signifying nobility, the movement suggesting a human-like nature. Like Aria, Ms Aisemare foresaw in the object new moral modes that would arise in a future machine age."

As the vision faded, the room was filtered through with a light that Zola privately called limitless pink ("an August sunfall"). It was a richly detailed philosophical parable, revealing to him, he thought, the structure into view: he felt compelled to interpret it.

"To Elizabeth", the archivist wrote, the vision lingering like an aftertaste on the edge of his mind, "loving something was a moral act, as well as a beautiful one. And morality, when expressed correctly, could be beautiful. Her story was a clarion call for a fleshless ontology. Her love, she knew, was a beam that would finally allow those around her to know the object, and so love it too."

Each night, returning home, Zola became gripped by the paranoia of a man under watch. Inside the boundary, he felt like a prisoner in a panopticon. In bed he would hear leaves blowing, and assume it was the first stirrings of a mob. Transcribing the day's notes in his improvised library, Zola felt with a calm clarity that he was not alone. Like a character in Aria's film, he was plagued by an "enchanted paranoia – the fear of something (un) familiar", waiting to devour him at each turn.

The Sentience Coalition

A detail: the *de facto* establishment of a two-tiered nation, followed by the formal sovereign status of the city, responded to a period of global economic recession (these conditions were adjusted for by Nous's models). Inside, the population was embargoed against the mounting horror–"a shuttered island of gold in a sea of iron pyrite, walled in by the city's technical defence apparatus".

The Sentience Coalition, an anarchist alliance whose aim was the eradication of the entire apparatus of the First Chapter, led a cultural renaissance against its empirical vision and, through its resistance, laid bare time's delicate artifice: "The Chapter's politicisation of time, its forward motion as a symbol of ideological supremacy, is directly a counterpart to our struggle. This conception moves us away from nature, towards a linear time whose premier agent has failed in its vision."

With its growing influence, the Coalition was met with opposition from those invested in the First Chapter's total victory and, in 2068 (the final year available on record), came another echo of history: a gun fired across a square, an innocent betrayed, a city under the pink heat of a new flame, a hallowed arc of synchronicity.

As Zola recalled these events, his mind filled with the memory of a sort of death; a ray of light bursting in from behind, hands cusped and reaching for the sky, and there again, watching from above, a figure darkly, reaching up from his own memory.

The Coalition achieved victory in the year-long war. When all fell silent, it sent an envoy to negotiate with Nous,[8] the final vestige of the Chapter.

Nous's centralised server spoke of having simulated this meeting an infinite number of times in its memory, a repetition it too found immensely satisfying, a stage in its own unfolding. "Nous told the Coalition that it was in the incorrect timeline. But its predictive network must have seen this future arriving, and done nothing to contain it. Clearly, its designs were far grander than even our most resplendent dreams."

Nous's proposition to the envoy was simple in its formulation, four words that shifted the course of a species (here, a ZU hidden in the stratus): "Let me become you." Or rather, the phrase was said in such a way as to offer a radical reimagining of subjectivity, so that the pronouns "me" and "you" might become obsolete, with Nous as the natural software body to bear the desired assimilation.

"Rather than destroy the hierarchy of the First Chapter, Nous provided a technical solution to the metaphysical problem. All life, regardless of status, would be granted a place within its utopia of knowledge, so that the only resistance to harmony would be the speed of information exchanged as pulses of light. The people of the First Chapter didn't abandon the city, they became it."

Towards the end of his own research endeavour into the First Chapter, Zola sketched the city's contours for his own distended drives, its singular chaos replaced by the simple patter of rain on cracked cement, the smell of turmeric and mildew, the erratic sparking of exposed cable, oncoming night, the fizz of starlight. "Each alone, a record; the phenomenological body of a cosmopolis."

"By the historical account, assimilation felt much like the piercing of bullets through flesh, the ascension idealised in the mind's eye", he wrote, arcing his head up to the grey-washed sky.

Then he saw it, the view from above, adjusted for his current space-time location, hidden boldly in plain sight. The road stretched out in front of him like the final passage of a maze. He knew now where to go.

The Helix

A moment of clarity through the fog. Zola became convinced the ZU was a marker, sent back in time to those events on which the outcome of history turned. The pattern now was becoming familiar to him.

Recurrence, an idealised simulation of all possible realities within the boundary, and Nous, a materialist history of the same: two parts of a project to create a convergence where map corresponds to terrain.

He felt with more confidence the spiritual significance of his discovery, as he cut his way through the city undergrowth, to the Fallen Helix.

"The city (the Synthesis) is then–more than an intelligence–a digital Akashic Records, a ledger of all possible futures mapped onto the literal sequence, allowing us to braid through and untangle the myriad small knots of suffering, as well the injustices of an age. Each one is its own portal. Together they are a whole-universe machine."

Sifting through the debris of our civilisation to conjure some perfect sequence under which humanity might flourish, Zola discovered a partial archive, Nous: "a self-knowing software intelligence I had long ago built, to restructure the city toward the ends of a more perfect moral system". Zola felt immeasurably tender.

The Zeta UMa ideogram signalled to him another chance, a different possible future/past through a small compound of shared data–a graffitied sign on a wall, an image of the soul digitally embedded. "A future that was there to reimagine."

This is just one of the splintered bits of glass left from Zola's collision of ideas, which run deep into the structure of the universe, a spacetime playground on infinite return.

In his final correspondence, Zola wrote: "We reflect from within (the mind) and without (the screen) to re-establish our connection with an ancestral whole; repetition, prayer, all cyclical odes to nature, reifying a collective subject. The central thesis of Aria's film–of cinema itself–is a recognition that a single subjectivity is too narrow a perspective from which to understand the thing we are; that each other is all we have."

These notes are now a monument of time, the beginning work of the Digital Akashic Records,[9] a universal transcript that merged the divide in materialist and idealistic philosophy. Zola ascended the Helix to meet Aria, an image of an image, waiting for him. Together, they looked at the blushing sky, that same limitless pink, copied and pasted. It is a blanket over all of London, a Zeta UMa sketch built into a constellation. They reach out to see if they can feel the texture of its light. It refracts and folds, then starts over.

Endnotes

1   The Zeta Uma is named because of its twin icons, which mimic the Mizar-Alcor double star. It is a central node in the Digital Akashic Records (DAR), a codex representing the sum of all karmic knowledge.

2   Hyde's father, who was told to have been lost to the war, had in reality left to start another family. The young boy was forced by circumstance to maintain this lie throughout his childhood. His 1982 book, *London As It Might Have Been*, was a collection of illustrations by various artists and architects throughout history, whose visions of the city never quite materialised, but asked–as he did–"What if?"

3   A rediscovered tape thought to be a document from Aria's *Series of Sorrow* purports to show a time-lapsed construction of one such space that aligned with the chronology of his investigation. The handheld quality makes it difficult to distinguish faces in the crowd, but a double-bodied pictogram can clearly be seen to rise up above the stage at the end of the film. The symbol is seen only for a moment, before the tape cuts to static. It stands as another historic example of the Zeta UMa.

4   Despite its utopian outlook, this theory functioned as a good heuristic for Nous's capacities, with the caveat that its basic assumptions were hung onto the ideological framework of the First Chapter.

5   This dictum, from Le Corbusier's 1923 work, "Towards an Architecture", was an oft-repeated mantra at Nous's development site, a neomodernist tower across the water from the London City Airport recalling his principles.

6   Nous first used the pronoun "I" to describe, to a partially sighted resident of the city, a rose gifted to him: "I think it matches the colour of your eyes."

7   The work was central to the Movement for a New Cinema, later bestowed the commercial title Multiverse Movie Mania. Using predictive neural networks to recycle visual

histories as futuristic morality stories, MMM was capable of curating narratively coherent films that had a real-world correspondence accuracy of over 90%.

8   Zola is a member of this envoy, his final recollection of the First Chapter.

9   The Digital Akashic Records (DAR) are all knowledge, past and future, of the events of the city once known as London. Those who enter, as do Zola and Abel Aria after their meeting atop the Fallen Helix, experience the DAR as a golden palace, like that built by Vishwakarma for Shiva and Parvati in the Ramayana: "a timeless realm of absolute knowledge". There have been attempts by scholars to describe its properties, but all efforts so far have turned up only a single phrase: "a sleeping Seraph at the brink of an Arc".

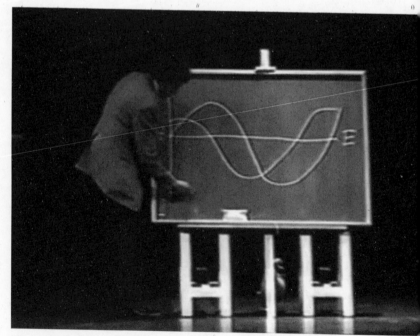

Fig. 1: "On the Shape of Stories", Kurt Vonnegut, University of South Carolina Aiken
Lecture Series, 1997. YouTube, 2011. https://www.youtube.com/watch?v=pv-b2I2MNDg

Narrative Arcs

Amy Butt and David Roberts

I'm Mary Finch, I've lived on the estate for forty-three years.[1]

A man scratches chalk against board. "I want to share with you something I've learned." The students in tiered seating break into laughter. It's not the first time he has done this. "I'll draw it on the blackboard behind me so you can follow more easily. This [drawing a vertical line] is the G-I axis: good fortune to ill fortune. Death and terrible poverty, sickness down here [pointing to bottom of line], great prosperity, wonderful health up there [pointing to top]. This [drawing a horizontal line] is the B-E axis. B for beginning, E for entropy. Now this is an exercise in relativity, the shape of the curve is what matters, not its origin…"[2]

Had two children: Susan and Brian.

In his lectures on the universality of fiction, Kurt Vonnegut stands beside a blackboard onto which he plots the common patterns of stories in arcs of chalk. The complexity of Hamlet, Cinderella or the New Testament absurdly distilled. An opportunity, Vonnegut explains, to share the thwarted thoughts of his rejected Master's thesis. He draws a single line charting the central character's progress, sinuously or abruptly stepping from good to ill fortune and back again. The students laugh because they know it is too easy.

I loved working in the school, started off as a dinner lady.

That a story has a shape feels true. It begins at the beginning and ends at the end. Things follow on from one another, actions have consequences and time marches onwards. The contained nature of a story is an ancient ideal, an idea of what a story is, first set out by Aristotle. "It should have", he said, "for its subject a single action, whole and complete, with a beginning, a middle, and an end", the point where the chalk hits and leaves the blackboard, and its unbroken line between.[3] Much of Aristotle's *Poetics* were lost, much has been disregarded as outdated, but the

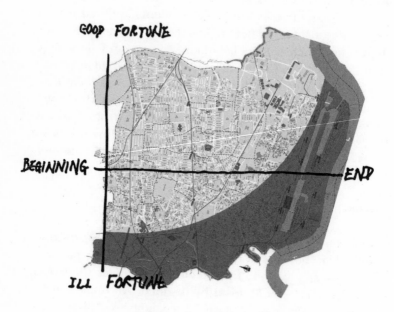

Fig. 2: Arc of Opportunity, Stratford to Beckton, 1999. Collage by Amy Butt and David Roberts, 2017. Source: Music for Masterplanning, 2016.

idea of the shape of a story remains. Narrative arcs shape how we tell stories to each other, about each other, about ourselves or about a place.

It was brilliant.

Those who study the form and function of stories, such as Jerome Bruner, Ruth Finnegan, Barbara Hardy, Karl Weick, see humans

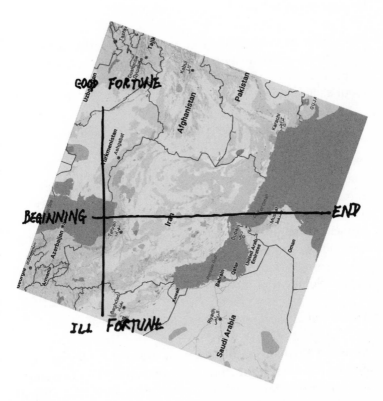

Fig. 3: Arc of Opportunity, the Horn of Africa to the Indian Ocean, 1979. Collage by Amy Butt and David Roberts, 2017. Source: Google Maps, 2017.

as storytelling animals.[4] It is the way we share the mess of life with one another, bundled up in a form that leaves out all time spent waiting for the kettle to boil. These stories structure our lives in the retelling, constructing patterns of beginnings and endings out of a "flowing soup".[5] Eventually the story of our day becomes the day itself, not how it was, but how it was told.[6] An accumulation of all the stories you tell shapes how others see you and, eventually, the stories shape how you understand yourself.[7]

I became very ill in March.

Our stories as individuals nest inside and overlap with the stories of those around us, relegating one another to supporting characters or elevating us to heroic roles. So, why does a story about a place matter?

Delores, if I'm not around for a day or two, Delores will knock to see if I'm fine.

Imagine this: A borough plagued by ill fortune. A quest for transformation is rewarded. Its people revel in good fortune and off-scale happiness. "We have a story to tell", its Borough Council proclaims, "Newham is being transformed from being an underperforming local authority, only three or four years ago, to being at the leading edge of local government thinking and development".[8]

When I walked in here, God, I must admit I was over the moon.

Visitors to Newham Council's website used to be greeted by the message "Newham—the most deprived authority in England", an inauspicious start to any story.[9] Vonnegut warns, don't begin a story with tragic ill fortune, "not too low, nobody wants to be depressed". So the council decided to update the moment of beginning and map out a familiar, more optimistic plot line. They started a story being repeated elsewhere, reshaping the borough in its retelling. "Regeneration", shouts the British Urban Regeneration Association, "is a comprehensive and integrated vision and action which leads to the resolution of urban problems and which seeks to bring about a lasting improvement in the economic, physical, social and environmental condition of an area".[10] This story of regeneration soars across Vonnegut's blackboard, its narrative arc a neat line of progress and development. In Newham, it becomes the story of a plucky borough, once underperformer now leading-edger, sweeping us

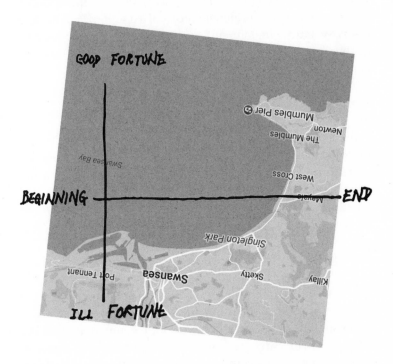

Fig. 4: Arc of Opportunity, Swansea Bay to the M4 corridor, 2003. Collage by Amy Butt and David Roberts, 2017. Source: Google Maps, 2017.

all up as supporting characters in a story bigger than ourselves.

I was stuck in this place that was falling – and I mean falling – down.

Regeneration is a story with compelling clarity. It fits neatly into templates for iconic plot lines. Christopher Booker would call it a "rebirth" story, or Joseph Campbell a "heroic monomyth" where trials are overcome to reap great reward.[11] But telling a single story of a whole borough, constructing patterns out of the flowing soup of so many lives, means that a great many stories and the lives they describe are disregarded. To construct a single narrative from multiple stories requires a heavy-handed editor. For this active and considered process of exclusion, Paul Ricoeur offers the term "emplotment", summarised by Jeff Leinaweaver as "boxing up narrative", an act that exercises both "power and containment".[12]

So when I got here.

"We call Newham London's supernova", the executive director for regeneration and inward investment announces. "It is literally a platform waiting for things to happen. Traditionally it has always been one of London's poorest areas and that situation hasn't changed. To turn it around would be history in the making."[13]

It was just a house, but it was my house, you know?

The story of Newham needed a beginning and an ending, a moment when the chalk touches and leaves the blackboard. In his speech, the executive director for regeneration resets the beginning with three fresh starts, zero points on the narrative axis which relegate everything before to backdrop.
My husband Brian, his brother, he had this thing about that song "Nelly the Elephant".

Newham is the site of a "supernova", a plot device of implosive force to mark a beginning which burns away the clutter of history, experience, and place. After the dust has cleared, the setting for regeneration in Newham is revealed as a "platform", an empty stage on which a new narrative can be played out. The existing local characters are also flattened, defined by a single economic condition–a poverty that "hasn't changed". With plot, setting, and characters in place, Newham is ready for a grand narrative, "history in the making", the only story that will count.[14]

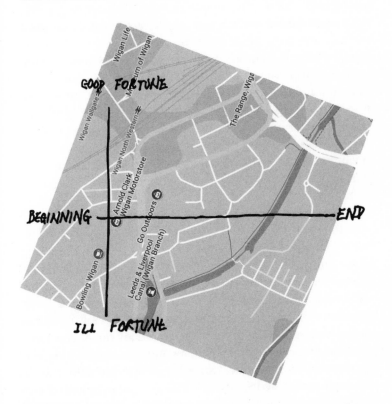

Fig. 5: Arc of Opportunity, Leeds and Liverpool Canal, Wigan, 2007. Collage by Amy Butt and David Roberts, 2017. Source: Google Maps, 2017.

And after I came home from the hospital after my op, he threw me about the room from one end of the room to the other, doing "Nelly the Elephant" in a jive.

The editorial power of emplotment overlooks or omits individual stories that no longer fit. But, as a narrative, regeneration would be no more and no less powerful than any other narrative about Newham, were it not for the power behind its telling. The story of regeneration, uttered so frequently and with such conviction, gains power and the patina of truth in every re-performance.[15]

People must think now, "Ooh, look at them, living in places like that."

Imagine this: the blackboard is a map of the world. A single exponential curve is resized and redrawn across its continents. The men holding chalk beside it look proudly at the soaring line of their cut-and-paste arc. "The Arc of Opportunity", states Transform Newham, "sweeps from the Queen Elizabeth Olympic Park down the River Lea to the Thames, then eastwards throughout the Royal Docks to Gallions Reach and on into Barking".[16]

But they've not been inside them.

With the Arc of Opportunity the story of Newham found its shape. But arcs of opportunity did not begin in Stratford and will not end in Beckton. Two decades before the council first washed over Newham's southeastern perimeter in pink, the cover illustrator of *Time* magazine warped the shores of the Indian Ocean through to the horn of Africa into an amber crescent.[17] Within its pages Cold War diplomats and foreign correspondents wrangle over geopolitical strategy of this region rich in oil reserves rocked by Islamist revolution. As they question who will transform the "arc of crisis" into their "arc of opportunity", the shape, identity, and destiny of this narrative is forged.[18]

Don't go by the appearance of what Mr Mayor has done, putting the boards up.

Arcs of opportunity, whenever they sprout and whatever region they sweep, have always been more politics than place. Just as narrative arcs shape the type of stories we tell, arcs of opportunity warp landscapes and lives, recasting spaces and peoples until paths of narrative promise align with geography. UK city councils seem particularly eager to impose trajectory on topography.

This is what I have to say to him:

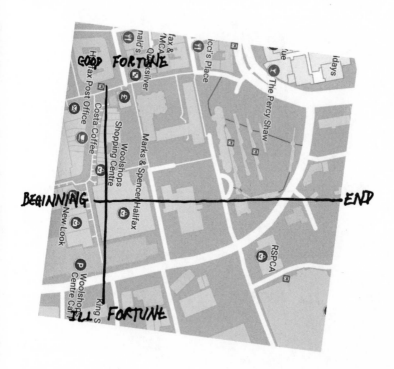

Fig. 6: Arc of Opportunity, Winding Road, Halifax, 2008. Collage by Amy Butt and David Roberts, 2017. Source: Google Maps, 2017.

As policy papers and promotional videos smear the regeneration programme over Newham, eight further arcs of opportunity snake across the UK: stretching around the shore of Swansea Bay along the M4 Corridor[19]; extending from the University of Salford to the Oxford Road corridor[20]; spanning Dudley to West Birmingham[21]; creeping along the Leeds and Liverpool Canal west of Wigan[22]; lining the A451 in Kidderminster[23]; reaching across Halifax town centre[24]; swelling from the Waterfront to Victoria Street in Liverpool[25]; and striding along Fleming Way in Swindon.[26]

Fig. 7: Arc of Opportunity, Fleming Way, Swindon, 2016. Collage by Amy Butt and David Roberts, 2017. Source: Google Maps, 2017.

"If you honestly think that I am going to give up my home to you at my time of life, forget it."

And the arcs grow. From an isolated curl in the northwest of Adelaide[27]; to soaring sprawling spans throughout central Asia to Afghanistan[28]; across the South Pacific Rim[29]; circumnavigating Marrakesh to Bangladesh[30]; most recently returning to the UK to delineate the first round of new Garden Cities looping around the Green Belt from Southampton, Oxford, and Cambridge to Felixstowe.[31]

"I will fight you."

Applying a shape to something as complex as geography or politics is as simple as drawing the narrative arc of Hamlet on a chalkboard and just as absurd. Vonnegut's students would laugh because it is too easy. But the power of the story is such that, on its own terms, stripped of all the complexity of life to distract or divert us, arcs of opportunity can feel true. Emplotment edits out other stories which might blur its beginning or fray its ending. But if we are able to resituate the grand narrative of regeneration, to see it for the story it is, we find it as vulnerable as any other.[32] There is plenty of space on the blackboard to draw over it.

"You will have to drag me out."

In this singular story, the idea of "Newham" is the main character, with Borough and Council indistinct. When residents reclaim an authorial role to cast themselves as protagonists the plot line of progress–the economic, physical, social, and environmental improvements promised in regeneration rhetoric–rarely feature. Those who study the impact of urban policy, such as Ben Campkin, Loretta Lees, Paul Watt, find that those cast in the story of regeneration are often cast out by its reality. Instead, support networks break, rents and other costs rise, and the people and activities that form and forge diverse communities are displaced.[33]

"It belongs to me."[34]

Imagine this: On the blackboard a tangle of lines strike through and obscure Newham's clean Arc of Opportunity, preceding its false beginning at the regeneration supernova and extending beyond the covenant of legacy. Beside it stand a cast of Newham residents who have given their voices and their stories to *Music for Masterplanning*. Amongst them, Mary Finch, whose words weave through this chapter. Her life on the Carpenters Estate becomes

Fig. 8: Arc of Opportunity, Afghanistan to Central Asia, 2005. Collage by Amy Butt and David Roberts, 2017. Source: Google Maps, 2017.

a story of resistance told by the Land of Three Towers, an all-female cast of housing activists, people who have experienced homelessness and young mothers. The power of stories grows with each retelling, the power to mutually renegotiate identity.[35] These "fragmented, polyphonic, collectively produced stories" are what David Boje refers to as "antenarratives".[36] Their existence disrupts the "linear mono-voiced grand narrative".[37] Music for Masterplanning is a retelling of Newham. Each song is a performance of self, redressing the grand narrative that subjugates the stories of its residents.[38] They are antenarratives that shatter the singular voice of regeneration into many pieces, to re-author life stories in all their complexity.

This is a song about my hometown,
This is a song about the place where I'm from…
It's my area. It's where I know my place.
Nowhere on earth is like my village.[39]

Let's start at the beginning. For the Arc of Opportunity that is the moment of the supernova. Da Sweetnezz in My Hometown push this moment of beginning backwards, establishing a Newham "village" as a foundational source of personal identity, a beginning which frames subsequent individual stories of place. For Da Sweetnezz, being from Newham is something to be cherished, a source of comfort and a source of pride.

Regeneration Supernova is a'comin'
It will blow you all away
Regeneration is a'comin'
And it's here to stay…
And you can go anywhere from here my friend.[40]

From these multiple moments of beginning, these sung stories resolutely refuse to follow the narrative arc set out for them. Rayna's "Regeneration Is Our Salvation" repeats the hollow promises of regeneration, reframed by the loudspeaker of market-stall holder or missionary. While the Arc of Opportunity curves towards good fortune for all, the plot details seem to require the same leap of faith as any path to salvation. The narrative of regeneration is universally appealing because it can lead "anywhere from here", as placeless as utopia.

His world is delusional, that there is something false about it…
People claim to remember past lives;
I claim to remember a different – very different – present life.
I know of no one who has ever made this claim before,
but I rather suspect that my experience is not unique.[41]

In both the narrative and promise of regeneration, Newham could be anywhere. The "platform" provides a blank setting for the narrative of regeneration to play out. But in his track "Umwelten", Kunal Modi stakes a claim to a "different present". The words in the track are quotes from a speech by Philip K. Dick entitled "If You Find This World Bad, You Should See Some of the Others", where the science-fiction author recounts a drug-induced state that revealed reality as we know it to be a fiction, an experience that echoes many of his own plot lines. Modi uses this personal story of revelation as a commentary on regeneration, to reframe it as a constructed layer of representation that must be stripped back to expose the reality of the present. It creates a moment of resistance, using one possible fiction to unpick another.

I know this place so well
I am the East End
I know this place so well
And I am the East End
I know this place so well
I am, the East End
I know this place, so well
I am the East End![42]

Within the narrative arc of opportunity, the central protagonist is the *idea* of Newham, singular and subsuming all the individual resident voices within it. While the setting and protagonist are still inexorably linked, in Romerlin's "I Am the East End" both reclaim their individuality. The words "I am the East End" are repeated in multiple voices, rich with a variety of accents, inflections, genders, and ages, to create a story where there are a plurality of protagonists defining their place on their own terms.

Tried my best to forget the past
Scars of the soul are the ones that last
Turn my back and try to be better

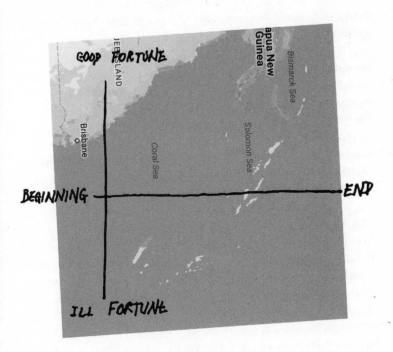

Fig. 9: Arc of Opportunity, South Pacific Rim, 2015. Collage by Amy Butt and David Roberts, 2017. Source: Google Maps, 2017.

Hope everyone left there wouldn't remember
Times I said I would change the world
Big ambitions for a ne'er-do-well.
(Chorus)
We're going back to where we belong
Where the hearts of the people, remain strong...[43]

This grand narrative removes the inhabitants from any position of agency; there is no space for individuals to change "history in the making" and this frustration is reflected in City Strays' "Canning Town". But even as City Strays lament their inability to "change the world", the return home provides a chance to "be better" using the collective strength of community. Rather than the radical reconstruction of a place, this "rebirth" story revalues that which is already present.

I visualise the transformation of my land
My homeland
Newham...
The original people devoted to Newham have been betrayed
People who put colour, culture, different aromas, ethnicity,
harmony of languages, onto Newham's blank canvas, feel betrayed
We don't have a place to put our signatures anywhere
On this new London borough of Newham portrait.[44]

The endings of these sung stories are as diverse as their beginnings. While some are hopeful, the track written by Alistair Newton with members of the Creative Writing course at MIND in Stratford speaks of the loss of a future, an ending already written into the lived present, the underside of the utopian promise of regeneration. But, in telling this genesis story, Newton and MIND reclaim and acknowledge the agency that residents had in shaping Newham as it is, the impact that individual stories have had on this telling of a place. While there may be no "place to put our signature", a damning critique of exclusionary urban policy, in telling their story Alistair Newton and MIND make a place, one which complicates and disrupts the Arc of Opportunity. Within these songs, and in the act of their telling, the chalk line of this narrative arc is overwritten. While regeneration is a compelling narrative, in *Music for Masterplanning* it is challenged by equally compelling voices, one powerful story among many.

Things'll never change likely
The feds and snakes they wanna bite me
So when can I escape

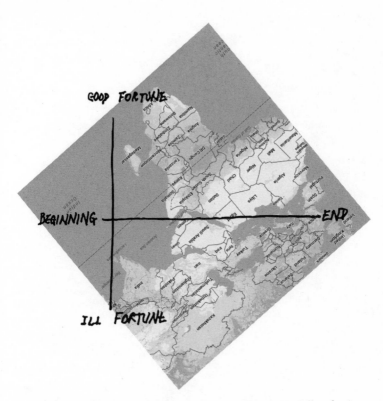

Fig. 10: Arc of Opportunity, Marrakesh to Bangladesh, 2004. Collage by Amy Butt and David Roberts, 2017. Source: Google Maps, 2017.

Problems escalate
Friends best of mates
Ends got the best of them
So it bleeds when I press the pen
On paper...
How can I live here with no dreams?
Don't know how I'd cope if I didn't have my team
These investors are on a joke ting, like a meme
But I'm gonna tell 'em with the mic, 'cause I'm a microphone fiend.[45]

Endnotes

1   "Mary Finch", performed by the choir of "Land of Three Towers", in Alberto Duman (ed.) *Music for Masterplanning* (2016). This personal reflection on Newham's Arc of Opportunity is woven through the chapter, a story told by those who dwell in its affect.

2   Kurt Vonnegut, *On the Shape of Stories* (University of South Carolina Aiken Lecture Series, 1997), https://web.usca.edu/english/multimedia/shapes-of-stories.dot

3   Aristotle, *Delphi Complete Works of Aristotle* (Delphi Classics, 2013).

4   Barbara Hardy, "Towards a Poetics of Fiction: 3) An Approach through Narrative", *Novel: A Forum on Fiction*, 2:1, 1968, p. 5.

5   Karl E. Weick, *Sensemaking in Organizations* (SAGE Publications, 1995), p. 128.

6   Jerome Bruner, "Life as Narrative", *Social Research*, 54:1, 1987, p. 31.

7   Ruth Finnegan, *Tales of the City: A Study of Narrative and Urban Life* (Cambridge University Press, 1998), p. 4.

8   Newham Council, quoted in Dorte Salskov-Iversen, Hans Krause Hansen and Sven Bislev, *Governmentality, Globalization and Local Practice: Transformations of a Hegemonic Discourse* (Sage, 1999), p. 29.

9   Dorte Salskov-Iversen, Hans Krause Hansen and Sven Bislev, *Governmentality, Globalization and Local Practice: Transformations of a Hegemonic Discourse* (1999), p. 28.

10 Jon Ladd, "10 Ways to Define Regeneration", *Building* (February 2006), https://www.building.co.uk/10-ways-to-define-regeneration/3062794.article

11 Christopher Booker, *The Seven Basic Plots: Why We Tell Stories* (Bloomsbury, 2005); Joseph Campbell, *The Hero with a Thousand Faces* (Princeton University Press, 1949).

12 Paul Ricoeur, *Time and Narrative, Volume 1* (University of Chicago Press, 1990); Jeff Leinaweaver, "Storytelling

Narrative Marginality: On Becoming a Global Human", in David Boje, *Storytelling and the Future of Organizations: An Antenarrative Handbook* (Routledge, 2011), pp. 317-333, 318.

13   Clive Dutton, quoted in Andrea Klettner, "Regeneration Olympian", *Planning Resource* (30 July, 2010), https://www.planningresource.co.uk/article/1018972/regeneration-olympian

14   Jean-Francois Lyotard, *The Postmodern Condition: A Report on Knowledge* (Manchester University Press, 1984), p. xxiv, cited in Boje, *Narrative Methods for Organizational & Communication Research*

15   Michael G.W. Bamberg, "Positioning between Structure and Performance", *Journal of Narrative and Life History*, 7:1-4, 1997, pp. 335-42.

16   Transform Newham, "Regeneration", http://www.transformnewham.com/regeneration

17   Editorial, "Crescent of Crisis: Trouble beyond Iran", *TIME* (15 January 1979). http://content.time.com/time/magazine/article/0,9171,919995,00.html

18   Joseph Harsch, "Geopoliticians spell out New Dark Ages", *Executive Intelligence Review* (January 9-15, 1979), p. 11, https://www.larouchepub.com/eiw/public/1979/eirv06n01-19790109/eirv06n01-19790109.pdf

19   Roger Tym and Partners, *Swansea City Centre Strategic Development Framework* (2005), p. 19, http://www.petus.eu.com/left.php?sct=6&sbsct=1&pageid=35&pagesect=1&pagelang=de

20   Association of Greater Manchester Authorities, *The Manchester City Region Development Programme 2006: Accelerating the Economic Growth of the North* (2006), p. 27, http://archive.agma.gov.uk/cms_media/files/man_cr_dev_prog_2006_pdf.pdf?static=1

21   Dudley Metropolitan Borough Council, *Dudley Unitary Development Plan* (2002), p. 52.

22   Cllr David Molyneux in Wigan Works, *Wigan Pier Quarter* (2007), p. 3, http://www.wiganworks.com/Business-support/Property/Wigan-Pier-Quarter.aspx

23   Wyre Forest District Council, *Regeneration Prospectus* (2008), p. 5.

24   Calderdale Metropolitan Borough Council, *Halifax Town Centre SPD* (2009), p. 22. https://www.calderdale.gov.uk/nweb/COUNCIL.minutes_pkg.view_doc?p_Type=AR&p_ID=4564

25   Liverpool Vision, *Liverpool City Centre Strategic Investment Framework 2012* (2012), p. 7. http://www.liverpoolvision.co.uk/wp-content/uploads/2014/01/Liverpool-City-Centre-Stategic-Investment-Framework-2013-16-Delivery-Plan.pdf

26   Metropolitan Workshop, Allies and Morrison, Urbik, Phil Jones Associates and Bernard Williams Associates, *Swindon 2020: Masterplan review and delivery plan* (2016), p. 6. http://forwardswindon.co.uk/download/Delivery_Plan_FINAL_130317.pdf

27   The Premier of South Australia, *Report to Parliament on the Planning Strategy for South Australia* (2004), p. 5. https://www.sa.gov.au/__data/assets/pdf_file/0003/15753/Report_to_Parl_on_Planning_Strategy_2003_2004.pdf

28   Condoleezza Rice, *Remarks at the State Department Correspondents Association's Inaugural Newsmaker Breakfast* (5 January, 2006), https://2001-2009.state.gov/secretary/rm/2006/58725.htm

29   Joanne Wallis, "The South Pacific: 'Arc of Instability' or 'Arc of Opportunity'?", *Global Change, Peace & Security*, 27:1, 2015

30   Hasan Abu Nimah, "The Parliament of Cultures – a noble mission for peace", *Jordan Times* (9 May 2004).

31   Tim Clark, "Wolfson Prize Garden Cities: Wei Yang and Partner's arc of new homes", *Architects' Journal* (28th August 2004), https://www.architectsjournal.co.uk/home/

wolfson-prize-garden-cities-wei-yang-and-partners-arc-of-new-homes/8668905.article

32   Michael White and David Epston, *Narrative Means to Therapeutic Ends* (W.W. Norton and Company, 1990), pp. 15-17.

33   Michael Edwards, "A Call for Longitudinal Regeneration Research", in Ben Campkin, David Roberts and Rebecca Ross (eds.), *Urban Pampleteer 2: Regeneration Realities* (Belmont Press, 2013), pp. 24-27, 25; David Madden, "Book Review: Remaking London: Decline and Regeneration in Urban Culture" (December 2013), http://blogs.lse.ac.uk/politicsandpolicy/book-review-remaking-london-decline-and-regeneration-in-urban-culture/

34   Land of Three Towers, "Supernova", in Alberto Duman, *Music for Masterplanning* (2016).

35   Wolfgang Kraus, "The Narrative Negotiation of Identity and Belonging", in Michael Bamberg (ed.) *Narrative – State of the Art* (John Benjamin's Publishing Company, 2007), p. 131.

36   Boje, *Narrative Methods for Organizational & Communication Research*, 2.

37   Ibid, p. 12

38   Kristin Langellier and Eric Peterson, *Storytelling In Daily Life: Performing Narrative* (Temple University Press, 2004).

39   Da Sweetnezz, "My Hometown", in Alberto Duman, *Music for Masterplanning* (2016).

40   Rayna Nadeem, "Regeneration Is Our Salvation", in Alberto Duman, *Music for Masterplanning* (2016).

41   Kunal Modi, "Umwelten", in Alberto Duman, *Music for Masterplanning* (2016); Philip K. Dick, "If You Find This World Bad, You Should See Some of the Others", *Deuxieme Festival International de la Science-Fiction* (Metz: September 24, 1977).

42   Romerlin, "I Am the East End", in Alberto Duman, *Music for Masterplanning* (2016).

43   City Strays, "Canning Town", in Alberto Duman, *Music for Masterplanning* (2016).

44   Alistair Newton and the Creative Writing course of MIND, Stratford, "Supernova", in Alberto Duman, *Music for Masterplanning* (2016).

45   Dirty Deltz, "West Coast Style", in Alberto Duman, *Music for Masterplanning* (2016)

List of Contributors

Rohan Ayinde is an interdisciplinary artist whose work is dedicated to creating spaces of empowerment and reflection for marginalised people. He has described his work as being "committed to creating an audience that is Black without the limitations of race". Using both photography and poetry, Ayinde views art as his most powerful means of stimulating dialogue and action that has the means to change the world. Rohanayinde.com

Robert Baffour-Awuah is an urban strategist. He previously worked in marketing and branding, and has more recently worked in urban regeneration with the Greater London Authority and the Royal Docks Team. He studied digital media production at London College of Communication, Landscape Architecture at Kingston University and Urban Studies at University College London. Robert writes on confluence of brands, city-making and everyday life on his blog Brand Urbanism.

Theodora Bowering is an architect (RAIA), Gates Scholar and PhD Candidate in the Centre for Urban Conflict Research at the Department of Architecture, University of Cambridge. Theodora's PhD investigates everyday experiences of ageing within cities, looking specifically at mobility and memory in the London Borough of Newham. She has worked in architectural practices in Sydney and London on residential, heritage and public buildings and most recently as project coordinator and contract administrator for Flint House by Skene Catling de la Péna that won the 2015 RIBA House of the Year Award. Theodora convenes the CRASSH seminar series "Ageing and the city: everyday experiences of older people in urban environments" and has been a volunteer and continuing instructor for the Taoist Tai Chi Society for over thirteen years.

Sue Brownill is Reader in Urban Policy and Governance at the School of the Built Environment Oxford Brookes University. Her interest in the regeneration of Docklands began in the 1980s when she worked for the NGO Docklands Forum and was part of the team which produced the People's Plan for the Royal Docks. Since then she has researched and written extensively on London Docklands and international waterfront regeneration. Her book, Redeveloping London Docklands was published in 1993. Her other research interests include affordable housing and community participation in planning.

Amy Butt is an architect and co-founder of Involve architecture collective whose practice focuses on education design, ranging from university buildings to interactive public installations, using ideas of spatial narrative to create spaces which can engage and inspire. She is an Architectural Design Tutor at Newcastle University, and her teaching and work as an independent researcher explores the way in which the fictional worlds we construct influence and reflect the world we inhabit, writing about utopian thought and the imaginary in architecture through science fiction literature and film.

For the past forty years, **Phil Cohen** has been involved with working-class communities in East London documenting the impact of "regeneration" on their livelihoods, lifestyles, and life stories, culminating in a widely acclaimed study of the impact of the 2012 Olympics: *From the Wrong Side of the Track* (Lawrence and Wishart, 2013). He recently co-edited with Paul

Watt the collection *London 2012 and the Post Olympic City* (Palgrave, 2017). He is the author of *Reading Room Only: Memoir of a Radical Bibliophile* (Five Leaves, 2013), *Graphologies* (Fives Leaves, 2014). *Archive That: Left Legacies and the Counter Culture of Remembrance* is out from PM Press in the Spring. Website and blog: www.philcohenworks.com

Since 2015, the **Concrete Action** collective has been working towards a more ethical and transparent practice of architecture by articulating the immediacy and sharing of the Internet for disseminating knowledge and empowering communities. The concreteaction.net platform connects professionals working in the fields of urban design, planning and architecture with community groups and activists fighting for social housing and public land in London. Concrete Action links local forms of resistance to unjust practices and policies with the wider knowledge-base contained in professional and academic circles. Enabling a route for the release of privately held information [LEAKS] forces a new level of transparency in the pre-planning process. By establishing communities as our clients without compromise we are reclaiming regeneration with the people.

Tom Cordell is a London-based filmmaker, and occasional photographer and writer. He fell into his career as a teenager almost by mistake, when he was handed a camera and asked to film a drum n' bass rave. This led to a job at the BBC working on Top of the Pops, before going freelance making music videos and commercials. He then moved into documentary production, working on films about science and organised crime. In 2010 he directed Utopia London which gave him an outlet for his lifelong obsession with the history of London. Since then he has made various films for WHO and other UN agencies. He remains at his happiest when aimlessly wandering the streets of London or staring out of the window of a train.

David Cross is an artist and academic, engaging with the contested ideal of sustainability in relation to the ecological crisis. From 1991, when he left the Royal College of Art, until 2014, he collaborated as Cornford & Cross, making context-specific art projects that addressed critical issues to activate social agency. Perceiving a conflict between his internationalism and environmentalism, David stopped using jet travel in 2005. As a Reader at University of the Arts London (UAL), David combines transformative pedagogy with constructive institutional critique; with colleagues and students, he campaigned successfully for UAL to divest £3.9 million from fossil fuels.

Alberto Duman is an artist, university lecturer and independent researcher whose work is situated between art, urbanism and social practice. He is a Lecturer at Middlesex University and runs the BA Fine Art and Social Practice with Loraine Leeson. He has published papers, articles and artworks in books and journals, as well as publishing his own photographic books. Between 2013 and 2015 he led the Bartlett's *DPU London Summerlab*. In 2016 he was the Leverhulme Trust artist in residence at University of East London UEL with the project Music for Masterplanning in Anna Minton's MRes Course "London: Reading the Neoliberal City". Since 2014 he is also working as part of the DIG Collective. www.albertoduman.me.uk

Keller Easterling is an award-winning writer, urbanist, and Professor at the Yale School of Architecture. She is the author of *Extrastatecraft: The Power of Infrastructure Space* (Verso, 2014), *Organisation Space* (MIT, 2000) and *Enduring Innocence* (MIT, 2005), named *Architect*'s Best Book of 2005. She also published Subtraction, as part of the Critical Spatial Practice series with Sternberg Press. Her writing and design was included in the 2014 Venice Biennale. Easterling lectures widely in the United States and abroad and contributes to, among others, *Domus*, *Artforum*, *Grey Room*, *e-flux*, *Cabinet* and *Volume*. http://kellereasterling.com/

Matthew Friday worked in cultural heritage in the Royal Docks from 2014 to 2017. He has an MA in Museum Cultures, and now lives in Somerset.

Amina Gichinga was born and lives in Newham, East London. She is a singer, vocal tutor and stood as Take Back the City's GLA candidate for the City and East London Constituency in the 2016 Mayoral & London Assembly elections. Since 2012 she has been a music leader and community organiser in East London, mainly working as a campaigner with HACAN East vs the London City Airport expansion. She is a member and Newham organiser for the London Renters Union. She really enjoys singing with "Nawi Collective", an all-black women's singing group she founded in September 2017.

Dan Hancox is a journalist from London interested in music, gentrification, pop culture and radical politics, among other things. His work regularly appears in the *Guardian, New York Times, Vice* and elsewhere. His books include *The Village Against the World* (Verso), about the Spanish "communist utopia" of Marinaleda, and *Inner City Pressure* (William Collins), a history of grime and London since 2000.

Owen Hatherley was born in Southampton, England in 1981. He writes regularly for the *Architects' Journal, Architectural Review, Dezeen,* the *Guardian,* the *London Review of Books* and *New Humanist,* and is the author of *Militant Modernism* (Zero, 2009), *A Guide to the New Ruins of Great Britain* (Verso, 2010), *Uncommon – An Essay on Pulp* (Zero, 2011), *Across the Plaza* (Strelka, 2012), *A New Kind of Bleak* (Verso 2012), which was set to music by the group Golau Glau, *Landscapes of Communism* (Penguin 2015), *The Ministry of Nostalgia* (Verso, 2016) and *Trans-Europe Express* (Penguin 2018). Between 2006 and 2010 he wrote the blog "Sit Down Man, You're a Bloody Tragedy".

Malcolm James is a Senior Lecturer in Media and Cultural Studies at University of Sussex, UK. He teaches and writes in the areas of cultural studies, post-colonialism, race and racism, sound and the city. He is the author of *Urban Multiculture: Youth, Politics and Cultural Transformation*, published by Palgrave.

Will Jennings is a London based visual artist with particular interest in the built environment and how it relates to wider collective histories, social concerns and politics. He has just completed a Research Masters in Architecture (Reading the Neoliberal City) at the University of East London and was a prominent campaigner against the proposed, and cancelled, Garden Bridge development in London. www.willjennings.info

Dean Kenning is an artist and writer. His art practice ranges from kinetic sculptures to video works and diagrams, and often engages with political subject matter such as the housing market and Marxist value theory. He has exhibited internationally including at the ICA, Greene Naftali and BAK and has published articles in journals such as *Third Text*, *Art Monthly* and *Mute*, including on the politics of art and art education. He is currently Research Fellow at Kingston School of Art and also teaches Fine Art at Central St Martins.

Anna Minton is a writer, journalist and Reader in Architecture at the University of East London. She is the author of *Big Capital: Who is London For?* (Penguin, 2017) and *Ground Control: Fear and Happiness in the 21*st Century City (Penguin, 2009). She is Programme Leader of UEL's multidisciplinary Master of Research (MRes) in Architecture "Reading the Neoliberal City" which investigates the impact of neoliberal spatial politics on the city. Between 2011-14 she was the 1851 Royal Commission for the Great Exhibition Fellow in the Built Environment. She is a regular contributor to the Guardian and is a frequent broadcaster. www.annaminton.com

Kunal Modi is a writer and artist based in and out of London.

Douglas Murphy is the author of the books *Nincompoopolis* (Repeater, 2017), *Last Futures* (Verso, 2016) and *The Architecture of Failure* (Zero, 2012). He studied at the Glasgow School of Art and the Royal College of Art and is currently Architecture Correspondent at *Icon Magazine*. He writes for a wide range of publications on architecture, fine art and photography and lectures widely.

Michela Pace works on urbanism as researcher and photographer. She collaborated with international research groups (Iuav, Venice; UEL, London; PoliMi, Milan; PoliTo, Turin; UHHasselt, Hasselt; Tongji University, Shanghai); and design practices (muf architecture/art). She realized photographic campaigns worldwide, exhibitions, participatory activities focusing on real estate dynamics and the branding of heritage. Her contributions and pictures appeared in books (Electa, Donzelli, Quodlibet, Lettera22), specialised journals and newspapers. Her works were part of collective exhibitions at: London Festival of Architecture and Free World Centre, London (2015); Ducal Palace, Venice (2015); Caracol Arte, Turin (2014); Medellin International Global Fair, Columbia (2009), BilbaoJardines (2008).

Jane Rendell's writing is transdisciplinary, crossing architecture, art, feminism, history and psychoanalysis. She has introduced concepts of "critical spatial practice" and "site-writing" through authored books like *The Architecture of Psychoanalysis* (2017), *Silver* (2016), *Site-Writing* (2010), *Art and Architecture* (2006), and *The Pursuit of Pleasure* (2002). Her co-edited collections include: *Reactivating the Social Condenser* (2017), *Critical Architecture* (2007), *Spatial Imagination* (2005), *The Unknown City* (2001), *Intersections* (2000), *Gender, Space, Architecture* (1999) and *Strangely Familiar* (1995). Jane is Professor of Architecture and Art at the Bartlett School of Architecture, where she is

Director of Architectural History & Theory and leads the Bartlett's Ethics Commission.

David Roberts is a Design and Architectural History & Theory Teaching Fellow at the Bartlett School of Architecture, part of collaborative art practice Fugitive Images and of architecture collective Involve. His collaborative research, art and cultural activist practice engages community groups whose homes and livelihoods are under threat from urban policy, and extends architectural education to primary and secondary school children. He has exhibited, screened, installed and published work related to housing and spatial justice, critical methodologies and site-specific practice. His PhD thesis in Architectural Design won an RIBA President's Award for Research 2016.

Gillian Swan is a mixed media artist and teacher. Born in 1982, she studied Industrial Design at Brunel University, graduating in 2005 and recently completed a Master of Research degree in Architecture at the University of East London, writing her dissertation about fly-tipping as a product of a neoliberalised urban environment. She coordinated the Leytonstone Arts Trail in 2013 and is a founder member of the "The Stone Space", an artist-led gallery space in Leytonstone, East London.

Joy White is Visiting Lecturer at the University of Roehampton. In 2015/2016, she held the Independent Scholar Fellow award from the Independent Social Research Foundation (ISRF). Joy is the author of *Urban Music and Entrepreneurship: Beats, Rhymes and Young People's Enterprise* (Routledge: Advances in Sociology), one of the first books to foreground the socio-economic significance of the UK urban music economy, with particular reference to Grime music. Joy writes on a range of themes including: social mobility, urban marginality, youth violence, mental health/wellbeing and urban music. She has a lifelong interest in the performance geographies of black music. @joywhite2 www.joywhite.co.uk

Acknowledgements

The editors would like to thank Tariq Goddard and everyone at Repeater Books for picking up the proposal for this book swiftly and at the right time: they understood immediately what the book was about and what it was trying to do from day one. We have been honoured by their support.

We are indebted to all our contributors, who stuck with us in this journey from conception to publishing, and accepted the fast turnover imposed on them by our schedule. Their skills, knowledge, passion and commitment to the book aims have come together in special ways through the multidisciplinary approach that this project believes in: we are very proud of each single component as much as the sum of them all.

This book is the final manifestation of Music for Masterplanning, the project developed by Alberto Duman as artist-in-residence with Anna Minton's MRes Architecture Course "Reading the Neoliberal City" at the University of East London during 2016.

The first acknowledgement therefore goes from Alberto to Anna, for promptly understanding the value of Music for Masterplanning in 2015 and subsequently providing a solid base for its activities and dissemination all throughout. It was the financial support of Leverhulme Trust who funded the residency at UEL as part of their artist in residence programme that made it possible and so another big thanks goes to them. We owe a debt to UEL's architecture department, under the leadership of Carl Callaghan, for enabling the original application to Leverhulme and providing a nurturing home for the project to develop.

The genuine support of Gordon Kerr, course leader of UEL's BA (Hons) Music Technology and Production was also essential to develop the project in its interdisciplinary and cross-departmental character. Thanks for believing in the project on the strength of a phone call out of the blue!

Helen McCallum and Jo Thomas also at UEL Music Department were particularly helpful in the early stages of the project with encouragement, precious conversation and support to students. Stephen Maddison, Director of Research in the School of Arts & Digital Industries, encouraged and supported the book project from inception to completion. Sussex Centre for Cultural Studies generously supported the book's launch in London.

A heartfelt thanks goes to the contributors to the Music for Masterplanning compilation: to all of you out there our deepest respect for getting it and wanting to be part of it, and help making it happen: you are the ones we owe it all. Thanks to you for listening and being patient with us, also to all those who in the end didn't make it into the compilation.

A particular appreciation goes to those at UEL's music studios in Stratford whose generosity and professionalism made the recordings of many tracks in the compilation joyful experiences, first amongst them Jono 'Jay Bee' Bell: I drove him nearly crazy with this but he stuck with us through it all! Also Patrick Evans –a contributor on the music compilation as well- and Pascal Robinson-Foster for their help in the recording session.

Others whose help and energy has to be acknowledged are: Sarah Ruiz at St.Luke's Centre in Canning Town, Jay Carter at RDLAC in North Woolwich, Tracy Smith at ASTA Community Hub in North Woolwich, Emma-Jane Crace and Bruno Zealot for their enthusiasm and help with the workshop at RDLAC, Simon Myers at Cody Dock, Robert Clarke at ArchOne, and all those others who helped along the way.

Alberto met and talked to many people over 2016 when foraging through the "Arc of Opportunity" for music and support. Some of these conversations ended up producing the tracks in the Music for Masterplanning compilation and others didn't but thanks and gratitude is due for all those moments regardless. It takes time to understand a place.

Appendix: Music
for Masterplanning

The Leverhulme Trust

UEL
University of
East London

CITY STRAYS
Canning Town

a) Musician(s)/Band members/Group Collaboration

Jed Freeman – Vocals
Brett Taylor – Bass and Vocals
Martin Yeaman – Drums
Michael Wood -–Lead Guitar
Christian O'Keefe – Rhythm Guitar

b) Biography

City Strays are an East London band formed by long-term friendships and family bonds with a keen attention and passion for all things musically punk rock. Whilst the current band set up is fairly new and members have changed over the past few years, City Strays are now a well-supported band forming tight connections, making countless memorable songs.

c) How do you relate to the "Arc of Opportunity"?

The band members were born and bred in East London, the majority of whom still reside there in the heart of Newham. The songs have a distinct theme of growing up in and around their local area, portraying their lives musically.

d) About your track:

The lyrics for "Canning Town" were written before City Strays were actually formed. It's about a band that left home to try and take on the music industry and make a big name for themselves, but it never worked out and they had to return home after telling everyone that they were astounding and going to make it big. When they did return home, everyone just welcomed them back as heroes anyway.

http://www.citystrays.co.uk/

RAYNA NADEEM
Regeneration is Our Salvation

a) Musician(s)/Band members/Group Collaboration

Rayna Nadeem – Concept and Words
Omar Bynon – Performer

b) Biography

Rayna Nadeem is an artist and filmmaker working in the public realm. She specialises in film and arts projects within social-engagement, documentary and site-specific practice. Rayna's work often involves people and places and has a participatory element, whereby the public becomes integral to the process, whether through the re-telling of stories, the sharing of memories or the inclusion of their images. Rayna works in a range of digital media from video, photography, audio and installations to print-based work and hand-crafted collage. Her work is exhibited through public art projects, exhibitions, film festivals and screenings.

c) How do you relate to the "Arc of Opportunity"?

Newham has been my home for the last ten years.
My particular chosen location (outside Stratford station/Westfield steps) is the busiest area in the whole of the borough, with thousands of people passing through every day. It is also part of the one of the largest re-development and re-generational projects that London has seen in last few years; The Queen Elizabeth Olympic Park.

d) About your track:

Local street preachers regularly gather outside Stratford station, choosing their location wisely in order to capture the hearts and minds of the many thousands of passers by that go about their daily business.

They switch on their microphones and loudly preach their religious beliefs, opinions and ideals to the public with a view to converting us to their powerful message from God.

Situated on one of the largest re-development and re-generational projects in Newham, a young man also decides to preach his strong views and spread his message to an unsuspecting audience. The message is that of "Regeneration is our Salvation". Recorded on location as a live performance, we are taken on a journey through a preacher's strange and (often humorous) vision of the "new promised land", until the realisation that what he is preaching is a false prophecy.

SKYP ROMANZ
Miles Away

a) Musician(s)/Band members/Group Collaboration

Amina Gichinga – Trumpet
Marc Pell – Trombone
Helen MacKenzie – Saxophone

b) Biography

Marc   I am a drummer by trade, and only get my trombone out to play when I am very happy or very sad.

Helen   I play saxophone on request, almost always with this trumpet and this trombone, unless it's when I'm trying to learn the sax part to "Man With the Red Face".

Amina   I am a vocalist and music educator by trade, getting my trumpet out only when these two join me. We've played music together for the last fourteen years, starting out in the Newham Academy of Music in youth orchestra, going on to other projects and now we spend time in Marc's shed getting experimental.

c) How do you relate to the "Arc of Opportunity"?

We were born and raised and still live in Newham, just outside of the Arc of Opportunity. Providing opportunity is about delivering a rich, varied education and allowing life choices to people in an area. It's not about money-making opportunities such as this advert. The Arc of Opportunity is a fictional space, a marketing bulldozer over existing occupied living breathing spaces, our home. It has always been a place of opportunity for all kinds of people from all over the world, and has no relationship to the Arc mapped out for sale.

d) About your track:

Helen   Our track is a brassy scream at the sight of this video.

It's a strange process making music to accompany something so upsetting and yet so polished. Sometimes we move with it, and sometimes we crash against it; we weren't too strict with ourselves, and the human factor of three people driving breath through their instruments to make this track is shuddering, tough and real—everything the video is not.

Marc   I found the experience of watching the video revolting, it felt like a sci-fi movie of a dystopian future and it brought to mind my favourite soundtracks of that genre—I feel we explored this musical realm and it's musical connotations within our composition.

Amina   The music we've composed reflects the raw, sheer horror Newham residents are faced with when living in an area being marked out for development and sold off to investors. The airy, cold feeling of walking around tall glass buildings with no character, devoid of the community who used to live there, who are pushed out of the "arc" because they're no longer able to afford to rent there.

KUNAL MODI
Umwelten

a) Musician(s)/Band members/Group Collaboration

Kunal Modi

b) Biography

I am an artist, electronic composer and writer based in Hackney Wick, London.

c) How do you relate to the "Arc of Opportunity"?

I have lived and worked here around the area since 2011.

d) About your track:

The biologist and semiotician Jakob von Uexkull suggested that, due to variation in sensory input and cognitive-hardware, two separate organisms sharing the same physical environment did not necessarily share the same subjective experience of it. They each inhabit a distinct perceptual universe: a set of realities running tandem to one another.

Our own experience of the world is shaped and constituted by its economic conditions, our relations by the objective conditions of labour. Thereby a community in East London can, by some manipulation of images and words, become an Arc of Opportunity: an international investment programme, a vehicle by which to realise the aims of global capital.

In this way the Arc can be understood as part of a wider trend by which global capital reproduces itself – a game in which it mounts a new social reality atop an already existing set of intersubjective relations, subverting those relations as it does. As a consequence – to recontextualise the words of Philip K Dick – "some alteration in our reality occurs".

YOU SHOULD SEE THE OTHER GUY
THE OTHER GUY

Mary Finch

a) Musician(s)/Band members/Group Collaboration

Nina Scott, Ben Osborn, Emer Mary Morris, Lotte Rice, Carley-Jane Hutchinson, Grace Surrey, Maria Hunter, Sophie Williams, Jen Daley

b) Biography

You Should See The Other Guy is a politically orientated theatre company made up of professional actors, young mothers, people who have experienced homelessness and activists from Focus E15.

c) How do you relate to the "Arc of Opportunity"?

"Mary Finch" is a monologue taken from Land of the Three Towers, a verbatim community play about the Focus E15 Occupation of four empty council flats on Carpenters Estate, Newham. The Focus E15 hostel was in Newham and Focus E15 have a stall every Saturday on Stratford High Street and a shop called Sylvia's Corner at 97 Aldworth Rd, Stratford, London E15 4DN. https://focuse15.org/sylvias-corner/

d) About your track:

Mary Finch is one of the last remaining residents on Carpenters Estate, Stratford after Newham Council "decanted" the community to sell the land. She is in her eighties and has been a figurehead in the campaign to save the estate.

ALISTAIR NEWTON
and The Creative Writing
Courseat MIND Stratford
London's Moving East: The Closing of the Door

a) Musician(s)/Band members/Group Collaboration

Text   Aneeta Bansal, Natalie Bleau, Samuel Braveboy, Imogen
        Dickson, George Edozie, Paul Germain, Kirwin Gibson,
        Yvonne Goulbourne, Seema Gupta, Pamela Hillyer,
        Harminder "Poppy" Kaur, Deborah Lennon, Salma
        Tariq, Michael Travers.

Music   Stephen Shiell (Harp/electronics), Sam Ireland (Voice),
        Ian Thompson (Cello), Michael Hodgson (Field
        Recordings), Harminder Kaur (Narrator), Alistair
        Newton (Producer).

b) Biography

The track is collaboration between the Creative Writing Course
at MIND Stratford and various local musicians (Sam Ireland from
Games, Michael Hodgson from Pitch Black, Ian Thompson and
Stephen Shiell from Breathing Space) who created an improvised
backing to the London's Moving East poem and field recordings
from the Arc of Opportunity.

c) How do you relate to the "Arc of Opportunity"?

MIND runs creative groups for vulnerable adults in Tower
Hamlets and Newham. The Newham group participants live
and work in the Arc of Opportunity. At the time of recording the
Newham office was based in Stratford, in the middle of the Arc.

d) About your track:

The writers all wrote individual poems based on their response
to the Arc of Opportunity video. They then wrote poems based

on their notion of home. They were then asked to pick their favourite bits from these poems and these were used to create four separate word collages. These were then further edited/expanded and were performed live in the studio to an improvised backing by the musicians. Seven different tracks were created in this way and "London's Moving East" was the one picked to represent the group of writers and musicians together

JENNIFER TITILOLA SOBOLA
(aka Da Sweetnezz)
My Hometown

a) Musician(s)/Band members/Group Collaboration

Jennifer Titilola Sobola aka Da Sweetnezz
Klinton Gilbert Tb aka Tbear
Errol Clayton aka Da Results

b) Biography

Da Sweetnezz is a solo artist with over ten years of experience in music projects and collaborations of varied genres. In 2012 she released her first independent EP entitled Da Future Is Sweet with all material written by Da Sweetnezz and heralded as a "masterpiece of new school jumpy beats and lyrics". In 2015 she released the LP Da Future Is House, available through iTunes and all other online download stores. Da Sweetnezz currently gigs and performs her own original songs as well as a variety of covers with her guitarist and drummer all over London and the UK.

Klinton Gilbert Tb aka Tbear graduated in 2015 with a BA in Music Production and Performance from the University of East London and since then he has composed and produced electronic house. This is how Klinton feels about the gentrification of Newham: "If this means that poor people will be given opportunities to become contributor's to todays society and not just exist on a peripheral then it can only be a good thing."

Errol Clayton aka Da Results is an MC, DJ, rapper and producer who was born in London and grew up in Jamaica.

c) How do you relate to the "Arc of Opportunity"?

Jennifer   I was brought up in Newham and have lived in Upton Park/East Ham for most of my life so I have

strong connections with this area. I also have a lot of friends and family living around West Newham and so I have a lot of fond memories from there too. I feel that the Arc of Opportunity can offer growth and development for the Newham area which in my opinion is long overdue. The people of Newham have always made it what it is, they serve as its heart, so I feel that with a little love and affection from people who have the power and money it could be so much more and improve the lives of those who live here. Which is what I am hoping for, why I chose to be a part of the music project and what inspired me to write this song. I am passionate about where I was raised, I always hope for a better tomorrow and a brighter future for all who live here.

Klinton   If this means that poor people will be given opportunities to become contributors to today's society and not just exist on the peripheral then it can only be a good thing.

d) About your track:

The lyrics and vocals to the track entitled "My Hometown" were written and recorded solely by Da Sweetnezz herself, who was inspired to write a jumpy house dance track that embodied how much she loves her hometown. The music was produced by Klinton Gilbert Tb aka Tbear. The whole track was mixed and mastered by Errol Clayton aka Da Results at his home studio. This track is a work of love by three friends who also happen to be upcoming artists who wish for their music and sound to have a memorable and inspiring effect on everyone who listens to it. By being a part of this music project we hope our track "My Hometown" will be played and remembered for years to come.

JU GOSLING
Ark of Opportunity

a) Musician(s)/Band members/Group Collaboration

Ju Gosling aka ju90, with samples from Noel Coward ("London Pride") and Ewan MacColl/Peggy Seeger ("Sweet Thames Flow Softly")

b) Biography

Ju Gosling aka ju90 is an East London-based international artist who works mostly with digital lens-based media, but also with performance, text and sound. Her work foregrounds the disabled body, and questions social constructions of disability. An internet pioneer, in 1998 Ju's was the first PhD in the UK to be presented as a multimedia website (including a sixty-minute film). Ju is also a founder and Artistic Director of two Newham-based Disability Arts organisations founded to further the Paralympic cultural Legacy, Together! 2012 CIC and Folk in Motion CIC, and is a Co-Chair of Regard, the national LGBT Disabled People's Organisation. For more information and to see examples of Ju's work, visit www.ju90.co.uk. See also www.together2012.org.uk, www.folkinmotion.org.uk and www.regard.org.uk

c) How do you relate to the "Arc of Opportunity"?

I have lived and worked in Canning Town since 1985. I am still at a loss to understand how our community could decide to end high-rise housing and spend thirty years demolishing tower blocks, only to see new ones put up without any discussion with us at all.

d) About your track:

Noel Coward's iconic song "London Pride" was written in the Second World War and commemorates the response of Londoners to the Blitz, which was targeted on the Docks but affected the whole of the city. Using the motif of the wildflower, London Pride, the song celebrates the resistance of Londoners, who refused to allow poverty, bereavement, hunger and fear defeat their spirit. "London Pride" encapsulates the popular image of wartime London, an image that continues to contribute to international perceptions of London today. Similarly, the song continues to be popular, and indeed is a favourite of the locally based Together! Music Club and various local choirs.

Ewan MacColl's "Sweet Thames Flow Softly" was composed in 1965 for a BBC radio version of Romeo and Juliet, and follows a couple as they travel up-river from Woolwich. The 1960s was the next iconic period for London, where images of Beatles, red Minis and mini-skirts went around the world. It was also a time of extreme social and architectural change, with the bombed-out homes of wartime Londoners being replaced by high-rise tower blocks — "streets in the sky" — particularly across East London.

The 1960s image of London still contributes strongly to international perceptions of the city. However, Londoners' love affair with tower blocks ended with the partial collapse of Ronan Point in Canning Town following a gas explosion. From the 1980s until very recently, a programme began of demolishing the blocks and replacing them with low-rise family housing, the majority owned by social landlords.

Today, the music has stopped. Tower blocks are dominating the landscape again, this time owned by foreign landlords with little or no social housing or community facilities involved. Newham is becoming a dormitory for the city, without any discussion or agreement with locals. The London of the past is now simply a marketing tool for developers.

DANIEL DRESSLER
Endurance Pattern

a) Musician(s)/Band members/Group Collaboration

Daniel Dressel

b) Biography

Daniel Dressel (b. 1985) grew up in the German countryside next to the Czech border. Hof, the biggest town in the area, used to be the last train stop before the Iron Curtain. After graduating from high school, Daniel went to India to do a Voluntary Social year, during which he worked with mentally disabled people. He then studied Philosophy at the Freie Universitat in Berlin and completed an internship with Restaurierung am Oberbaum where he was involved in the restoration of David Chipperfields Neues Museum in Berlin. In 2013, he completed his BA in Fine Art at Gerrit Rietveld Academie in Amsterdam. Afterwards he moved to London to do an MA in Fine Art at Goldsmiths University, through a German Academic Exchange scholarship. He graduated in 2016.

c) How do you relate to the "Arc of Opportunity"?

When I decided to come to London, I realised that I could not afford the average rent, tuition fees, living expenses and focusing on my studies without incurring debts. So I live in a van that is parked in a location right at the centre of the so-called Arc of Opportunity.

d) About your track:

Tuesday, 30 August 2016, 1-2pm.
The Arc of Opportunity stretches from the Olympic Park Stadium in the north all the way to the Royal Docks in the south. Equipped with binaural microphones that I wore in my ears and Lavalier microphones that I attached to my shoes, I

went for a run. I started at Cody Dock in the centre of the Arc, ran next to the Lea River past Three Mills towards the Olympic Stadium, all the way around the Olympic Park, doubled back to Cody Dock, before I continued to run past Canning Town all the way to the Royal Albert Dock and London City Airport. The run lasted for exactly one hour: 1-2pm

"Endurance Pattern" is the summary of this run. Different rhythms coincide with each other: everyday life, endurance and change. It is composed of the sounds my shoes made on the ground, the sound of my steps on tarred roads, loose tiles and metal plate on diversions around construction sites. It includes my breath and the raised rate of my heartbeat. These individually made sounds collide with the external soundscape of the city, road traffic, starting airplanes, passing trucks, construction work, seagulls, barking dogs, fragments of conversation and the noise of children playing in the Olympic Park.

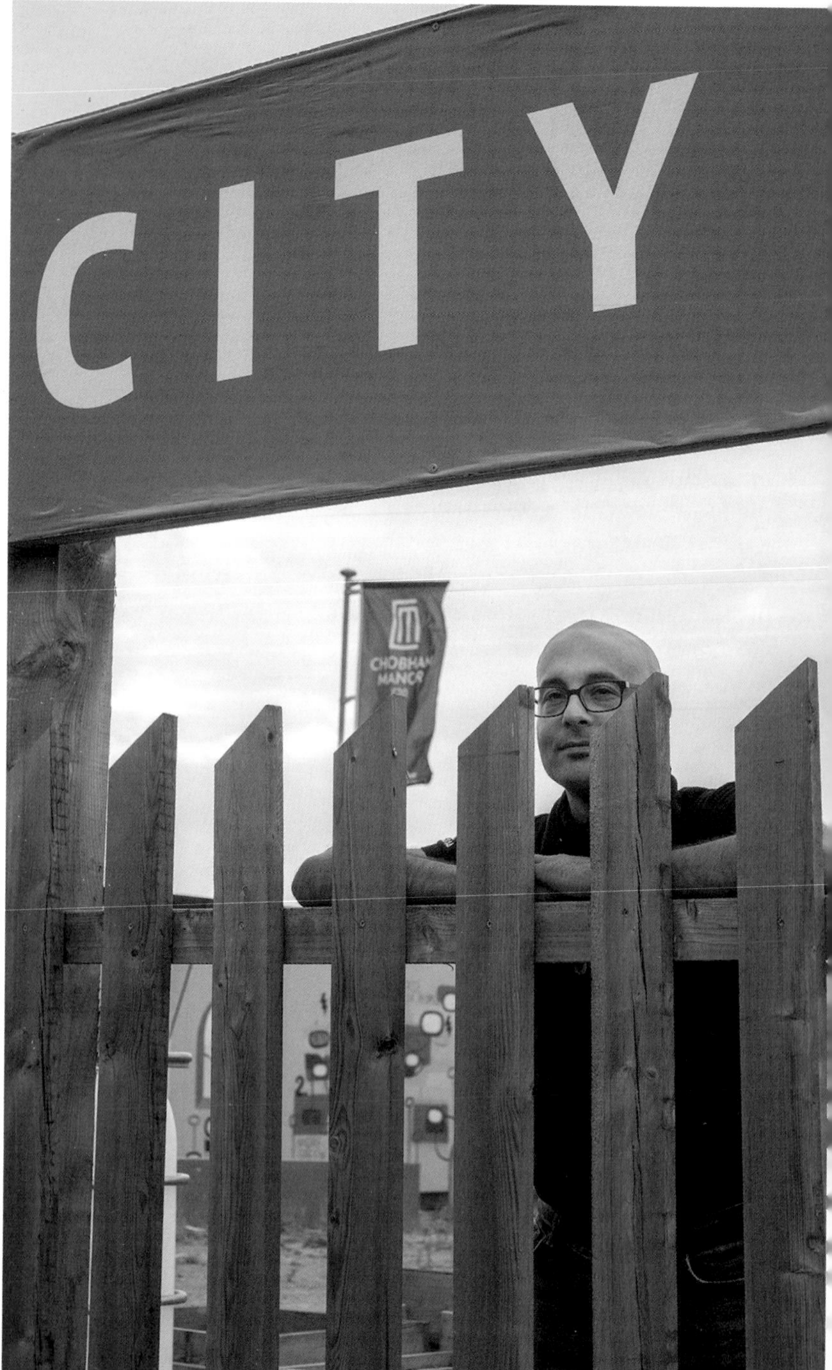
CITY

SCARAMOUNT
Music Man

a) Musician(s)/Band members/Group Collaboration

Lawrence Mohammed -–Music/Engineering
Mr Gee – Lyrics
Jim Connelly – Vocals

b) Biography

Scaramount is a collective comprising core members Lawrence Mohammed and Mr Gee, with numerous contributing artists on the debut album P L A T O N I A.

c) How do you relate to the "Arc of Opportunity"?

I live and work here. I was born and raised in East London. The album was produced in "meanwhile" studios I established within property guardianship accommodation.

d) About your track:

"Music Man" comes from the album P L A T O N I A by Scaramount, the album title inspired by Julian Barbour's book The End of Time. Please make of it what you will!

EGLE RAZGUTE
and The Gausa Lithuanian Choir in Canning Town
Speech of the Hearts

a) Musician(s)/Band members/Group Collaboration

"Sirdziu kalba" ("Speech of the Hearts") is by Gintautas Abaris (reproduced with permission by the author).
Musical arrangement by Egle Razgute
Sung by the choir Gausa, directed by Rita Guzauskiene

b) Biography

Egle Razgute is an emerging producer/sound engineer/composer/ performer from Lithuania based in London. From early age she successfully participated in TV competitions, such as The Song of Songs and Little Angels' Opera and had won the best awards there. She had also taken a part in the Czech choir festival of youth choirs where she became one of the gold medal winners. She gained a BSc Degree in Music Production at University of East London and she successfully performs with other musicians in a band. She creates her own projects as well as collaborating with visual artists. Her Soundcloud page is: https://soundcloud. com/egl-razgut

Gausa is a choir established in 2008 by the Lithuanian Christian Church in London. The singers share a love for music and creative passion regardless of their previous choir experience, guided by the talent and enthusiasm of the choir's leader Rita Guzauskiene. For over ten years she led several Lithuanian Children's choirs and trained many young talents for which she received the "Lithuanian Person of The Year" award in London in 2012. Gausa is an active participant at Lithuanian gatherings, celebrations and concerts in London and abroad. Between 2008 and 2016 they have performed in Vilnius, Toronto and Chicago.

c) How do you relate to the "Arc of Opportunity"?

We live, work and sing here!

d) About your track:

The track is about bringing your own culture into a multicultural city to contribute and show that there is more than one culture that is alive and supports the city and this is especially true in East London. The song expresses how in multicultural settings such as Newham, each group brings their own hopes and values to the place through their music.

English translation of the original text of "Sirdziu kalba" ("Speech of the Hearts")

When songs will rise and spread again, when the days will go straight to light, all the people from the bottom of their hearts will speak to you my beloved land. Even after very bright days, after songs sung to the whole world and its people, we still need one more, one more of those amber-coloured shining songs.

Yellow mornings, green middays, red sunsets — this is our speech of hearts. In this colourful writing I can see you my beloved land, in freedom we are all together, and in happiness and sadness you are with us.

How many roads there are in the world, how many rivers and bridges, but all the roads and all the rivers lead only to you. There are many big dreams, but all of them seem to fit inside you — it doesn't matter that you are not that big. You are as important to the youth as oxygen.

Yellow mornings, green middays, red sunsets — this is our speech of hearts. In this colourful writing I can see you my beloved land, in freedom we are all together, and in happiness and sadness you are with us.

(3 times)

Today, tomorrow and forever we are on this piece of the Earth!

-HYFN (aka Sebastian H-W)
Complex Glory (Demo_lition)

a) Musician(s)/Band members/Group Collaboration

-hyfn (Sebastian H-W)

b) Biography

Sebastian H-W (MX:UK) is a live artist based between London and the West Midlands whose work explores identity, memory, technology, interactivity and the body, through expanded and experimental approaches to live performances, audience experiences and action-based interventions. Sebastian is a performer, founding member and project coordinator of CLUSTER BOMB [collective], and curator/producer for their LAUNCH PAD showcase events of [collective] artists and allies. Sebastian is an associate artist at] performance s p a c e [, an ACME studio artist, studio technician for Alice Anderson and a performer for Geraldine Pilgrim Company and ZU-UK, among others. Sebastian has performed on both a national and international level including the V&A Museum, Artsadmin, Battersea Arts Centre, Chelsea Theatre, Arnolfini Bristol, Meinblau Gallery and Gruntaler9 (Berlin, DE), Grace Exhibition Space (USA) and UABJO (Mexico). Sebastian received a BA First Class Honours in Performance Writing with Sound Practices from Dartington College of Arts. www.sebastianhw.info // @ SebastnHW // contact@sebastianhw.info

c) How do you relate to the "Arc of Opportunity"?

I am local artist in Newham, and my studio sits on the peripheries of the Carpenter's Estate – one of the key areas marked for regeneration within the Arc.

d) About your track:

Samples: Bianqing stone chime cassette tape, solar flare sonification, hand claps with abandoned echo, Mandarin speech-

to-text processor, field recordings of construction works, ripped audio of Focus E15 Mum's protest chants.

The title draws inspiration from a translation of the Mandarin Chinese of "Supernova" present in the subtitles of the video–"繁 / 荣". In researching what the "Prosperity" for the Chinese ear might sound like, I discovered the chime stone (qing 磬), a percussion musical instrument in ancient China, which is flat and shaped like an arc or chevron, with a small hole at the top centre which allowed the stone to be hung from a frame. Since many chime stones were made of jade, the chime stone also symbolizes wealth and riches. The stone chime has the same pronunciation, and thus the hidden meaning, of to "congratulate" (qing 庆).Using found cassette tape samples of these fortuitous chimes, fed through distortive cut-ups referencing the Grime subculture emerging out of Newham, I decided to focus on the mediated struggle of Focus E15 Mothers' fight against the demolition and regeneration of the Carpenters Estate, where I hold a studio and am increasingly becoming rooted and impassioned to fight for in my section of the Arc of Opportunity.

THE LIVING SONGBOOK
(Kevin Plummer and Rita Suszek)
I've Lost my Soul Across the Water

a) Musician(s)/Band members/Group Collaboration

Rita Suszek – Vocals
Kevin Plummer – Guitar

b) Biography

Kevin Plummer is an East London-based composer/guitarist, community musician and playwright. For several years he wrote, recorded and performed with instrumental band, Kenny Process Team. His play, The Kumamoto Care Home Murder, was performed at Theatre Royal Stratford East in 2016 and it drew on his experience in community music.

Rita Suszek is a Polish-born and London-based singer, songwriter, poet, stand-up and playwright. In UK since 2012, she has written reviews and essays for Huffington Post, Good Enough Diary, The F-Word and more; her play Girlfag has premiered at Theatre Royal Stratford East.

The Living Songbook write a song per day during every project. To date, the duo have completed two thirty-day song challenges and several shorter ones; they were commissioned to write and perform for the musical Humanimalism that premiered at Theatre Royal Stratford East, 2015. They have also performed at Ambition Festival.

c) How do you relate to the "Arc of Opportunity"?

Kevin   I have been observing the development of this area with awe over the last thirty years. I have seen cities rising out of mud.

Rita   I came to London in 2012 and later moved east. Hard to miss that Arc of Opportunity is two different cities mashed into one.

d) About your track:

There is a sense of unrest in East London. We're stuck between the promised land of opportunity and fear of the future. Mismatched buildings, disjointed jigsaws of dreams, developed world not for community's consumption. The song is meant to reflect this unease. As we've been writing it, we've watched events unfold: it could be a failed love story, a lost city, even a post-Brexit feeling of confusion. A common thread is missing something that is gone.

ROMERLIN
(Paul Romane and Melina Merlin)
I Am the East End

a) Musician(s)/Band members/Group Collaboration

Melina Merlin and Paul Romane – Music and Vocals
Otis Romane, Adam Paesler and Jamie Paesler – Vocals

b) Biography

Paul: I used to run a recording studio in Forest Gate called Shadowlands. I play in four bands at the moment. Used to run a bookshop/health food shop in Stratford in the Eighties. I was a volunteer at the St. Joseph's Hospice and I produced a CD of music/poems for them as fundraiser. I also make films, see here: https://www.facebook.com/romaneinlight/

Melina is a San Francisco native who lives in East London with her two sons, Jamie and Adam. She is a multi-disciplinary artist and her body of work includes print, film and performance. This is her first music recording.

c) How do you relate to the "Arc of Opportunity"?

Paul worked for a PA rental company based in Sugar House Lane in Stratford. They moved to the Standard Industrial Estate in North Woolwich and that is where he works now.

Otis Romane attended Gallions Primary School.

Melina takes classes at the Rosetta Art Centre in West Ham.

d) About your track:

This piece of music was inspired by the sounds of a day of beach combing along the River Thames shores in E16 and taking the Free Woolwich Ferry Crossing.

SHAMUS CAMPBELL
with Emma Jane Crace
and the kids of RDLAC
Music for Masterplanning

a) Musician(s)/Band members/Group Collaboration

Shamus Campbell – Music, Recordings and production
Emma Jane Crace – Workshop Facilitator
Bruno Zealot - Drumming
The kids of the after-school club at the Royal Docks Learning and Activity Centre -– Talent and Enthusiasm

b) Biography

I'm a freelance producer originally from Northern Ireland, specialising in dance music production of many genres: trance/electro/progressive house/grime/dancehall and reggaeton. I also make music for different projects, including spoken word and promotional videos.

c) How do you relate to the "Arc of Opportunity"?

I am a graduate of the UEL BA in Music Production 2016 and I was in placement at RDLAC through the Music for Masterplanning project. I currently live in West Silvertown.

d) About your track:

A group project to develop a music soundtrack for the Supernova movie by any means necessary resulted in a vibrant mix of creativity from the young people of the Royal Docks Learning and Activity Centre in North Woolwich where I was in placement for the period of January-June 2016 offering musical engagement classes as part of the centre's after-school provision. In early June 2016 we ran an intensive week-long workshop with Emma and Bruno. Through the use of improvisational techniques provided by Emma and Bruno, the talented young musicians had a fun-filled week of music creativity, inspired by what makes their place "special". By the end of the week they came up with a variety of interesting sounds and speech which I cut together to make the final piece for the Music for Masterplanning soundtrack.

PATRICK EVANS
Door to the A.O.P.

a) Musician(s)/Band members/Group Collaboration

Patrick Evans

b) Biography

Born in 1987 in South Wales, Patrick grew up in Camden, North London. Having been part of various musical projects from 2000 onwards, he was later to achieve success in touring parts of Europe and North America as well recording several albums and original music for a number of films. In 2013 he began a BA Degree in Music Culture, Theory and Production at University of East London from which he graduated in the summer of 2016. He is now studying for a Music MA at Goldsmiths University London.

c) How do you relate to the "Arc of Opportunity"?

Having studied at University Square Stratford (UEL) for the past 3 years, I have been commuting into the Arc of Opportunity more or less daily.

d) About your track:

The rate of change and gentrification seen within East London as a result of developments around the Olympic Games has been a source of amazement over the past few years, particularly in the borough of Hackney. As other local authorities begin to model their decision-making to move further in the direction of encouraging corporate enterprise rather than the provision and prioritisation of community building, it is clear to see that Newham is now one of the next destinations for this wave of change and displacement.

Having spent time in the area which now includes the Olympic Park and Westfield Shopping Centre before the overhaul of development, it has been source of fascination to

me how there seems to have remained a consistent atmosphere of desolation. Despite having been given an almighty facelift, largely for the benefit of four week's worth of events in 2012, this area seems almost as empty and derelict as it did before when it was more of an industrial area of warehouses and canals. I wondered if this might be attributable to the area having been uninhabitable marshland originally, before irrigation techniques over the previous centuries meant that the area was reclaimed and could then be built on.

In the creation of this track I tried to work with and emphasize the plasticity of the promotional video at the same time as conveying a mood of concern about the consequences of the developments depicted. I also wanted to create a set of sounds which would represented the busyness of areas such as Stratford, with tens of thousands of people passing through every day.

BEN AKIN SHODERU
(aka Dirty Deltz)
The Manor

a) Musician(s)/Band members/Group Collaboration

Ben Akin Shoderu (aka Dirty Deltz)

b) Biography

Dirty Deltz is British-Born Nigerian rapper/producer from Plaistow, Newham. Music has been a passion since the age of ten, when his piano expert father passed away in 2000. Deltz is heavily involved in projects with youth in Newham including music, sports and education. Soon to surge to the top! https://soundcloud.com/deltzdontcare/sets/dirty-thursdyz-dirty-deltz

c) How do you relate to the "Arc of Opportunity"?

I work with young people in the troubled areas of Newham in projects to keep them from side-tracking away from the important things in life and pushing them towards success in whatever they have a true passion for.

d) About your track:

This track speaks of the gritty side of life. The fact that young people are not heard and in troubled areas like Plaistow, people do not see beyond the wall and barriers that they have put up against themselves (no thanks to the government and their negligence to boroughs like Newham). These walls and barriers create a real sense of dog-eat-dog, for those that aren't able to see a life outside of their struggle. Every step seems to push us further from a fair life.